ANNUAL REVIEW OF COMPARATIVE AND INTERNATIONAL EDUCATION 2023

INTERNATIONAL PERSPECTIVES ON EDUCATION AND SOCIETY

Series Editor: Alexander W. Wiseman

Recent Volumes:

Series Editor from Volume 11: Alexander W. Wiseman

Volume 21:	The Development of Higher Education in Africa: Prospects and Challenges
Volume 22:	Out of the Shadows: The Global Intensification of Supplementary Education
Volume 23:	International Education Innovation and Public Sector Entrepreneurship
Volume 24:	Education for a Knowledge Society in Arabian Gulf Countries
Volume 25:	Annual Review of Comparative and International Education 2014
Volume 26:	Comparative Sciences: Interdisciplinary Approaches
Volume 27:	Promoting and Sustaining a Quality Teacher Workforce Worldwide
Volume 28:	Annual Review of Comparative and International Education 2015
Volume 29:	Post-Education-For-All and Sustainable Development Paradigm: Structural Changes with Diversifying Actors and Norms
Volume 30:	Annual Review of Comparative and International Education 2016
Volume 31:	The Impact of the OECD on Education Worldwide
Volume 32:	Work-integrated Learning in the 21st Century: Global Perspectives on the Future
Volume 33:	The Century of Science: The Global Triumph of the Research University
Volume 34:	Annual Review of Comparative and International Education 2017
Volume 35:	Cross-nationally Comparative, Evidence-based Educational Policymaking and Reform 2018
Volume 36:	Comparative and International Education: Survey of an Infinite Field 2019
Volume 37:	Annual Review of Comparative and International Education 2018
Volume 38:	The Educational Intelligent Economy: Big Data, Artificial Intelligence, Machine Learning and the Internet of Things in Education
Volume 39:	Annual Review of Comparative and International Education 2019
Volume 40:	Annual Review of Comparative and International Education 2020
Volume 41:	Building Teacher Quality in India: Examining Policy Frameworks and Implementation Outcomes
Volume 42A:	Annual Review of Comparative and International Education 2021
Volume 42B:	Annual Review of Comparative and International Education 2021
Volume 43A:	World Education Patterns in the Global North: The Ebb of Global Forces and the Flow of Contextual Imperatives
Volume 43B:	World Education Patterns in the Global South: The Ebb of Global Forces and the Flow of Contextual Imperatives
Volume 44:	Internationalization and Imprints of the Pandemic on Higher Education Worldwide
Volume 45:	Education for Refugees and Forced (Im)Migrants Across Time and Context
Volume 46A:	Annual Review of Comparative and International Education 2022
Volume 46A:	Annual Review of Comparative and International Education 2022
Volume 47:	How Universities Transform Occupations and Work in the 21st Century: The Academization of German and American Economies

INTERNATIONAL PERSPECTIVES ON EDUCATION
AND SOCIETY   VOLUME 48

ANNUAL REVIEW OF COMPARATIVE AND INTERNATIONAL EDUCATION 2023

EDITED BY

ALEXANDER W. WISEMAN
Texas Tech University, USA

United Kingdom – North America – Japan
India – Malaysia – China

Emerald Publishing Limited
Emerald Publishing, Floor 5, Northspring, 21-23 Wellington Street, Leeds LS1 4DL.

First edition 2025

Editorial matter and selection © 2025 Alexander W. Wiseman.
Published under exclusive licence. Individual chapters © 2025 Emerald Publishing Limited.

Reprints and permissions service
Contact: www.copyright.com

No part of this book may be reproduced, stored in a retrieval system, transmitted in any form or by any means electronic, mechanical, photocopying, recording or otherwise without either the prior written permission of the publisher or a licence permitting restricted copying issued in the UK by The Copyright Licensing Agency and in the USA by The Copyright Clearance Center. Any opinions expressed in the chapters are those of the authors. Whilst Emerald makes every effort to ensure the quality and accuracy of its content, Emerald makes no representation implied or otherwise, as to the chapters' suitability and application and disclaims any warranties, express or implied, to their use.

British Library Cataloguing in Publication Data
A catalogue record for this book is available from the British Library

ISBN: 978-1-83549-319-9 (Print)
ISBN: 978-1-83549-318-2 (Online)
ISBN: 978-1-83549-320-5 (Epub)

ISSN: 1479-3679 (Series)

INVESTOR IN PEOPLE

CONTENTS

About the Editor	*ix*
About the Contributors	*x*
Preface	*xxi*

PART 1
COMPARATIVE EDUCATION TRENDS
AND DIRECTIONS

**Comparative and International Education Entering a
New Century: Impressions Gleaned From the** *Review*
C. C. Wolhuter, Oscar Espinoza and Noel McGinn   *3*

**Comparative Education at the Crossroads: A View from
Hong Kong**
Liz Jackson   *19*

**Reflections on Comparative and International Education
in Mexico**
Carlos Ornelas and Zaira Navarrete-Cazales   *27*

PART 2
CONCEPTUAL AND METHODOLOGICAL
DEVELOPMENTS

Educational Contestations in a Changing World Society
Jieun Song, Minju Choi and Francisco O. Ramirez   *39*

**How Should Comparative Research Be Conducted and
What Purpose Does it Serve?**
Renata Nowakowska-Siuta   *57*

**Rethinking Our Embrace of Decolonization: A Slippery Slope
Leading to Nationalist Ideologies and Agendas**
Supriya Baily   *81*

QuantCrit in Comparative Education Research: Tackling
Methodological Nationalism when Examining Differences in
Learning Outcomes Between Indigenous and Non-Indigenous
Children in Peru
Miriam Broeks 99

PART 3
RESEARCH-TO-PRACTICE

Into the Void: Teachers' Experiences With Student
Well-Being, Program (In)Consistency, and Communication
at International Schools
Rebecca Stroud and Shamiga Arumuhathas 135

Can Teaching Overcome Socioeconomic Inequality in Latin
America? A Trend Analysis Using Erce Data
Pablo Fraser, Fabián Fuentealba, Francisco Gatica,
Alvaro Otaegui and Carlos Henríquez Calderón 157

Contextualizing the Civic Roles of Postsecondary Institutions
with Insights from Different Traditions
Jakob Kost, Leping Mou and Michael O'Shea 175

PART 4
AREA STUDIES AND REGIONAL DEVELOPMENTS

Education and Economic Development in South Asia
Amrit Thapa, Mary Khan, Will L. H. Zemp and
James Gazawie 199

Educational Shift or New Age for Teaching and Learning:
Examining the Journey of the Indian Educational System
During the COVID-19 Pandemic
Praveen K. Dubey 219

Global Injustices of Colonial Schools: Educational
Reparations and Representations of the Human
Benjamin D. Scherrer, Brandon Folson, Chevy R. J. Eugene,
Ellie Ernst, Tinesh Indrarajah, tavis d. jules,
Madeleine Lutterman and Anastasia Toland 235

Contents   vii

PART 5
DIVERSIFICATION OF THE FIELD

**International Schools For LGBTQ+ Youth: A Comparative
Case Study of the Educational Function of International
Schools in Poland**
Joanna Leek, Marcin Rojek and Elżbieta Szulewicz   *251*

Index   *273*

ABOUT THE EDITOR

Alexander W. Wiseman, PhD, is Professor of Educational Leadership and Policy in the College of Education and Director of the Center for Innovative Research in Change, Leadership, and Education (CIRCLE) at Texas Tech University, USA. He holds a dual-degree PhD in Comparative and International Education and Educational Theory and Policy from Pennsylvania State University, an MA in International Comparative Education from Stanford University, an MA in Education from The University of Tulsa, and a BA in Letters from the University of Oklahoma. He conducts comparative educational research on educational policy and practice using large-scale education datasets on math and science education, information and communication technology (ICT), teacher preparation, professional development and curriculum, as well as school principal's instructional leadership activity. He is the author of many research-to-practice articles and books, and serves as Senior Editor of the online journal, *FIRE: Forum for International Research in Education*, and as Series Editor for the *International Perspectives on Education and Society volume series* (Emerald Publishing).

ABOUT THE CONTRIBUTORS

Shamiga Arumuhathas, a doctoral student at Western University of Ontario Faculty of Education, is an instructor in the international teacher education cohort and a secondary teacher in the Greater Toronto Area. Informed by her international teaching experiences in East Asia, her scholarly work focuses on understanding the experiences of racialized international students in settler-colonial universities. She investigates systemic barriers hindering their academic persistence and advocates for the decolonization of higher education, teacher education, and equitable inclusion of marginalized groups. As a research practitioner and educator, she provides intercultural interventions for students during crises, emphasizing sustainable secondary and post-secondary education practices.

Supriya Baily, PhD, is an activist, scholar, and educator. Currently, she is Professor of Education at George Mason University, focusing social justice issues in education, the marginalization of girls and women in educational policy and practice, and the role of teacher education to address educational inequity. She serves also as the Co-Director for the Centre for International Education and served as the President of the Comparative and International Education Society (2022–2023). She has co-edited four books, including *Experiments in Agency: A Global Partnership to Transform Teacher Research* (2017), *Educating Adolescent Girls Around the Globe: Challenges and Opportunities* (2015), and *Internationalizing Teacher Education in the US* (2012), published numerous articles and book chapters, and has secured nearly $2m in collaborative grant partnerships. Her new book, *Bangalore Girls: Witnessing the Rise of Nationalism in a Progressive City*, will be released in November 2024.

Miriam Broeks is a PhD candidate at the Faculty of Education, University of Cambridge. She is a member of the Research for Equitable Access and Learning Centre. Her interests include policy analysis and evaluation, comparative education research, and critical quantitative approaches to tackle educational inequalities. She has experience in international survey design, mixed-methods research, impact evaluations, and pilot studies. Her doctoral research focuses on disentangling the factors driving educational inequalities affecting Indigenous pupils in Peru using longitudinal survey data. As Senior Analyst at RAND Europe, she managed a variety of education research projects for the Education Endowment Foundation, the OECD, the European Commission, and other public and private organizations. She holds an MSc in Comparative Social Policy from the University of Oxford and a BA in Human Geography and Sociology, from the University College Roosevelt in the Netherlands.

About the Contributors

Minju Choi is a doctoral candidate in the International and Comparative Education program at Stanford University. Her dissertation is a cross-national, comparative study of the right to education for non-citizens as framed in national constitutions. More broadly, her research interests include the comparison of human rights and human capital ideologies in education, as well as tensions between nation-building purposes of schooling and the universal right to education for all. She has been examining these issues in the context of educational curricula, organizations, laws, and policies. Her recent publications may be found in *Comparative Education Review, Globalisation, Societies, and Education, Sociology of Education*, and the *Oxford Handbook on Education and Globalization*. Currently, she is a PhD Fellow at the Stanford Philanthropy and Civil Society Center and an active member of the Center's Global Civil Society and Sustainable Development Lab. Prior to her PhD studies, she worked in several international governmental and non-governmental organizations, including the World Bank, UNICEF, and UNESCO Bangkok.

Praveen Dubey, PhD, is Assistant Professor of Education and Director of Clinical Experiences and Partnerships at Montana State University Northern. His research interest focuses in the areas of multicultural education, diversity, equity, and inclusivity, leadership and change, technology in education (digital equity), STEM education, immigrant education, comparative and international education, teacher quality, and teacher choice for diverse classrooms. He uses the statistical tools of structural education modeling (SEM), mediation and moderation, and R programming in his research to address the issues that intersect in improving the learning experiences of diverse, immigrant/refugee, and minority students. He has presented research papers at several national research conferences such as the American Educational Research Association and the University Council for Educational Administration and is currently working on different projects and grants.

Ellie Ernst is an undergraduate student at Loyola University Chicago double majoring in Economics and Political Science. She has focused her research on reparative economic justice and exploring the best method of delivery for reparations. She is recognized in the Interdisciplinary Honors College and Dean's List.

Oscar Espinoza is full-time Professor at the Universidad de Tarapacá. He is also a researcher at the Interdisciplinary Program of Educational Research. In the past, he has worked in research projects funded by international agencies (e.g., USAID, UNESCO, World Bank, UNDP, and Ford Foundation) and national agencies (Ministry of Education, National Commission of Science and Technological Research, and the National Council for the Innovation and Competitiveness) in issues associated with access, equity, quality assurance, academic performance, accreditation, management, and higher education policies. Currently, he participates in various networks including the Comparative International Education Society, Latin American Studies Association, and Network of Epistemological and Theoretical Studies in Educational Policy. Author of numerous publications,

xii ABOUT THE CONTRIBUTORS

including 10 books, 60 book chapters, and 95 articles. He holds an EdD in Policy, Planning, and Evaluation in Education from the University of Pittsburgh, USA.

Chevy R. J. Eugene is Lecturer in the Black and African Diaspora Studies Program in the Department of Political Science at Dalhousie University. He is recognized as one of the Global Top 100 Most Influential People of African Descent Under 40 in politics and governance. Currently, he is completing a Social Science Humanities Research Council funded PhD entitled "Decolonizing the Caribbean Community's Reparations Campaign" in the Social and Political Thought Program at York University, Canada. His research takes up the historical struggles for reparations by conceptualizing it as a liberation praxis for conquest, enslavement, colonialism, and neocolonialism in new worldmaking, in the Caribbean context. It proposes a decolonial reparations framework that seeks to delink demands for reparations from neoliberal epistemologies and mechanisms that perpetuate the continuation of neocolonial governmentalities in the Caribbean. His research explores the role of the arts and social movements in the politicization and mobilization of civil society in the Caribbean and its diasporas on the issue of reparatory justice.

Brandon Folson is an enrolled member of the Oceti Sakowin (Seven Counsel Fire), belonging to the Ihanktonwan Nakota, federally recognized as the Yankton Sioux Tribe and the Tetonwan: Oglala Lakota, federally recognized as the Oglala Sioux Tribe, of South Dakota. His mother was compelled to attend the St. Paul's Mission Indian Boarding School in Marty, South Dakota, in the 1960s and 1970s. At Loyola University Chicago, he is pursuing a degree in Economics, Philosophy, and Arab Language. Engaging in independent research through the Cura Scholar Research program, he explores indigenous economics with the intention of optimizing economic systems within his Lakota/Nakota heritage. He holds the position of President on the Dakota County Technical College Alumni Board in Rosemount, MN. He aspires to earn a dual JD/PhD, utilizing his education, experience, and relationships to enhance the quality of life for American Indians both on and off the reservation.

Pablo Fraser holds a PhD in Comparative and International Education Policy from the Pennsylvania State University and is a Sociologist from the Pontificia Universidad Católica de Chile. He is currently the Coordinator for Teacher Research at the UNESCO Santiago office. Previously, he was a Policy Analyst in the Teaching and Learning International Survey at the OECD from 2015 to 2022. His research involves teacher training programs, teacher effectiveness, and teacher working conditions from an international comparative perspective.

Fabián Fuentealba holds graduate and master's degrees in Statistics from the Pontificia Universidad Católica de Chile, with experience in psychometrics, educational measurement, and evaluation. He works as an Educational Assessment Specialist at the Latin American Laboratory for Evaluation of the Quality of Education at UNESCO Santiago, leading the design, analysis, and

About the Contributors

implementation of the Regional Comparative and Explanatory Study and being a technical counterpart to consultants and collaborating institutions.

Francisco Gatica holds a master's degree in Management and Public Policy, and is currently pursuing a master's degree in Education Research at the University of Chile. Additionally, he earned his undergraduate degree in Social Work from the Pontificia Universidad Católica de Chile. He brings a decade of expertise to the field of education, particularly in the design and implementation of large-scale educational assessments. Currently, he serves as an Educational Researcher at the Latin American Laboratory for Assessment of the Quality of Education, affiliated with UNESCO Santiago.

James Gazawie serves as Assistant Development Officer at the University of Pennsylvania, contributing to the organization, coordination, and execution of fundraising efforts for specific domains within the Perelman School of Medicine. He is currently pursuing a Master of Science in Education at the University of Pennsylvania. He has a diverse professional history encompassing academia, non-profit work, and even experience in cosmetology and construction. With a passion for education, he is dedicated to making a positive impact in the field of international educational development.

Carlos Henríquez Calderón holds a master's degree in Management and Public Policies from the University of Chile. He is an Engineer from the University of Santiago de Chile. He was General Manager of the Measurement Center, Mide UC, of the Pontificia Universidad Católica de Chile and Executive Secretary of the Quality Agency of Education of the Ministry of Education of Chile, during the period 2014–2019. He currently works as Coordinator of the Latin American Laboratory for Evaluation of the Quality of Education, of the Regional Office of Education for Latin America and the Caribbean of UNESCO.

Tinesh Indrarajah is a PhD in Higher Education student at Loyola University Chicago researching on university wellbeing practices, minoritized student experiences, racial capitalism in education, reparative justice movements, and ASEAN regionalism policies. He is also the Managing Editor of the *Comparative Education Review*, the flagship journal of Comparative and International Education. He graduated from Yale-NUS College with a BA with Honors in History and a Master in Public Policy from the Lee Kuan Yew School of Public Policy.

Liz Jackson is Professor and Assistant Dean of Research in the Faculty of Education at the University of Hong Kong. She is the President of the Comparative Education Society of Hong Kong and a former Director of the Comparative Education Research Centre at the University of Hong Kong Faculty of Education. She is also currently Editor-in-Chief of Educational Philosophy and Theory and a Fellow and Past President of the Philosophy of Education Society of Australasia. She has published broadly in philosophy of education, global studies in education, and citizenship education and has

xiv ABOUT THE CONTRIBUTORS

conducted research in various societies in North America, Europe Africa, and Asia. Her single-authored books include *Emotions: Philosophy of Education in Practice* (Bloomsbury, 2024), *Contesting Education and Identity in Hong Kong* (Routledge, 2021), *Beyond Virtue: The Politics of Educating Emotions* (Cambridge University Press, 2020), and *Questioning Allegiance: Resituating Civic Education* (Routledge, 2019).

tavis d. jules is Professor of Higher Education at Loyola University Chicago; his focus and expertise lie in comparative and international education, specifically on decoloniality, racial capitalism, race/racism, terrorism, regionalism, and dictatorial transition issues. He is Past President of the Caribbean Studies Association, the immediate Past Book and Media Reviews Editor for the Comparative Education Review, an International Institute of Islamic Thought Fellow, a Senior Fellow at NORRAG and current Co-Editor-in-Chief of the *Comparative Education Review* (with Florin D. Salajan). His vast professional and academic experiences have led to research and publications across the Caribbean and North Africa. He has authored, co-authored, and edited over sixty refereed articles and book chapters, three monographs, and seven edited books. At Loyola, he is a Magis Fellow, Diversity Advocate, and Diversity and Equity Liasion.

Mary Khan is Presidential Management Fellow at the US Department of Education, where she oversees the nation's grants aimed at addressing learning losses due to Covid-19. She holds a Master of Science in Education from the University of Pennsylvania. She previously worked as a teacher in alternative high school programs in both Bangladesh and the USA. Her dedication lies in supporting underserved students.

Jakob Kost, PhD, is Lecturer in Education at Bern University of Teacher Education Switzerland. His research interests focus on international comparative (vocational) education research, upper secondary and higher education policy, educational and labor market pathways, and the relation between education and labor market policy. He published two books in German and several articles in German and English on topics such as the permeability of the Swiss education system, success of vocational education and training students with migration background, upward mobility in education systems, teacher education, and teacher shortage. He is an Expert on vocational education and training pathways and social disparities and was Advisor to the Swiss Science Council and the German Federal Institute for Vocational Education and Training. He studied at the University of Teacher Education Zürich, Humboldt University Berlin, and did his master's and PhD at the University of Fribourg, Switzerland. He was a Visiting Scholar with the Centre for the Study of Canadian and International Higher Education at the Ontario Institute for Studies in Education at the University of Toronto between 2021 and 2023.

Joanna Leek, PhD in Education, is a Researcher, Lecturer, and Teacher Trainer at the Faculty of Educational Sciences, University of Lodz, Poland. She has

About the Contributors xv

extensive experience in teaching and training pedagogy students in the areas of educational law and international education. Her research interests include international education, global citizenship education, multicultural education, mobility of students and teachers, digital mobility in Europe, curriculum development, early school leaving, and teacher education. She is passionate about promoting intercultural dialogue, diversity, and inclusion in education. In 2020–2023, she led a project on a comparative study of the functions of international programs in Poland, funded by the National Science Centre Poland.

Madeleine Lutterman is an undergraduate student at Loyola University Chicago double majoring in French and Global Studies with minors in Political Science and Photography. Her academic career has been centered around French cultural and language studies, international relations policy, and international law. Her research is focused on international reparative justice movements along with former French colonial relations and current decolonization efforts. She is recognized as an Interdisciplinary Honors student and on the Dean's List. She is also a member of Sigma Iota Rho Global Studies Honors Society and Pi Delta Phi French Honors Society.

Noel McGinn received his PhD in Social Psychology from the University of Michigan. He is Professor Emeritus of the Harvard University Graduate School of Education and Fellow Emeritus of the Harvard Institute for International Development. His authored books include *Build a Mill, Build a City, Build a School: Education and the Modernization of Korea; Framing Questions, Constructing Answers: Linking Research with Education Policy for Developing Countries; Decentralization of Education: Why, When, What and How?;* and *Learning to Educate: Proposals for the Reconstruction of Education in Developing Countries.* He is the Co-editor of the *Handbook of Modern Education and Its Alternatives* and *Comparative Perspectives on the Role of Education in Democratization.* He is the Editor of *Crossing Lines: Research and Policy Networks for Developing Country Education* and *Learning Through Collaborative Research.* He is Past President of the Comparative and International Education Society. In 1998, he received the Andres Bello Award of the Organization of American States for Outstanding Contribution to Education in Latin America.

Leping Mou, PhD, is Lecturer (Assistant Professor) in Postsecondary Education (Higher Education and the College Sector) and Comparative International Education at the School of Education, University of Glasgow, UK. Prior to joining Glasgow in 2023, he held academic positions at various institutions including the Ontario Institute for Studies of Education (OISE) University of Toronto, York University, and University of Toronto Mississauga. He obtained his PhD in Higher Education and Comparative International Development Education from OISE at the University of Toronto. His Postdoctoral project, "Liberal Arts Education in Asia: Through the Lens of Decolonization," won the Postdoctoral Fellowship of the Social Sciences and Humanities Research Council of Canada. His research explores how higher education models in different social

xvi

contexts contribute to students' capabilities development and future life flour ishing. His research interests include liberal arts education, the role of universities and colleges in a changing society, outcomes of higher education through the capabilities approach, student development, and success through the lens of social justice.

Zaira Navarrete-Cazales is a Professor of Pedagogy at the Faculty of Philosophy and Letters of the Universidad Nacional Autónoma de México. She teaches pedagogy and gender studies. She is a National Researcher Level II. She earned a PhD in Educational Research from the Department of Educational Studies at the Center for Research and Advanced Studies of the National Polytechnic Institute. She was honored with the "Premio Arturo Rosenblueth 2016" for the best doctoral thesis in Social Sciences and Humanities and the "National University Distinguished Young Scholars Award 2023" for Teaching in Humanities. Her research interests include policies for inclusion, the construction of identities, the history of pedagogy, and comparative and international education. She participated in 12 editorial boards and as reviewer in another 20. She is an Honorary President of the Iberoamerican Society of Comparative Education and the Mexican Society of Comparative Education. She has published books, chapters, and articles.

Renata Nowakowska-Siuta, PhD, is Professor in Education and Dean of the Faculty of Social Sciences at The Christian Academy of Theology in Warsaw. She is a Specialist in Comparative Education and Educational Policy in Europe. She finished her master's in Education in 1994 at the University of Warsaw, obtained the PhD title at the University of Warsaw in 1998, habilitated in 2009 at The Maria Grzegorzewska University in Warsaw, and obtained a Professorship in 2020. She is an expert evaluator with several programs of scientific exchange and research (including European Commission Horizon 2020, National Erasmus + Agency & European Solidarity Corps, The National Centre for Research and Development, and Foundation for Polish Science). She has been awarded for her scientific, didactical, and organizational merits by the state, chancellors, foundations, and students. She is also a member and Specialist of the Committee of Pedagogical Sciences of the Polish Academy of Sciences.

Alvaro Otaegui is a Sociologist with a master's degree in Sociology from Alberto Hurtado University and a master's in Public Policies from the University of Chile. Presently, he is working as an Analyst and Project Manager at the Latin American Laboratory for the Evaluation of Education Quality (LLECE) under UNESCO. Previously, he held the position of Research Manager at the Abdul Latif Jameel Poverty Action Lab. His current primary research areas include social inequalities, education, and evaluation of social programs and policies.

Carlos Ornelas is Professor of Education and Communications at the Universidad Autónoma Metropolitana Xochimilco Campus in Mexico City. His teaching experience includes being Visiting Professor at Hiroshima University, Visiting

About the Contributors   xvii

Professor of Comparative Education and Transcultural Studies at Teacher College Columbia University, and Visiting Lecturer and Fulbright Scholar in Residence at Harvard University Graduate School of Education. He earned a PhD in Education (1980) and an MA in International Education from Stanford University (1978). He is the author of 7 books as a single author, editor or co-editor of 15 other books, 60 chapters in academic compilations, and 39 articles in professional journals (in Spanish, English, and French). He has also authored 99 reviews, extended essay reviews, and other professional articles. He is also the author of 22 additional unpublished policy and research reports. He writes a column each week in *Excélsior*, a Mexican national newspaper.

Michael O'Shea, PhD, is a higher education scholar and practitioner passionate about supporting student success and building more equitable, democratic education systems. Supported by competitive Canadian and US federal and university research grants, his interdisciplinary research probes equity, diversity, inclusion, and decolonization questions in higher education policy and governance, Indigenous student mobility, qualitative methods, and science (astronomy) education. A proud product of the City of Chicago and its public schools, he has worked in a range of higher education, K-12, community non-profit, and public service roles in the USA and Canada. He has lent his energy to serving organizations that strengthen advance equity, diversity, inclusion, and decolonizing agendas – including the New Leaders Council, a national progressive organization, and the Massey College Anti-Black Racism Council. In recognition of both his scholarship and community service, he has been awarded a Canadian Social Sciences and Humanities Research Council Doctoral Grant, New Leaders Council Fellowship, Massey College Fellowship, Fulbright Student Award, among others. His published work has appeared in *The Walrus, Irish Echo, Irish-American News, National Post, Hill Times*, the *Chicago Sun-Times, University Affairs, Canadian Journal of Higher Education*, and *Higher Education Policy*.

Francisco O. Ramirez is the Vida Jacks Professor of Education and (by courtesy) Sociology at Stanford University. His current research interests focus on the worldwide rationalization of university structures and processes and on terms of inclusion issues as regards gender and education. His recent publications may be found in *Sociology of Education, Comparative Education Review, Social Forces*, and *International Sociology*. He is also the Co-editor of *Universities as Agencies: Reputation and Professionalization* (2019). His work has contributed to the development of the world society perspective in the social sciences and in international comparative education. He was the Director of the Scandinavian Consortium for Organizational Studies at the Graduate School of Education at Stanford (2017–2022). He has been a Fellow at the Center for the Advanced Studies of the Behavioral Sciences (2006–2007) and at the Swedish Collegium for Advanced Studies (2017). He has been inducted into the honor societies of the American Sociological Association and the Comparative and International Education Society.

xviii ABOUT THE CONTRIBUTORS

Marcin Rojek, PhD in Education, is a researcher, lecturer, and teacher trainer at the University of Lodz, Faculty of Educational Sciences, Poland. His research interests are adult education, especially teacher intergenerational learning, teacher workplace learning, learning from working life, students mobility, and digital tools in education. He published two monographs and several articles in this research field. He took part in several European and national funding research projects where he paid attention to how adults learn in formal and non-formal educational situations and what is digital tools role in intergenerational learning. He cooperates with scientists from Latvia, the Czech Republic and Hungary. He participated four times in Lifelong Learning Erasmus Intensive Programme and conducted academic internships in Arhus University. He is initiator and coordinator of the university's cooperation with employers and the social partners. He is also involved in improving the quality of education at the University of Lodz.

Benjamin D. Scherrer completed his PhD at the University of Massachusetts Amherst in Education Policy where he was a W.E.B. Du Bois Fellow. His scholarship draws from Black Studies, political ecology, and critical cartographic methods. In his current project on flooding and ongoing catastrophes, he examines climate change education through methods of epistemic deciphering across the curriculum. He is interested in educational practices located materially outside or outdoors, in esthetic engagement with affective elements that enliven what is put on the page. He has been a public school teacher, school founder, and curriculum author.

Jieun Song is a doctoral candidate in the International and Comparative Education and the Sociology of Education at Stanford University. Her research interests revolve around equitable and inclusive education, global initiatives and discourses and their impact on national education policies and practices, and the evolving roles and expectations for universities. She often employs quantitative methods with longitudinal, cross-national data to explore these issues. Her dissertation investigates how education for marginalized groups and individuals has evolved over time globally and in US higher education and the kinds of sociocultural factors that have shaped these changes. She is currently involved in the Diversity and Inclusion in Higher Education project as well as the World Education Reform Database project at the Stanford Graduate School of Education. Prior to starting doctoral studies, she worked for the Korean National Commission for UNESCO as a Program Specialist in the education and culture sectors, engaging in important discussions around education for all and cultural diversity.

Rebecca Stroud, PhD, is a K-12 teacher, an adjunct instructor, and a researcher, drawing from intersectionality, intercultural learning, and interdisciplinary scholarship, most notably in education and sociology. She is a Postdoctoral Fellow at Carleton University conducting comparative and international research on youth homelessness prevention. She has recently been awarded an Social Science Humanities Research Council Postdoctoral Fellow at Wilfrid Laurier University

About the Contributors xix

to explore inclusive education at international schools, at the intersections of "special education," international host cultures, and school leadership. Other projects include youth mentoring, educational leadership, service learning, community programs for underserviced youth, student, and teacher well-being, and systemic factors contributing to experiences of student marginalization. She is a published poet, she writes short fiction, hikes, and enjoys spending time outdoors and traveling.

Elżbieta Szulewicz is a PhD candidate in Doctoral School of Social Sciences, University of Lodz, Poland. Her research interests are related to constructivist didactics, schoolwork methods, early school education, and broadly understood education. She conducts research on the ways of working of teachers, who in their activities are guided by the interests and needs of their students. She took part in Erasmus projects concerning young people withdrawing from school. The goal was to create tools to help teachers and educators work with students. In 2023, she joined as a scholarship holder a project on a comparative study of the functions of international programs in Poland.

Amrit Thapa is Senior Lecturer in the International Educational Development Program at Graduate School of Education, University of Pennsylvania (Penn GSE). He received his bachelor's and master's degrees in Economics from Sri Sathya Sai University, India, and MPhil and PhD in Economics and Education from Columbia University. He is also a Research Affiliate at Penn's Population Studies Center, a Fulbright Specialist, an Affiliated Researcher for the Center for Benefit–Cost Studies of Education at Penn GSE, Consultant to UNESCO Institute of Statistics, and an Advisory Board Member of the *International Journal of Educational Development*. In 2019, he was honored with the prestigious Penn GSE Excellence in Teaching Award. Prior to Penn GSE, he worked as a Research Director at the National School Climate Center, an educational non-profit organization, where he was involved in a number of school climate-related projects such as development and validity/reliability studies of school climate/SEL metrics. He was honored with the prestigious 2019 Penn GSE Excellence in Teaching Award.

Anastasia Toland is an undergraduate student at Loyola University Chicago. Majoring in Political Science and minoring in Criminal Justice and Sociolegal Studies, she has focused her academic career around engaging in policy and the legal system. She is recognized as both an Interdisciplinary Honors student and a Political Science Honors student.

C. C. Wolhuter has studied at the University of Johannesburg, the University of Pretoria, the University of South Africa, and the University of Stellenbosch. His doctorate was awarded in Comparative Education at the University of Stellenbosch. He is former Junior Lecturer in the Department History of Education and Comparative Education at the University of Pretoria, and former

Senior Lecturer in the Department of History of Education and Comparative Education at the University of Zululand. Currently, he is Comparative and International Education Professor at North-West University, Potchefstroom Campus, South Africa, and Adjunct Professor, University of Fort Hare, South Africa. He is the author of several articles and books in the fields of History of Education and Comparative and International Education. He has been Visiting Professor at i.a. Brock University, Ontario, Canada; Mount Union University, Ohio, USA; University of Crete, Greece; University of Queensland, Australia; Driestar Pedagogical University, Netherlands; Canterbury Christ University, UK; Mauritius Institute of Education, Mauritius; The University of Namibia; University of Modena and Reggio Emilia, Italy; Mata Bel University, Slovakia, Boris Grinchenko University, Ukraine; the Education University of Hong Kong; The University of Ljubljana, Slovenia; Tarapaca University, Chile, and San Martin University, Argentina.

Will L. H. Zemp is an international education professional with six years of experience in the ESL sector in the Middle East and North Africa (MENA). He holds a Master of Science in Education from the University of Pennsylvania. A teacher by trade, he is passionate about teachers' rights and recognizing educators as key agents of change within education systems. His specific areas of interest lie at the intersection of emergent technology, impact assessment, and educational development with regional focuses in the MENA, West/Central Asia, and the Caucasus.

PREFACE

As the *Annual Review of Comparative and International Education* enters its second decade of continuous publication, it is a good time to re-evaluate the purpose of an annual review and how it is specifically relevant to the field of comparative and international education. In the inaugural *Annual Review*, Wiseman and Anderson (2013) articulated the vision of an annual review becoming a tool for both reflective practice among those who identify with comparative and international education and a medium through which the field could both professionalize and coalesce. This ambitious vision persists; however, in those 10 years in between the world has changed dramatically in ways that were unpredictable at the time the inaugural volume was prepared. The COVID-19 pandemic, for example, created a fundamental shift in – and in many ways both broke and re-oriented – formal education worldwide (Grek & Landri, 2021). Global crises have resulted in the most documented forced migration of humans that has ever been experienced worldwide, even in times of world war (Fransen & de Haas, 2019). A rise in populist politics and fascist-like regimes worldwide has called into question the effectiveness of mass education for creating democratic citizens and systems (Sant, 2021). And, new technologies employing artificial intelligence have disrupted the ways that people work, think, communicate, and exchange information, ideas, goods, and services (Zhai et al, 2021). Even though these changes and others may seem like insurmountable challenges, they have both inspired and required innovations and unique entrepreneurial approaches to teaching, learning, and other aspects of education, which have been necessary to continue the work of education regardless of other ongoing challenges (e.g., González-Pérez & Ramírez-Montoya, 2022).

Since 2013, the *Annual Review of Comparative and International Education* has published both clear review-oriented pieces (e.g., Turner, 2022) as well as more empirical studies of comparative and international education (e.g., Polat & Arslan, 2022) over the first decade, but one of the shifts moving forward from the editorial team should and will be a more purposeful attempt to review the past in order to understand what is happening in education during the review year. This may mean a reduction in the number of empirical studies published in the *Annual Review*, but it may also increase the number of meta-analyses and meta-syntheses published as part of the review each year. Another focus of the *Annual Review of Comparative and International Education* that has been a challenge during its first decade is the review or analysis of professional practice in the field, especially by development organizations, non-governmental organizations, and other entities outside of traditional educational systems and schools. So much of education occurs outside of formal, national systems (e.g., Tisza et al., 2020) that it is imperative to examine and review education and educational influences originating outside of formal, mass schooling. Therefore, a specific effort should and will be made to focus more evenly on comparative and international education taking place inside traditional education systems but also to the education and educational influences that comprise both the public and private sectors as well as informal and non-formal teaching and learning occurring outside of formal education.

At the same time, less emphasis on establishing comparative and international education as a distinct field and more recognition and review of ways that comparative and international education is celebrated and incorporated into other disciplines is needed in the *Annual Review*. Social science disciplines such as sociology, psychology, philosophy, history, and economics have produced just as much, if not more, comparative and international education research, and professionals working in the field of comparative and international education, especially in development and policy roles, are rarely if ever trained in comparative and international education specifically (e.g., Jones, 2007). So, instead of wishing or willing a distinct field or discipline of comparative and international education to exist, the *Annual Review*'s editorial team should and will be more explicit about the contributions and contributors to the field coming from other disciplines and from non-education-specific sources.

With these challenges and objectives in mind, the second decade of the *Annual Review of Comparative and International Education* will continue to be a foundation for reflective practice in the field and for the development and enhancement of comparative and international education research and practice.

Alexander W. Wiseman
Editor, *Annual Review of Comparative and International Education*
Series Editor, International Perspectives on Education and Society

REFERENCES

Fransen, S., & de Haas, H. (2019). *The volume and geography of forced migration* [IMI Working Paper Series 2019, No. 156]. International Migration Institute (IMI).

González-Pérez, L. I., & Ramírez-Montoya, M. S. (2022). Components of Education 4.0 in 21st century skills frameworks: systematic review. *Sustainability*, *14*(3), 1493.

Grek, S., & Landri, P. (2021). Education in Europe and the COVID-19 pandemic. *European Educational Research Journal*, *20*(4), 393–402.

Jones, P. W. (2007). *World Bank financing of education: Lending, learning and development*. Routledge.

Polat, M., & Arslan, K. (2022). International mobility of academics: Science mapping the existing knowledge base. In A. W. Wiseman (Ed.), *Annual review of comparative and international education, volume 46A* (pp. 45–55). Emerald Publishing Limited.

Sant, E. (2021). *Political education in times of populism*. Springer International Publishing.

Tisza, G., Papavlasopoulou, S., Christidou, D., Iivari, N., Kinnula, M., & Voulgari, I. (2020). Patterns in informal and non-formal science learning activities for children – A Europe-wide survey study. *International Journal of Child–Computer Interaction*, *25*, 100184.

Turner, D. A. (2022). Underwhelmed by research in comparative and international education. In A. W. Wiseman (Ed.), *Annual review of comparative and international education, volume 46A* (pp. 161–171). Emerald Publishing Limited.

Wiseman, A. W., & Anderson, E. (Eds.). (2013). *Annual review of comparative and international education 2013* (International Perspectives on Education and Society Series, Volume 20). Emerald Publishing Limited.

Zhai, X., Chu, X., Chai, C. S., Jong, M. S. Y., Istenic, A., Spector, M., Liu, J.-B., Yuan, J., & Li, Y. (2021). A review of artificial intelligence (AI) in education from 2010 to 2020. *Complexity*, *2021*(1), 8812542.

PART 1

COMPARATIVE EDUCATION TRENDS AND DIRECTIONS

COMPARATIVE AND INTERNATIONAL EDUCATION ENTERING A NEW CENTURY: IMPRESSIONS GLEANED FROM THE *REVIEW*

C. C. Wolhuter[a], Oscar Espinoza[b] and Noel McGinn[c]

[a]*North-West University, South Africa*
[b]*Universidad de Tarapaca, Chile*
[c]*Harvard University, USA*

ABSTRACT

This paper takes stock of developments in, and the state of, the field of comparative and international education at the beginning of the 21st century, using as data base articles published in the journal Comparative Education Review *during the second decade of the 21st century and to compare results with a content analysis done on the first 50 years of the existence of the* Review *and which was published in 2008. The 246 articles that were published in the* Comparative Education Review *during the decade 2010–2019 were analyzed under the following metrics: levels of analysis of articles; number of units covered by articles; research methods; narrative basis; phase of education articles cover; and mode of education articles deal with. Compared to the first 50 years of the existence of the* Review, *single-unit national-level studies still dominate the field, though less so. A case can be made out for a deconcentration to allow more space for research at geographic levels both larger and smaller than the nation-state. The most prominent narrative in which articles*

Annual Review of Comparative and International Education 2023
International Perspectives on Education and Society, Volume 48, 3–18
Copyright © 2025 by Emerald Publishing Limited
All rights of reproduction in any form reserved
ISSN: 1479-3679/doi:10.1108/S1479-367920240000048001

are framed is that of the social justice narrative. The neo-liberal economic narrative stands strong too, while the poor standing of the human rights narrative is disappointing. Turning to modes and phases of education is concerned, the shadow education system has registered on the comparative and international education research agenda, while there seems to be a modest upswing in interest in pre-primary education. Thoughts about the future trajectory of the field are suggested.

Keywords: Comparative and international education; *Comparative Education Review*; human capabilities theory; human rights; international test series; journal analysis; neo-liberal economics; shadow education system; social justice

INTRODUCTION

Comparative and international education has been typified as a field of scholarship that is gaining new relevance in a changing world (Powell, 2020). On the other hand, it has also been described as a field where there is constantly much discussion of the future road the field should take and has also been criticized as a field that is not remotely living up to its potential (Wolhuter, 2008). Such a situation necessitates regular stocktaking and attendant critical reflection as to the state of the field. One method of gaining a picture of the state of the field is a content analysis of the articles published in its most esteemed journals, as has been done by scholars in the field such as Schweisfurth (2015), Davidson et al. (2017), Nordtveit (2016), Flessa et al. (2021), Jing et al. (2023), Schweisfurth et al. (2020), and Wolhuter (2008).

The aim of this research was to take stock of the field of comparative and international education by means of a content analysis of the articles published recently over a decade in one of the top (based on impact factor) journals in the field – the *Comparative Education Review* or, in short, the *Review*. Based on an analysis of the articles published in the *Comparative Education Review* during the decade 2010–2019, this paper constructs a picture of the current state of comparative and international education. As a base reference point, the paper will use the results of a content analysis of the articles published in the *Comparative Education Review* during the first 50 years of its existence, from 1957 to 2006 (Wolhuter, 2008). This will indicate movements in the field during the decade 2010–2019, compared to the state of the field in the past.

LITERATURE SURVEY

Comparative and international education has been described as an amorphous field (see Bereday, 1957; Halls, 1990; Wilson, 1994), a field neither stable nor well defined (Nordtveit, 2015), or an eclectic, diverse field with adjustable borders

Comparative and International Education Entering a New Century

and contours that are difficult to demarcate (Epstein & Carroll, 2005), but at the same time also as a dynamic or even an infinite field, constantly testing new frontiers (Wolhuter & Wiseman, 2019) and aiming to adjust and rise to the occasion brought about by new times and contexts (Arnove, 2001). That it is a field with a growing corpus of literature accumulating at an increasing rate is clear from Easton's (2016) analysis of the *Comparative Education Review* bibliography, which was published annually in the Review (until discontinued in 2015). Easton traces the growth of the *Comparative Education Review* bibliography and describes it as "galloping." The number of references increased from 606 in 1990 to 1,232 in 2000, to 2,071 in 2010, and to 4,300 in 2015 (Easton, 2016). Indeed, reflecting on his experience as the editor of the *Comparative Education Review* for 10 years, 2013–2023, and studying the archives of the journal since its inception in 1957, Nordtveit (2023, p. 701) remarks that the rate of change in the field, as reflected in publications in the journal, is accelerating.

An analysis of articles published during the first 50 years of the history of the *Comparative Education Review* (1957–2006) came to the conclusion that during that half century in the *Review*, two equally strong trends were visible in the field – a remarkable resilience or constancy amid a broadening of the field (Wolhuter, 2008). While new vistas that were beckoning were constantly identified by scholars active in the field, at the same time, strong inertia was detectable, as scholars tenaciously stuck to established traditions and patterns of scholarship (Wolhuter, 2008). This inertia prevented the field from developing to its maximum capacity and use. The inertia hampering the field was evident in four aspects of scholarship: the methodology that scholars used, the paradigms extant in the field, the modes of education, and the phases of education that scholars tended to focus on (Wolhuter, 2008).

To commence with research methods, some comparativists argue that "comparison" is a research methodology in itself (Schriewer, 2014, see also Manzon, 2011, pp. 158–177). Erwin Epstein (2008) maintains that comparative education is nothing but an applied study; that is, the conceptual and methodological tools of the entire range of social sciences are applied to solve education problems or challenges. However, it can also be argued that comparative and international education has a dual nature, simultaneously being a field of study with a clearly specified object of study and representing a method of study (Wolhuter, 2024). The object of study is then education systems in their societal contextual interrelationships. Various education systems in their societal contextual interrelationships are compared to highlight these interrelationships and to gain a more complete understanding of education systems and the interrelationships between education systems and their societal contexts (Wolhuter, 2024). However, even conceding that comparative education is a method or contains an element of the method of comparison, in carrying out this comparison, other methods of research are subsumed.

In the published analysis of the first 50 years of the *Comparative Education Review*, it was found that, despite all the clamor of the field entering a social science phase in the 1960s, with an attendant quantitative revolution, a literature study remained the most common method of conducting research, although its dominance declined over those 50 years (Wolhuter, 2008). During the first five years of the journal, 72% of the articles it published were on research entailing a literature study as method. This decreased to 48% during the last five years of the first 50 years (Wolhuter, 2008). The second most common research method, making its appearance in the 1960s (the time of the proclaimed social science phase), was the calculation of correlation coefficients (Wolhuter, 2008). The conclusion reached in the analysis was that this was a very limited selection of the range of social science research methods that scholars in the field employed, to the detriment and impoverishment of the field.

The article that surveyed the first 50 years of the *Review* analyzed the paradigmatic affiliation of the articles it had published (Wolhuter, 2008). Analyzing the paradigmatic affiliation of authors and publications was judged to be important, as a paradigm specifies what kind of problems or issues scholars regard as worthy of being studied and what concepts and methods are viewed as legitimate. In that analysis, it was found that, despite theoreticians of the field proclaiming that the field was beset by an impressive and growing assortment of paradigms as a hallmark of its stage of development (e.g., Epstein, 1983; Jules et al., 2021; Paulston, 1977, 1994, 1996, 1999; Psacharopoulos, 1990; Rust, 1991), actual studies on education remained tenaciously stuck in the two conventional, historical frameworks, namely the factors and forces framework and the framework of structural functionalism. These two frameworks stem from, respectively, the 1930s and 1960s (see Epstein, 1983; Noah & Eckstein, 1969; Stone, 1983), and in view of developments in both the scholarly world (e.g., Jules et al., 2021; Suter et al., 2019) and the world of education practice (e.g., Baker, 2014; Coombs, 1968, 1985; Wolhuter & Wiseman, 2022a, 2022b), now seem to be anachronistic.

Turning to foci on various phases of education, the analysis of articles published during the first 50 years of the *Comparative Education Review* found that the two main foci were higher education and secondary education. While over those 50 years, the exact proportion of articles dealing with these two phases varied, typically over any five-year period, roughly 20% of the articles published focused on higher education and 15% on secondary education (Wolhuter, 2008). Criticism was expressed about the low interest in pre-primary education (at most 2% of the articles in any five-year cycle), adult education (less than 10%), and primary education (10% or less of the articles in any five-year cycle).

Finally, turning to mode of education, this was perhaps the aspect of scholarship where the feature of scholars being stuck in trodden paths, thereby impoverishing the field, was most evident. The article that analyzed the first 50 years of the *Comparative Education Review* recognized four modes of education. The first three – formal, informal, and nonformal education – are used as defined by Phillip Coombs (1985). As in the article reviewing the first 50 years of the *Review*, a fourth category was added, namely pre-formal education. Pre-formal refers to what children learn from family, especially parental influences, especially in the years before formal schooling commences (Wolhuter, 2008).

Throughout the first 50 years of the existence of the *Review*, over 90% of the articles it published focused on formal education. The comment was made that in view of the rise of stimuli of informal education (television and the Internet) and in-service training, the existence of ample (occupation and other) training systems outside of the formal education system, and the impact of the preschool years on the subsequent lives of students, there are strong imperatives for scholars to give more attention to informal, nonformal, and pre-formal education. In view of the rise of social media and fake news, also noted by scholars of comparative and international education (e.g., Nordtveit, 2023, pp. 703–704), the call for more attention to the informal mode of education is even more compelling today than in 2008.

This need is even more accentuated with the rise of artificial intelligence, underscored by the sudden emergence of ChatGTP. ChatGTP was released in 2022, and a year later, in 2023, it became the fastest growing computer software in history (Hu, 2023, as cited by Nordtveit, 2023, p. 704). Similarly, in view of the importance of family background in the overall life and development of children and young people (e.g., Acar et al., 2018), also noted in comparative and international education circles (e.g., in 2020 the journal *Comparative Education* had a Special Issue on "Competing Interests: Parents, schools and nation states"; see also Proctor et al., 2020), more attention by comparative and international education scholars to the pre-formal mode of education is needed too.

Evidently, there is now a need to investigate whether scholars have, in recent times, moved away or evolved from the historical patterns of scholarship regarding methodology, narratives, and the phases and modes of education.

RESEARCH METHODOLOGY

The 246 articles that were published in the *Comparative Education Review* during the decade 2010–2019 were analyzed in terms of the following parameters:

- research methods;
- narrative bases (i.e., in which of the four basic narratives extant in the field the article falls);
- the phase of education (pre-primary education, primary education, secondary education, post-secondary education, or higher education) the article covers; and
- the mode of education (formal, non-formal, informal, pre-formal education, and supplementary tutoring) the article deals with.

These four parameters were chosen because they deal with features that have, as emerged in the literature survey above, simultaneously defined the field and prevented the field from reaching its maximum potential. This statement is explained and substantiated with respect to each parameter, as the results of the investigation of each parameter are now discussed in turn.

The research method followed in this study is not a review (not any of the 14 review types identified by Grant & Booth, 2009) but a content analysis (see Vaismoradi et al., 2013). Content analysis is an established and accepted method of research in the social sciences (Leedy & Ormrod, 2001). Content analysis entails a systematic coding and categorizing approach used for exploring large amounts of textual information unobtrusively to determine trends and patterns of the words used, their frequency, their relationships, and the structures and discourses of communication (Gbrich, 2007; Mayring, 2000; Pope et al., 2006; Sarantakos, 1998). Leedy and Ormrod (2001) describe the steps of content analysis as follows:

1. The researcher selects the specific material to be studied.
2. The researcher decides on the features to be studied.
3. The features are divided into small, manageable segments or categories.
4. The material is investigated with respect to the features of Step 2 and the categories of Step 3.

Subjecting leading journals to content analysis is an accepted and time-tested method of gaining a picture of the state of a particular scholarly field, including in comparative and international education (see, e.g., Davidson et al., 2020; Jing et al., 2023; Manzon, 2011; Wolhuter, 2008).

RESULTS

Research Methods Employed by Scholars

This paper differs from the approach of the analysis of research methods published in the article that reviewed the first 50 years of the *Review* (Wolhuter, 2008). In the current paper, a distinction is made between three levels of research methods. Following Robson (2011), whose framework for research methods was also used by the publication of Val Rust et al. (1999) on research methods in comparative education, this paper distinguishes between research methods on three levels. These are the level of data collection, methods at the level of data processing, and methods at the level of data interpretation. In surveying the articles used as the source for this analysis, the reality that transpired was that researchers used a variety of methods, which could comfortably be categorized into the three levels of methods of data collection, methods of data processing, and methods of data interpretation.

Methods of Data Collection

The frequency of each of the 10 most used data collection methods, instruments of data collection, or sources of data collection is presented in Table 1.

A small number of methods, sources, or instruments of data collection dominate. While literature studies and documents were the prime method of data collection (75 of the 246 articles), as it was for the first 50 years of the *Review*, it is

Comparative and International Education Entering a New Century

Table 1. Frequency of the 10 Most Used Data Collection Methods, Sources of Data Collection, or Instruments of Data Collection.

Method	Number of Articles
1. Literature survey and documentary analysis	75
2. Existing data sets (PISA[a] and IEA[b] test results, UNESCO data, census data, PIAAC[c], and national test series results)	67
3. Interviews	53
4. Questionnaires	15
5. Observation	7
6. Artefacts and work of students (e.g., essays), textbooks, or newspapers	7
7. Tests	4
8. Focus group discussions	4
9. Experiments	2
10. Own experience, autobiographies	2

[a]PISA: Programme for International Student Assessment.
[b]IEA: International Association for the Evaluation of Educational Achievement.
[c]PIAAC: The Programme for the International Assessment of Adult Competencies is a worldwide study by the Organisation for Economic Co-operation and Development in 24 countries of cognitive and workplace skills.

no longer as dominating (see Wolhuter, 2008). What is new is the rise of the use of large data sets. This method constitutes the second most common method of data collection (67 of the 246 articles). Hence it seems that Martin Carnoy's (2019) depiction of a general preoccupation with big data as the hallmark of the current phase in the development of the field at Stanford University is an accurate comment on developments in the field at large. This method reflects the rise of international league tests in the world in the past quarter of a century (especially the International Programme for Student Assessment of PISA tests since 2001), the importance of which in turn, can be traced back to the neo-liberal economic revolution and the place of education or human capital in the competition between nations in a competitive globalized world. It should be mentioned that the international league tests and the importance attached to these tests have drawn its share of criticism too, including from scholars in the field (see Denman, 2019; Meyer & Benavot, 2013).

The third most common method of data collection was interviews. Fifty-three articles in the *Review* had interviews as the prime method of data collection. This can be related to the standing of qualitative research in the social sciences in general and in comparative education in particular – a backlash that has developed since the elevation of quantitative methods in the 1960s.

The value of autobiography as data collection method in comparative and international education research has recently been illustrated in the Doctoral Degree dissertation of Kamani (2021), in the Comparative and International Education Society Presidential Address of Karen Mundy (2016), and in the publication of renowned comparativist David Turner (2022) and is slowly registering in articles published in the *Comparative Education Review* too. The same can be said about observation as a method of data collection. This is also shown in the

Comparative Education Review. The call for observation to be used as a method of data collection by comparativists is also evident in recent comparative and international education literature, for example, in the recently published article of Luoto (2023). The employment of observation as a data collection method by scholars in the field has also been facilitated and made more attractive by the development of measuring instruments such as the International System for Observation and Feedback (ISTOF).

Methods of Data Processing

The frequency of each of the 10 most used data-processing methods is presented in Table 2.

As in the case of methods of data collection, a few methods of data processing dominate. The most common method is a synthesis of information collected, which ties in with literature and documents being the most common sources of data collection. The second most used method is correlation and regression analyses (and related methods, such as factor analysis), which is consistent with an expectation of using large databases as data sources.

Methods of Data Interpretation

Based on the explanation above as to what comparative and international education entails, it can be argued that the use of the comparative method is part of the essential features of the field of comparative and international education. Furthermore, this method, as used in comparative and international education, is aimed at an explication of the interrelations between education (systems) and their societal contexts. Also, the comparative method is a method of interpretation. The overwhelmingly largest part of the articles surveyed in the study displayed this method of data interpretation: 221 in total. The few others, while they all could comfortably fit into this method of data interpretation, explicitly used one of the following acknowledged methods of data interpretation: symbolic interactionism, ethnography, phenomenology, critical ethnography, and methodological individualism.

Table 2. Frequency of the 10 Most Used Data-Processing Methods.

Method of Data Processing	Number of Articles
1. Synthesis of information collected	116
2. Calculation of correlation, regression coefficients, effect sizes, factor analysis, and diffusion analysis	74
3. Content analysis	13
4. Inferential statistics and calculation of probabilities	12
5. Descriptive statistics	9
6. Discourse analysis	7
7. Historical reconstruction	6
8. Critical discourse analysis	2
9. Reflection	2
10. Phenomenography	2

Comparative and International Education Entering a New Century

To summarize the information on research methods, while the assortment of methods with which scholars in the field let themselves be served has widened compared to the past, a limited sample of the rich range of available research methods in the social sciences (see Morin et al., 2021) is still dominating the field.

Narratives

In the analysis reported in this paper, the authors opted to use the notion of narratives as a heuristic device, for reasons explained (Wolhuter et al., 2022). A narrative, being defined as a story or account of events (Ibid.), is believed to be a more meaningful depiction of what takes place in the field. Mapping the field along the dimension of narratives, having identified a small number of narratives, provides a more easily digestible or comprehensible panoptic view of the field than the identification of a large number of paradigms. Another major reason for opting for the notion of narratives is that these, being present in both the (comparative and international education) scholarly and the public discourse of education, also serve to bridge the theory – practice gap – a long-standing problem in the field that has been pointed out by many scholars (e.g., Psacharopoulos, 1990, in his Comparative and International Education Presidential Address; Welch, 2000). The following four narratives, identified by Wolhuter et al. (2022), were taken for the analysis reported in this paper: capabilities theory, the neo-liberal economic narrative, the human rights narrative, and the social justice narrative. The frequency of the different narratives in the articles surveyed is presented in Table 3.

The fact that all four narratives register visibly in publications indicates a broadening of the field and moving with the times, from the fixation on the forces and factors paradigm and the structural functionalism paradigm that dominated until the end of the 20th century. However, on the relative salience of the four narratives, a few notes are apt.

The strongest of the four narratives are the social justice and neo-liberal economics narratives. The strong position of the social justice narrative can be linked to a number of factors. These include the function of the university to critique society and act as its conscience, as well as longstanding traditions or strands in comparative and international education. These traditions include the following: (1) the quest for equality or equity in education as a dominant motive for both the expansion and the reform of education (see Espinoza, 2007; Farrel, 1999); (2) over the past 70 years, the significance or purpose of the field as an ameliorative force in society (see Levin & Kelley, 1994; Lutz & Klingholz, 2017; Switzer, 2018; Unterhalter et al., 2014; Wolhuter, 2017); and (3) the existence of theories

Table 3. Number of Articles Being Part of Various Narratives.

Narrative	Number of Articles
Capabilities theory	30
Neo-liberal economics narrative	95
Human rights narrative	29
Social justice narrative	92

such as socio-economic reproduction, cultural reproduction, neo-colonialism, and post-colonialism – all are very strong within the field (see Gerber & Hout, 1995; Jules et al., 2021).

The strong standing of the neo-liberal narrative can be linked to the largely undisputed and unchecked free rein with which neo-liberal economics has operated in most of the world for the past 30 years (see Stiglitz, 2019) also as a driving force of education reform (see Wolhuter & Van der Walt, 2019) and also to the rather instrumental use of large data tables in this regard (explained earlier). The rise of individualism, global competitiveness, and creativity may be factors explaining why some authors chose to fit their research into the narrative of the capability theory.

What is disappointing, and unexpected, is the poor standing of the human rights narrative. Although it has been criticized for limited participation in its drafting, the Creed of Human Rights has emerged as a moral code for the globalized world. The poor standing of the narrative of the Creed of Human Rights is also standing at variance with major events and drives in the world of education praxis, where the Creed of Human Rights is visible as one of the major drives of education expansion and reform, at both the national and the global levels (see Wolhuter & Van der Walt, 2019). The right to education has been included in many national constitutions and education acts. At the global level, the narrative of education as a human right has provided an underpinning for the work of the United Nations Educational, Scientific, and Cultural Organisation (UNESCO), including its Human Rights Education drive and UNESCO declaring the decade 2005–2015 the Decade of Human Rights Education (see UNESCO, 2006), the United Nations Declaration of Human Rights Education in 2011 (United Nations, 2011), and the Education for All movement.

The poor standing of the human capabilities narrative is also disappointing. In view of the rise of knowledge economies, their significance in a competitive, globalized world, and the role of the creative class in such economies, there seems to be much scope and much reason for the development of this narrative in the field. The value of this approach for education studies has been highlighted by scholars (e.g., Walker & Unterhalter, 2007), including scholars in the field of comparative and international education in particular (e.g., Khanal et al., 2023). In the most recent Comparative and International Education (CIES) Presidential Address, Supriya Baily (2023) links the merits of a capability approach to the issue of social justice, arguing that social justice can only be obtained if people are accorded the agency to realize their vision/ideals through their capabilities.

Phases

The frequency of articles focusing on the various phases of education is presented in Table 4.

The preponderance of articles focuses on secondary (especially) or primary education. This corresponds to the pattern during the first 50 years of the *Review* (see Wolhuter, 2008). Compared to the patterns then, the substantial interest in higher education has been sustained during the 10-year period of 2010–2019 (understandable in view of the global higher education revolution, see Altbach

Table 4. Frequency of Articles Focusing on Various Phases of Education.

Phase(s)	Number of Articles
All phases or no focus on any particular phase	30
Pre-primary	8
Primary	23
Secondary	68
Primary and secondary	65
Primary, secondary, and post-secondary	1
Secondary and post-secondary	1
Post-secondary	2
Primary, secondary, and higher	1
Higher	36
Adult	10
Lifelong learning	1

et al., 2010). There seems to be a small but growing interest in pre-primary education. While a case can be made that since 1990, the world has experienced a global higher education revolution and that (relative to the 1990 base) the largest expansion of education in recent times was on the level of higher education, the importance of pre-primary education (evident again in the goals of the 2015 Incheon Declaration, spelling out a vision of universal pre-primary education of at least one year by 2030, see UNICEF, 2015). and adult education (against the background of, e.g., the changing age pyramid all over the world), the minuscule attention paid to pre-primary education and adult education is objectionable.

MODES OF EDUCATION

In this analysis, another category was added to the four used in the analysis of the first 50 years of the *Comparative Education Review* (explained earlier), namely the shadow education system (or tutoring). This category has, more recently, become visible in education practice and in the field, including articles published from 2010 through 2019 in the *Review* (see Bray & Khubakidze, 2014) and also in publications (e.g., Bennell, 2023) and fora in the field outside the *Review*, for example Mark Bray's 2017 CIES Presidential Address (Bray, 2017).

The number of articles dealing with the various modes of education is presented in Table 5.

Table 5. Number of Articles Focusing on Various Modes of Education.

Mode(s)	Number of Articles
Not mode-specific	11
Formal	204
Nonformal	18
Formal and nonformal	2
Informal	2
Pre-formal	3
Shadow education system	6

As was the case during the first 50 years of the *Review*, the preponderance of articles published during the period of 2010–2019 dealt with formal education, though now somewhat less so. There is a small rise in articles focusing on nonformal education. Different from the first 50 years, the shadow education system has now registered, and there is a small rise in articles dealing with pre-formal education as well. However, the persistent neglect of nonformal and especially informal education continues to impoverish the field. This is now even more cause for concern than was the case 20 years ago because of the rise of social media as a source of informal education (and, at that, a mode of education very controversial and challenging). So significant is the rise of social media and electronic media in (informal) education praxis that Strohmaier (2014) identifies it as a new mode of knowledge: Mode 3 knowledge – extending the classification of Gibbons et al. (2003) of Mode 1 and Mode 2 knowledge. The imperative for scholars attending to nonformal and adult education is now more compelling too, in view of the rise of the continuing adult and old population pyramid worldwide, the emphasis now placed on lifelong learning (it is, e.g., mentioned explicitly in Goal 4 of the Sustainable Development Goals), and the rise of micro-credentials (visible in, e.g., the rise of MOOCS or mass online open courses, which were unknown 20 years ago – a topic attended to by none of the 246 articles surveyed). It is regrettable that the work of pioneer comparativists on adult and lifelong learning, Peter Jarvis (1937–2018) (see Arthur & Crossley, 2017, 2020; Holford, 2017), was not continued after his passing.

CONCLUSION

Measured by the articles published in the *Comparative Education Review*, the recent decade (2010–2019) has been one of a marginal broadening of the field compared to past patterns, as pertaining to the research methods which scholars let themselves be served by, as well as by phase of education and mode of education being the object of scholarship. As far as research methods are concerned, what is new in the field is the use of mass databases, notably those containing the results of international test series. Turning to modes and phases of education, the shadow education system has registered on the comparative and international education research agenda, while there seems to be a modest upswing in interest in pre-primary education too. However, on all three facets of research methods, and modes of education, scholars in the field are not by a far stretch realizing the full potential of the field.

While there are articles that are linked to all the major narratives extant in the public discourse of education, the balance of these narratives is lopsided. The most prominent narratives detectable in the field are those of social justice and neo-liberal economics. The poor showing of the human rights narrative is disappointing. Turning to modes and phases of education, the shadow education system has registered on the comparative and international education research agenda, while there seems to be a modest upswing in interest in pre-primary education too.

Comparative and International Education Entering a New Century   15

At present, the COVID-19 pandemic has brought massive changes to education worldwide. The two most salient changes were the increase in home schooling (Hamlin & Peterson, 2022) (albeit more to supplement, rather than replace school education) and the harnessing of technology to assist teachers in teaching and learners in learning (Breslin, 2021). While it is uncertain how permanent these changes will prove to be, it can also be stated that it is unlikely that education will fully return to the old "normal." This gives comparativists an opportunity to rise to the occasion to conduct research as to how home schooling and technology can be used to augment the effort in schools in a variety of contexts.

Much has certainly been learnt from the mining of large databases – one of the hallmarks of the field in the past generation (as has been shown by the analysis reported in this paper). But such large databases – at least in their existing form, for example, the results of the PISA test – seem at prima facie to be of limited value in the new tasks proposed for the field. Instead, more emphasis should be given to the study of home schooling (thus far eschewed by comparativists) as another mode of education, and then finer textured (geographical levels smaller than the nation state) analyses. This shift may address the imbalance of studies at various geographical levels (shown in this study). Changes in emphasis may improve the ability of the field to contribute to reforms intended to create more equitable, high-quality, lifelong education for all. This would help in the achievement of Goal 4 of the Sustainable Development Goals, the construction of humanity's collective vision for education in the world of 2030.

REFERENCES

Acar, I. H., Evans, M. Y. Q., Rudasill, K. M., & Ykduz, S. (2018). The contributions of relationship with parents and teachers to Turkish children's anti-social behaviour. *Educational Psychology: An International Journal of Experimental Educational Psychology, 38*(7), 877–897. https://doi.org/10.1080/01443410.2018.1441377

Altbach, P. G., Reisberg, L., & Rumbley, L. E. (2010). Tracking a global academic revolution. *Change: The Magazine of Higher Learning, 42*(2), 30–39. http://dx.doi.org/10.1080/0091381003590845

Arnove, R. F. (2001). CIES facing the twenty-first century: Challenges and contributions. *Comparative Education Review, 45*(4), 477–503. http://dx.doi.org/10.1086/447689

Arthur, L., & Crossley, M. (2017). Wide horizons and blurred boundaries: Comparative perspectives on adult and lifelong learning. *International Journal of Lifelong Education, 36*(1–2), 181–194. https://doi.org/10.1080/02601370.2017.1268833

Arthur, L., & Crossley, M. (2020). Peter Jarvis (1937–2020). In D. Phillips (Ed.), *British scholars of comparative education: Examining the work and influence of notable 19th and 20th century comparativists*. Routledge.

Baily, S. (2023). Reclaiming idealism in a hyperpolitical global landscape: The power of the comparative. *Comparative Education Review, 67*(4), 710–726.

Baker, D. P. (2014). *The schooled society: The educational transformation of global culture*. Stanford University Press.

Bennell, P. (2023). Out of the shadows: The incidence and patterns of private tuition provision in Francophone West and Central Africa. *Compare: A Journal of Comparative and International Education, 53*(8), 1323–1338. http://dx.doi.org/10.1080/03057925.2021.2022461

Bereday, G. Z. F. (1957). Some discussions of methods in comparative education. *Comparative Education Review, 1*(1), 13–15. http://dx.doi.org/10.1086/444747

Bray, M. (2017). Schooling and its supplements: Changing global patterns and implications for comparative education. *Comparative Education Review, 61*(3), 1–20. https://doi.org/10.1086/692709

Bray, M., & Khubakidze, M. (2014). Measurement issues in research on shadow education: Challenges and pitfalls encountered in TIMSS and PISA. *Comparative Education Review, 58*(4), 590–620.

Breslin, T. (2021). *Lessons from the lockdown: The education legacy of COVID-19.* Routledge.

Carnoy, M. (2019). *Transforming comparative education: Fifty years of theory building at Stanford.* Stanford University Press.

Coombs, P. H. (1968). *The world education crisis: A systems approach.* Oxford University Press.

Coombs, P. H. (1985). *The world crisis in education: The view from the eighties.* Oxford University Press.

Davidson, P., Dzotsenidze, N., Park, M., & Wiseman, A. (2020). Compare in contrast: A 50 year retrospective examination of compare. *Journal Retrospective Study Report.* https://baice.ac.uk/compare/journal-retrospective-study-report/

Davidson, P., Taylor, S., Park, C., Dzotsenidze, N., & Wiseman, A. (2017). Reflecting on trends in comparative and international education: A three-year examination of research publications. *Annual Review of Comparative and International Education, 2017,* 1–27.

Denman, B. D. (2019). Critical challenges in approaches and experience in comparative education research. In L. E. Suter, E. Smith, & B. D. Denman (Eds.), *The SAGE handbook of comparative studies in education* (pp. 25–49). SAGE.

Easton, P. B. (2016). *Comparative Education Review* bibliography 2015: Galloping growth and concluding reflections. *Comparative Education Review, 60*(4), 833–843. https://www.jstor.org/stable/26544681

Epstein, E. (1983). Currents left and right: Ideology in comparative education. *Comparative Education Review, 27*(1), 3–19.

Epstein, E. (2008). Setting the normative boundaries: Crucial epistemological benchmarks in comparative education. *Comparative Education, 44*(4), 373–386.

Epstein, E., & Carroll, K. T. (2005). Abusing ancestors: Historical functionalism and the postmodern deviation in comparative education. *Comparative Education Review, 49*(1), 62–88.

Espinoza, O. (2007). Solving the equity–equality conceptual dilemma: A new model for analysis of the educational process. *Educational Research, 49*(1), 343–363.

Farrel, J. (1999). Changing conceptions of equality of education: Forty years of comparative evidence. In R. Arnove & C. Torres (Eds.), *Comparative education: The dialectic of the global and the local* (pp. 149–178). Rowan & Littlefield.

Flessa, J., Bramwell, D., & Mindreau, G. C. (2021). Educational administration research in comparative education, 1995–2018. *Comparative Education Review, 65*(3), 419–444.

Gbrich, C. (2007). *Qualitative data analysis: An introduction.* Sage.

Gerber, T. P., & Hout, M. (1995). Educational stratification in Russia during the Soviet period. *American Journal of Sociology, 101*(3), 611–660.

Gibbons, M., Limoges, C., Nowotny, H., Schwartzman, S., Scott, P., & Trow, M. (2003). *The new production of knowledge: The dynamics of science and research in contemporary societies.* Sage.

Grant, M. J., & Booth, A. A. (2009). Typology of reviews: An analysis of 14 review types and associated methodologies. *Health and Information Libraries Journal, 26,* 91–108.

Halls, W. D. (1990). *Comparative education: Current issues and trends.* Jessica Kingsley.

Hamlin, D., & Peterson, P. E. (2022). Homeschooling skyrocketed during the pandemic, but what does the future hold? *Education Next, 22*(2), 18–24.

Holford, J. (2017). Local and global in the formation of a learning theorist: Peter Jarvis and adult education. *International Journal of Lifelong Education, 36*(1–2), 2–21.

Jing, X., Ghosh, R., Liu, B., & Fruchier, T. (2023). A decade review and bibliometric analysis of the journal "Compare". *Compare: A Journal of Comparative and International Education, 53*(3), 506–524.

Jules, T. D., Shields, R., & Thomas, M. A. M. (Eds.). (2021). *The Bloomsbury handbook of theory in comparative and international education.* Bloomsbury.

Kamani, F. (2021). *An autobiographical snapshot: The impact of Covid-19 on online adult learning in international development* [Unpublished Doctoral Thesis, University of Toronto].

Khanal, S., Pokhrel, S. R., & Dewey, R. (2023). Propagation of Inequality: An analysis of capability development opportunities of Dalits in higher education on the Indian subcontinent. *Compare: A Journal of Comparative and International Education.* https://doi-org.nwulib.idm.oclc.org/10.1080/03057925.2023.2254214

Leedy, P. D., & Ormrod, J. E. (2001). *Practical research: Planning and design*. Prentice Hall.

Levin, H. M., & Kelley, C. (1994). Can education do it alone? *Economics of Education Review, 13*(2), 97–108.

Luoto, J. M. (2023). Comparative education and comparative classroom observation systems. *Comparative Education, 59*(4), 564–583, http://dx.doi.org/10.1080/03050068.2023.2173917

Lutz, W., & Klingholz, R. (2017). *Education first! From Martin Luther to sustainable development*. SUNMEDIA.

Manzon, M. (2011). *Comparative education: Construction of a field*. Springer and University of Hong Kong Centre for Comparative Education.

Mayring, P. (2000). Qualitative content analysis. *Qualitative Social Research, 1*(2), Article 20. http://www.qualitative-research.net/index.php/fqs/article/view/1089/2385

Meyer, H-D., & Benavot, A. (Eds.). (2013). *PISA, power, and policy: The emergence of global educational governance*. Symposium Books.

Morin, J-F., Olsson, C., & Atikcan, E. Ö. (2021). *Research methods in the social sciences: An A-Z of key concepts*. Oxford University Press.

Mundy, K. (2016). "Learning" in on education for all. *Comparative Education Review, 60*(1), 1–26.

Noah, H., & Eckstein, M. (1969). *Toward a science of comparative education*. Macmillan.

Nordtveit, B. (2015). Knowledge production in a constructed field: Reflections on comparative and international education. *Asia Pacific Education Review, 30*(1), 1–11.

Nordtveit, B. (2016). Trends in comparative and international education: Perspectives from the *Comparative Education Review. Annual Review of Comparative and International Education, 30*, 27–37. https://doi.org/10.1108/S1479-367920160000030001

Nordtveit, B. (2023). Transition and change: A decade of comparative and international education. *Comparative Education Review, 67*(4), 701–709.

Paulston, R. G. (1977). Social and educational change: Conceptual frameworks. *Comparative Education Review, 21*(2/3), 37–39.

Paulston, R. G. (1994). Comparative and international education: Paradigms and theories. In T. Husén & T. N. Postlethwaite (Eds.), *The international encyclopedia of education* (2nd ed., pp. 922–933). Pergamon.

Paulston, R. G. (1996). Four principles in a non-innocent social cartography. In R. G. Paulston (Ed.), *Social cartography: Mapping ways of seeing social and educational change* (pp. xv–xxiv). Garland.

Paulston, R. G. (1999). Mapping comparative education after postmodernity. *Comparative Education Review, 43*(3), 438–463.

Pope, C., Ziebland, S., & Mays, N. (2006). Analysing qualitative data. In C. Pope & N. Mays (Eds.), *Qualitative research in health care* (3rd ed., pp. 63–81). Blackwell.

Powell, J. J. W. (2020). Comparative education in an age of competition and collaboration. *Comparative Education, 56*, 1–22.

Proctor, P., Roch, A., Breidenstein, G., & Forsey, M. 2020. Parents, schools and the twenty-first-century state: Comparative perspectives. *Comparative Education, 56*(3), 317–330. http://dx.doi.org/10.1080/03050068.2020.1781422

Psacharopoulos, G. (1990). Comparative education: From theory to practice, or are you A:\neo* or B:*ist? *Comparative Education Review, 34*(3), 369–380.

Roberts, K. (2017). Socio-economic reproduction, In A. Furlong (Ed.), *Routledge handbook of youth and young adulthood* (2nd ed.). Routledge.

Robson, C. (2011). *Real world research: A resource for users of social science research methods in applied settings*. John Wiley.

Rust, V. D. (1991). Postmodernism and its comparative education implications. *Comparative Education Review, 35*(4), 615–626.

Rust, V. D., Soumaré, A., Pescador, O., & Shibuya, M. (1999). Research strategies in comparative education. *Comparative Education Review, 43*(1), 86–109.

Sarantakos, S. (1998). *Social research*. Macmillan.

Schriewer, J. (2014). Neither orthodoxy nor randomness: Differing logics of conducting comparative and international studies in education. *Comparative Education, 50*(1), 84–101. https://doi.org/10.1080/03050068.2014.883745

Schweisfurth, M. (2015). *Fifty years of comparative education*. Routledge.

Schweisfurth, M., Thomas, M., & Smail, A. (2020). Revisiting comparative pedagogy: Methodologies, themes and research communities since 2000. *Compare: A Journal of Comparative and International Education, 52*(4), 560–580. https://doi.org/10.1080/03057925.2020.1797475

Stiglitz, J. E. (2019). *People, power, and profits: Progressive capitalism for an age of discontent*. Penguin.

Stone, H. J. S. (1983). *The common and the diverse: A profile of comparative education*. McGraw-Hill.

Strohmaier, L. (2014, February 17). *Mode 3 knowledge production, or the difference between a blog post and a scientific article*. Intentialicious: Markus Strohmaier's Weblog. https://mstrohm.wordpress.com/2014/02/17/mode-3-knowledge-production-or-the-differences-between-a-blog-post-and-a-scientific-article/

Suter, L. E., Smith, E., & Denman, D. B. (Eds.). (2019). *The SAGE handbook of comparative studies in education* (pp. 25–49). SAGE.

Switzer, H. D. (2018). *When the light is fire: Maasai schoolgirls in contemporary Kenya*. University of Illinois Press.

Turner, D. A. (2022). *Comparative education: A field in discussion*. Brill.

UNESCO/Office of the United Nations High Commissioner for Human Rights. (2006). *Plan of action: World programme for human rights education, first phase*. UNESCO/United Nations.

UNICEF. (2015). *Incheon declaration: Education 2030: Towards inclusive and equitable, quality education for all*. UNICEF.

United Nations. (2011). *United Nations declaration on human rights education*.

Unterhalter, E., North, A., Arnot, M., Lloyd, C., Moletsane, L., Murphy-Graham, E., Parkes, J., & Saito, M. (2014). Interventions to enhance girls' education and gender equality. *Education Rigorous Literature Review*. Department for International Development.

Vaismoradi, M., Turunen, H., & Bondas, T. (2013). Content analysis and thematic analysis: Implications for conducting a qualitative descriptive study. *Nursing Health Science, 15*(3), 398–405.

Walker, M., & Unterhalter, E. (2007). *Amartya Sen's capability approach and social justice in education*. Springer.

Welch, A. R. (2000). New times, hard times: Re-reading comparative education in an age of discontent. In J. Schriewer (Ed.), *Discourse formation in comparative education* (pp. 189–222). Peter Lang.

Wilson, D. N. (1994). Comparative and international education: Fraternal or Siamese twins? A preliminary genealogy of our twin fields. *Comparative Education Review, 38*(4), 161–177. http://dx.doi.org/10.1086/447271

Wolhuter, C. C. (2008). Review of the review: Constructing the identity of comparative education. *Research in Comparative and International Education, 3*(4), 323–344.

Wolhuter, C. C. (2017). The philanthropic mission of comparative and international education bequethed by Jullien: Continuing capstone of the field. *Compare: A Journal of Comparative and International Education, 47*(3), 303–316.

Wolhuter, C. C. (2024). *The global south in comparative and international education: Past, present and future trajectories*. AOSIS (Forthcoming).

Wolhuter, C. C., Espinoza, O., & McGinn, N. (2022). Narratives as a way of conceptualising the field of comparative education. *Compare: A Journal of Comparative and International Education, 54*(2), 259–276. http://dx.doi.org/10.1080/03057925.2022.2093160

Wolhuter, C. C., & Van der Walt, J. L. (2019). Neo-liberalism and the human right creed: Conflicting forces vying for control of the global education agenda. *South African Journal of Education, 39*(4), 1–12

Wolhuter, C. C., & Wiseman, A. W. (Eds.). (2019). *Comparative and international education: Survey of an infinite field*. Emerald.

Wolhuter, C. C., & Wiseman, A. W. (Eds.). (2022a). *World education patterns in the global north: The ebb of global forces and the flow of contextual imperatives*. Emerald.

Wolhuter, C. C., & Wiseman, A. W. (Eds.). (2022b). *World education patterns in the global south: The ebb of global forces and the flow of contextual imperatives*. Emerald.

COMPARATIVE EDUCATION AT THE CROSSROADS: A VIEW FROM HONG KONG

Liz Jackson

University of Hong Kong, Hong Kong

ABSTRACT

This brief reflective piece considers the experience of academics in the field of comparative and international education in Hong Kong. It begins by examining the state of international higher education and the continued dominance of Western contexts and perspectives in publishing in comparative education even in the so-called global era. It contrasts Western-oriented historical and contemporary views of the field with the situation in East Asia and particularly Hong Kong, where lively international dialogue has always been a key theme of academic and intellectual life. Against pronouncements in recent decades of "the death" of Hong Kong, the paper asserts that comparative and international education remains a thriving domain in Hong Kong since the handover and provides further reflections on the history and state of the field today as well as its future promise.

Keywords: Comparative education; Hong Kong; comparative and international education; educational history; East Asian education

Despite waves of negative press the region has faced in recent years, Hong Kong higher education continues to benefit from the challenging lessons of navigating a tenuous position, wedged by historical forces between two giants of ideological, political, and cultural influence: the Western world and China. In 2023, Hong Kong is a postcolonial context indelibly marked by global dialogue and diaspora

---

Annual Review of Comparative and International Education 2023
International Perspectives on Education and Society, Volume 48, 19–25
Copyright © 2025 by Emerald Publishing Limited
All rights of reproduction in any form reserved
ISSN: 1479-3679/doi:10.1108/S1479-367920240000048002

and gifted with rich intellectual and institutional resources to draw upon. As the world around us appears to re-fragment with the rise of populism in the last decade into "the west" and "the rest," there is a potential for Hong Kong scholars to pave a new way in-between ongoing Western imperialism in higher education and the field of comparative and international education for global mutual understanding and learning.

THE WEST AND "THE REST"

Universities in Hong Kong (and, increasingly, in Mainland China) are consistently considered among the best in the world according to many global rankings, with most other regular top contenders from Western countries (Postiglione & Jung, 2017). Some might see this as a mere result of the history of Western colonialism in the region. Indeed, at the same time that Hong Kong higher education perseveres, Western media and Western leaders steadily sketch and retrace simplified pictures of Hong Kong as "dead." While the purpose of this paper is not to delve into recent or historical events, it is worth noting that Hong Kong has been pronounced dead in *Fortune* magazine in 1995, by Milton Friedman in 1999, in *Time* magazine in 2001, and by the last British Governor of Hong Kong Chris Patten in 2020. The regular obituaries are difficult and eerie to read when one is sipping their coffee and working on essays and grading student work while in Hong Kong. While the Covid-19 experience was very hard in Hong Kong and the Mainland (Jandrić et al., 2022), my home seems to me to be as "alive" as anywhere else today; my regular trips abroad do not suggest the vital signs here are weaker than in the States or the United Kingdom (see Jackson, 2021, 2025).

On the other hand, in Hong Kong, we know what makes us special. Although any critical scholar will reflexively ask what exactly is meant by "east" and "west," historical forces have positioned Hong Kong-based scholars to benefit uniquely from insights from Western European liberal and progressive epistemological and educational traditions, as well as from the historical and ongoing dialogues among ancient and modern forms of thought with roots in East Asia, such as Confucianism, Taoism, and Buddhism, among others (Jackson, 2019; Yang, 2019). This goes far beyond the notion that Hong Kong's Western colonial heritage has been its only or primary source of intellectual richness and strength.

In Western or "global" higher education, a colonialist legacy persists. Time and again throughout history, Western thinkers have recognized their position as exceptional across the world: As the best, most enlightened, most progressive (Wallerstein, 1997). It may appear to scholars in the Western world that this is an exaggeration or a historical rather than contemporary feature of so-called international academic communities. After all, most academics aspire to be and think that they are open-minded and wary against any kind of undue cultural or social bias as individuals. But for "the rest," we know Western supremacy still reigns.

In East Asia, scholars have, on the whole, been open-minded as well and interested in learning from the best of traditions around the world. In relation, there have always been active projects for mutual learning. It has been customary for

Comparative Education at the Crossroads 21

East Asian scholars in most societies and across most historical periods to actively seek out opportunities to learn and collaborate with thinkers from around the world (Yang, 2017). Throughout the 20th century, it has been commonplace for students and academics, particularly from Hong Kong, to spend some formative period of higher education abroad, in such countries as the United States, United Kingdom, Canada, and Australia, as well as other parts of Asia (Jackson, 2019; Ninomiya, 2008; Sweeting, 1999; Yang, 2019). The overwhelming majority of academics in Hong Kong today regard international collaboration as vital to their work (Wong & Fairbrother, 2008).

However, Asian scholars have observed, time and time again, that mutual learning does not go both ways. When scholars from outside the Western world enter the United States or the United Kingdom, they are expected to leave their traditions, values, and cultural ways of thinking and living at the airport (Grigorenko, 2007). To most Western scholars, to know anything substantive about the world beyond the West represents a niche interest (Yang, 2013). An American professor might have dozens of students studying with them from East Asia over the span of their careers but remain reluctant throughout to learn anything systematic about education or knowledge where their students come from, outside the West.

This is not something that non-Western academics tend to complain loudly about, because we experience a unique opportunity compared to others to enter into and understand two very different worlds. We learn from the juxtaposition of the two, from experiencing center and periphery perspectives simultaneously, and from refined skills of position taking and epistemological and discursive tone changing (Yang, 2017). Yet Western disinterest, ignorance, and arrogance about the position, values, and traditions of the West relative to those of others are also a source of injustice. Global research assessment frameworks continue to define what is important and distinctive in scholarship from a Western view. This means that non-Western scholars who are committed to improving educational practice and educational scholarship in the context where they live are disadvantaged, facing a burden to communicate why Westerners should care about Asia. Meanwhile, scholars who assimilate their research agendas to Western values and approaches have it easier (Hwang, 2016; Yang, 2019). Following a hidden curriculum of doctoral education, they learn to speak to Western scholars about things that interest Western scholars (and in ways that they like, which implicitly reflect Western prominence and superiority and Asian irrelevance and inferiority), further enabling those in North America and Western Europe to remain happily oblivious and content that they already know about everything important there is to know about.

When producing journal articles, we face obvious bias in apparently double-anonymous peer reviews (Jackson et al., 2018). Fluent, native English speakers who write on topics in or about the non-Western world are criticized in double-anonymous peer-review processes for their language capacity, with additional audacious pleas to kindly explain to the reviewers why they, living in Boston or Edinburgh, for example, should have any interest in what is taking place elsewhere (Davids, 2022). At the same time, we see Western scholars who read and write on Asian themes and traditions build a name for themselves above and apart from local scholars, ultimately extracting the themes and traditions from their historical and practical contexts. The assumption is still that Western scholars are in the best position to explore the global significance of Asian ideas or make them palatable globally, in comparison with a scholar who has been educated within that cultural and social sphere (Wallerstein, 1997). This reiterates the traditional Western anthropological view that the impartial, enlightened scholar (as subject) coming from the West is tasked with studying and scrutinizing the native (as object) and knows better than they do what is of value from their world (Lugones & Spelman, 1983).

We also see something tragic in the way most Western scholars continue to assume the universality of Western frameworks (Latouche, 1996). This can take a few different shapes. On the one hand, there may be the attitude that Western thought has taken over the world, incidentally or by necessity, so that is all there really is to work with anymore. On the other hand, many in the West do not recognize that they have and work and live from traditions. Following a liberal view (Rawls, 1971), they see their tradition minimally, as a consciously, critically chosen way of life, apart from those of people living in "traditional societies" (Taylor, 1992). In this case, they are wary to suggest or imagine that traditions matter to anyone, anywhere, because it is part of their tradition to deny that traditions have value.

So, when a scholar from the non-Western world introduces the idea of significant cultural variation as a noteworthy feature of the world, they are regarded as quaint relics out of touch with our contemporary global reality at best, or at worst as purveyors of cultural stereotypes and biases. Either way, they blame the messengers for sharing ideas that they would prefer not to face. Incredibly, as our world becomes more polarized, Western scholarly interest in other world views remains low, while universalism is taken for granted as the ideal or tolerable, rather than asking questions or meeting global others from a position of equity or humility (Jackson, 2023; Yang, 2019).

THE ROLE OF COMPARATIVE AND INTERNATIONAL EDUCATION

One might hope that the field of comparative and international education would be light years ahead of others when it comes to openness to traditions and ways of thought and life outside the Western center. But this is unfortunately not our experience. International handbooks for comparative and international education describe the field as founded by European scholars, overlooking the practices of international study found elsewhere around the globe and which root the field more widely (e.g., Bray, 2004; Epstein, 2017; Yang, 2019). With a legacy steeped in colonialist anthropological attitudes of Westerners exploring the world and comparing it to their own assumptions, Western-based approaches and measurements remain foregrounded that mark the world as developed or deficient (Jackson, 2013).

Comparative Education at the Crossroads

Intellectually, a great deal of comparative and international education scholarship remains enmeshed in global development projects that assume the superiority of Western-based and Western-rooted so-called international organizations that aim (and succeed) in part to make the world more uniform, standardized, and homogenous rather than more equitable or just (Arnove & Bull, 2015). Here, abstracted empiricism and gathering increasingly more data are preferred approaches, with little consideration for how and why data matter from a more critical view (Cossa, 2016; Epstein, 2016; Jackson, 2022; Mason, 2014). Thus, the West continued to collect data from "the rest" and analyze it according to highly particular schemas and imaginaries of progress and development with little attention paid to the assumptions beneath the surface and the effects of this work in re-entrenching the west-periphery worldview given the remaining global hierarchy in higher education and knowledge production.

THE FIELD IN HONG KONG

In Hong Kong, there is a strong history of comparative and international education. Before the institutionalization of the field, international exchanges and comparative and international curricula were the norm at many Hong Kong higher education institutions, with the University of Hong Kong publishing comparative educational scholarship in the 1920s and offering its first postgraduate diploma with a focus on comparative education in 1939 (Bray, 2004; Sweeting, 1999). The Comparative Education Society of Hong Kong celebrates its 35th birthday this year, while the Comparative Education Research Centre at the University of Hong Kong celebrates its 30th birthday. Scholars from these communities have made an impact on global leadership in the field, for example, serving as presidents of the (American) Comparative and International Education Society and the World Council of Comparative Education Societies (Bray, 2004; Wong & Fairbrother, 2008).

Today our leading scholars come from China, Hong Kong, the United States, Korea, the United Kingdom, Georgia, Cambodia, and Japan, and draw on rich experience in other parts of the world including South Africa, Australia, and other parts of Europe and Asia. Our Society and Centre activities, as well as our Master of Education program in Comparative and Global Studies in Education and Development, continue to attract scholars and students to visit Hong Kong for short- or long-term stays, enriching the academic environment locally while impressing upon visitors the dynamic, engaged, critical nature of our perspectives and our projects.

Most recently, the Comparative Education Research Centre, long known for its strengths in such areas as international comparison and shadow education, has begun a new special interest group on comparative education traditions, involving junior and senior scholars from Europe, North America, Japan, China, and other parts of South and East Asia. Inspired by the University of Hong Kong Faculty of Education Dean Yang Rui, colleagues involved are hopeful to promote awareness that cultural embeddedness is not only a feature of the peripheral "other" but also a feature of all people, that traditions are important parts of everyday life around the world, and that traditions make a difference for educational research, higher education collaboration, and internationally oriented teaching and learning (and for educating diverse learners).

In connection, I am currently leading a multi-volume handbook on philosophies of education of Asia which will include six volumes and leading scholars from around the world who are devoted to ameliorating epistemic injustice in knowledge creation and publication steadily with small if imperfect steps. Thus, with revitalized book series and research projects, connections to leading international journals, and new energy in the post-Covid-19 era for conferences and other events, comparative and international education scholars in Hong Kong are ready to demonstrate proof of life against pronouncements of death and lead global conversations in terms of orientations which make sense to us, where we are not dead, deficient, or the "other."

The experiences of Hong Kong scholars as global leaders in a field that otherwise is heavily Western based, equipped with rich international experiences as individual researchers and as a collective, enable us to trace out the role of tradition across societies while at the same time recognizing the continuing role of global power politics and Western supremacy in the field, including its nature and how it progresses. Indeed, we may be uniquely positioned to help develop mutual understanding at this time, identify gaps in apparent openness, and facilitate dialogues on a more balanced playing field than is possible in the United States, the United Kingdom, or elsewhere in the Western world.

REFERENCES

Arnove, R., & Bull, B. (2015). Education as an ethical concern in the global era. *FIRE: Forum for International Research in Education, 2*(2), 76–87.

Bray, M. (2004). *Comparative education: Traditions, applications, and the role of HKU.* Lecture at the 20th Anniversary Celebration of the Faculty of Education at the University of Hong Kong, and the Annual Conference of the CESHK. Faculty of Education, The University of Hong Kong.

Cossa, J. (2016). Shaping the intellectual landscape. In E. Epstein (Ed.), *Crafting of a global field: Six decades of the Comparative and International Education Society* (pp. 129–139). Comparative Education Research Centre.

Davids, N. (2022). *Out of place: An autoethnography of postcolonial citizenship.* African Minds Publishers.

Epstein, E. (Ed.) (2016). *Crafting of a global field: Six decades of the Comparative and International Education Society.* Comparative Education Research Centre.

Epstein, E. (2017). Is Marc-Antoine Jullien de Paris the 'father' of comparative education? *Compare: A Journal of Comparative and International Education, 47*(3), 317–331.

Grigorenko, E. L. (2007). Hitting, missing, and in between: A typology of the impact of western education on the non-western world. *Comparative Education, 43*(1), 165–186.

Hwang, K. K. (2016). From cultural rehabilitation to cultural renaissance. In C. P. Chou & J. Spangler (Eds.), *Chinese education models in a global age* (pp. 87–101). Springer.

Jackson, L. (2013). They don't *not* want babies: Globalizing philosophy of education and the social imaginary of international development. *Philosophy of Education, 69*(1), 353–361.

Jackson, L. (2019). *Contesting education and identity in Hong Kong.* Routledge.

Jackson, L. (2021). Free speech, false polarization, and the paradox of tolerance. *Philosophy of Education, 77*(3), 139–145.

Jackson, L. (2022). Philosophy of education: Contributions to comparative education. In L. Misiaszek, R. Arnove, & C. A. Torres (Eds.), *Emergent trends in comparative education: The dialectic of the global and the local* (pp. 59–76). Rowman & Littlefield.

Jackson, L. (2023). Humility versus the desire to throw hands up or slam fists down. *Philosophy of Education, 78*(4), 49–53.

Jackson, L. (2025). Beyond Western ideals: Academic freedom, capabilities, and social knowledge. In M. Slowey & R. Taylor (Eds.), *Academic freedom in higher education: Core value or elite privilege?* (pp. 113–129). Routledge (in production).

Jackson, L., Peters, M. A., Benade, L., Devine, N., Arndt, S., Forster, D., Gibbons, A., Grierson, E., Jandrić, P., Lazaroiu, G., Locke, K., Mihaila, R., Stewart, G., Tesar, M., Roberts, P., & Ozoliņš, J. J. (2018). Is peer review in academic publishing still working? *Open Review of Educational Research, 5*(1), 95–112.

Jandrić, P., Martinez, A. F., Reitz, C., Jackson, L., Grauslund, D., Hayes, D., Lukoko, H. O., Hogan, M., Mozelius, P., Aldous-Arantes, J., Levinson, P., Ozoliņš, J. J., Kirylo, J. D., Carr, P. R., Hood, N., Tesar, M., Sturm, S., Abegglen, S., Burns, T., ... Hayes, S. (2022). Teaching in the age of Covid-19: The new normal. *Postdigital Science and Education, 4*, 877–1015.

Latouche, S. (1996). *The westernization of the world: The significance, scope, and limits of the drive towards global uniformity*. Polity Press.

Lugones, M. C., & Spelman, E. V. (1983). Have we got a theory for you! Feminist theory, cultural imperialism and the demand for 'the woman's voice'. *Women's Studies International Forum, 6*(6), 573–581.

Mason, M. (2014). Comparing cultures. In M. Bray, B. Adamson, & M. Mason (Eds.), *Comparative education research: Approaches and methods* (pp. 221–258). Comparative Education Research Centre.

Ninomiya, A. (2008). The Japan Comparative Education Society (JCES). In V. Masemann, M. Bray, & M. Manzon (Eds.), *Common interests, uncommon goals—Histories of the World Council of Comparative Education Societies and its members* (pp. 128–138). Comparative Education Research Centre.

Postiglione, G., & Jung, J. (Eds.). (2017). *The changing academic profession in Hong Kong*. Singapore: Springer.

Rawls, J. (1971). *A theory of justice*. Harvard University Press.

Sweeting, A. (1999). Doing comparative historical education research: Problems and issues from and about Hong Kong. *Compare: A Journal of Comparative Education, 9*(3), 269–285.

Taylor, C. (1992). The politics of recognition. In A. Gutmann (Ed.), *Multiculturalism and the politics of recognition* (pp. 25–74). Princeton University Press.

Wallerstein, I. (1997). Eurocentrism and its avatars: The dilemmas of social science. *Sociological Bulletin, 46*(1), 21–39.

Wong, S.-Y., & Fairbrother, G. P. (2008). The Comparative Education Society of Hong Kong (CESHK). In V. Masemann, M. Bray, & M. Manzon (Eds.), *Common interests, uncommon goals—Histories of the World Council of Comparative Education Societies and its members* (pp. 245–255). Comparative Education Research Centre.

Yang, R. (2013). Indigenizing the western concept of the university: Chinese experience. *Asia Pacific Education Review, 14*, 85–92.

Yang, R. (2017). The cultural mission of China's elite universities: Examples from Peking and Tsinghua. *Studies in Higher Education, 42*(10), 1825–1838.

Yang, R. (2019). Riddled with gaping wounds: A methodological critique of comparative and international studies in education: Views of a professor. In L. Suter, E. Smith, & B. D. Denman (Eds.), *The SAGE handbook of comparative studies in education* (pp. 63–78). Sage.

REFLECTIONS ON COMPARATIVE AND INTERNATIONAL EDUCATION IN MEXICO

Carlos Ornelas[a] and Zaira Navarrete-Cazales[b]

[a]Universidad Autónoma Metropolitana-Xochimilco, Mexico
[b]Universidad Nacional Autónoma de México, Mexico

ABSTRACT

The creation of the Mexican Society for Comparative Education (SOMEC) in 2004 led to increased academic activity, such as designing research projects, picking up speed on publications by Mexican scholars, and developing and importing theoretical approaches. SOMEC has been a significant catalyst in expanding and strengthening comparative education in Mexico and Ibero-America by making studies and research in this discipline accessible to teachers and scholars. SOMEC has contributed substantially to consolidating a robust and diverse academic community in comparative education. SOMEC members have focused on several areas to promote the development and dissemination of comparative education. One of these areas is the publication of specialized volumes, which serve as platforms for sharing research, theories, and pioneering practices. Through critique and debate, SOMEC attempts to influence educational policies. Its work in facilitating access to research and promoting academic exchange has been fundamental to the growth and consolidation of the field of comparative education in Mexico and Ibero-America.

Keywords: Comparative education; educational politics; equity; innovation; inclusion; curriculum; communication technologies

---

Annual Review of Comparative and International Education 2023
International Perspectives on Education and Society, Volume 48, 27–35
Copyright © 2025 by Emerald Publishing Limited
All rights of reproduction in any form reserved
ISSN: 1479-3679/doi:10.1108/S1479-367920240000048003

INTRODUCTION

In 2013, Marco Aurelio Navarro and Carlos Ornelas reported that the field of comparative and international education (CIE) in Mexico was under construction at the beginning of the 21st century. However, the creation of the Mexican Society for Comparative Education (SOMEC) in 2004 led to increased academic activity, such as designing research projects, picking up speed on publications by Mexican scholars, and developing and importing theoretical approaches (Navarro-Leal & Ornelas, 2013). These authors predicted that the future of comparative education in Mexico would likely enjoy increased funding for educational research from various government agencies, international organizations, and private foundations. They were wrong in predicting more financial resources but asserted in forecasting an increase in SOMEC's activity.

SOMEC assumed the identity of a civil association with legal personality and the capacity to convene public events for its members, students, and other academic institutions. To demonstrate its internationalist spirit, SOMEC became affiliated with the World Congress of Comparative Education Societies in 2004 and, in 2007, joined the Ibero-American Society of Comparative Education Societies during the XIII World Congress of Comparative Education held in Sarajevo, Bosnia (Navarro-Leal & Ornelas, 2013).

Twenty years after SOMEC's founding and 11 years after the report published by Navarro-Leal and Ornelas, it is worth asking whether the definition of CIE in Mexico has changed. It is also worth reflecting on SOMEC's role in academic research and CIE dissemination. Finally, what are the responsibilities of researchers and practitioners in CIE?

SOMEC has been a significant catalyst in the expansion and strengthening of comparative education, both in Mexico and in Ibero-America, by making studies and research in this discipline accessible to teachers and researchers. SOMEC has contributed substantially to consolidating a robust and diverse academic community in comparative education. Nevertheless, the CIE field is still under construction and constantly evolving, although minor innovations may occur.

COMPARATIVE EDUCATION RATIONALE

Alexander Wiseman reasons that in the 10 years since the first edition of the *Annual Review of Comparative Education* was published, the field remains siloed into broad but distinct communities focused on (1) economics and development, (2) critical politics and power, (3) empirical research – both qualitative and quantitative –, and (4) program implementation and practical evaluation (Wiseman, 2023). In Mexico, SOMEC members have focused on several areas to promote the development and dissemination of comparative education. One of these areas is the publication of specialized volumes, which serve as platforms for sharing research, theories, and pioneering practices. These books expand existing knowledge and offer theoretical frameworks and methodological approaches to address contemporary educational challenges. There is little research that brings the economics of education into play; SOMEC's books put more emphasis on educational equity, policy and politics, assessment, and new technologies, and even more on the pursuit of understanding and scholarly debates of CIE and its scope. Since its foundation, SOMEC has published 23 books, mostly in editions of its academic meetings.

As at the beginning of the century – when a few Mexican scholars, members of the Comparative and International Education Society (CIES), promoted the founding of SOMEC – there is no official definition of CIE. It is not a balanced academic field with unique theoretical approaches or homogeneous research methods. Most scholars define CIE according to their needs or their working disciplines, such as economics, sociology, politics, history, or philosophy of education (De Sierra-Neves & Navarrete-Cazales, 2019; Iturralde Guerrero et al., 2017; Schmelkes, 2001). Others reason it according to the purposes of their work, be it scientific research or public policy suggestions.

> Still, other groups define comparative education concerning the study site, such as classrooms, schools, states, institutions, systems, or processes. Furthermore, other academics or research groups embrace CIE according to the human subjects they study, such as students, teachers, administrators, and decision-makers. (Navarro-Leal & Ornelas, 2013, p. 52)

Nevertheless, despite no consensus on the CIE definition, SOMEC's effect on comparative education encompasses generating knowledge and forming academic communities. Through critique and debate, it attempts to influence the formulation of educational policies. Its work in facilitating access to research and promoting academic exchange has been fundamental to the growth and consolidation of the field of comparative education, both in Mexico and Ibero-America. Yet, the field of CIE remains siloed in a few areas of study. The number of members of SOMEC is close to 300, distributed in 155 higher education institutions in Mexico and countries of Latin America like Colombia, Peru, and Chile, as well as in the United States and the United Kingdom.

THE IMPETUS OF SOMEC

Although SOMEC is a relatively young society, it has clear purposes that it tries to put into practice through collaboration among its members and fellows of sister societies, especially with the CIES. Its leaders decided not to have a periodical journal but to produce books and propose – after rigorous arbitration – certain papers presented at its symposia and other forums to journals of Latin American and the Spanish Peninsula societies.

SOMEC has three main purposes: (1) To promote the study of CIE and to raise its academic status. (2) To use comparative education to contribute to the solution of educational problems and to facilitate cooperation between CIE practitioners and researchers from different countries and regions. (3) To structure research projects for which there is a particular need. In the spirit of these aims, SOMEC leaders collaborate with sister societies to organize analysis forums in Mexico. Highlights include the 62nd Annual CIES Conference: "Re-Mapping

Global Education: South-North Dialogue," in 2018; the XVII World Congress of Comparative Education Societies: "The Future of Education," in 2019; and the IV Ibero-American Congress of Comparative Education: "Education and Democracy," convened by the Ibero-American Society of Comparative Education (SIBEC), in 2023. However, most of SOMEC's work is domestic, manifested in the meetings it has organized since 2013, resulting in several books.

In these volumes, the members of SOMEC report on the growth of comparative education in Mexico and Latin America, compare education systems in different countries and conduct assessments in different units. Alternatively, from different perspectives, they try to emulate the achievements of renowned researchers who study trends, paradigms, and ideological debates in the broad territories of CIE (for instance, Altbach & Kelly, 1988; Arnove et al., 2022; Baker & Wiseman, 2007; Bray et al., 2010; Carnoy, 1974; Steiner-Khamsi, 2012). Mexican scholars do not scrounge approaches and trends as if they were static knowledge; they try to keep up with theoretical, epistemological, and practical developments and apply them to their concrete studies. Table 1 summarizes the fields and modes in which members of the Society work, publish, and, not infrequently, try to replicate in their teaching activities.

The first book produced by SOMEC after the 2013 report was a compilation by Marco Aurelio Navarro-Leal of renowned authors in the field of CIE, *Comparative Education: Views from Latin America*. He stressed that quite a few SOMEC members were moving toward a Latin American network of researchers interested in establishing a dialogue with non-Spanish-speaking colleagues from the rest of the world. The book's authors raised questions, historical descriptions, reflections, discussions, and cases from Argentina, Chile, Uruguay, Brazil, Peru, Venezuela, Costa Rica, and Mexico to present their points of view (Navarro-Leal, 2013). In 2014, SOMEC published the second book, *Las tecnologías de la información y la comunicación en el sistema educativo mexicano* (*Information and Communication Technologies in the Mexican Education System*) (Manzanilla-Granados & Rojas-Moreno, 2014). The authors emphasized the pervasive presence of information and communication technologies in everyday life, transforming strategies for producing and circulating knowledge and increasingly generating new ways of thinking and living. The authors of the essays did not make predictions, but they did conjecture – and they were correct – that the use of information technologies would not be a panacea, nor would teachers automatically make them their own, perhaps for their particular tasks but not for

Table 1. Comparison Modes.

Locations	Curricula
Systems	Modes of school organization
Times	Varieties in the ways of learning
Cultures	Pedagogical innovations
Values	Programs
Educational performance	Educational reforms

Source: Navarrete-Cazales et al. (2020).

mass teaching. The exception came with the COVID-19 pandemic, but almost a decade later.

These two volumes were traditional compilations, but in 2013, SOMEC held its First Meeting on International and Comparative Education. After a selection and refereeing process, Marco Aurelio Navarro and Zaira Navarrete edited two books of distinction: *Comparar en educación: diversidad de intereses, diversidad de enfoques* (*Benchmarking in Education: Diversity of Interests, Diversity of Approaches*) (Navarro-Leal & Navarrete-Cazales, 2013), and *Internacionalización y educación superior* (*Internationalization and Higher Education*) (Navarrete-Cazales & Navarro-Leal, 2014). They included cases and comparisons from Argentina, Brazil, Chile, the Caribbean, Sweden, and Mexico in educational and institutional contexts of national education systems' various levels and modalities. They dealt with the aims of the educating state and the social meaning of education in the socio-cultural context, the pedagogical structure of schooling processes, their articulation with cultural practices, and internal and external evaluation processes. Few essays analyzed the gap between urban and rural social segments, middle-class students and those living in vulnerable areas, and the differences between public and private schools. Inequity was the hallmark of most of Latin America's educational systems. They concluded that educational research was growing in quantity and quality in the region at the beginning of the second decade of the 21st century.

Beyond the results of the first national meeting organized by SOMEC, Marco Aurelio Navarro and Zaira Navarrete compiled essays to analyze comparative education studies linked to economist approaches and development ideology. In *Educación comparada: internacional y nacional* (*Comparative Education: International and National*) (Navarro-Leal & Navarrete Cazales, 2015), several of the authors argued that the rise of linear theories allowed for transfers or "loans" of models or educational innovations from more advanced countries to less developed ones. However, the intention was to improve education systems and incorporate them into the development path of advanced countries. The most influential theoretical approaches and analyses considered lightly local conditions. Many researchers of advanced countries underrate the conditions and structures of the education systems of less-developed nations. Several chapters argue for an approach that harmonizes analyses of national systems with world trends and globalization.

The same editors took up multiple ideas of this dialectical relationship between national challenges and global development in *Globalización, internacionalización y educación comparada* (*Globalization, Internationalization and Comparative Education*) (Navarrete-Cazales & Navarro-Leal, 2016), with essays and papers resulting from the IInd International and Comparative Education Meeting organized by SOMEC at the Faculty of Philosophy and Letters of the National Autonomous University of Mexico in 2015. This book stressed that the relations between society and education represent a vital axis in comparative education studies and that the debate on globalization and internationalization raises new questions and objects of inquiry but also new opportunities to conduct cross-cultural and comparative research on education and its secular dilemmas such as equity, equality, and quality in education around the world. The volume editors took sides, criticized the inequity or absence of social justice, and favored the search for a democratic, quality, and inclusive education.

As Wiseman (2023) reviews for other parts of the world, the concerns of Latin American researchers also work on discourses that include innovation in educational practice and power within school systems and classrooms. The Third International and Comparative Education Meeting, "Innovación en Educación: Organismos, Instituciones y Actores en Perspectiva Internacional y Comparada" (Innovation in Education: Organizations: Institutions and Actors in an International and Comparative Perspective) generated two books: *Innovación en educación: gestión, currículo y tecnologías* (*Innovation in Education: Management, Curriculum and Technologies*) (Navarrete-Cazales & Navarro-Leal, 2017) and *Política educativa, actores y pedagogía* (*Education Policy, Stakeholders and Pedagogy*) (Ornelas et al., 2018). In the first of those, several authors argue that innovation concerning education is a priority issue to strengthen the processes of administration and implementation of policies, as well as the practices of teaching and learning. This volume focused on pedagogical approaches, the work of teachers – victims and perpetrators –, classroom work, and issues of gender and school violence.

The second echoes classical authors when analyzing the relationship between knowledge and power (Machiavelli and Weber). Various arguments in the collected essays claim that while there may be dominant politics and pedagogy, they are not the only ones. Different interests about education, its purposes, contents, and resources converge in the public space, as do different pedagogical perspectives (explicit and implicit). However, they do not necessarily present antagonistic positions; there are also confluences and alliances. Topics include official knowledge, cultural hegemony, ideological struggles, domination and resistance, and analysis of social actors such as trade unions, civil society organizations, and churches that try to influence children's education.

As Erwin Epstein (2010) pointed out, for the field of CIE in general, the authors of books published by SOMEC have not settled accounts with the positivist past nor with neo-Marxist or institutionalist tendencies. They are ecumenical; they do not disdain any analytical approach. They embark on empirical studies – with emphasis on numbers – and on ethnographic research, consuming hours, days, weeks, and months of observation. They address the role played by institutional actors and the purposes that drive innovators of all kinds. Much of their research focuses on teachers' roles, the main actors in formal education systems. They study their aspirations, credentials, knowledge, dreams, claims, and achievements. They also examine teachers' unions and the political networks woven between them and authorities or political parties. Education reforms are a key theme in many studies (Cordero Arroyo & Vázquez Cruz, 2022; Ornelas, 2017)

In recent years, SOMEC texts address decolonial approaches and a growing emphasis on innovation, inclusion, social justice, and the right to education. For instance, *Innovación e inclusión en educación: Políticas y estrategias de implementación* (*Innovation and Inclusion in Education: Policies and Implementation Strategies*) (Monkman et al., 2021), and *Inclusión en educación* (*Inclusion in*

Education) (Navarrete-Cazales, 2022). These texts discussed the role of the most conspicuous intergovernmental organizations and their advocacy for educational innovations and reforms. There was – and still is – no homogeneous view; the innovations promoted by the World Bank and the OECD are one thing, while those of UNSECO are quite another. The former emphasizes training human capital to increase productivity and make countries more competitive in the global economy. UNESCO does not deny such purposes, but in its proposals, it dominates the idea that education is a human right and that national states must include in their school systems all children without discrimination of any kind. The editors showed some agreement with UNESCO's Incheon Declaration: "Education 2030: Towards Inclusive and Equitable Quality Education and Lifelong Learning for All". This document ratified the principles of Education for All and established 17 Millennium Development Goals. Goal 4 embodied the "transformative and universal vision" of education and culture. The vision is inspired by a humanistic conception of development based on human rights, dignity, social justice, inclusion, protection, cultural, linguistic, and ethnic diversity, shared responsibility, and accountability. Most authors of SOMEC's books agree that education is a public good, a fundamental human right, and the basis for guaranteeing the realization of other rights. It is essential for peace, tolerance, human accomplishment, and sustainable development.

SOMEC also developed a first approach to the analysis of the consequences brought about by COVID-19 and the responses offered by education systems: *Educar en el confinamiento: actores, experiencias y estrategias* (*Educating in Confinement: Actors, Experiences and Strategies*) (Navarro-Leal & Navarrete Cazales, 2023). The editors prepared a summary of the book's arguments. The confinement caused disruptions not only in family routines but also in the production processes of goods. One of the lessons learned was that telework requires both technologies and connectivity robust enough for superior performance and the development of computer skills, especially the formation of habits for remote work and collaboration. In the field of education, confinement also brought great experiences. The disruption of face-to-face classes led to the emergence of a remote education process that adopted different modalities according to the socioeconomic condition of families, connectivity and equipment, and teachers' skills and initiatives. The volume contains 21 papers generated during this time; they proposed alternatives, innovations, and reflections on new directions.

In sum, SOMEC's impact on comparative education in the Ibero-American region is perceptible in several territories. Its congresses are increasingly well attended, and thanks to distance communication, leaders of sister societies, distinguished scholars, and executives of international organizations deliver lectures. Its publications are increasingly popular (several books are out of print); some are required reading or reference in graduate courses and receive favorable reviews. Several of its members publish columns in national or regional newspapers, providing information on their research and comparative education. SOMEC's future looks bright despite the political uncertainty and violence in Mexico.

RESPONSIBILITIES OF CIE RESEARCHERS AND PRACTITIONERS

Most SOMEC members are professors at higher education institutions; others are graduate students, although few have specific credentials in comparative education. Nevertheless, despite from different disciplines and specialties, they converge in their interest in education and making comparisons. The professors' primary responsibility is teaching. Most SOMEC members offer seminars and graduate courses, though few do so in comparative education courses, at times sociology of education, educational policy, economics of education. or seminars with titles that elude the silo to which Wiseman (2023) referred, for example, "Educational Problems of Mexico," "Contemporary Society and Education," "Education, Innovation and Information and Communication Technologies," and "Intercultural, Indigenous and Bilingual Education." However, in all of them, there are explicit glimpses of comparative education approaches. In the teaching tasks, SOMEC members – especially the most productive and well known – inspire students who seek to become scholars. These will be the successors.

Although teaching is a fundamental task, most higher education institutions require their full-time professors (still a minority in Mexico) to do research. What can be observed in SOMEC – without being able to quantify – is that the number of research projects that involve aspects of comparative education is growing. Increasingly, others deal with international issues. Most scholars who cultivate comparative education believe it is a moral obligation to make known the products of their research work. They submit it through presentations in various forums, popular articles, journal papers, chapters in collective books, and a few authored books.

At the end of this report, we move to the first person. We are right when we point out that the SOMEC members – although we do not completely banish the models of analysis and the consolidated theoretical approaches – share, as Regina Cortina (2019) expressed, the passion for the possible. We advocate for equality and social justice in communities at both the local and global levels.

REFERENCES

Altbach, P. G., & Kelly, G. P. (Eds.). (1988). *Textbooks in the third world: Policy Content and context.* Garland.

Arnove, R. F., Franz, S., Ornelas, C., & Torres, C. A. (2022). Education in Latin America: From dependency and neoliberalism to alternative paths of development. In C. A. Torres, R. F. Arnove, & L. I. Misiaszek (Eds.), *Comparative education: The dialectic of the global and the local* (5th ed., pp. 343–376). Rowman & Littlefield.

Baker, D. P., & Wiseman, A. W. (Eds.). (2007). *The impact of comparative education research on institutional theory.* Emerald Publishing Limited.

Bray, M., Adamson, B., & Mason, M. (2010). *Educación Comparada: enfoques y métodos.* Granica.

Carnoy, M. (1974). *Education as cultural imperialism.* David McKay.

Cordero Arroyo, G., & Vázquez Cruz, M. d. Á. (2022). *La formación continua del profesorado de educación básica en el sexenio de la reforma educativa.* Juan Pablos Editor.

Reflections on Comparative and International Education in Mexico

Cortina, R. (2019). Presidential address. "The passion for what is possible". *Comparative Educational Review, 63*(4), 463–479. https://doi.org/10.1086/705411

De Sierra-Neves, M. T., & Navarrete-Cazales, Z. (Eds.). (2019). *Políticas y prácticas educativas en perspectiva comparada.* Universidad Pedagógica Nacional/Sociedad Mexicana de Educación Comparada.

Epstein, E. (2010). Huellas vitales en el desarrollo epistemológico de la educación comparada. In M. A. Navarro (Ed.), *Educación comparada. perspectivas y casos* (pp. 9–16). Consejo Mundial de Sociedades de Educación Comparada/Sociedad Mexicana de Educación Comparada/Planea Editorial.

Iturralde Guerrero, D., Maya, S. P., & Silva, M. L. G. (2017). *La reforma educativa en México, Chile, Ecuador y Uruguay: aportes para un análisis comparado.* Crefal.

Manzanilla-Granados, H. M., & Rojas-Moreno, I. (Eds.). (2014). *Las tecnologías de la información y la comunicación en el sistema educativo mexicano.* Palibrio/Sociedad Mexicana de Educación Comparada.

Monkman, K., Navarrete Cazales, Z., & Ornelas, C. (Eds.). (2021). *Innovación e inclusión en educación: políticas y estrategias de implementación.* Plaza y Valdés Editores/Sociedad Mexicana de Educación Comparada.

Navarrete-Cazales, Z. (Ed.). (2022). *Inclusión en educación.* Plaza y Valdés Editores/Sociedad Mexicana de Educación Comparada.

Navarrete-Cazales, Z., & Navarro-Leal, M. A. (Eds.). (2014). *Internacionalización y educación superior.* Sociedad Mexicana de Educación Comparada/Palibrio.

Navarrete-Cazales, Z., & Navarro-Leal, M. A. (Eds.). (2016). *Globalización, internacionalización y educación comparada.* Plaza y Valdés/Sociedad Mexicana de Educación Comparada.

Navarrete-Cazales, Z., & Navarro-Leal, M. A. (Eds.). (2017). *Innovación en educación: gestión, currículo y tecnologías.* Plaza y Valdés/Sociedad Mexicana de Educación Comparada.

Navarrete-Cazales, Z., Ornelas, C., & Navarro-Leal, M. A. (Eds.). (2020). *Educación comparada: tendencias teóricas y empíricas internacionales y nacionales.* Somec/Plaza y Valdés Editores.

Navarro-Leal, M. A. (Ed.). (2013). *Comparative education: Views from Latin America.* Palibrio, Sociedad Mexicana de Educación Comparada/El Colegio de Tamaulipas.

Navarro-Leal, M. A., & Navarrete-Cazales, Z. (Eds.). (2013). *Comparar en educación: diversidad de intereses, diversidad de enfoques.* El Colegio de Tamaulipas/Sociedad Mexicana de Educación Comparada.

Navarro-Leal, M. A., & Navarrete Cazales, Z. (Eds.). (2015). *Educación comparada internacional y nacional.* Plaza y Valdés/Sociedad Mexicana de Educación Comparada.

Navarro-Leal, M. A., & Navarrete Cazales, Z. (Eds.). (2023). *Educar en el confinamiento: actores, experiencias y estrategias.* Plaza y Valdés Editores/Sociedad Mexicana de Educación Comparada.

Navarro-Leal, M. A., & Ornelas, C. (2013). Mexican perspectives in comparative and international education. In A. Wiseman & E. Anderson (Eds.), *Annual review of comparative and international education 2013* (Vol. 20, pp. 51–56). Emerald.

Ornelas, C. (2017). Mexican educational reform: Politics in the frontline. In J. Zajda (Ed.), *Globalisation and education reforms: Paradigms and ideologies* (pp. 137–153). Springer.

Ornelas, C., Navarro-Leal, M. A., & Navarrete-Cazales, Z. (Eds.). (2018). *Política educativa, actores y pedagogía.* Plaza y Valdés Editores/Sociedad Mexicana de Educación Comparada.

Schmelkes, S. (2001, March 14–17). *Teacher evaluation mechanisms and student achievement: The case of Carrera Magisterial in Mexico.* Annual conference of the Comparative and International Education Society, Washington, DC.

Steiner-Khamsi, G. (2012). Introduction. Understanding policy borrowing and lending: Building comparative policy studies. In G. Steiner-Khamsi & F. Waldow (Eds.), *World yearbook of education 2012: Policy borrowing and lending in education* (pp. 3–19). Routledge.

Wiseman, A. W. (2023). 10 years of reflection on the field of comparative and international education: What difference does it make? In A. W. Wiseman (Ed.), *Annual review of comparative and international education 2022* (Vol. 46B, pp. 1–17). Emerald Publishing Limited.

PART 2

CONCEPTUAL AND METHODOLOGICAL DEVELOPMENTS

EDUCATIONAL CONTESTATIONS IN A CHANGING WORLD SOCIETY

Jieun Song, Minju Choi and Francisco O. Ramirez

Stanford University, USA

ABSTRACT

From a world society perspective, common national educational developments are driven by global cultural models that dominated an international liberal order. These models emphasized the centrality of education as an institution, both as a source of human capital and as an inherent human right. Epistemic communities and international organizations circulated these models influencing national educational policies and reforms. However, in recent decades the international liberal order has been challenged with social movements across the political spectrum questioning the value and authority of education in this order. Earlier educational mandates to be more inclusive are attacked with the rights of women, immigrants, and minorities often targeted. Confidence in knowledge grounded in education and science also gets undercut. In a more fragmented world society, educational contestations increase, reflecting surges in nationalist, populist, and traditional illiberal ideas. We reflect on the impact of these challenges on the centrality of education and propose future research directions to ascertain which educational developments are likely to continue to be globally valued and which are more apt to erode.

Keywords: Liberal/illiberal culture; education as an institution; educational contestations; diversity; equity; inclusion; human rights; human capital; authority of science

---

Annual Review of Comparative and International Education 2023
International Perspectives on Education and Society, Volume 48, 39–56
Copyright © 2025 by Emerald Publishing Limited
All rights of reproduction in any form reserved
ISSN: 1479-3679/doi:10.1108/S1479-367920240000048004

INTRODUCTION

A global liberal order emerged after World War II and deeply influenced national-states and national educational systems. Models of the good nation-state were transmitted through epistemic communities and international organizations and in varying degrees enacted throughout the world (Meyer et al., 1997; Ramirez & Lee, 2023). Nation-states were expected to pursue development and equity goals, and education was central to both of these endeavors. The worldwide expansion of mass schooling and higher education reflected the triumph of education as both human rights and human capital (Baker, 2014). Educated individuals were seen as crucial to national development as well as champions of equity programs. The good nation-state was one with a lot of highly educated and empowered individuals with expanded citizenship rights. The good nation-state was also one where educationally credentialed professionals and scientists enjoyed authority and influence over an expanding number of domains (Drori et al., 2003; Powell et al., 2017).

In this global liberal order, citizenship rights were increasingly framed as human rights (Soysal, 1994). The celebration of these rights often implied limits on national state sovereignty (Sassen, 2006). All humans were entitled to these rights, regardless of the national flag to which they paid allegiance. The authority of professionals and especially scientists was also transnational in character. This liberal order was positively imagined as populated by global citizens and experts without borders. The transformative power of education was a core feature of the liberal imagination. A world with more educated people and more educated experts would surely be a better world. Belief in education driven progress was widespread.

However, this imaginary is now questioned. The global liberal culture today is very much contested (see the chapters in Börzel et al., 2024). Nationalist, populist, and authoritarian social movements revitalize earlier assumptions about who counts and what counts. Nationalists pit themselves against globalists, populists against elites, and conservatives against "woke" liberals (Cole & Schofer, 2023). Illiberal narratives emerge and these percolate in emergent illiberal international organizations and alliances (Bob, 2012; Lake et al., 2021). These narratives vary, from re-emphasizing the virtues of the nation and the national interest to recognizing the genius of "the people" and common sense to celebrating "the family" as the main building block of society. Finally, these social movements highlight the internal contradictions of liberalism, clashes between the rights of individuals and the authority of scientists, for example (Cole et al., 2023).

This paper first explores the role of education in the global liberal order. We focus on the relationship between educational expansion and human rights. Next, we examine the links between education and the authority of science. This paper then turns to illiberal challenges and assesses its educational repercussions. We conclude by sketching research directions to ascertain which dimensions of liberalism and education are most vulnerable to the challenges, and on the other hand, which are more resilient.

Educational Contestations in a Changing World Society   41

We contribute to the comparative and international education literature by examining changes in world models of development and equity and by reflecting on their educational impacts. It is imperative to understand the cultural assumptions and forces that shape educational policies and practices worldwide. Earlier world society scholarship emphasized a growing cultural consensus but in a period of contestation it behooves us to directly address cracks in the global liberal models.

LIBERAL WORLD ORDER AND EDUCATION AS AN INSTITUTION

In this paper, we examine three core cultural assumptions underlying the liberal world order: (1) The centrality of individual rights, freedom, and choice; (2) the rationalization of authority on the basis of scientific expertise; and (3) the value of international institutions that support individual rights and scientific expertise. The liberal culture that underpinned global changes in education emphasized the right and capability of individual persons to make societal progress through learning (Meyer & Jepperson, 2000). As Eleanor Roosevelt (1958) declared during a speech at the United Nations, the goals of equality, equity, and justice were envisioned as achievable by empowering individual persons with rights and utmost dignity:

> Where, after all, do universal human rights begin? In small places, close to home – so close and so small that they cannot be seen on any maps of the world. Yet they are the world of the individual person; the neighborhood he lives in; the school or college he attends; the factory, farm, or office where he works. Such are the places where every man, woman, and child seeks equal justice, equal opportunity, equal dignity without discrimination.

The right to education was one of these enshrined rights in the United Nations (1948), for which Roosevelt played a leading role in drafting. Improving access to education became an increasingly legitimate and universalized goal for countries. As Fig. 1 demonstrates, primary education achieved nearly universal enrollment since the 1980s and other levels of education show steadily increasing rates of enrollment since the 1990s and 2000s. Education thus became deeply institutionalized at all stages of human life, further generating ideas like "lifelong learning" in which learning should be a continuous endeavor in individuals' entire lifespan (Zapp & Dahmen, 2017).

The liberal notion of the "empowered individual" led to not only the expansion of education at all age groups but also the protection of educational rights for various social groups, particularly the historically marginalized. The human rights movement gave greater visibility to the rights of women, children, racial, ethnic, linguistic, religious minorities, and other minoritized groups (Elliott, 2007). Various international human rights treaties were drafted during the peak of the liberal order in which global norms pressured countries to better protect the rights of all individuals (Elliott, 2011; Wotipka & Tsutsui, 2008). Norms emphasizing the common humanity and diversity were reflected in education and

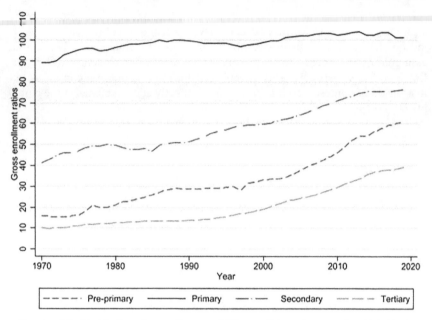

Fig. 1. Worldwide Enrollment Rates at Different Education Levels, 1970–2019.
Source: UNESCO Institute for Statistics (2022).

society at large (Ramirez et al., 2009). For example, a greater number of educational curricula used in schools worldwide have incorporated discussions of women (Nakagawa & Wotipka, 2016), migrants (Choi & Lerch, 2024), and other marginalized groups (Jiménez & Lerch, 2019).

To be sure, some of these rights can be conceptualized as collective or group rights, the right of indigenous peoples to their ancestral lands or more broadly their culture (Tsutsui, 2018). However, the individual was the entity most emphasized in the rights narratives (Boli, 2006; Elliott, 2007, 2011). The triumph of liberal individualism is evident when one considers which rights were more taken for granted and which were more contested in the post-World War II era. In earlier periods, whether women had the right to vote or obtain a higher education degree was much disputed. In these periods the individual was indisputably a man, and in the Western world, a white man (Ferree, 2012; Orloff, 1993). Women's movements in some respects succeeded in de-masculinizing the individual so that women also could enjoy these political and educational rights. To this day these rights are more secure than rights that only pertain to women, reproduction rights, for example (Boyle et al., 2015; Lerch & Ramirez, 2024).

De-racializing the individual also facilitated the acquisition of rights by people of color, but here again, most of these rights were framed as individual rights earlier acquired by white men. The same liberal logic applies to migrants. For both people of color and migrants, the right to education is taken for granted. More contested is whether migrants and minoritized groups have a right to be educated in their language of origin or have their collective histories embodied in school

Educational Contestations in a Changing World Society 43

curricula. The right to be taught in "mother tongue" is in fact a right affirmed in the Convention on the Rights of the Child. But it involves invoking collectives or groups, as indeed does much of the valorization of diversity dynamic (Lee et al., 2024). The international human rights regime mostly but not solely supports the liberal emphasis on the individual as the center of all things. We return to this point in the section on illiberal reactions and their educational repercussions.

The international human rights regime evolved to emphasize human rights education (Ramirez & Choi, 2024; Suárez, 2006). Textbook convergence of human rights increased worldwide (Meyer et al., 2010) as did a student centered focus (Bromley et al., 2011). Students were not only rights bearers themselves but also rights advocates and change agents (Wotipka et al., 2023). But these history and social studies textbook studies also revealed that the nation-state continued to be a central topic (Lerch et al., 2017b). Moreover, while the influence of liberal models was broadly evident, equity concerns in the textbooks also highlighted collective justice issues (Skinner & Bromley, 2019).

The expanded status of the individual from the liberal era intensified in the neoliberal era, generating other developments like the entrance of free market principles into the education space. Dominant explanations have focused on the political economy of the neoliberal era in which privatization of education or school choice policies widely diffused (Ball, 2012; Verger, 2016). In addition to these arguments, we suggest a cultural explanation that expanded individualism has further galvanized the idea that individuals and organizations are "active agents of change" that can make rational and informed decisions (Lerch et al., 2017b, p. 39). As individuals are believed to assume greater agency, they are encouraged to choose from a variety of school types and characteristics, based on their circumstances and preferences. All types of organizational actors assume greater responsibility in providing education, as evidenced by the dramatic increase in the number of private and non-state organizations in education worldwide (Choi et al., 2023).

Critiques of neoliberal principles in education point to the risk of burdening individuals with "choice," in which existing inequalities could exacerbate (Apple, 2001; Waitoller & Super, 2017). Other critics fear that the celebration of choice undercuts the earlier expectation that schools would transform the masses into common citizens (Fuller, 2003). But this assimilationist and liberal assumption faced multiple challenges, from both multiculturalism and cosmopolitanism. Efforts to reconcile liberalism with multiculturalism acknowledge the tensions (Reich, 2002) and as we shall later see, tensions have escalated.

To summarize, a rights-centered global culture facilitated the expansion and celebration of education. Greater educational accessibility was clearly a virtue. Not only were all to be more educated, but all were to be exposed to the rights of their fellow humans. Most of these rights were framed as individual rights. The right to education is globally institutionalized. Other less individual-centered educational rights are more contested.

A second cultural assumption is the rationalization of authority on the basis of scientific expertise. In the liberal imagination neither tradition nor charisma warrant authority and influence. Nor does bureaucracy suffice (in pacem Weber).

Instead, scientific expertise emerges as the favored rationale and justification of authority. Expanded higher education has gone hand in hand with increased scientific expertise (Schofer et al., 2021) and the scientization of society has also propelled the growth of higher education (Schofer & Meyer, 2005). In the liberal imagination what counts as knowledge is produced in universities, or by people who are highly educated. The educationally certified count and play a huge role in shaping what counts in their societies and indeed in the world. This has not always been the case; earlier captains of industry often thought of the highly educated as irrelevant or worse. Academic knowledge was often derided as not connected to the "real world." However, higher education triumphed during the liberal era, becoming the most legitimate source of knowledge (what counts) and allocation of personnel (who counts) (Meyer, 1977). Efforts to become a legitimate source of knowledge inevitably push for standing in universities, from computer science to women's studies (see Fourcade, 2006 for the rise of economics as a science).

In what follows we briefly consider the emergence of a global testing culture as an illustration of the rationalizing authority of scientific expertise (Ramirez et al., 2018; see also the chapters in Smith, 2016). Some very strong (and some would argue unrealistic) assumptions gave rise to this regime. No less than national economic success was presumed to be at stake, driven by how young people performed in standardized mathematics and science tests. Subject matter as well as test and measurement experts crafted the tests. This undertaking would allow national educational policy makers to know how well their children were learning in comparison to the children in other countries. Furthermore, testing advocates contended that countries with low achievers could learn from countries with high achievers, subsequently, initiating the necessary reforms to catch up or even exceed the winners. National science commissions and international organizations supported these multiple endeavors.

The global testing culture has been critiqued on technical and political grounds (Sjøberg, 2016; Zhao, 2020). However, the number of countries participating in international tests has increased and so have the numbers of assessments (Liu, 2016). More recently, a great deal of attention has been mobilized to measure previously unmeasured dimensions of human life like socioemotional learning (Hoffman, 2009) or early childhood development (Fernald et al., 2009). The World Bank's Human Development Index (HDI) similarly assesses various dimensions of human capital, including health, education, and standard of living. The merits and shortcomings of international testing aside, the global testing culture is shaped by core elements of the dominant liberal world culture. There is the universalistic presumption that scientific expertise transcends national differences in gauging learning outcomes (Frank et al., 1995). There is also the optimism that individuals and their societies can learn "best practices" that also transcend national borders.

Lastly, we turn to the role of international institutions supportive of a global liberal order and the centrality of education as a driver of progress. Several scholars point to the birth of the United Nations and the Universal Declaration of Human Rights as fundamental developments in the emergence of the liberal a world order (Ruggie, 1982). Subsequently, international organizations such as

Educational Contestations in a Changing World Society

UNESCO and UNICEF were founded in 1945 and 1946, respectively, as special UN agencies dedicated to education and issues related to children. These organizations have played a central role in establishing education as a universal human right and leading the Education for All (EFA) movement in the late 1990s and early 2000s (Chabbott, 2003). Education as human capital had earlier gained ascendancy and economic development was widely seen as contingent on human development (Chabbott, 2015). The World Bank, earlier skeptical about higher education, would shift gears and join the education for development normative bandwagon (Heyneman, 2003).

The collapse of the Soviet Union gave rise to new democracies in Eastern Europe in the 1990s and elsewhere. Liberal democracies were ubiquitous as were market economies. The transformation of China in the direction of a market economy led to speculation that it would also embrace more liberal ideas in other spaces. These global developments gave rise to the end of the history thesis (Fukuyama, 1992). There appeared to be no viable alternatives to the liberal models of progress.

ILLIBERAL REACTION TO EDUCATION

In what follows, we first focus on the decline of liberal democracies supportive of the rights of individuals and of scientific expertise as rationalizing authority. We discuss which of these two pillars of liberal culture are confronted by which illiberal social movement. Next, we reflect on issues regarding the centrality of education to national progress. We deal with both the perceived value of education in general and the legitimacy of authority based on scientific expertise. Finally, we reflect on contestations of liberal models that arise not from external shocks but rather from internal contradictions.

Although illiberalism can surface in various ways, including through authoritarianism, nationalism, or populism, its core is defined by opposition to liberal ideas and principles, such as individual human rights, liberal democracy, and international cooperation (Bonikowski, 2017; Diamond, 2016; Kurlantzick, 2013; Moffitt, 2016; Norris & Inglehart, 2019). Several studies have documented the decline of democracies in the world as part of the breakdown of the global liberal order (Diamond, 2015). As demonstrated in Fig. 2, the proportion of liberal democracies in the world seems to be declining since the 2010s (using the Varieties of Democracy's measure of liberal democracy). This recent decrease is in contrast to the steadily rising proportion of democracies since the 1970s, illustrating the spread of liberal democratic forms of government across the world during the dominance of the global liberal order. In our paper, the global liberal order is not solely defined by liberal democracy as a type of political regime but speaks to a broader liberal democratic culture in which the dignity and rights of individual persons are presupposed.

The liberal world order is challenged by alternative visions of society. The nationalist movement reaffirms the sanctity of national borders and challenges international institutions that limit state sovereignty. Several developments in this

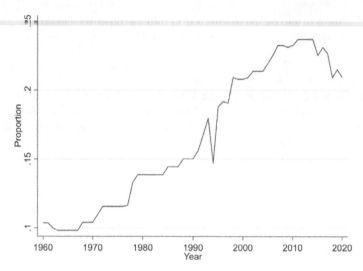

Fig. 2. Proportion of Liberal Democracies in the World, 1960–2020.
Source: Varieties of Democracy Dataset (Version 13) (Coppedge et al., 2023).

direction come to mind. Famously, the election of Donald Trump in the United States and the subsequent actions advanced by the Trump administration – anti-immigration policies, withdrawal from the Paris Climate Accord, and exiting from UNESCO, to name a few – showed how arguably the leading liberal nation in the world could deviate from its cultural anchor. Brexit generated fundamental questions about liberal values, such as international cooperation and human rights – particularly in relation to refugee issues – in contrast to national interest and domestic priorities. From the Global South countries that earlier joined the International Criminal Court have exited, with state sovereignty as the overriding justification for their departure (see the chapters in Steinberg, 2020).

Populist movements target elites and institutions identified with elites. Illiberal populist leaders in Hungary and Poland have sought to control higher education and mass media, often via exclusionary policies and censorship practices (Buzogány & Varga, 2023; Pirro & Stanley, 2022; Surowiec et al., 2020). Similar trends have appeared in other parts of the world, including Hong Kong, Turkey, and Brazil, highlighting the global nature of illiberalism's rise (Hunter & Power, 2019; Öktem & Akkoyunlu, 2018; Thomas, 2018). Right- and left-wing populists differ in some important respects but disenchantment with elites and opposition to their institutions is what they have in common (Cole & Schofer, 2023).

Authoritarian movements directly challenge the idea that individuals are the building blocks of societies and that nothing should be prioritized over their rights. The challenges often invoke religious or traditional family norms, as in debates about women's reproductive or LGBT rights (Velasco, 2023). But communitarian perspectives also raise questions about whether a good society should be individual-centric. An early political economy theorist coined the phrase "possessive individualism" as part of his overarching critique of liberalism (Macpherson, 1962).

Educational Contestations in a Changing World Society 47

In practice, there is of course overlap among the nationalist, populist, and authoritarian movements. But what mostly fuels their activism varies, from anti-globalization to anti-elites to anti individualism. We keep these distinctions in mind as we shift to consider the educational repercussions of illiberal reactions. We are also mindful of the fact that these movements have gained traction, as documented by the World Illiberalism Index (Lerch et al., 2017a). We consider three educational repercussions: (1) Confidence in education as key to individual and national development, (2) confidence in authority rationalized by scientific expertise, and (3) confidence in international educational institutions.

There are different ways of gauging confidence in education. One is to ascertain whether demand for education continues to manifest itself in increased enrollments. Fig. 1 shows that even at the level of higher education, enrollment rates continue to increase. On the other hand, some national surveys indicate that confidence in higher education is declining. In the United States, for example, a 2023 Gallup poll found that only 36% of Americans had high levels of confidence in higher education, a decline of about 20% from 2005. Alternatively, one can scrutinize how education is framed to garner public support. In the heyday of liberalism, both human rights and human capital rationales were activated to foster confidence in education. Both rationales played a role in how education was positively framed in public policies. Jakobi (2011), for instance, found that political parties from 25 OECD countries increasingly supported the expansion of education between 1945 and 2003.

Party ideological differences became less evident since the 1980s. However, a more recent analysis of the Manifesto Dataset demonstrates that political parties are increasingly discussing the cutdown of state budget for education in the recent decades, in comparison to the 1990s (Furuta et al., 2023). Moreover, Choi (2024) observes a recent divergence in which human rights discourse in reforms decreases slightly while human capital discourse continues to rise. Reliance on only an instrumental justification for education may result in more pragmatic and more vulnerable policies. Confidence in institutions often requires a logic of confidence, not just a results logic (Meyer & Rowan, 1977).

Another approach is to think in terms of educational reforms. Belief in progress via education generates reforms time and time again (Tyack & Cuban, 1997). A demise of educational reform efforts raises questions about belief in the centrality of education in the pursuit of progress. Working with an original large cross-national data set of educational reforms, Bromley et al. (2020) show that the rate of educational reforms declined in the post-2008 era. Fig. 3 displays the number of education reforms for three different marginalized groups globally, from the 1970s to the 2010s, as recorded in the World Education Reform Database (Bromley et al., 2023). All three groups – racial/ethnic minorities, girls, and economically marginalized individuals – experienced a rapid increase in reforms during the 1990s and 2000s. However, in the last decade, albeit in varying degrees, the number of education reforms for these groups has markedly decreased. Two main explanations for the decline are possible: First, there was less belief in and enthusiasm for education and education reform in general in the 2010s compared to the 2000s. Second, these particular marginalized groups received less policy attention

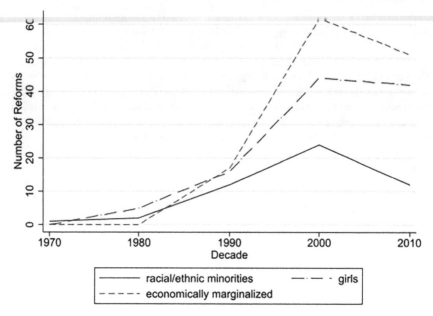

Fig. 3. Number of Education Reforms for Different Marginalized Groups by Decades, 1970–2019. *Source*: World Education Reform Database (Version 1) (Bromley et al., 2023).

in the last decade. Both explanations are linked to the weakening of the liberal world order. In a more illiberal world in the 2010s, perhaps education as an institution saw its influence wane, and many marginalized groups were overlooked or ostracized. That said, it can be observed that the number of reforms for the three marginalized groups was still higher than in the pre-1990s era. This may suggest that, while the centrality of education and the attention paid to marginalized groups might have weakened in the 2010s, the liberal understanding of education as a human right and a pathway to progress and justice has not fully faded.

Much scientific expertise was mobilized in the liberal era to promote more inclusive educational policies for women. Both human rights and human capital rationales were also activated to promote their greater participation in education (European Technology Assessment Network, 2000). And indeed, women's share of higher education has greatly expanded, even in the science, technology, engineering, and math fields of study (Kwak & Ramirez, 2019). This has led some observers to confidently depict women as destined for equality (Jackson, 1998). However, bumps on the road to equality cannot be overlooked. An extreme example is Afghanistan's Taliban entirely banning the education of girls (Akbari and True, 2022). Working with cross-national longitudinal data, Lerch et al. (2022) show women's participation in higher education slowing down more recently. More importantly, the negative period effect is greater for countries with links to illiberal international non-governmental organizations. The emergence and expansion of these organizations is part of the illiberal reaction (Bob, 2012; Lake et al., 2021).

Educational Contestations in a Changing World Society 49

Much scientific expertise has also been used to dispel race and ethnic biases that add up to education barriers. This has led to international declarations against discriminatory practices, often emphasizing common humanity as a core liberal value. This has become a contentious issue with respect to the rights of migrants and various marginalized groups. Nationalist sentiments characterize migrants not as individuals seeking a better life but as an alien force threatening "our" way of life. In authoritarian regimes, these sentiments lead to educational policies that undermine educational opportunities for migrants and other marginalized groups (Agbaria, 2018; Hadj-Abdou, 2021; Siebers, 2019).

Challenges to scientific expertise are also reflected in attacks on the university, including efforts to dismantle academic freedom norms. Given that the university plays a central role in creating and legitimizing scientific knowledge in contemporary society, an attack on science is equivalent to an attack on higher education as an institution (Frank & Meyer, 2020; Meyer et al., 2007). Recent studies are informative. Schofer et al. (2022) showed that societies linked to illiberal organizations have lower higher education enrollments, reduced funding for universities, and more academic repression. Relatedly, Lerch et al. (2024) found that academic freedom, which grew rapidly during the liberal era, has started to decline in recent years. They provided evidence that academic freedom in a country tends to diminish when illiberalism is prominent at a global level and when the country is more connected to such illiberal institutions. Easier access to the Internet facilities challenges to the authority of science and more broadly educationally certified expertise (Eyal, 2019).

Finally, the recent surge in nationalism and ethnocentrism has cast doubt upon the internationalization of higher education, which had made significant progress over the past few decades (Douglass, 2021; Rumbley et al., 2022). The internationalization of higher education has been driven not only by universities' ambitions to be globally competitive but also by countries' commitment to national and global development, and by the encouragement of international organizations for universities to engage in global issues (Altbach & Knight, 2007; Buckner, 2019; Knight, 2004; Song, 2024). All these drivers of internationalization can be seen as derivative of the underlying global liberal culture that promotes the idea of exchange and cooperation across national borders. Based on the liberal idea that the world is connected, knowledge is universal, and that students and faculty should be equipped with global perspectives, universities around the world have invested a lot of their resources into internationalizing their curricula and personnel.

However, the rise of illiberalism is changing the global landscape of higher education. Altbach and De Wit (2018) contend that "the era of higher education internationalization" might be over or "at least, be on life support" due to recent geopolitical trends. In fact, tensions surrounding internationalization are increasingly being identified worldwide. For example, Brexit propelled concerns about research collaboration between the United Kingdom and other (mostly European) countries, while the Trump administration caused many international students to worry about their alien status (Zeleza, 2017). Furthermore, international students face greater discrimination in a largely nationalistic environment (Ortaçtepe & Burhan-Horasanli, 2023).

AREAS FOR FUTURE INQUIRY

Challenges to the global liberal order can be further investigated guided by three broad questions: (1) Do some of the challenges arise out of the contradictions inherent to liberalism? (2) Are there some rights and some science authorities that are more secure and others more contested? (3) Are some societies more at risk of abandoning liberal institutions?

A global liberal culture fostered both highly empowered individuals and authority and influence legitimated by scientific expertise. Highly educated people are supposed to "listen to science." But this culture also fosters individual choice and valorizes individual opinion independent of the knowledge base that anchors opinion. Jepperson (1992), for example, finds that in liberal America people are less likely to check the "I do not know" or "no opinion" box in surveys than citizens from less liberal societies. Vaccine rates have declined in recent years and more so in more individualistic societies (Cole & Schofer, 2023). These findings suggest that we are in an era where the relationship between empowered individuals and scientific authority has become more problematic. Contradictions within liberalism may become more intense in light of illiberal populism.

A second contradiction is whether individuals have rights that require recognition of them as collectives or groups. The rise of unions in the 19th century was opposed to the liberal premise that individual workers should be negotiating with individual employers (Bendix, 1978). But the post-World War II liberal culture increasingly favored expanded individual rights that included invoking group rights based on collective identities. Anti-discrimination law morphed into affirmative action and later diversity, equity, and inclusion initiatives (Gavrila et al., 2024). These developments were framed as liberal ones and diversity initiatives flourished in other countries as well (Baltaru, 2018; Oertel, 2018). The educational repercussions varied from efforts to diversify the composition of the student and faculty bodies to calls to incorporate the lived experiences of women and minoritized groups in curricula to stressing the need for an overall sensitivity to the previously excluded. In American universities diversity, equity, and inclusion offices emerged and diffused, with almost eighty percent of four-year universities displaying a diversity office by 2020 (Gavrila et al., 2024).

We are now in the backlash era characterized by direct attacks on DEI (Gavrila et al., 2024). Much of the reaction is framed as opposition to "woke liberalism." Indeed, a lot of the reaction is a feature of overall critiques of higher education that combine elements of the three strands of illiberalism. There are calls to return to a more traditional curriculum with a revitalized nationalist focus. There are also calls for so-called color-blind admission policies, as reflected in the *Fair Admissions* v. *President and Fellows of Harvard College* decision. From a 21st-century liberal perspective, the backlash is itself a reactionary attempt to turn the clock back and halt inclusionary policies designed to rectify past exclusionary ones. However, a careful reading of the Fair Admissions decision reveals the tension between a sole focus on individual rights and collective rights. Universities could take race into account in a way that only considered individuals, not their groups. Justice Roberts wrote that universities could assign:

Educational Contestations in a Changing World Society 51

> benefit to a student who overcame racial discrimination, for example, must be tied to that student's courage and determination. Or, a benefit to a student whose heritage or couture motivated him or her to assume a leadership role or attain particular goal must be tied to that student's unique ability to contribute to the university. (*Students for Fair Admissions* v. *President and Fellows of Harvard College*, 2002, p. 40)

We see this as another example of contradictions within liberalism. Highly empowered individuals from previously excluded groups activate their group-based identities and make collective demands. These are not just demands for greater inclusion but also for having their collective lived experiences and aspirations reflected in what counts (curricula) and who counts (faculty and university leaders). In coping with the tensions between liberalism and multiculturalism, universities (and other institutions) increasingly adopted a "diversity leads to excellence" rationale. That rationale is now either directly challenged under the banner of meritocracy or reframed as applied only to individuals and not to groups. The tensions arise because liberal culture fosters both empowered individuals who go on to assert rights that invoke their group-based identities and the mantra that the individual is the center of all things.

To summarize, we have highlighted two contradictions that can be attributed to liberalism itself. The first pits the rights endowed individuals versus the authority of science and the second features the right of empowered individuals to make collective demands that collide with the liberal assumption that society is mostly an aggregation of individuals. Research that addresses these tensions is much needed.

We conclude by briefly reflecting on the second and third future areas of research. We start from the premise that not all rights and not all educationally certified authority are as firmly grounded in liberal culture. Those less well established are more at risk of eroding given the rise of illiberal contestations. Attempts to systematically exclude segments of the population from schools and universities are less likely to thrive than efforts to restrict what counts as knowledge in these educational institutions. Illiberal nationalist revivals, for example, may target global citizenship narratives more assiduously than bar entry on ethnic criteria. The right to education was in place as an individual citizenship right long before its declaration as a human right. Global citizenship more recently gained traction and rather directly impedes a revival of nationalism (Huntington, 2004).

With respect to what gets taught, evolution grounded in biological science is probably less at risk than social science-based understandings of human sexuality. The authority of the natural sciences is more secure and especially if it does not impose straightforward mandates on human behavior, basic versus medical science, for instance. Mathematicians and theoretical physicists are less likely to draw populist ire and get caught up in culture wars than social scientists.

Research is needed to ascertain whether it is indeed the case that some rights are "more sticky" and why that is the case. Research is also needed to figure out whether some forms of scientific expertise are more taken for granted and thus more likely to not be challenged or to endure contestations if these arise.

Finally, it behooves us to recognize that the impacts of illiberalism may vary depending on the historical legacies of the societies that experience its surges. Do historically weak liberal institutions account for the triumph of the autocratic regimes in Turkey and Hungary and attacks on universities therein? Stronger lib eral traditions did not spare America a populist uprising that almost prevented the peaceful transition of executive power. Early world society scholarship showed that historical legacies mattered more so in the early stages of a policy or organizational diffusion. Beyond some tipping point though, what other societies adopted worldwide or in their regions was more consequential. This process has been referred to as a normative cascade (Finnemore & Sikkink, 1998). The same analytical strategy can be utilized to examine the growth of illiberal challenges to ascertain what factors lead to earlier adopters and whether over time an anti-liberal normative cascade emerges.

It is of course possible that this era of contestations will not result in the over-throw of a liberal culture. Instead of a new global illiberal culture we may have a fragmented global culture characterized by greater inconsistencies on what con-stitutes a good nation state and a good educational system. The high priests of nationalism, populism, and traditionalism may still have to contend with persis-tent liberal deities and their influence.

REFERENCES

Agbaria, A. K. (2018). The 'Right' education in Israel: Segregation, religious ethnonationalism, and depoliticized professionalism. *Critical Studies in Education, 59*(1), 18–34.

Akbari, F., & True, J. (2022). One year on from the Taliban takeover of Afghanistan: Re-instituting gender apartheid. *Australian Journal of International Affairs, 76*(6), 624–633.

Altbach, P. G., & De Wit, H. (2018). Are we facing a fundamental challenge to higher education inter-nationalization? *International Higher Education, 93*, 2–4.

Altbach, P. G., & Knight, J. (2007). The internationalisation of higher education: Motivations and realities. *Journal of Studies in International Education, 11*(3–4), 290–305

Apple, M. W. (2001). Comparing neo-liberal projects and inequality in education. *Comparative Education, 37*(4), 409–423.

Ball, S. J. (2012). *Global Education Inc.: New policy networks and the neoliberal imaginary.* Routledge.

Baker, D. (2014). *The schooled society: The educational transformation of global culture.* Stanford University Press.

Baltaru, R.-D. (2018). Universities' pursuit of inclusion and its effects on professional staff: The case of the United Kingdom. *Higher Education, 77*(4), 641–656.

Bendix, R. (1978). *Kings or people: Power and the mandate to rule.* University of California Press.

Bob, C. (2012). *The global right wing and the clash of world politics.* Cambridge University Press.

Boli, J. (2006). The rationalization of virtue and virtuosity in world society. In M.-L. Djelic & K. Sahlin-Andersson (Eds.), *Transnational governance: Institutional dynamics of regulation* (pp. 95–118). Cambridge University Press.

Bonikowski, B. (2017). Ethno-nationalist populism and the mobilization of collective resentment. *The British Journal of Sociology, 68*(S1), S181–S213.

Börzel, T., Gerschewski, J., & Zürn, M. (Eds.). (2024). *The liberal script at the beginning of the 21st century: Conceptions, components, and tensions.* Oxford University Press.

Boyle, E. H., Kim, M., & Longhofer, W. (2015). Abortion liberalization in world society, 1960–2009. *American Journal of Sociology, 121*(3), 882–913.

Bromley, P., Kijima, R., Overbey, L., Furuta, J., Choi, M., & Santos, H. (2023). World Education Reform Database, v1.

Bromley, P., Meyer, J. W., & Ramirez, F. O. (2011). Student-centeredness in social science textbooks, 1970–2008: A cross-national study. *Social Forces, 90*(2), 547–570.

Bromley, P., Overbey, L., Furuta, J., & Kijima, R. (2020). Education reform in the twenty-first century: Declining emphases in international organisation reports, 1998–2018. *Globalisation, Societies and Education, 19*(1), 23–40.

Educational Contestations in a Changing World Society   53

Buckner, E. (2019). The internationalization of higher education: National interpretations of a global model. *Comparative Education Review, 63*(3), 315–336.

Buzogány, A., & Varga, M. (2023). Illiberal thought collectives and policy networks in Hungary and Poland. *European Politics and Society, 24*(1), 40–58.

Chabbott, C. (2003). *Constructing education for development: International organizations and education for all.* RoutledgeFalmer.

Chabbott, C. (2015). *Institutionalizing health and education for all: Global goals, innovations, and scaling up.* Teachers College Press.

Choi, M. (2024). Human Rights and human capital discourse in national education reforms, 1960-2018. *Comparative Education Review, 68*(1), 15–40.

Choi, M., D'Apice, H. K., Skinner, N. A., & Bromley, P. (2023). World culture, education, and organization. In P. Mattei, X. Dumay, E. Mangez, & J. Behrends (Eds.), *Oxford handbook on education and globalization* (pp. 119–146). Oxford University Press.

Choi, M., & Lerch, J. C. (2024). Portrayal of immigrants and refugees in textbooks worldwide, 1963-2011. *International Sociology, 39*(4), 399–421.

Cole, W. M., & Schofer, E. (2023). Destroying democracy for the people: The economic, social, and political consequences of populist rule, 1990 to 2017. *Social Problems*, 1–29.

Cole, W. M., Schofer, E., & Velasco, K. (2023). Individual empowerment, institutional confidence, and vaccination rates in cross-national perspective, 1995 to 2018. *American Sociological Review, 88*(3), 379–417.

Coppedge, M., Gerring, J., Knutsen, C. H., Lindberg, S. I., Teorell, J., Altman, D., Bernhard, M., Cornell, A., Fish, M. S., Gastaldi, L., Gjerløw, H., Glynn, A., Good God, A., Grahn, S., Hicken, A., Kinzelbach, K., Krusell, J., Marquardt, K. L., McMann, K., … Ziblatt, D. (2023). V-Dem [Country-Year/Country-Date] Dataset v13. Varieties of Democracy (V-Dem) Project. https://doi.org/10.23696/vdemds23

Diamond, L. (2015). Facing up to the democratic recession. *Journal of Democracy, 26*(1), 141–155.

Diamond, L. (2016). Democracy in decline: How Washington can reverse the tide. *Foreign Affairs, 95*(4), 151–159.

Douglass, J. A. (2021). *Neo-nationalism and universities: Populists, autocrats, and the future of higher education.* Johns Hopkins University Press.

Drori, G. S., Meyer, J. W., Ramirez, F. O., & Schofer, E. (2003). *Science in the modern world polity: Institutionalization and globalization.* Stanford University Press.

Eleanor, R. (1958, March 27). *Where do universal human rights begin?* United Nations.

Elliott, M. A. (2007). Human rights and the triumph of the individual in world culture. *Cultural Sociology, 1*(3), 343–363.

Elliott, M. A. (2011). The institutional expansion of human rights, 1863-2003: A comprehensive dataset of international instruments. *Journal of Peace Research, 48*(4), 537–546.

European Technology Assessment Network. (2000). *Science policies in the European Union: Promoting excellence through mainstreaming gender equality.* European Union.

Eyal, G. (2019). *The crisis of expertise.* Polity Press.

Fernald, L. C. H., Kariger, P., Engle, P., & Raikes, A. (2009). *Examining early child development in low-income countries: A toolkit for the assessment of children in the first five years of life.* The International Bank for Reconstruction and Development/The World Bank.

Ferree, M. M. (2012). *Varieties of feminism: German gender politics in global perspective.* Stanford University Press.

Finnemore, M., & Sikkink, K. (1998). International norm dynamics and political change. *International Organization, 52*(4), 887–917.

Fourcade, M. (2006). The construction of a global profession: The transnationalization of economics. *American Journal of Sociology, 112*(1), 145–194.

Frank, D., & Meyer, J. W. (2020). *The university and the global knowledge society.* Princeton University Press.

Frank, D., Meyer, J. W., & Miyahara, D. (1995). The individualist polity and the prevalence of professionalized psychology: A cross-national study. *American Sociological Review, 60*(3), 360–377.

Fukuyama, F. (1992). *The end of history and the last man.* Free Press.

Fuller, B. (2003). Education policy under cultural pluralism. *Educational Researcher, 32*(9), 15–24.

Furuta, J., Meyer, J. W., & Bromley, P. (2023). Education in a post-liberal world society. In X. Dumay, E. Mangez, P. Mattei, & J. Behrends (Eds.), *Oxford handbook on education and globalization* (pp. 96–118). Oxford University Press.

Gavrila, G., Overvey, L., & Ramirez, F. (2024) "In the name of diveristy: Analyzing the adoptions of diveristy-related offices in American higher education, 1969-2020". Under review.

Hadj-Abdou, L. (2021). Illiberal democracy and the politicization of immigration. In A. Sajó, R. Uitz, & S. Holmes (Eds.), *Routledge handbook of illiberalism* (pp. 299–312). Routledge.

Heyneman, S. P. (2003). The history and problems in the making of education policy at the World Bank 1960-2000. *International Journal of Educational Development, 23*(3), 315–337.

Hoffman, D. M. (2009). Reflecting on social emotional learning: A critical perspective on trends in the United States. *Review of Educational Research, 79*(2), 533–556.

Hunter, W., & Power, T. J. (2019). Bolsonaro and Brazil's illiberal backlash. *Journal of Democracy, 30*, 68–82.

Huntington, S. P. (2004). *Who are we? The challenges to America's national identity*. Simon & Schuster.

Jackson, R. M. (1998). *Destined for equality: The inevitable rise of women's status*. Harvard University Press.

Jakobi, A. P. (2011). Political parties and the institutionalization of education: A comparative analysis of party manifestos. *Comparative Education Review, 55*(2), 189–209.

Jepperson, R. L. (1992). *National scripts: The varying construction of individualism and opinion across the modern nation-states* [Ph.D. dissertation]. Yale University.

Jiménez, J. D., & Lerch, J. C. (2019). Waves of diversity: Depictions of marginalized groups and their rights in social science textbooks, 1900–2013. *Comparative Education Review, 63*(2), 166–188.

Knight, J. (2004). Internationalization remodeled: Definition, approaches, and rationales. *Journal of Studies in International Education, 8*(1), 5–31.

Kurlantzick, J. (2013). *Democracy in retreat: The revolt of the middle class and the worldwide decline of representative government*. Yale University Press.

Kwak, N., & Ramirez, F. O. (2019). Is engineering harder to crack than science? A cross-national analysis of women's participation in male-dominated fields of study in higher education. In *Annual review of comparative and international education 2018* (Vol. 37, pp. 159–183). Emerald Group Publishing Limited.

Lake, D. A., Martin, L. L., & Risse, T. (2021). Challenges to the liberal order: Reflections on international organization. *International Organization, 75*, 225–257.

Lee, S. S., Wotipka, C. M., Ramirez, F. O., & Song, J. (2024). To STEM or not to STEM: A cross-national analysis of gender and tertiary graduates in science, technology, engineering, and math, 1998–2018. *International Journal of Comparative Sociology*.

Lerch, J. C., Bromley, P., Ramirez, F. O., & Meyer, J. W. (2017a). The rise of individual agency in conceptions of society: Textbooks worldwide, 1950-2011. *International Sociology, 32*(1), 38–60.

Lerch, J. C., Frank, D. J., & Schofer, E. (2024). The social foundations of academic freedom: Heterogenous institutions in world society, 1960 to 2022. *American Sociological Review, 89*(1), 88–125.

Lerch, J. C., & Ramirez, F. O. (2024). Global liberalism and women's rights. In T. Börzel, J. Gerschewski, & M. Zürn (Eds.), *The liberal script at the beginning of the 21st century: Conceptions, components, and tensions* (pp. 322–352). Oxford University Press.

Lerch, J. C., Russell, S. G., & Ramirez, F. O. (2017b). Wither the nation-state? A comparative analysis of nationalism in textbooks. *Social Forces, 96*(1), 153–180.

Lerch, J. C., Schofer, E., Frank, D. J., Longhofer, W., Ramirez, F. O., Wotipka, C. M., & Velasco, K. (2022). Women's participation and challenges to the liberal script: A global perspective. *International Sociology, 37*(3), 305–329.

Liu, J. (2016). Student achievement and PISA rankings: Policy effects or cultural explanation? In W. C. Smith (Ed.), *The global testing culture: Shaping education policy, perceptions, and practice* (pp. 85–100). Symposium Books.

Macpherson, C. B. (1962). *The political theory of possessive individualism: Hobbes to Locke*. Oxford University Press.

Meyer, J. W. (1977). The effects of education as an institution. *American Journal of Sociology, 83*(1), 55–77.

Educational Contestations in a Changing World Society

Meyer, J. W., Boli, J., Thomas, G. M., & Ramirez, F. O. (1997). World society and the nation-state. *American Journal of Sociology*, *103*(1), 144–181. https://doi.org/10.1086/231174

Meyer, J. W., Bromley, P., & Ramirez, F. O. (2010). Human rights in social science textbooks: Cross-national analyses, 1970–2008. *Sociology of Education*, *83*(2), 111–134.

Meyer, J. W., & Jepperson, R. L. (2000). The "Actors" of modern society: The cultural construction of social agency. *Sociological Theory*, *18*(1), 100–120.

Meyer, J. W., Ramirez, F. O., Frank, D. J., & Schofer, E. (2007). Higher education as an institution. In P. J. Gumport (Ed.), *Sociology of higher education: Contributions and their contexts* (pp. 187–221). Johns Hopkins University Press.

Meyer, J. W., & Rowan, B. (1977). Institutionalized organizations: Formal structure as myth and ceremony. *American Journal of Sociology*, *83*(2), 340–363.

Moffitt, B. (2016). *The global rise of populism: Performance, political style, and representation*. Stanford University Press.

Nakagawa, M., & Wotipka, C. M. (2016). The worldwide incorporation of women and women's rights discourse in social science textbooks, 1970–2008. *Comparative Education Review*, *60*(3), 501–529.

Norris, P., & Inglehart, R. (2019). *Cultural backlash: Trump, Brexit, and authoritarian populism*. Cambridge University Press.

Oertel, S. (2018). The role of imprinting on the adoption of diversity management in German universities. *Public Administration*, *96*(1), 104–118.

Öktem, K., & Akkoyunlu, K. (Eds.). (2018). *Exit from democracy: Illiberal governance in Turkey and beyond*. Routledge.

Orloff, A. S. (1993). Gender and the social rights of citizenship: The comparative analysis of gender relations and welfare states. *American Sociological Review*, *58*(3), 303–328.

Ortaçtepe, H. D., & Burhan-Horasanli, E. (2023). Neo-nationalism and Turkish higher education: A phenomenological case study of a multilingual scholar's identity (re) construction. *Studies in Higher Education*, *49*(8), 1451–1462.

Pirro, A. L. P., & Stanley, B. (2022). Forging, bending, and breaking: Enacting the "illiberal playbook" in Hungary and Poland. *Perspectives on Politics*, *20*(1), 86–101.

Powell, J. J. W., Baker, D. P., & Fernandez, F. (2017). *The century of science: The global triumph of the research university*. Emerald Group Publishing.

Ramirez, F. O., Bromley, P., & Russell, S. G. (2009). The valorization of humanity and diversity. *Multicultural Education Review*, *1*(1), 29–54.

Ramirez, F. O., & Choi, M. (2024). Educational expansion and human rights. In M. Berends, B. Schneider, & S. Lamb (Eds.), *SAGE handbook on the sociology of education* (pp. 612–628). SAGE Publications.

Ramirez, F. O., & Lee, S. S. (2023). Globalizing nation states and national education projects. In P. Mattei, X. Dumay, E. Mangez, & J. Behrend (Eds.), *The Oxford handbook of education and globalization* (pp. 29–50). Oxford University Press.

Ramirez, F. O., Meyer, J. W., & Schofer, E. (2018). International tests, national assessments, and educational development (1970–2012). *Comparative Education Review*, *62*(3), 344–364.

Reich, R. (2002). *Bridging liberalism and multiculturalism in American education*. University of Chicago Press.

Roosevelt, E. (1958). *IN YOUR HANDS: A guide for community action for the tenth anniversary of the universal declaration of human rights*. UN Commission on Human Rights.

Ruggie, J. G. (1982). International regimes, transactions, and change: Embedded liberalism in the postwar economic order. *International Organization*, *36*(2), 379–415.

Rumbley, L. E., Altbach, P. G., Reisberg, L., & Leask, B. (2022). Trends in global higher education and the future of internationalization: Beyond 2020. In D. K. Deardorff, H. de Wit, B. Leask, & H. Charles (Eds.), *The handbook of international higher education* (pp. 64–80). Routledge.

Sassen, S. (2006). *Territory, authority, rights: From medieval to global assemblages*. Princeton University Press.

Schofer, E., Lerch, J. C., & Meyer, J. W. (2022). Illiberal reactions to higher education. *Minerva*, *60*(4), 509–534.

Schofer, E., & Meyer, J. W. (2005). The worldwide expansion of higher education in the twentieth century. *American Sociological Review*, *70*, 898–920.

Schofer, E., Ramirez, F. O., & Meyer, J. W. (2021). The societal consequences of higher education. *Sociology of Education, 94*(1), 1–19.

Siebers, H. (2019). Are education and nationalism a happy marriage? Ethno-nationalist disruptions of education in Dutch classrooms. *British Journal of Sociology of Education, 40*(1), 33–49.

Sjøberg, S. (2016). OECD, PISA, and globalization: The influence of the international assessment regime. In C. H. Tienken & C. A. Mullen (Eds.), *Education policy perils: Tackling the tough issues* (pp. 102–133). Routledge.

Skinner, N., & Bromley, P. (2019). Individual and collective social justice education: Comparing emphases on human rights and social movements in textbooks worldwide. *Comparative Education Review, 63*(4), 502–528.

Smith, W. C. (Ed.). (2016). *The global testing culture: Shaping education policy, perceptions, and practice.* Symposium Books.

Song, J. (2024). Bridging universities and the world: A cross-national analysis of countries' participation in the UNITWIN/UNESCO chairs programme, 1992–2020. *Compare: A Journal of Comparative and International Education,* 1–19.

Soysal, Y. N. (1994). *Limits of citizenship: Migrants and postnational membership in Europe.* University of Chicago Press.

Steinberg, R. H. (Ed.). (2020). *The international criminal court: Contemporary challenges and reform proposals.* Brill.

Students for Fair Admissions v. *President and Fellows of Harvard College*, 40, U.S. (2002).

Suárez, D. (2006). The institutionalization of human rights education. In A. W. Wiseman & D. P. Baker (Eds.), *The impact of comparative education research on neoinstitutional theory* (Vol. 7, pp. 95–120). Emerald Group Publishing Limited.

Surowiec, P., Kania-Lundholm, M., & Winiarska-Brodowska, M. (2020). Towards illiberal conditioning? New politics of media regulations in Poland (2015–2018). *East European Politics, 36*(1), 27–43.

Thomas, N. (2018). *Democracy denied: Identity, civil society and illiberal democracy in Hong Kong.* Routledge.

Tsutsui, K. (2018). *Rights make might: Global human rights and minority social movements in Japan.* Oxford University Press.

Tyack, D., & Cuban, L. (1997). *Tinkering toward Utopia: A century of public school reform.* Harvard University Press.

UNESCO Institute for Statistics (2022). *Database.* https://data.uis.unesco.org/

United Nations. (1948). *Universal declaration of human rights.* https://www.un.org/en/about-us/universal-declaration-of-human-rights

Velasco, K. (2023). Transnational backlash and the deinstitutionalization of liberal norms: LGBT + rights in a contested World. *American Journal of Sociology, 128*(5), 1381–1429.

Verger, A. (2016). The global diffusion of education privatization: Unpacking and theorizing policy adoption. In K. Mundy, B. Lingard, & A. Verger (Eds.), *The handbook of global education policy* (1st ed., pp. 64–80). John Wiley & Sons, Ltd.

Waitoller, F. R., & Super, G. (2017). School choice or the politics of desperation? Black and Latinx parents of students with dis/abilities selecting charter schools in Chicago. *Education Policy Analysis Archive, 25*(55), 1–41.

Wotipka, C. M., Svec, J., Yiu, L., & Ramirez, F. O. (2021). The status and agency of children in school textbooks, 1970–2012: A cross-national analysis. *Compare: A Journal of Comparative and International Education, 53*(6), 949–966.

Wotipka, C. M., & Tsutsui, K. (2008). Global human rights and state sovereignty: Nation-states' ratifications of international human rights treaties, 1965–2001. *Sociological Forum, 23*(4), 724–754.

Zapp, M., & Dahmen, C. (2017). The diffusion of educational ideas among international organizations: An event history analysis of lifelong learning, 1990–2013. *Comparative Education Review, 61*(3), 492–518.

Zeleza, P. T. (2017). Internationalization of higher education in the era of xenophobic nationalisms. In *NAFSA 2017 annual conference and expo* (pp. 1–10). NAFSA.

Zhao, Y. (2020). Two decades of havoc: A synthesis of criticism against PISA. *Journal of Educational Change, 21*, 245–266.

HOW SHOULD COMPARATIVE RESEARCH BE CONDUCTED AND WHAT PURPOSE DOES IT SERVE?

Renata Nowakowska-Siuta

Christian Theological Academy in Warsaw, Poland

ABSTRACT

Comparative analyses in education science have traditionally focused on the category of geographic location as the comparative unit. However, comparison may involve many other units of analysis, such as culture, politics, curricula, education systems, social phenomena, and other categories of the lives of societies. Still, categories are inseparably linked to one or several geographic locations. Comparative approaches are often also dictated by the availability heuristic. Studying geographic units as the foci of comparative research is a necessary step for comparative presentation of the topic. According to Bray and Thomas, a researcher must always seek preliminary insight in the geographic unit to be analyzed before making the comparison. In social science research, a unit of analysis relates to the main object of the research, as it answers the question of "who" or "what" is going to be analyzed. The most common units of analysis are people, groups, organizations, artifacts or phenomena, and social interactions. Ragin and Amoroso have noted that comparative methods can be used to explain the commonness or diversity of results. This paper shows how comparative research can be approached in ways that have not been discussed, grounded in the historically variable understanding of the very term "comparison." They are, for example, The Ogden-Richards triangle,

---

Annual Review of Comparative and International Education 2023
International Perspectives on Education and Society, Volume 48, 57–79
Copyright © 2025 by Emerald Publishing Limited
All rights of reproduction in any form reserved
ISSN: 1479-3679/doi:10.1108/S1479-367920240000048005

58 RENATA NOWAKOWSKA-SIUTA

The Porphyrian Tree. Classification strategies – Mill's Canons. The chaos of the world – the order of science, Weber's ideal types, Raymond Boudon's formula, and the Möbius strip in comparativism.

Keywords: Comparative education; compare; comparative research in education; methodology contexts in comparative research; comparative methods; new approaches in comparativism

INTRODUCTION

The pioneers of comparative research, by which I'm referring to Marc-Antoine Jullien de Paris (1775–1848) and Pedro Rosselló (1897–1970), thought that the basic task of comparative education was primarily to collect data and to examine basic aspects of the functioning of education in different countries, and the results were to be compared and published, whereas the research procedure was to provide a basis for determining the progress of the education (or the lack thereof) in a given country. This stage in the development of comparative educational studies can be called the first phase of its development. In the second phase of the research, the emphasis was primarily on explaining phenomena, and describing the education and higher education systems was of less interest to researchers involved in international comparisons. The theories and related research of Michael E. Sadler (1861–1943), Nicholas Hans (1888–1969), and Isaac Kandel (1881–1965) gained recognition during this phase. It became important to analyze the social and cultural context of education and its reforms.

What happens outside the school is fundamental to understanding the system of education and upbringing. It was thought impossible to analyze the contemporary educational changes taking place in the world without the traditions and stories from which the education systems have grown. After all, each of them is a unique product of its own past. The new qualitative understanding of comparative pedagogical studies proposed at that time was broad and included both a description of the educational system and theoretical explanations of its functioning, as well as proper comparative analysis, often not without utilitarian ambitions. When looking for traces of this methodological approach in successive concepts appearing in the 20th century as well as in the present one, one should remember that comparative analysis must not only include up-to-date information about the system of education, upbringing or higher education, as it is also necessary to be aware of the complexity of the historical and cultural context (contextual analysis) in which they developed, and to skillfully interpret educational phenomena, providing grounds for predicting changes.

A constitutive feature of comparative studies is, therefore, its knowledge-generating character. New knowledge is acquired in the final stage of the comparatists' work, that is, when they make a value comparison. Comparative education is not a nomothetic science, because it does not detect regularities, rather it determines the meaning of pedagogical phenomena. The meaning, on the other hand, can only be grasped when the entirety (or at least a meaningful context) of the educational reality is revealed, that is, the links between specific phenomena and their historical, social, political, and cultural references. Pedagogical comparison is therefore a scientific method that starts from the phenomena of education and upbringing situated in time and related to society, in order to reveal the underlying regularities by contrasting different views and products, to assign them according to the rule of domination, and thus to reach genuine understanding. George Bereday (1920–1983) wrote about this, arguing that comparatists should be taught to observe facts objectively and then to put them together to learn about the circumstances preceding the occurrence of an educational event and its consequences, and to make a proper comparison for the purpose of formulating general pedagogical claims (Bereday, 1964).

These steps correspond to John S. Mill's description of the steps of the research procedure using the inductive method (Mill, 1962). The established concepts of Isaac Kandel, Franz Schneider, but also Margaret Scotford Archer, creator of the concept of elisionism in the social sciences (Archer, 1995), fall within a similar paradigm. Comparative education can thus be a means of planning the development of educational reform and policy, as it very often helps to establish rules that explain the functioning of educational systems. The research instrument is the problem-based method, through which predictions can be made and possible educational policy options can be formulated.

In contrast to the historical method, which is based on a temporal overview of the occurrence of phenomena, the problem-based method illuminates educational issues in an interdisciplinary manner by showing them only in a specific time period. It should be noted that educational problems are usually multidimensional and identifying possible solutions is often an extremely complex and difficult procedure. Generalizing phenomena usually involves personal choice and judgment on the part of the researchers, which very often leads to accusations of arbitrariness. Many comparatists believed that comparative education should not be considered as a special type of history of education or a subdiscipline of sociology or political science, but as a synthesis of these and other fields of study. Comparative research was considered to be a monograph of one country or a comparative study of many countries conducted at the same time. Applying this methodology in practical terms proves difficult, as it is almost impossible to separate description from interpretation. Another difficulty is the skillful accumulation of knowledge from several scientific disciplines and the equally accurate synthesis of this knowledge, so that it forms the basis for appropriate comparisons.

The necessary conditions for methodological correctness are: knowledge of the languages and culture of the researched countries, correct comparison of the quantitative data collected, discovery of antecedents, establishment of the historical, philosophical, economic, sociological, and political contexts in which educational phenomena are set, and, finally, making of comparisons appropriate for the purpose of formulating general pedagogical claims. The difficulty in applying the methodological assumptions of comparative studies is the time-consuming nature of in-depth monographs of the examined countries and the thorough generalization of what we know about education once data has been collected and correct scientific analyses have been carried out. However, it is only when the indicated research path is followed that comparative work is not necessarily limited to the creation of theoretical models (as it may be) but can also present educational phenomena in practical terms (how to make a change for the better). An important element of comparative work is to prevent oversimplifications caused by drawing conclusions solely from the experiences of one's own country and generalizing them.

COMPARATIVE EDUCATION AMONG OTHER SUB-DISCIPLINES OF THE PEDAGOGICAL SCIENCES

The source of academic interest in comparative pedagogical studies and the subsequent integration of comparative pedagogical studies into pedagogical curricula in the 19th and early 20th centuries stemmed from the desire to explain observable and documented differences between educational systems in place in different countries. The pioneers of comparative pedagogical studies – Marc Antoine Jullien de Paris (1775–1848), Michael E. Sadler (1861–1943), Nicholas Hans (1888–1969), Isaac Kandel (1881–1965), and Pedro Rosselló (1897–1970) – were primarily interested in the number of schools and children attending school and the expansion of secondary education systems, as well as the quality of education. Attention was also drawn to terminological ambiguities and the need to classify data. The latter was made possible, in part, by Brian Holmes (1920–1993) and the work of the UNESCO Institute for Education in Hamburg. William Torrey Harris was the first person to justify the need for models that allowed statistical data to be compared without having to deal with the translation of the terms "primary school," "secondary school," "college," etc. into native languages (Harris, 1891).

Over time, the need not only for a review of quantitative data but also for comparative analysis of the education systems of different countries (and in particular the educational experiences of highly developed countries) began to be discussed more widely. Comparative research began to be used as an implication for the construction of new educational solutions. As G. Shiel and J. Cosgrove note, "the particular benefit that international comparisons provide is to help us see the links between the various aspects of education and how they vary from country to country" (Shiel & Cosgrove, 2002b, p. 690). It should also, as the cited authors emphasize, "motivate individual countries to analyse their own situation in a more critical way and to make the necessary changes" (Shiel & Cosgrove, 2002a, p. 690).

Since the end of the Second World War, the search also began for other paradigms, most notably a move away from the dominant positivist approach – mainly through Alvin Gouldner's then groundbreaking book: *The Coming Crisis of Western Sociology* (Gouldner, 1970). New paradigmatic approaches began to be proposed, which rejected not only the assumptions of the comparative historical-philosophical school represented by Isaac Kandel, Nicolas Hans, and Franz Schneider. This school was dominated by the conviction that in comparative research, it was necessary to identify the so-called driving forces (German: Triebkräfte), that is, the social, religious, economic, etc., factors determining the development of education in a given country. The assumptions made by epistemically oriented comparatists such as Thorsten Husén, Neville Postlethwaite, and Michael Debeuvais, who recognize that an epistemic conception of truth, because of the theoretical perspective taken, reduces reality to our individualized creation, have also been revised (Husén & Postlethwaite, 1996).

Comparative education, more or less since the 1980s, is still in a state of identifying its distinctiveness. For, on the one hand, it is firmly rooted in pedagogical issues, but on the other hand, it remains connected to other disciplines, above all sociology, political geography, political science, philosophy, and general history. This versatility of comparative education, combined with the dynamics of changes taking place in many countries, makes it seem a difficult research field that is especially poorly represented in Polish pedagogy – a permanent trend for several decades. The fact that comparative research is costly does not help either, just like the difficulties in obtaining funding for comparative research, which is often due to a lack of understanding of its nature and importance. Decision-makers often see comparative research as a superfluous add-on to "higher-level" research, but this does not prevent them from using knowledge about other countries' education systems to legitimize a variety of problem areas, which through comparative data provide evidence in support of their theses. The problem is that scientific comparative analysis is often replaced by information taken from the Internet or simple statistical data with no proper interpretation.

Comparative international research is not and never has been merely a description of external factors influencing the shape, structure, and functioning of various elements of social life, however it used to be perceived that way, especially in the Polish tradition of comparative pedagogical studies. Comparison is part of the consciousness of every researcher, regardless of the discipline they represent. It is also easy to see the pressures and resulting comparisons in the field of science through which individual communities position themselves in relation to others: social well-being, demographic indicators, social phenomena, economic and military levels, standards of rule of law and education, degree of democratization, etc. In the case of all these and countless other issues, specialized institutions, as well as ordinary citizens, constantly compare their societies with others, pondering what to mimic and what to avoid.

Besides comparisons, an important factor in the development of societies is their interdependence and dependence on other societies. It seems obvious, therefore, that any building of a theory of social change (which is the purpose of comparative research) must include the interactive dimension of the social world. Unfortunately, comparative pedagogical studies failed to fully handle this task. It has experienced, like other social disciplines and sub-disciplines, theoretical pluralism, extending the theoretical consensus established in the 1980s based on the rules of liberalism, realism, and Marxism with new paradigms: critical theory, constructivism, feminism, post-structuralism, post-modernism, post-colonialism, environmentalism, and others. Researchers working in the field of broadly defined international research have also voiced opinions emphasizing the importance of structural realism for the methodological basis of this area of research. Kenneth N. Waltz (2004), for example, believed that constructivism is not really a theory, and, in fact, it is difficult to say what specifically constructivism explains (p. 5). Waltz describes it as an optimistic view of the world, recognizing that people and states, rather than pursuing their own interests, can and do act for the benefit of others. This is just an example of the current disputes.

Science wants to be an objective description of reality. The very choice of topic is a value judgment – by focusing on one sphere of research rather than another, we signal: this is important! The researcher even projects the values of the society in which they live onto the physical world and the natural world. What is relevant in one society is completely irrelevant in another, or more likely, irrelevant to those currently deciding on the values that shape society. Science, aimed at cultural institutions and processes, historically speaking, originated from practical impulses. Its first purpose was to form value judgments about the socio-political and economic undertakings of the state. As Max Weber wrote, it was a "technique" in the same way that the clinical branches of medicine are a "technique" (Weber, 1982).

The perception of science gradually changed, but this change did not lead to a fundamental separation of the cognition of what exists from what should exist. This process was hindered by the view of the immutability of natural laws, then of unambiguous developmental regularities that influence economic, social, and business phenomena. Many researchers thought, and still think, that what ought to exist is compatible with what invariably exists or will inevitably arise as a result of the regularities of development. The historical sense has mastered science in the sense that it has led to a combination of ethics and relativism, giving all possible cultural ideals the stigma of "morality." The particular dignity of ethical imperatives has been weakened, without achieving anything that would strengthen the objectivity of cognition.

Of course, value judgments should by no means be excluded from scientific discussion, for they are based on certain ideals and thus have the character of subjective judgments. After all, the criticism and doubt that constitute the essence of science do not circumvent value judgments. Should we avoid value judgments and questions of duty in comparative pedagogical studies? Every reasonable human action is linked to categories of ends and means. We want something precisely for its own sake or we want to use something in an instrumental way to achieve a particular end. A fundamental question in research, including that belonging to comparative education, is the appropriateness of ends and means. What means are adequate to achieve certain ends? How should we assess the meaningfulness or meaninglessness of the research objective? How can we determine (anticipate) the consequences of the means required to achieve the end in relation to the context of the activities undertaken?

The existence of multiple disciplines continuously suggests that different features of the external world require distinct ways of exploring it. It also leads us to believe that the world of science has been permanently divided and that the boundaries marking the divisions are reflected in the ways in which we see and describe them. Gałganek (2019, p. 13) writes

> The disciplines and fields of research that have been constructed appear to so obviously attest to the existence of a close correspondence between what we say and what we think we see that many researchers have begun to treat this illusion, or what they themselves have invented, as a justification for their research.

Science is what we can discover using the scientific method: the truth, or at least an approximation of it.

In logic and mathematics, the unspoken rule is that as few words as possible should be used to represent the world. Consequently, it should come as no surprise that analytical philosophy, the philosophy of science, has its origins in the positivist way of understanding reality. The philosophy of science in the 20th century, especially between 1930 and 1960, as Jan Woleński writes, was dominated by a formal approach (reconstructionism), derived from logical empiricism, and advocated the research into scientific products (theories, laws, hypotheses, statements about experimental results, explanations, predictions, as well as linguistic means of coding scientific statements) by means of formal–logical methods (Woleński, 2014). It was assumed that there is a strict criterion distinguishing science from what is not science.

According to the proponents of the formal methodological orientation, science always manifests itself in the same way, regardless of the historical period, the main object of research in the field of science is scientific products and not scientific activities, the context of justification and not the context of discovery is important. According to the reconstructionists, it is possible to formulate a rule that characterizes science (empirical science – that is, formal science such as logic and mathematics is omitted here) and at the same time contrasts it with non-science, that is, pseudoscience.

The early empiricists proposed the criterion of verification (a statement is scientific if it is empirically verifiable), others, such as Karl Popper, falsifiability (a statement is scientific if it is empirically falsifiable), and still others, such as Rudolf Carnap, expressibility through definability and/or reducibility in empirical language (a statement is scientific if it can be expressed in empirical language, with the particular aim of defining theoretical constructs in such a way that they make empirical sense). The methodology of reconstructionism was apragmatic, focused on products rather than activities, and its model was to be metamathematics. Reconstructionism maintained that, in most cases, activities are accessed through their products, so the latter are more important. We should note that various paths, including irrational ones, can lead to scientific discovery. Justification is therefore important in science, as it is subject to logical standardization, with the burden of proof (onus probandi) always resting on the one who creates the theory. Consequently, the context of justification is always subject to logical analysis, whereas the context of discovery is subject to logical analysis only in specific cases.

The last few decades have been characterized by a shift in emphasis on the views of the role of science, including that of its trustees, the researchers. Science needs to be accessible, easy to understand and, above all, useful in many ways. As John A. Bargh writes in his book *Social Psychology and Unconscious: The Automaticity of Higher Mental Processes* (Bargh, 2006), the evidence is piling up that we do not control our judgments and behavior as much as we think we do.

We tend not to realize that unconscious or automatic forms of mental and behavioral processes occur without our intention or consent, even though they affect us in important ways every day. Automatic processing influences our liking and disliking of almost everything, as do the ways in which we perceive other people.

So, since many of our choices are made unconsciously or controlled unintentionally by our prior experiences, are we able to make objective judgments in any area of science? Are the choices we make really our own? Are the processes of identifying research objectives really dictated only by our cognitive curiosity and absolutely free? Are they not determined by our individual perceptions, as well as by our prior, often unconscious life scripts? Perhaps by making various choices, whether in our personal or scientific lives, we automatically generate preferences or aversions toward objects and events. In fact, there are no completely indifferent stimuli in the human environment.

HEURISTIC OF AVAILABILITY, ANCHORING AND FALSE ACCESSIBILITY, I.E., HOW MISTAKES CAN BE MADE IN CHOOSING A RESEARCH TOPIC AND HOW TO AVOID THEM

Humans are rational beings. Some can solve complex mathematical problems and make inferences using sophisticated logic. We can be rational, considerate, and analytical. Fritz Heider showed in the 1950s that humans are motivated by two main needs – the need to formulate a coherent vision of the world and the need to exercise control over the world around us. Heider believed that we behave like naïve scientists, rationally and logically testing our hypotheses about the reality in which we function (Heider, 1958). In particular, we have within us the need to attribute causes to effects and to create a meaningful and stable world in which everything is comprehensible. However, human beings also have a complexity of mental processes. Just as we seek rational justifications, we can also explain reality under the influence of various emotions. Comparison can therefore be a rational procedure, but it can just as well be a purely emotional one. The methodology of comparative pedagogical studies assumes that the rule of rationality must be followed. But are we capable, when conducting research, of completely switching off our emotions? And if not, what accompanies us in choosing a topic, guiding it, making analyses, and drawing conclusions?

It is difficult to find a theory in the social sciences that does not explicitly or implicitly refer to the concept of similarity. Without this category, scientists would be unable to describe, let alone explain, most of the phenomena they study. Nor would they be able to verify the veracity of the hypotheses they formulate by any means. Many also suggest that these remarks do not apply only to psychological or pedagogical theories or, more broadly, to the field of social sciences, but to cognition of the world in general. Amos Tversky, a psychologist and mathematician, shows us a model of feature similarity which, although most often used in mathematics and cognitive psychology, can serve as a theoretical basis for comparative education. Similarity, Tversky (1977) argued, can refer to features with different weights, so it is necessary to introduce feature weights, although the weights can be selected due to different criteria.

Through the use of concepts, people make use of knowledge about the world and the possibility of certain correlations in it, referring to the causes that explain these correlations. Many of the existing models of similarities or differences are used in comparative pedagogical studies as determinants of methodological proceedings. In the vast majority of these models, an important role is given to context. This is also the case in Tversky's model, in which the assessment of the degree of similarity between a pair of objects depends not only on the attribute values but also on the context in which the comparison is made. This context depends both on the task the similarity assessment serves and on the other objects described in the available dataset. Similarity can be thought of as a binary relationship τ between the objects in the considered universe Ω.

A lot of empirical research by psychologists and cognitive scientists has shown that people's perception of similar objects is significantly dependent on external factors, such as the available information, the subjects' previous life experiences and the context. The last factor is particularly important. One example context for assessing similarity is the decision attribute of the objects under consideration. In this context, we can distinguish a useful property of similarity relations – if two objects are similar, they must belong to the same decision class. Special functions, called similarity functions or measures, are very often used to approximate similarity relations.

Thus, similarity in Tversky's concept is defined on the basis of the number of common features that characterize a certain group of objects and the number of features that differentiate these objects. In addition, each feature that determines similarity or difference is weighted for its salience or importance. In assessing similarity, context is always taken into account. In Tversky's feature contrast model, objects are not represented by vectors of attribute values, but by sets of their high-level, sometimes abstract features.

As the equation of this model, Tversky proposed:

$$Sim(x, y) = \theta f(X \cap Y) - \left(\alpha f(Y \setminus X) + \beta f(X \setminus Y) \right)$$

where the sets X and Y are binary features of the objects, f is an interval scale, and the non-negative constants θ, α, β are the model parameters.

Selecting appropriate features allows the Tversky model to capture the context in which similarity is assessed. Furthermore, depending on the values of the parameters θ, α, β, the similarity approximations obtained using the feature contrast model may have different properties. For example, if $\alpha 6 = \beta$, the resulting relationship is not symmetric. In practical terms, it is difficult to properly identify the set of possible high-level features of the objects, however, which significantly limits the applications of this model.

Tversky made heuristic in decision-making – rules that are only approximately valid – an important indication of comparison. For comparative pedagogical studies, this mechanism is important in selecting the object of comparison and the indicators by which we can make this comparison. So how do we use Tversky's theory for comparison methodology in pedagogy? Let us first consider how we select the object of comparison. As a rule, we are guided, similar to the mechanisms of cognitive psychology, by the representativeness heuristic, or availability heuristic, or anchoring and adjustment heuristic.

With the representativeness heuristic, we evaluate events or samples of events based on their similarity to the entire category of events they appear to represent (Kosonen & Winne, 1995). A sample of events can be as much a coin toss made six times in relation to an infinity of such tosses (population) as it can be a selected event in a learning process in relation to an infinite number of similar events (population). The representativeness heuristic suggests a rule for predicting the degree of probability of a particular sequence of events (inferring their occurrence) based on a reference to the degree of occurrence of similar events in the population as a whole.

The availability heuristic occurs when we make judgments about the frequency or probability of events based on the ease with which we judge in thought the occurrence of known similar instances (events). If someone were to ask us, for example, at what age children are most often sent to school, without knowing the statistics, we would probably give an answer based on the knowledge we have of how starting school is structured in the countries for which we know this. The anchoring and adjustment heuristic, on the other hand, is an expression of the inertia of our judgments about the world. When we form judgments or opinions, we usually have some initial belief that acts as an anchor for our judgment. When we receive additional information, we adapt this initial belief to it, though this occasionally comes with difficulty. Sometimes it is also not based on rationale but on our prior judgments. Let us illustrate this mathematically with two cases of multiplication:

$$8 \times 7 \times 6 \times 5 \times 4 \times 3 \times 2 \times 1$$

$$1 \times 2 \times 3 \times 4 \times 5 \times 6 \times 7 \times 8$$

If we asked several random people to estimate in three seconds the supposed result of the calculations, what estimates would we get? Of course, the actual result is identical in both cases, because numbers multiplied by each other are identical. Tversky and Kahneman asked students to estimate each product, and the estimates were significantly higher when the sequence started with large numbers than when it started with small numbers. In the first case, the average estimate was 2,250 and in the second case, it was 512. The estimates were therefore higher when the anchor was the number 8 rather than 1 (Tversky & Kahneman, 1982). Anchoring is the tendency to use a certain value (anchor) as a starting point when making a quantitative assessment. Our judgments on many issues are highly dependent on the point at which we begin our deliberations. The anchoring heuristic is seen as different from the availability heuristic. In essence, they both boil down to the same psychological mechanisms.

The starting point has an impact on assessments because it is the most accessible source of information related to the issue under consideration. Such an error not only has certain consequences in social situations but is also relevant to the undertaken research. This is because we assess reality through the lens of the information and impressions most available to us as researchers. It is enough to include in the title of an article or monograph a claim that we offer the reader a unique description of the issue, that this issue is unique, unusual, presenting the best solutions in the world and right from the outset, thanks to the anchoring heuristic, we give in to the suggestion and follow the conviction that we are dealing with an exceptional or even outstanding work.

The subjects that we subject to analysis and the conclusions that we draw from our analyses can also be the result of the anchoring and adjustment heuristic. In this case, conclusions may be falsified or distorted.

The availability heuristic is also responsible for the development of a serious error called the false consensus effect (Gross & Miller, 1997). In social psychology, it describes the tendency to overestimate someone's opinions in comparison to the general population. Our own beliefs are easily recalled from memory and are more accessible when we are asked to judge whether others agree with us. It is possible that how I judge the attitudes and opinions of others is, to some extent, influenced by my own beliefs. This is how social psychology puts it. But what is the relevance of this heuristic to research? It is possible that, in choosing a research topic, analyzing it and even making citations, we are guided by the false consensus effect. We fixate on what is universally desirable and known and are rarely willing to take a non-conformist approach.

Fearing misunderstanding, negative opinions, or rejection of our own views, we protect ourselves by choosing topics that are well-known and well-established in the perception of others, especially specialists in a given field and discipline, because it is their opinion that researchers care most about, especially at the beginning of the academic career.

We are afraid to express our own views, so, on the one hand, we prefer to hide them behind statements of universally accepted experts. On the other hand, we choose topics that we think are widely accepted and universally demanded. Hence, it is easier for us, for example, in comparative education to turn to well-known areas of scientific research than to explore those that have been completely neglected so far and are distant from the experience of our geographical region or socio-political context.

This strategy may result in neglecting or giving little attention to topics that are interesting but poorly represented, for example, in the media discourse or in the interests of influential scientific bodies. There have also been cases of abandoning research due to the failure of the first research steps, especially when the researcher faces a lack of understanding, unconstructive criticism of the chosen research strategy, ridicule, or exclusion from the mainstream, recognized way of carrying out research, etc.

SELECTED METHODS IN COMPARATIVE RESEARCH

William James wrote that he who values certainty too highly avoids error at the expense of neglecting the pursuit of truth (cf. James & Murphy, 1995, first edition 1897). When desiring cognitive gains, one must therefore risk error.

The crucial question that arises in choosing a research area in comparative education is not only that of the topic – relevant, socially important, serving to anticipate change – but also whether it can be grasped in terms of a logically connected argument. Ontology imposes epistemology and research methods. If one treats a non-human or human being as an object being, then in learning about it, one will attempt to explain it. When undertaking explanation, it is assumed that impersonal laws are at work in the subject being, of which the explained facts are a singular example. Because it is these general laws that are discovered in natural science, the natural (and technical) science is called nomothetic (Windelband) or generalizing (Rickert). If we treat a non-human or human being, capture it as a subjective being, we seek to understand it. What is understanding? In the simplest terms, the result of an explanation.

Explaining is not easy, because we are dealing with the effects of certain laws – we have to search for laws themselves by putting forward hypotheses. Understanding is also difficult, because we deal with the effects of human acts, and we must tediously reconstruct the knowledge and values that guided the person performing the act. Understanding is an art, and the art of understanding is called hermeneutics. Positivist scientism, with its reverence for natural science, regarded explanation as the only scientific form of cognition. Therefore, the positivists considered that only natural science deserved to be called a science, a true science, while the humanities would either adopt the methodological patterns of natural science (i.e., it would explain), or it could not be considered a science. This was the case until the turn of the 20th century, when (thanks to Dilthey, as well as Windelband and Rickert, and many other philosophers of the hermeneutic school), the so-called anti-positivist breakthrough in the humanities took place. It amounted to an acknowledgement of the peculiarity of the humanities: natural science explains, humanities understand – because the examined objects in both cases are different (objective–subjective), so they should be accompanied by a different methodology (and different criteria for the results achieved).

Let us first consider whether quantitative methods are possible in comparative education. We acknowledge, following textbooks on comparative research, that the overarching goal of quantitative research methods in comparative education is to identify laws that contribute to the explanation and prediction of educational phenomena (Ary et al., 2009; Bryman, 1988; Hartas, 2010; Cowen, 2018). The laws of association assume a functional relationship between objects, whereas the laws of causality imply a fixed succession of events. The adherence of quantitative approaches to a nomothetic mode of reasoning would imply that researchers consider such laws to be universal, regardless of cultural, temporal, etc., differences. One of the primary interests of quantitative research is to establish causality. This is because explanations or "why" questions imply the search for causes and the identification of causal relationships.

A particularly effective method of testing these is through experimentation, but many researchers rely on correlational research of variables through data collected via intentionally created or standardized survey questionnaires as a way of accessing causality. Bryman noted that in order to make such arguments, the researcher must demonstrate a logical relationship between the variables in a particular temporal order. The quantitative paradigm assumes nomothetic reasoning, generalizing research findings, relating them to broader cohorts and populations, as well as broader cultural contexts, through the use of random, representative samples in experimental and survey research. Maximizing variation is said to be possible at the level of societies and is also justified in cross-national and cross-cultural research (van de Vijver & Leung, 1997). Another purpose of quantitative research is deduction, theory building, or hypothesis testing and verification.

The research process generally begins with the adoption of a general theory, the setting of hypotheses, the operationalization of variables, the collection of data, and its subsequent statistical analysis. Researchers using quantitative methods, including experimental methods, determine the specific issues to focus on at the beginning of the research before moving on to tool selection and data collection. Hard data are collected using structured, systematic procedures and are susceptible to verification by others. Standardized and coordinated random sampling activities are intended to reduce or even eliminate human bias. Some of the issues identified above related to the use of quantitative and qualitative methods are of particular relevance in comparative research. On the one hand, there is a certain methodological pressure to use quantitative methods, which goes hand in hand with a paradigmatic shift in the field of comparative education from a historical explanatory approach toward research using statistical information and quantitative data analysis procedures.

On the other hand, some researchers are interested in the search for generalized explanations and universal rules applicable to educational phenomena in societies and cultures. At the same time, other scholars and policymakers are encouraging topics in the transfer of educational theories, practices and policies from other countries and regions of the world and report a demand for seeking solutions to global problems. Hence, large-scale databases from international research on educational achievements and educational statistics collected by international agencies are becoming more important.

There is, however, just as much pressure for qualitative research in comparative studies. Qualitative researchers in comparative education strongly believe in the importance of cultural, political, and social contexts and claim that education cannot be detached from its cultural context. Qualitative research is also recommended because of an awareness of the shortcomings and problems associated with large sets of international statistics that are difficult to interpret, often used indiscriminately without consideration of their potential bias in comparison with local (national) contexts, and without taking into account the internal variability of such a micro set.

Traditionally, the quantitative research approach in comparative research has been considered positivist, while the qualitative approach has been considered interpretative. The positivist position is the theoretically grounded belief that there is an objective reality that the researcher can know if they use the right methods and apply those methods in the right way. The positivist paradigm of exploring social reality is based on the philosophical ideas of French philosopher August Comte, according to whom true knowledge is based on sense experience and can be obtained through observation and experiment. These assumptions today are translated into methodological treatments, such as determinism, empiricism and generality. Interpretive views in methodology can be divided into various disciplines. The views of Alfred Schutz, Aaron Cicourel, and Harold Garfinkel (phenomenology/sociology), the "Chicago School of Sociology" (sociology), and Franz Uri Boas and Bronisław Malinowski (anthropology) are often associated with the emergence of an interpretive paradigm.

With interpretive approaches relying heavily on naturalistic methods (interviews and observations, and analyses of existing texts). The Chicago sociological school refers primarily to the category of *Lebenswelt* (life-world, world of lived experience). The original genesis of the meaning of human knowledge is sought in the subjective experience of the surrounding reality. Sociologists such as Schutz, Cicourel, and Garfinkel adopt the Husserlian thesis of the human "natural attitude" toward the external world. They believe that in scientific cognition, humans do not suspend their belief in the reality of the world's existence but ignore the doubt that the world is different from what appears to their consciousness. The human "being-in-the-world" is constituted not only by the meaning of the surrounding objects but also by one's own reactions and actions. Schutz uses the phenomenological apparatus to develop, for example, Max Weber's concepts.

For him, Weber's notion of meaningful action is extended and supplemented by the concept of the natural attitude maintained by the individual in the world of everyday life. According to Max Weber, social actions are determined and guided by the meaning given to them by the acting individual entity, while Schutz draws attention to the importance of situational context. In his view, and that of other proponents of this school of sociology, the scientific research of human activity must be based on the interpretation of subjective meaning in terms of the acting individual (Schutz, 1962). These methods provide an appropriate dialogue between researchers and those with whom they interact in order to jointly construct meanings in the domain of a given reality. In general, it is important to note that meanings emerge from the research process.

Egon Guba and Yvonna Lincoln (1994) define the concept of reliability as a criterion for qualitative evaluation and point to comparative relevance understood as "the appropriateness, meaningfulness and usefulness of comparative inference." There seem to be other important issues to consider in comparative research. First, the use of other scientific disciplines, such as economics, sociology, and cultural anthropology. This is because beliefs, customs, traditions, characteristics of moral, and social, economic, and political justifications influence educational processes. A comparative study should, therefore, always be conducted according to a holistic approach. Second, methods should always be used according to the paradigmatic position and the objective of the comparative research.

The debate on the methodology of comparative education has been stimulated from time to time by the need for accurate answers and a better understanding of education systems, theories, practices and problems. One of the functions of comparative education is to help solve problems. As with other social sciences, comparative education has been examined at different stages of its development through different methodologies. Starting from simple narratives about education abroad in the "travelers' tale" phase, the disciplines' methodological approaches have gradually evolved to the current application of sophisticated social science methods that are empirically based. Due to its diverse clientele, resulting from its multidisciplinary nature, comparative education has not developed a single, universally accepted research methodology.

Consequently, it is currently characterized by a multitude of debates and opinions as to which method is the most suitable (Melosik, 2023). The statistical/quantitative method emphasizes the collection, interpretation, verification, and comparison of data in education by means of statistical and, therefore, quantitative analytical data. The main purpose was to facilitate the collection and sharing of information about other countries or to show quantitative indicators characterizing specific features of education systems or the socio-political or economic context in which these systems operate. In this method, quite obviously, different types of data are collected about a specific country. For example, data are collected on the number of students at different stages of education, expenditure on education and higher education, non-formal education, etc., failure rates at different stages of education, expenditure on teachers' salaries, the size of the educational infrastructure and other elements in comparison with identical data from another country.

Although this method is still in use, its shortcomings have been pointed out, such as the unreliability of statistical data, in particular the inaccuracies of local registers, compiled by officials who may try to hide any shortcomings and omissions. There is also often a lack of due diligence in the collection of data, so a lot of the data may be false. There is also a lack of precision in defining certain non-standardized terms used in a different cultural context. In many cases, the terms used do not mean the same thing, and this can also lead to erroneous assignments of indicators and consequently to errors in interpretation.

In addition, it must be taken into account that with the statistical method, we cannot understand the educational characteristics that may result from the social, cultural, economic, political, and religious situation of a given country.

The descriptive method in comparative education began to be used in the 19th century, as the main objective of researchers at that time became to consider the advantages and disadvantages of another country. Such an approach required a detailed account of the ways in which another country's educational systems functioned, and many comparative pedagogs therefore provided such detailed accounts of social phenomena and interesting solutions in the education and universities of the countries visited. Among them were Marc Antoinne Jullien de Paris, Horace Man, Henry Bernard, and Mathew Arnold. John Griscom, an American researcher, visited Britain, France, the Netherlands, Switzerland, and Italy between 1918 and 1919 and wrote a book entitled *One Year in Europe*, detailing the educational systems of these countries. He was also concerned with relating the educational issues he observed to American solutions.

Griscom's book, hitherto unpublished as a work on comparative education, may nevertheless be a good example of comparative research undertaken in the 19th century. Matthew Arnold from the United Kingdom and Horace Man from the United States have also done some work in the area of the descriptive method.

M. Arnold studied the educational systems of France and Germany and published a report on France in 1859 and on Germany in 1865. In his description, he drew the readers' attention to those factors which distinguish the educational system of one country from the other. Arnold's method was also followed by Sir Michael Sadder and Paul Monroe. Their views helped to better organize the study of comparative education. Horace Man visited Germany, Ireland, Great Britain, France, and the Netherlands. In 1843, he published a report on the educational systems of these countries in which he drew attention to the peculiarities of these systems and identified specific elements that others should follow.

He drew attention to the evaluation of the educational methods used in each country. Henry Bernard published 31 volumes of *The American Journal of Education* between 1856 and 1881. In these volumes, he described the educational systems of the various states of the USA and other countries of the world. He carefully outlined the historical and social background of each educational system he described. Michael Sadder emphasized that we should examine all the national factors that influence a country's education system and are responsible for its growth or decline. He believed that the study of comparative education was useful for understanding one's own education system.

Similarly monumental was a work so far undervalued in the research on comparative education, but in my opinion important, namely: "Le tour de Monde. Noveau Journal des Voyages," a beautifully illustrated weekly journal. "Around the world, a new travel journal" was created in January 1860 by Édouard Charton, designer of the Magasin Pittoresque, and was published under the aegis of Librairie Hachette until 1914. The weekly booklets, sold through a network of railway stations, were then collected into volumes. Today, they are extremely rare. A second series was inaugurated in 1895 under the title "Le Tour du monde, journal des voyages et des voyageurs." This was a much more modern series, no longer containing drawings, but reproductions of photographs. The weekly magazine was addressed to readers curious about travel, detailing most of the great expeditions that marked the end of the 19th and beginning of the 20th century, the last great period of exploration of the globe by Western travelers.

The magazine included descriptions of every region of the world, covering the period from the discovery of the source of the Nile in the early 1860s to the conquest of the South Pole in late 1911. The incalculable value of this publication lies in its meticulous coverage of the richness of each continent and country of the world, including their natural, social, political, and educational wealth. "Le tour du Monde" is also a record of the complexity of the perception of the world in the 19th century. What was then considered a travel magazine, aimed at a wide audience, today we would consider a strictly scientific message, characterized by an extraordinary meticulousness, reliability, a unique perspective as observers of the world and people, and at the same time extremely esthetic in its presentation.

The woodcuts inside "Le tour du Monde" are now extraordinary testimonies to the era and the insight of the people living in it, their love of the world and their reading of the meaning of the beauty that surrounds us. The Polish reader was first introduced to a similar comparative approach through Friedrich Wilhelm Foerster's books entitled *School and Character. Moral and Pedagogical*

Issues of School Life (1908) and *Raising a Human Being"* (1913). In the latter, in the chapter "A Glance at Moral-Pedagogical Trials and Experiences in Various Countries," we can read about the ways of teaching and education in America, England, France, and Switzerland (Foerster, 1913, pp. 133–190). Foerster's travels to America, England, and Switzerland and observing the misery of the people living in the industrial districts of the big cities, as well as his time spent on personal ethical reflections, became the catalyst not only for his Christocentric views but also for framing pedagogical questions from an ethnographic and comparative perspective.

Another method used in pedagogy is the historical method. It allows us to grasp contemporary educational problems through the foundations that led to them in a temporal sense. It should be noted that we use the historical method not only to learn about the past, but above all to better understand the present and to improve the functioning of the educational system in the future, pointing out those factors that may be the most functional, sensible, and rational for the creation of education in a country. In this approach, we also try to understand all the geographical, social, political, religious and linguistic factors that influence the image of education in a country. Researchers such as Nicholas Hans, Isaac Kandel, Schneider, and Michael Sadler are known for popularizing this method. They generally agreed that selective cultural borrowing was possible and stressed that educational policies and practices had both a cause and effect to be found in the unique historical experience of each society, already referred to by Horace as "national character." These scholars portrayed comparative education as a sub-discipline of the educational sciences for discovering the universal causes or conditions of educational practices, as well as for determining the best conditions for education. Although the scholars who have favored this approach have not proposed a specific methodological procedure, they are considered to distinguish three necessary procedures in comparative research:

(1) Each national system should be studied separately in its historical context, paying attention to differences in terminology and methods of data collection and classification.
(2) The forces and factors responsible for the differences noted must be equally analyzed, which must then be grouped into four categories: natural, religious, socio-economic, and political.
(3) Only those ideas and practices that best approximate and can be adapted to the historical context of the country in which they are to be applied should be adopted as models for indigenous educational solutions.

However, such an approach suffers from the following shortcomings: the data on which a single study is based may not be reliable because, again, due diligence is often not exercised in its collection, and therefore the conclusions drawn may not be very reliable and thus useful. It should be borne in mind that historical material on the education systems of different countries is often unreliable and this, in turn, limits the usefulness of historical data. Another disadvantage is that historians are generally not impartial in their accounts. In most cases they want to

74 RENATA NOWAKOWSKA-SIUTA

hide undesirable elements of their own country's history or glorify selected ones without presenting them objectively; sometimes facts about other countries are also interpreted incorrectly, with obvious prejudices and stereotypes. In such a situation, the truth is lost, and it is therefore difficult to draw the right conclusions.

A third limitation of this approach is that it often overemphasizes the past, treats it as a benchmark, and ignores the changing social and political contexts. This is because it is not possible to relate the contemporary situation, even if the facts point to its similarity, to a bygone era, to a different past context. This is a fundamental methodological error, involving the use of categories that are not appropriate to the era under analysis. Another method used in comparative research is the analytical method. This approach links the relationships that exist between a country's educational system and its social, political, and economic conditions. It is clear that in any comparative analysis research, we must use analytical analysis, because through analysis, the different elements can be separated and the meaning of each can be understood independently. However, the analytical method is only considered useful in comparative research when comparing selected social and educational organizations. This is because it is not conducive to generalization, to drawing complete conclusions about the overall picture of the education system.

The analytical method therefore takes into account three main rules to guide the analysis.

(1) Educational data should be analyzed with the prior use of other methods – descriptive and statistical – which form the basis of the analytical method.
(2) Interpretation should always be made of interrelated social, political, economic, and historical data, as it is essential to understand the similarities and differences found in the educational systems of different countries.
(3) The analytical method often makes it possible to formulate a standard of comparison between different educational systems, which helps to indicate the similarities and differences of different educational systems. For example, political philosophy, educational objectives and educational control methods are good examples of standards for comparison. It is on the basis of these standards that one can analyze and understand the similarities and differences of the disparate educational systems found in different countries of the world. However, the use of the analytical method also encounters its own peculiar limitations. First of all, this method does not pay due attention to educational systems as certain wholes. Second of all, it is inclined to ignore the inherent similarity that exists in educational systems in spite of differences.

QUALITATIVE RESEARCH IN COMPARATIVE STUDIES

Qualitative research is intended to examine people's perceptions of the world around them and their experiences, including people's perspectives on social phenomena such as education, health and social care services and wider policies and processes related to the system of social organization. In recent years, systematic reviews of qualitative research (also known as Qualitative Evidence Syntheses – QES) have become commonplace, and the procedures for conducting these syntheses are now well developed. Results obtained from QES are increasingly often being incorporated into decision-making processes and the formulation of national policies for the purpose of showing the possible effects of interventions and the use of existing resources. Qualitative syntheses are also currently used in decision support tools, and to inform researchers and public opinion in many countries about decisions on social policy implementation strategies.

Qualitative research has a long history. The term "qualitative research" is used as a generic name for many research approaches in the social sciences. They are also referred to as hermeneutic, reconstructive or interpretative approaches (Flick, 2012, p. 23). Sometimes, the term "research" is replaced by the term "inquiry" or neither is used, and the activities undertaken are referred to as ethnography. The term "qualitative research" has long been used as an alternative to "quantitative research. However, it cannot be defined by negation: qualitative research as non-quantitative. Qualitative research generally uses text instead of numbers as empirical material. They start from the concept of the social creation of the realities under investigation and focus attention on the research participants' points of view, practices, and knowledge of the object of research.

Comparative research is generally dominated by three different analytical approaches: internalism (methodological nationalism), externalism, and correlationism. What we call internalism consists in capturing the conceptualization of a system of social life and the educational canons in force within it in its singularity. Internalism imports the explanation of internationalism through the interiority of a given country. A researcher undertaking comparative research from this perspective is interested in what happens inside the examined society. This methodological approach to conducting comparative research can only be considered useful to a certain extent, for it may ultimately lead to the creation of an ideal social model, but it also ignores the need to distinguish between the internal (particularistic, country-specific) and the external (social action, universal ethics, phenomena, etc.).

Similarly, externalism ignores the internal, the individual, focusing attention primarily on what influences the image of a given country and comes from outside, is universal and global. Comparative education has the task of mapping the fields of research, it must be an analysis of the relations between these fields, it should be oriented horizontally and look for what we usually identify as national and global, and it should try to understand the meaning and correlations of the different fields. This issue is illustrated by the metaphor of the circle as a kind of border. Researchers either give value to the boundary as relevant to the study of a given system, phenomenon, society, etc., or they point to connections beyond the boundary. In addition to this duality in thinking about the boundary, some also add a reflection on the individual bringing the boundary into existence, drawing the circle.

They thus pose questions such as on what basis the individual drawing the boundary of the analysis – putting the problem boundary in the form of a circle – determined the size of that circle, the height of the wall and the thickness of the walls of the boundary wall. Even if the boundary maker delineates their circle, determines the height and thickness of the walls, the sky above the cylinder remains open. As a result, "hopes and fears can travel above the walls, connecting what was inside with what was outside". Closure is never complete and crossing the boundary is always cognitively more interesting. The dialectic is always more complex than drawing dividing lines.

Thus, we move toward correlationism. Bigo and Walker use the model of the Möbius strip, which is a unique, one-sided surface. The Möbius strip is often cited as an aid to thinking about (conceptualizing) international comparative research, as a topos (place). All human activities – wars, expansions, writing, reading – have places. Everything that cannot be mapped is beyond the horizon of our consciousness. The Möbius strip is intended to provide a vivid illustration of the methodological difficulty in comparative analysis – for there is no clear definition when researching a given country of the educational system, social phenomena, relations with other countries, etc., of what is inside and what is outside. In fact, the shape of a phenomenon occurring in a given country is always going to be influenced by what is happening in neighboring countries, on a given continent and in the world in general. It is purely a matter of perspective that determines who the researcher sees inside or outside the Möbius strip. An analysis of internationalism that takes into account the topology of the Möbius strip leads one to recognize the thesis that social development has never been the result of the internal history of a given society alone. Comparative education, to use Martin Heidegger's term, means "throwing into the world" (German: Geworfenheit), a recognition of the interdependence of societies and states, and only in this way can it be conducted as a science.

CONCLUSIONS

The diversity of comparative education can be captured by four of its types. We can call the first one informational comparative education, i.e. one that collects data and produces analyses focused on the needs of educational decision-makers. The second is critical comparative education, which identifies the characteristics of societies and nations as well as social phenomena and, sometimes taking into account its utilitarian character, proposes a variety of solutions taking into account the national or international context. The third is comparative studies, aimed at evoking emotion through pictorial descriptions of social phenomena. It can be characterized as expressive. The fourth type, the cognitive type, considers its aim to be the explanation of often puzzling, obscure or so far poorly explored social phenomena. Its motive is usually curiosity about a different culture.

The four orientations, in my opinion, characterize classical and contemporary comparative education, with – historically speaking – the earliest type being the first, but all are equally present in the conduct of comparative research today. The decision to choose a research paradigm and also the type and methods of conducting comparative research is always left to the researcher. It is important, irrespective of the research path chosen, to maintain reliability, objectivity of judgments, rationality of analysis, and respect for contextual thinking, embedded in cultural and linguistic contexts. I believe that comparative research allows for a contextualized analysis of educational systems.

Comparative analyses make it possible to understand the entanglement of school systems in social, cultural, economic, and political dependencies. Moreover, to quote Hans J. Noah, it is "comparative studies that provide the most desirable approach to understanding education" (Noah, 1984). The variation in the sphere of modes and effects of contemporary education systems is – it seems – largely due to the educational policies outlined and implemented by the authorities of a given country. This is based on specific political and educational ideologies, which often have a significantly different perception of the functions and tasks that an education system should fulfill.

What, then, are the objectives of comparative education today? It examines and analyzes educational systems as historically established models of education and upbringing operating in a particular society, and focuses attention not only on the external (structural) features of educational systems but also makes the "inside" of these systems the object of its interest, including the educational policy of a given country, the particular functional solutions, the historical, cultural, economic and social conditions that form the external image of a given educational system.

Comparative education is interdisciplinary in nature and therefore draws information from sociology, the economics of educational processes, the history and contemporary educational policy of the countries analyzed. Comparative research can and should be characterized by utilitarianism. Both quantitative and qualitative methods are used in comparative research, with both groups of methods complementing each other. With quantitative analysis, not only the relatively permanent elements of educational systems can be described, but also their variable elements. Qualitative data analysis deepens the knowledge of the characteristics of educational systems and allows for their multifaceted consideration. By combining quantitative and qualitative approaches, we can not only identify what an educational system is like but also determine why proposed educational solutions take certain forms.

Contemporary comparative studies also seek to impart intercultural competence, with the purpose of providing the individual with knowledge of other nations and of containing, mitigating and avoiding conflicts arising from the clash of rigidly separated world religions and, more broadly, cultures (Nowakowska-Siuta, 2003). The historical aspects of the development of individual states and peoples are an important element of contemporary comparative studies. They are the ones that make it possible to avoid the rather frequent error of ahistorical thinking, of neglecting the role of cultural tradition or of building beliefs based on stereotypes or common knowledge. In my opinion, the history of education should always precede the introduction of comparative content, and it is also worth including in its curriculum a synthesis of the history not only of Europe but also of other, much less frequently studied continents.

By showing the relations between Europe and other regions of the world in a historical perspective, attempts can be made to build comparative knowledge

RENATA NOWAKOWSKA-SIUTA

based on a European perspective, but without ignoring other, no less important (and affecting, for example, the functioning of contemporary education) ways of perceiving the world around us. Without a history of education, moreover, without a history understood from the perspective of the memory of a given nation, there can be no reliable comparative research, and without comparative studies, there can be no rational and forward-looking educational policy devoid of xenophobia.

REFERENCES

Archer, M. S. (1995). *Realist social theory: The morphogenetic approach*. University Press. https://doi.org/10.1017/CBO9780511557675.

Ary, D., Jacobs, L. C., & Sorensen, C. (2009). Introduction to research in education (8th edn). Cengage Learning.

Bargh, J. A. (2006). *Social psychology and the unconscious. The automaticity of higher mental processes*. Psychology Press. https://doi.org/10.4324/9780203783016

Bereday, J. (1964). *Comparative method in education*. Holt Rienehart and Winston, Inc.

Bryman, A. (1988). *Quantity and quality in social research* (1st edn.). Routledge. https://doi.org/10.4324/9780203410028

Cowen, R. (2018). Reflections on comparative education: Telling tales in honor of Andreas Kazamias. *European Education, 50*(2), 201–215. https://doi.org/10.1080/10564934.2018.1455057

Flick, U. (2012). *Introducción a la investigación cualitativa* [An introduction to qualitative research]. Morata.

Foerster, F. W. (1908). Schule und charakter: beiträge zur pädagogik des gehorsams und zur reform der schuldisziplin. Schultheß & Co, Zürich.

Foerster, F. W. (1913). *Wychowanie człowieka [Raising a human being]*. tłum. W. Osterloff, wyd. III, Gebethner i Wolff.

Gałganek, A. (2019), Deduction and induction in theorizing of international relations. *Przegląd Politologiczny, 4*(24). https://doi.org/10.14746/pp.2019.24.4.4

Gouldner, A. (1970). *The coming crisis of Western sociology*. Basic Books.

Gross, S. R., & Miller, N. (1997). The 'golden section' and bias in perceptions of social consensus. *Personality and Social Psychology Review, 1*(3), 241–271.

Guba, E. G., & Lincoln, Y. S. (1994). Competing paradigms in qualitative research. In N. K. Denzin & Y. S. Lincoln (Eds.), *Handbook of qualitative research* (pp. 105–117). Sage.

Harris, W. T. (1891). *Annual report of the Commissioner of Education for the year 1888–89*. Government Printing Office. Retrieved December 28, 2023, from https://files.eric.ed.gov/fulltext/ED542895.pdf

Hartas, D. (2010). Educational research and inquiry: Key issues and debates. In D. Hartas (Ed.), *Educational research and inquiry: Qualitative and quantitative approaches* (pp. 13–29). Continuum.

Heider, F. (1958). The psychology of interpersonal relations. *American Sociological Review, 23*(6), 742. https://doi.org/10.2307/2089062

Holmes, B. (1984). Paradigm shifts in comparative education. *Comparative Education Review, 1984*(4), 584–604.

Husén, T., & Postlethwaite, T. N. (1996). A brief history of the International Association for the Evaluation of Educational Achievement (TEA). *Assessment in Education: Principles, Policy & Practice, 3*(2), 129–141. https://doi.org/10.1080/0969594960030202

James, W., & Murphy, T. (1995). The will to believe: And other writings from William James. In Doubleday eBooks. https://ci.nii.ac.jp/ncid/BA29874778

Kosonen, P., & Winne, P. H. (1995). Effects of teaching statistical laws on reasoning about everyday problems. *Journal of Educational Psychology, 87*(1), 33–46.

Melosik, Z. (2023). Comparative education: The status controversy and dynamics of scientific development. *Studia z Teorii Wychowania, XIV, 3*(44), 9–26. https://doi.org/10.5604/01.3001.0053.9192

How Should Comparative Research Be Conducted 79

Mill, J. S. (1962). *System logiki dedukcyjnej i indukcyjnej*, t. 1–2 (C. Znamierowski, Trans.). Państwowe Wydawnictwo Naukowe.

Noah, H. J. (1984). The use and abuse of comparative education. *Comparative Education Review*, *28*(4), 560.

Nowakowska-Siuta, R. (2003). *Pedagogika porownawcza: Problemy, stan badań i perspektywy rozwoju*. Impuls.

Sadler, M. (1902). The unrest in secondary education and elsewhere. *Board of Education special reports on education subjects. Vol. 9: Education in Germany*. HMSO.

Schütz, A. (1962). *The problem of social reality: collected papers I*. The Hague: Martinus Nijhoff.

Shiel, G., & Cosgrove, J. (2002a). Owning technology. *The Reading Teacher*, *55*(7), 690–692.

Shiel, G., & Cosgrove, J. (2002b). International assessments of reading literacy. *The Reading Teacher*, *55*(7), 690.

Tversky, A. (1977). Features of similarity. *Psychological Review*, *84*(4), 327–352. https://doi.org/10.1037/0033-295X.84.4.327

Tversky, A., & Kahneman, D. (1982). *Judgment under uncertainty: Heuristics and biases* (pp. 3–20). University Press.

van de Vijver, F. J. R., & Leung, K. (1997). *Methods and data analysis for cross-cultural research*. Sage Publications, Inc.

Waltz, K. N. (2004). Neorealism: Confusions and criticism. *Journal of Politics and Society*, *15*(1), 2–6. Retrieved January 2, 2024, from https://ir101.co.uk/wp-content/uploads/2018/11/Waltz-Neorealism-Confusions-and-Criticisms.pdf

Weber, M. (1982). *Gesammelte Aufsätze zur Wissenschaftslehre [Collected essays on the teaching of science]*. Johann Winckelmann, J.B.C. Mohr (Paul Siebeck).

Woleński, J. (2014). *John Vulsky: I Believe in What I Can Understand*. The Copernicus Center Press.

RETHINKING OUR EMBRACE OF DECOLONIZATION: A SLIPPERY SLOPE LEADING TO NATIONALIST IDEOLOGIES AND AGENDAS

Supriya Baily

George Mason University, USA

ABSTRACT

Over the past decade, the popularity of authoritarian governments and/or authoritarian leaning leaders has steadily grown. Much of the acceptance of and/or allegiance to such forms of leadership and governance structures stems from a rightward shift among voting blocs, who are increasingly comfortable with nationalist, nativist, and insular arguments in an effort to ensure a sense of stability and safety. In scholarly circles, there has been a parallel rise with scholars increasingly using decolonial theories, research, and practices in an effort to destabilize norms of colonial, Western, and patriarchal knowledge creation and dissemination. These two movements might, on the outside, appear to be disconnected but are in fact coupled together in ways that can constrain progressive movements around human rights, education and justice. The paper frames a selection of political battles in education to highlight the emergence, journey, and outcomes that have led to the successful rise of right-wing ideologies in education as well as offer a critique on the ambiguity inherent in decolonial theories that impede current decolonizing ways of knowing. These ambiguities exacerbate the emergence of a neo-decolonial perspective. This exploration of a neo-decolonial narrative is predicated on the evolution and co-option of the public space, or argued by Habermas, the "bourgeois public sphere." This shift often leaves the liberal, progressive, and human rights-orientated individuals out of the dialogue on the future of education, in part,

Annual Review of Comparative and International Education 2023
International Perspectives on Education and Society, Volume 48, 81–97
Copyright © 2025 by Emerald Publishing Limited
All rights of reproduction in any form reserved
ISSN: 1479-3679/doi:10.1108/S1479-367920240000048006

readying a public willing to engage in new forms of decolonial thinking, resulting in more sophisticated right-wing intersections in policy and practice that directly affect educational equity and access.

Keywords: Decolonization; nationalism; educational access; equity; feminist inquiry; neo-decolonial narratives

INTRODUCTION

It should be no surprise to most people with access to news and information that the current state of politics is resulting in a growing attraction and increasing allegiances to leaders who represent authoritarian leanings and temperaments. From Brazil to India, Turkey and China and France, as well as Russia and the United States among others, there is no dearth of examples of successful authoritarian movements and the growing complacency and acceptance voters are affording such leaders.

The right-ward shift of politics has been hypothesized as a result of a confluence of factors. Among those factors include the backlash to the burgeoning globalization and internationalization movements of the early 21st century (Frieden, 2019), the fears of working and middle-class voters about a more insecure future (Kojola, 2019) and/or the belief that the push for rights for those who would be considered in the minority (women, BIPOC and LBGTQ+ populations, linguistic and religious minorities, and others) have reached an apex (Cammaerts, 2022). These concerns have created a new "imagined community" (Anderson, 2005) where those who have been historically able to dominate structures and corridors of power feel as if they are no longer in control.

Educational systems have been directly impacted by the changing political environment. From national and local policies to curriculum changes, teacher preparation and in the day-to-day business of schools and classrooms, there have been more overt and endemic efforts to influence education from early childhood to post-secondary and higher education. While schools have always played a vital role in creating both "national identities and loyalties" (Spring, 2018, p. 42), the current environment is shifting how education is being perceived. While politics have always played a part in education and those who control government often also control how the stories of nation, citizenship, and belonging are represented, much of the control depends on the ethos and values held by those at the height of their political power. If a country takes a progressive, inclusive, and critical approach, the education system might embody similar values. If there is a restrictive or conservative shift, similar swings are manifested in educational spaces as well (Natanson et al, 2024).

While there are parts of the world where these ideological shifts have been explicit, sometimes veering toward violence (recent incidents around the return to power of the Taliban in Afghanistan or the protests around women's rights in Iran), efforts around reaching and meeting the needs of marginalized students in inequitable educational structures have usually proceeded with limited counterattack. Nearly a century of efforts around critical pedagogy, half a century of scholarship around critical race theory and the recent efforts around decolonization of educational policies and practices have been relatively ignored by conservative movements. Yet, as authoritarianism has expanded its reach to engage in more explicit attacks on progressive, pluralist, and humanist values, the work of schools to guarantee a singular identity and loyalty among students (future citizens) are increasingly playing a central role. These attacks, particularly around diversity, equity, and inclusion (DEI) have seen widespread animus since 2020. These DEI initiatives have seen greater political scapegoating, particularly under the guise that such efforts waste resources and reallocate priorities. This focus has been widely prevalent in the United States, but what has tended to be ignored is language around decolonization efforts. Both DEI and decolonization efforts are presented where "discrete cultures, races, and peoples whose views, approaches and histories have been suppressed, lost or marginalized" (Fatima & Jacobson, 2022, p. 208) and as such portend the same level of threat in changing political times. In the vein of DEI efforts, attacks on decolonization too are at risk to become a potent weapon in the hands of authoritarian leaders, especially when wielded by those who have limited or superficial understanding of the colonial enterprise. Part of the weaponization is due to the sophistication of the messages being crafted by authoritarian leaders and the relative lack of nuance in the spaces being occupied by scholars who seek to engage in decolonial praxis.

This paper offers a perspective on these topics as a theoretical exercise to raise concerns on the dangers of the use of decolonization where there is limited understanding of how it is being used by those who oppose the spread of progressive/humanist/secular values. The paper aims to present the dilemma embedded in the decolonization debate, provide current examples of the weaponization of education by authoritarian movements that might illustrate the predicament, and urge scholars and practitioners to engage in calls for progressive, liberal, humanist, and rights-based approaches, instead of potentially aligning with neo-decolonial models of educational liberation.

THE CHALLENGE OF DECOLONIALITY

The challenge of embracing decoloniality as a potential framework under which people seek to dismantle structures of power and oppression is, while seductive, laden with a complex lexicon that can be both weighty and opaque. To understand that complexity we might need to place it in context and as part of the timeline of the larger colonial exercise.

The entirety of the colonial endeavor remains to ensure domination through the "direct political, economic and educational control of one nation over another" (Altbach, 1971, p. 237). The ways that nationhood is contextualized and the subsequent domination of place include large swathes of territories in almost every continent. The persecution of indigenous/local/subaltern/native populations by the colonizer resulted in economic, political, and social structures that continue to influence many aspects of modern life today. The colonial influence was felt across all facets of life, including education where Carnoy (2019) argued that "colonial education was structured to reproduce the colonizer's power over the colonized." These practices would remain consistent event when local leaders took over, or other interests dominated to ensure the desire to "reproduce the power of the powerful over the less powerful" (p. 95).

As many countries shook off the vestiges of the 19th–20th century models of colonization, a new era of post-colonialism emerged. This period is indelibly linked to the colonial past, and often depended on how newly independent countries sought to re-establish nationhood in the shadow of the structures of colonization. Mishra and Hodge (2005) argue that this period of time, in part due to the lack of transparency on what post-colonialism was actually supposed to entail, has led to the evolution of the term, noting that the term itself is enmeshed in hybridity, resulting in slippage of meaning especially as it relates to its intersections with theory and practice. Mishra and Hodge (2005) construe that post-colonialism as a "result" is always connected to the past in order to exist in the present. As such, post-colonialism operates more as a time period in relation to the colonial movement shifting away from imperialism/colonialism toward a version of self-actualization in whatever forms was/is defined by nation-states or independent regions and territories.

Yet, while countries were just beginning to grapple with what a post-colonial identity might look like, new forms of colonial enterprises were already paying attention. The emergence of neo-colonialism was predicated on the rise of globalization and the preponderance of entities that could benefit from new models of oppressed/oppressor relationships, framed in more *in*-direct forms of exploitation of political economic and educational control. The role of industry and multi-national companies as well as the emergence of a "development-industrial complex" began to engage in new forms of unequal relationships. The influence of the neo-colonial movement sought to replicate systems of unequal power between the haves and the have nots. Schools, knowledge sharing, and the educational agendas of nations were also impacted in many ways in similar fashion to the colonial era. It was these constantly inequitable structures of education that would give rise to the movement to consider the value of decolonizing education. Decolonizing schools, decolonizing curriculum, and decolonizing education generally have become a rallying cry in many progressive circles as a way to rethink the colonial and neo-colonial influence on educational policies and practices.

The argument for decolonial practices is that:

> decoloniality, in this sense, is not a static condition, an individual attribute, or a lineal point of arrival or enlightenment. Instead, decoloniality seeks to make visible, open up, and advance radically, distinct perspectives, and positionalities that displace Western rationality as the only framework and possibility of existence, analysis, and thought. (Walsh, 2018, p. 17)

The movement to decolonize education, curriculum, teaching practices, and other areas of schooling has been rising over the past decade, reaching a zenith in the post-COVID-19 years, where activities around decolonization have resulted in programs, certificates, and other efforts around teaching and learning on what it means to be a decolonizing practitioner. Since most educational systems "on almost all levels, remain rooted in the administrative structures of the former colonial rulers ... the structure and organization of the schools reflect a foreign model necessarily has an impact on the nature of the education provided" (Altbach, 1971, p. 237). Even early in the post-colonial era, scholars such as Altbach argued that the curriculum of schools and colleges often "reflects orientations of the former colonial rulers or of other advanced countries" (p. 237), while imported textbooks, teacher preparation, language of instruction, and the values that are to be inculcated in schools are often still imports from and remnants of the colonial legacies of Western countries in non-Western contexts. This concern remains prevalent today as well. Most non-Western countries are heavily influenced by educational policies and practices that are grounded in the "legacy of Western colonization" which "remains too powerful," and the ways in which measurement, comparison, and our understanding of education systems emerge out of the binary of the west and the "analytical frameworks that are used to understand education remain imbued with the Western experience" (Silova et al., 2020, p. 4). As Fatima and Jacobson (2022) put it, "the colonial period lives on in one form or another in the social institutions and schisms of all postcolonial societies" (p. 210).

Yet, the increasing popularity of calls for decolonization are beginning to see critique and cracks. Vickers (2020) argues that the pitting a west/non-west dichotomy in decolonial studies is unsustainable. In a 2021 medical blog post, Opara (2021) called for the healthcare industry to decolonize the decolonization movement, arguing that it is "emblematic of the ego-centrism and lack of self-introspection" (n.p.) that is inherent in well-intentioned but relatively uninformed actors who themselves are oftentimes plagued by guilt but are absent from truly engaging in the rebalancing of power structures as would be expected within a truly decolonizing movement. In other critiques, Iyer (2020) reasons that decolonization is often conflated with supporting inclusion and diversity, which she then maintains leads to superficiality and a lack of deep reflection on one's role in the colonial enterprise. Finally, there are the words of Tuck and Yang (2012) who maintain that decoloniality is not a metaphor, saying:

> the easy absorption, adoption, and transposing of decolonization is yet another form of settler appropriation. When we write about decolonization, we are not offering it as a metaphor; it is not an approximation of other experiences of oppression. *Decolonization is not a swappable term for other things we want to do to improve our societies and schools.* Decolonization doesn't have a synonym. (p. 3, italics inserted)

These critiques and observations are important. First, they are united in that they contend that we are not doing enough to engage authentically with the true essence of decolonization. They put on notice those who might utilize the framing of decolonization as an effort to portray allyship, yet are gaining the benefits of using a convenient "buzzword" (Iyer, 2020, p. 1) in an effort to capitalize on the popularity of the movement around decolonization. These scholars critique the decolonization bandwagon, in an effort to ensure the integrity of what true decolonization ought to mean.

While these assessments have important value for scholars in fields where decolonization is popular, there is a parallel, more dangerous aspect to superficial engagement with decoloniality that hinders the desire to "make visible, open up, and advance radically, distinct perspectives, and positionalities that displace Western rationality as the only framework and possibility of existence, analysis, and thought" (Walsh, 2018, p. 17). This danger is embedded in the rhetoric of authoritarian leaders and nationalist ideologues. The increased popularity and convergence of these leaders center around brands of populism that are grounded in nationalist rhetoric and overt forms of patriotic behaviors (Kumar, 2020). Such ideologies offer a narrative that is rather unpretentious and direct, which appeals to busy, anxious, and vulnerable groups of people in an era of headline driven news snippets (Bang et al., 2017). The message is simple, where an authoritarian leader might say "I am a true patriot, I am a true (insert stated nationality here), and others who speak against me are nothing more than enemies of our country and our way of living and are in fact seeking to oppress us from (somewhere else)."

This message has been effective in labeling non-followers as unpatriotic at best, treasonous at worst (Lee, 2012). This increases the frequency with such attacks are oftentimes directed at those who have benefited from higher education, labeling them as elitist and out of touch with common people (Bonikowski & DiMaggio, 2016).

Within this context of nationalist political ideologies that depend on exploiting inter-group tensions, the argument about "who" is the "true decolonizer" becomes more fraught. The nationalist often argues, convincingly to their followers, that the shackles of colonization can only be lifted by someone who is a hyper-patriot. By embracing the role of the decolonizer, the neo-nationalist creates a narrative claiming that values often seen as progressive, humanist, feminist or secular are Western, colonizing imports. By imprinting that these ideas are linked to colonization, the response to countering them is then, naturally, a decolonizing effort. By calling these ideas vestiges of the colonial legacy, neo-nationalists argue that the use of local knowledges, a return to traditional ways of living, and "historic or cultural exceptionalism" (Lewis & Lall, 2024, n.p.) as defined by them, is in fact actual decolonization. This is in part due to the shifts in understanding who is considered elite, who has access to power, and the fight over the public sphere by vastly different ideological movements.

THE CO-OPTION OF PUBLIC SPACE

I ground the above argument in the evolution of the notion of the public sphere as argued by Jürgen Habermas, where the social realm moves from being a space that is merely public, to the co-option of that space by those who seek special interests. The use of the term "special interests" is centered around the ways in which those who have access to power also then have a vested interest in shaping the public narrative to protect their space. Habermas describes this group as the bourgeoisie and that vested space as the bourgeois public space.

Habermas et al. (1974) defines the concept of the public sphere as a "realm of social life in which something approaching public opinion can be formed" (p. 49). The bourgeoisie "are private individuals [who] do not 'rule,'" and Habermas describes this group as having a claim on power through the direction of public

Rethinking Our Embrace of Decolonization 87

authority, opting for the shared concentration of power between the public authority and the bourgeoisie. This would follow the current state of popularity for authoritarian leaders by primarily middle class voters (Rosenfeld, 2020) where middle-class voters could be defined as private individuals who are seeking to both control and maintain power in light of the changing perceptions of loss and insecurity. The re-emergence of authoritarian leadership often depends on the willingness of the public to recognize the need to capture, hold, and maintain political power. By consolidating their power over the public square to control public discussion, the bourgeoisie are able influence thinking in the public space where:

> public discussions about the exercise of political power which are both critical in intent and institutionally guaranteed have not always existed - they grew out of a specific phase of bourgeois society and could enter into the order of the bourgeois constitutional state only a result of a particular constellation of interests. (p. 50)

The "constellation of interests" allows populist movements to shift entire discourses around public opinion. The evolution of the public sphere to cater to the needs of the bourgeoisie who are in search of and seek to hoard power allows the state to engage more directly in public actions. Habermas warns that "group needs which can expect no satisfaction from a self-regulating market now tend towards a regulation by the state" (p. 54). This state regulation is then how authoritarian leaders develop policies and practices to assist those who would be sympathetic to their vision, leading to a consolidation of economic, social and political capital among a smaller fraction of the populace.

The public sphere, which must now mediate these demands, "becomes a field for the competition of interests, which assume the form of violent conflict" (p. 54) where any opposing viewpoints are considered unpatriotic or unnational. While who makes up the bourgeoisie has shifted over time, the power of the bourgeois in the public sphere has frequently centered on maintaining control over structures of oppression and labor. For instance, Marx's critique of the power of the public sphere could not ignore the role of labor relations, patriarchy, and property control (Calhoun, 1993), much of which is still controlled by those who find sympathy and cooperation with authoritarian and nationalist ideologies. Calhoun's studies of Habermas' ideas on the public sphere further offers that controlling public space serves the narrow self-interests of those who anoint themselves as the arbiters of the nation. In turn:

> the public sphere has become more an arena for advertising than a setting for rational critical debate. Legislators stage displays for constituents. Special interest organizations use publicity work to increase the prestige of their own positions, without making the topics to which those positions refer subjects of genuine public debate. The media are used to create occasions for consumers to identify with the public positions or personas of others. (Calhoun, 1993, p. 26)

If the "colonial matrix of power" demands control over economics, authority, knowledge, and the public sphere (Tlostanova & Mignolo, 2009), it is also clear that the matrix of authoritarian leaders operates in very similar ways. What is different however, is that in the current battle for ideologies, the control of who is seen as the credible authority on decolonization can be co-opted by nationalist regimes in an effort to (1) disqualify the efforts of those whose influence is deemed unwanted or unwelcome and (?) elevate policies and practices that are untenable for certain populations, by arguing that those efforts are "not the way we do it." A frequent example of this is the limitation of access to education for women and girls in many parts of the world by contending that this is a western, white, non-local practice. Claiming that educating women and girls is a legacy of the colonial influence engenders patriarchy and the continued control of men over women. Similarly, the co-option of decoloniality becomes the weapon of progressive, humanist, and liberal ideas, making those ideas the enemy of the true patriot.

With education at the center of most global authoritarian movements, there are more than a few examples of how progressive educational practices have become critical to populist and nationalist ideologues. The following examples offer insights into how such movements have shifted both the narrative and its representation in the public sphere.

THE WEAPONIZATION OF PROGRESSIVE EDUCATIONAL PRACTICES

The current argument is that in a post-colonial world, there has been increased efforts to engage in a movement to decolonize education while also seeing rising neo-nationalist agendas. These efforts are occurring in parallel as neo-nationalist movements require a foil for their efforts to engage in acts of "authentic patriotism." Authentic patriotism allows authoritarian leaders to claim their supremacy on how true patriotism is defined and how it is manifested which in turn creates a space to make changes that often appear to be decolonial in practice but are anti-progressive at best. By arguing that those who espouse decoloniality are embedded in Western, progressive thinking, schooled in ways that replicate the colonial hierarchy, and are complicit with forms of neo-colonialism, offers authoritarian leaders a way to reshape and co-opt, decolonization (Lewis & Lall, 2024).

In the operationalization of education as a vehicle for authoritarian regimes to promote the success of nationalist movements, I can identify three examples of what happens when ideologies collide. Each of these examples is drawn from current tensions between the political right and left but is also situated in the imaginary of the battle between the populace and the elite. These framings have shifted public perceptions on each of these issues, creating a sense of allegiance between people and leaders of authoritarian movements. The creation of a category of educated "out of touch elite" also represents the misunderstanding how moving away from a colonial past is also a method to move away from progressive values and systems.

The three illustrative examples of the weaponization of educational policy and practices center around the battles for and against free speech; the creation of a mythical "war on merit" that tends to inflate tensions between groups of already marginalized people; and directed anger at "western curriculum." Each of these is presented in different ways in many contexts and countries, but the examples are primarily drawn from the United States, India, and Nigeria.

FREE SPEECH

The battle over free speech within educational spaces but particularly in higher education has been a hot button issue over the past decade. Most aspects of higher education practices from what faculty teach to the choices of readings and texts and the dialogue that is controlled in classrooms are often situated under the auspices of free speech. In testing the limits of free speech, it does appear to be one of the most fundamental flashpoints in the current context of political polarization.

Free speech on college campuses emerged as a point of contention as more right-wing speakers were either disinvited from speaking on college campuses, or faced fervent protests when they did speak. Part of this has to do with a need to frame the idea of free speech in a more nuanced and thoughtful way. Writing for the American Association of University Professors (AAUP), Michael Behrant of Appalachia State University argues that there are two political sides to this debate. On one hand, there are the free speech absolutists, those who tend to be on the political right who argue that anyone should get to say what they want to say, when they want to say, and where they want to say it. On the other side, often the political left, the perspective around free speech tends to suggest consideration of the "utopia of inclusion," where time, context, and manner matters before free speech is justified and that some voices are impossible to fairly welcome, or another way to say it might be that "there really are not good people on both sides" (n.p.).

Continuing to fan these flames, former United States President Donald Trump signed an Executive Order in 2019 to "protect" free speech on campuses solidifying the myth that universities were unfriendly to conservative voices (Kreighbaum, 2019). There were repeated threats to end federal funding for colleges and universities, further cementing education as a space of political polarization. Newman (2020) cites Adam Harris, a journalist for *The Atlantic*, who claimed that this signing was just "red meat" for Trump's supporters (p. 20). More descriptively, Newman also goes on to say that this order was an act of symbolic politics where "what is signalled matters more than any substantive result. Trump's executive order can be understood as yet another volley in the 'culture wars' that American conservatives have been fighting for decades" (p. 22). Yet, even after the signing of the executive order, in 2022, at Cornell University, conservative pundit Ann Coulter spoke, was heckled, and then left early. She was invited despite the campus newspaper protesting her visit saying that Cornell was turning a "blind eye to extremism that may pose a threat to vulnerable students" (Moslemi & DiLizia, 2022, n.p.). At the time of the writing of this paper, Coulter has been reinvited to speak at Cornell, with similar concerns of absolutism and inclusion being debated.

The Cornell University situation might represent a classic case of seeking to balance free speech absolutism with the utopia of inclusion in the same space, there have been shifts in what is perceived to be free speech. Between 2019 and 2022, the promotion of free speech was often a coded message to ensure that any critique of conservative voices was swiftly attacked no matter what was said.

Yet, by 2023–2024, the issue of free speech has ricocheted to turn the previous assertion on its head. Nationalist and right-wing groups are moving from previous support of free speech absolutism to the utopia of inclusion to build political capital with new groups. For instance, the issue of protecting and challenging free speech guidelines is seen as much more of a political exercise than an academic one. Reporting from Texas, Friedersdorf (2023) found that an administrator canceled a performance by citing that the show in question would be offensive to women. Quoting the administrator who said they would be offended by the use of blackface (thereby aligning themselves with African Americans), the administrator argued that this performance would similarly be offensive to women. What was the piece? It was a drag performance to support LGBTQ+ efforts to support suicide prevention. By engaging in performative inclusion, the conservative effort allowed for further marginalization of LGBTQ+ students. In addition, the efforts on college campuses to tamp down on any efforts to protest the war in Gaza and to call for an immediate ceasefire in Gaza have come up against former free speech efforts (Lumpkin, 2023).

These battles over free speech and in shifting allegiances between demanding a voice for all with no censure on the message and the use of censure as a way to protect those whom one is looking for political capital create a way for authoritarian leaders to remove progressive voices from the public sphere. The framing of the messages in the public sphere remains in control of the bourgeoisie. By doing so, the messages of what is allowable, what is in the best interests of the nation, and who is protecting the true patriot becomes a way to convincingly argue that the any efforts to decolonize are embedded in the inclusion of nationalist voices.

THE HYPOTHETICAL "WAR ON MERIT"

Another educational issue that is playing a central role in the politics of right-wing ideologies is the use of any programs or projects designed to ensure greater representation of historically marginalized groups in society in general, and in education in particular. From affirmative action programs in the United States to the Indian reservation system, such endeavors are increasingly seen as targets for nationalist ideologues to tap into voter anger. In the United States, the creation of a hypothetical "War on Merit" is creating a false assumption that by including historically under-represented minorities, other groups are being "punished" for their abilities and losing their opportunities for admissions into selective schools and colleges (Riley, 2023). By inserting such programs into political narratives, subsequent battles have led to the diminishment of the more just and equitable goals such programs were expected to deliver.

In India, immediately after India's independence from the British, in some of its first efforts in the post-colonial period, Indian leaders sought to dismantle the structures of oppression that existed in the Hindu-created, pre-colonial caste system. Broadly, the Indian caste system was predicated on the roles

Rethinking Our Embrace of Decolonization 91

individuals played in society, but over centuries, the accumulation of power and privilege by those who were deemed to have higher ranks in the caste system led to wide injustice and systemic marginalization and oppression of those who were in "lower" castes. The labeling of who could benefit from the system would not just include lower caste Hindus, but other minority groups such as those from tribal regions of the country, as well as certain groups of religious minorities including Christians and Muslims. After India's independence and facing greater backlash and violence against inequitable opportunities for some (Osborne, 2001), the Reservation System came into effect, offering marginalized populations the prospect of accessing government jobs, educational seats, political representation, and government assistance as a way to remedy historic wrongs.

These structural changes to support greater access and opportunity for those who had/have experienced severe and generational marginalization due to their caste were often met with resistance by the middle class. This is not unusual as most affirmative action programs around the world have often been unwelcome by middle-class groups. The established middle classes of the post-independence era held on to the idea of merit as a guiding force for progress. They saw the Indian reservation system as a threat to their own progress (Alam, 2009).

While much of what has resulted from the provision of such reservations (or quotas) is conflicted, areas of uncertainty focus on how the precise definitions of caste and who is seen as "backward" (the official term for those who are meant to be the focus of the policies) have been blurred. Other areas with unclear outcomes include how the subsequent outcomes of such programs affected political parties and finally, in the ways in which, if any, goals around social justice and equity have been met (Kumar, 2022). For many high-caste Hindus, the creation of the Reservation System limited their control over and access to jobs, education, and political power. As such, this issue became a clear political winner for Hindu nationalist parties which could promote inter-caste divisions to garner votes and elicit support. Therefore, for much of the 20th century, support for Hindu majoritarianism and condemnation of preferential treatment for historically disadvantaged groups were a winning (and mutually reinforcing) political combination (Vaishnav, 2019).

The concerns of middle-class voters around access and their sense of insecurity around the future, in part due to fears that a more global world leads to greater competition, reinforced the power of education as a vehicle for stability. By limiting access to those who have been able to benefit from decades, if not centuries, of advantages, due purely to the chance of birth, arouses strong emotional responses, which are often more negative for dominant group membership (whites in the case of affirmative action, for instance) (Haley & Sidanius, 2006). Capitalizing on the animus that is created in response to these systems allows nationalists to argue for a vision of the country that is grounded in the precedence of one group over the other, Hindus over non-Hindus in the Indian context, or whites over non-whites in other contexts. The ability to control access, in this situation, also elicits inter-group animosity between high-caste Hindus and low-caste Hindus, but also between Hindus and Muslims as well as Christians who were able to benefit from the Reservation System. In their study on who opposes reservations and why, Chhibber and Verma (2018) found that:

> Only 28 percent of upper-caste respondents supported reservations for Muslims, with only 34 percent of OBC [other backward communities] respondents and 36 percent of Dalit [low-caste Hindus] respondents also expressing support [for Muslims]. Support for reservations for OBCs, and for continued reservations for Dalits, was predominant among OBC and Dalit respondents, respectively, but OBC and Dalit respondents alike seemed to oppose the extension of the reservations policy to Muslims. (p. 101)

The authors argue that such inherent biases toward the provision of public services (such as the Reservation System) between groups are then weaponized by political parties to ensure latent and overt messaging that ties religious identity to political support (Chhibber & Verma, 2018). They argue there are both prejudicial and policy-oriented concerns around Hindu opposition to the system of reservations where Hindus

> oppose reservations because they perceive such a policy leads to negative outcomes for them ... [and] any government policy that aims to target a "section of beneficiary" (such as the reservation system in India) will also open up space for reactionary mobilization. (p. 102)

By influencing the public sphere, the bourgeoisie, or here the middle-class, upper-caste Hindu, works in tandem with public authority (political parties) to ensure their grasp on access to educational opportunities. This in turn cements a larger narrative that the inclusion particularly of Muslims and Christians is based on a colonial past where India was led by both Muslim and Christian rulers (colonizers). As such, by providing them with special privileges would undercut and diminish the Hindu-first ideology, an identity that embraces the true vision of nationalism. In returning to a caste-based hierarchy by hoarding opportunity, nationalist leaders identify themselves as engaging in decolonizing practices. The backlash against the Reservation System, the description of the beneficiaries as members of the colonizing powers, and the anger toward secularists accusing them of betraying their "own" people are all consolidated in the public sphere.

THE CHALLENGE OF "WESTERN" CURRICULUM

The final example to draw from on the ways in which nationalist movements are co-opting education to challenge progressive, secular or feminist ideologies is by engaging in removing or eliminating curriculum that in sum or in parts is deemed infiltering historical or local norms. The most extreme example is the terrorist organization Boko Haram which has terrorized women and girls in Nigeria in many parts due to the group's focus on the "reform and purification of the Nigerian political system against Western values and culture, which it argues are the cause of corruption and economic hardship" (Iyekekpolo, 2016, p. 2213).

Iyekekpolo (2020) documents the emergence of Boko Haram as a direct reaction to the shifting political discourse in Nigeria from the emergence of a

Rethinking Our Embrace of Decolonization 93

post-colonial elite to a more nationalist and identity-based movement for autonomy and agency for those who were not able to reap social, economic, and political rewards in the immediate post-colonial epoch. By outlining how different groups of political elites engage in competition for political power at the national level, identity becomes the most critical aspect of allegiance, which in turn births a multitude of subgroups who are also battling for political influence and visibility. This finally leads to one group becoming politically "relevant" making "extremist demands which spark antagonism between it and the ruling political elites. Finally, the rise of fundamentalist insurgencies goes unchecked in a partial democracy with political elites factionalized along identity lines" (Iyekekpolo, 2020, p. 750). In Nigeria, this power struggle, as it has in India, is predicated on religious lines which creates a new bourgeois society that operates in the interchange between religion and politics.

The very essence of Boko Haram is designed to be both anti-western and anti-education where "education is seen as a corrupting influence—a tool for western imperialism that undermines Islamic values" (Kingsley 2023, n.p.). By instrumentalizing religion (Islam), the leaders of the organization have been able to gain access to legitimate power, engage in the radicalization of the populace and have been able to become more appealing to new converts (Brakoniecka, 2024). By politicizing religion (as is seen in India with Hindu Nationalism and the United States, with rising Christian nationalism), the use of Islam as a vehicle through which anti-Western propaganda is spread, is then aligned with further efforts to decolonize the country from its colonial past. The banning of secularism from the public space could be construed as a European practice leaving Boko Haram to argue that the removal of religion into purely private spaces is not Nigerian (Idahosa, 2015). This creates a perception in the public sphere that Boko Haram is in fact pushing back against colonial influences and post-colonial practices that are being maintained by cultural elites.

THE NEO-DECOLONIAL TRAP

In their essay on modernity in the age of anti-colonialism and decolonization, Fatima and Jacobson (2022) remind readers that in the immediate aftermath of the removal of colonial powers, many emerging leaders were oftentimes educated in institutions that were within or under the control of imperial powers. They cite the examples of Sun Yat-Sen and Jomo Kenyatta, but this was also true in India of Jawaharlal Nehru as well as Mohandas Gandhi. Fatima and Jacobson (2022) argue that these leaders often sought to reject previous elite rules and norms (pre-colonial influences) for a more modern engagement with "science and progress, while of course rejecting the hegemony, conquest and racism of the imperial powers" (p. 208). The current Hindu nationalist movement disavows both Nehru and his commitment to secularism as well have sought to increasingly valorize the Hindu nationalist, Nathuram Godse who assassinated Gandhi, as a hero of their efforts (Tripathi, 2023). The ilk of those who were committed to modernity, secularism, and democracy are often seen as the "other" (Wojczewski, 2020), and not just a foreign other but one that is an internal foreigner allowing them to then be cast in the role of a threat. Wojczewski (2020) claims that:

> Through such "boundary-producing political performances"… the populist Hindutva discourse seeks to construct a homogenous, secure, and strong Hindu nation-state through the externalization of difference and danger—that is, it marks a series of Others and accuses them of preventing or threatening the realization of a strong and monolithic Hindu identity. Significantly, the discourse does not locate the foreign Other primarily or exclusively in the state's outside – the international system – but within the confines of the Indian state and within the political establishment in particular.

These ideas link directly to the ways in which public spheres can be co-opted by neo-nationalists to create a narrative for their movements to ensure greater buy-in from the broader public within which they seek allegiance and control. The shift in the public sphere offers a way for neo-nationalists to use decolonizing principles to "promote exclusionary structures, elevating a singular national identity and its political needs at the expense of plural-versality and minority representation" (Lewis & Lall, 2024, n.p.). In many ways, this particular co-option and shift of educational narratives create a new layer in the continuum of colonial experiences. The practice of neo-decolonization which I introduce here is the melding of neo-nationalist ideologies with theories of decolonization, developed in an effort to distort the emergence of more inclusive forms of knowledge production, greater engagement on issues of global inequities and the incorporation of more varied and secular lenses through which issues are studied. Engaging in neo-decolonizing practices creates a space to blame progressive thinking for non-nationalist practices in education – which in turn then results in the reversal, if not the complete ebbing away from progressive, inclusive and secular practices to something that resonates with neo-nationalist, authoritarian, fundamental, and patriarchal systems. These forms of hegemonic hierarchies offer their own models of suppression and oppression, which in turn makes them no better than the worst aspects of colonial power, even if these efforts are described as decolonization in practice.

As scholars continue to overuse the term "decolonization," there is also a lack of deep understanding and meaningful engagement with the principles and values embedded in the idea of decolonial practices. Performative actions like labeling curriculum, programs, and practices in education as efforts at decolonization can do more harm than good. It might be more valuable to engage in inclusive, secular, feminist, and humanist practices, rather than promote the removal of all aspects of colonial influence. Where a little knowledge is a dangerous thing, the lack of a full comprehension of how neo-national powers are capitalizing and finding willing audiences to appreciate their own decolonizing agendas can result in reversal of equitable rights for large swathes of people. In using the term loosely, well-intentioned scholars offer more danger than support to these efforts. Recognizing that the era of neo-decolonization is upon us, maybe it is time to retire our engagement with decolonization as a viable effort in educational research and practice.

CONCLUSIONS

Neo-decolonial efforts are wholly underway, in education and beyond. The examples provided in this paper are used to illustrate the ways in which neo-nationalists have co-opted and strengthened their positions by framing and messaging of issues as being contrary to national pride, national development, and national identity. The larger concern for us has to do with our relatively unsophisticated understanding and oftentimes kindly, but misguided efforts to argue for decolonization, when in fact, we might mean progressive, liberal, secularist, feminist, or humanist values. The backlash then will be particularly felt by those who might be seen as colonial proxies, leading to potential ostracism, silencing, and other forms of overt and covert violence. Decolonization, as a term, suited a particular and critical purpose in the post-colonial period. However, in the current context of nationalism, the potential for a headlong collision between those who might espouse the values that Tuck and Yang (2012) called for such as plurality, inclusion, and de-centering hegemonic thinking with those who see decolonization as an agenda from which to pursue insularity, patriarchy, homogeneity, and fundamentalism can be dangerous. In this paper, I seek to encourage scholars, practitioners, and students of education to reframe their approaches to decolonization, discard the term if it is truly not aligned with their missions, and to argue more robustly for humanist, pluralist, and progressive values. By decoupling educational work from the neo-decolonial efforts of nationalist movements, we might be able to reach our aspirations that speak to the spirit and essence of decolonial endeavors.

REFERENCES

Alam, J. (2009). Democracy in India and the quest for equality. *Community Development Journal, 44*(3), 291–304.

Altbach, P. G. (1971). Education and neocolonialism. *Teachers College Record, 72*(4), 1–10

Anderson, B. (2005). Imagined communities. In P. Spencer & H. Wollman (Eds.), *Nations and nationalism: A reader* (pp. 48–60). Rutgers University Press.

Bang, H., Yoo, J. J., & Choi, D. (2017). The carryover effect of national identity activation on consumers' evaluations of ads with patriotic appeals. *Journal of Business Research, 79*, 66–78.

Bonikowski, B., & DiMaggio, P. (2016). Varieties of American popular nationalism. *American Sociological Review, 81*(5), 949–980.

Brakoniecka, S. (2024). The role of religion in triggering radicalism in Northern Nigeria: The case of Boko Haram. *Journal of Religion in Africa, 1*(aop), 1–24.

Calhoun, C. (Ed.). (1993). *Habermas and the public sphere*. MIT Press.

Cammaerts, B. (2022). The abnormalisation of social justice: The 'anti-woke culture war' discourse in the UK. *Discourse & Society, 33*(6), 730–743.

Carnoy, M. (2019). *Transforming comparative education: Fifty years of theory building at Stanford*. Stanford University Press.

Chhibber, P. K., & Verma, R. (2018). Who opposes reservations and why? In P. K. Chhibber & R. Verma (Eds.), *Ideology and identity: The changing party systems of India* (pp. 85–102). Oxford University Press.

Fatima, S., & Jacobson, D. (2022). Project modernity: From anti-colonialism to decolonization. In H. Akil & S. Maddanu (Eds.), *Global modernity from coloniality to pandemic* (p. 207). Amsterdam University Press.

Frieden, J. (2019), *The political economy of the globalization backlash. Sources and implications.* SSRN. https://papers.ssrn.com/sol3/papers.cfm?abstract_id=3355610.

Friedersdorf, C. (2023, April 3). Free speech is not just for conservatives. *Atlantic Online.* https://advance-lexis-com.mutex.gmu.edu/api/document?collection=news&id=urn:contentItem:67XT-YG01-DYY9-J007-00000-00&context=1516831

Habermas, J., Lennox, S., & Lennox, F. (1974). The public sphere: An encyclopedia article (1964). *New German Critique, 3,* 45–55.

Haley, H., & Sidanius, J. (2006). The positive and negative framing of affirmative action: A group dominance perspective. *Personality and Social Psychology Bulletin, 32*(5), 656–668.

Idahosa, O. (2015). Boko Haram and the Nigerian state: A different perspective. *Glocalism, 3,* 1–28.

Iyekekpolo, W. O. (2016). Boko Haram: Understanding the context. *Third World Quarterly, 37*(12), 2211–2228.

Iyekekpolo, W. O. (2020). Political elites and the rise of the Boko Haram insurgency in Nigeria. *Terrorism and Political Violence, 32*(4), 749–767.

Iyer, P. (2020, Summer). Do not colonize decolonization. *The Peace Chronicle.* https://www.peacejustice studies.org/chronicle/do-not-colonize-decolonization/

Kingsley, J. (2023, December 19). Boko Haram's assault on education in Northern Nigeria. *The Diplomatic Courier.* https://www.diplomaticourier.com/posts/boko-haram-assault-education-nigeria#:~:text=Boko%20Haram's%20ideology%20is%20deeply,imperialism%20that%20undermines%20Islamic%20values

Kojola, E. (2019). Bringing back the mines and a way of life: Populism and the politics of extraction. *Annals of the American Association of Geographers, 109*(2), 371–381

Kreighbaum, A. (2019). Trump signs broad executive order. *Inside Higher ED.* https://ir.westcliff.edu/wp-content/uploads/2019/06/Trump-Signs-Broad-Executive-Order.pdf

Kumar, R. (2022). Fluid identities, contested categories: Jats, Patels and the demand for reservation in India. *Asian Ethnicity, 23*(4), 658–675.

Kumar, S. (2020). Verdict 2019: The expanded support base of the Bharatiya Janata Party. *Asian Journal of Comparative Politics, 5*(1), 6–22.

Lee, Y. (2012). Punishing disloyalty? Treason, espionage, and the transgression of political boundaries. *Law and Philosophy, 31*(3), 299–342.

Lewis, A., & Lall, M. (2024). From decolonisation to authoritarianism: The co-option of the decolonial agenda in higher education by right-wing nationalist elites in Russia and India. *Higher Education, 87*(5), 1471–1488.

Lumpkin, L. (2023). At a DC school, proposed film event sparks outrage amid Israel-Gaza war. *The Washington Post,* NA-NA.

Mishra, V., & Hodge, B. (2005). What was postcolonialism?. *New Literary History, 36*(3), 375–402.

Moslemi, T., & DiLizia, I. (2022, November 7). Ann Coulter is not welcome here. *The Cornell Daily Sun.* https://cornellsun.com/2022/11/07/guest-room-ann-coulter-is-not-welcome-here/.

Natanson, H., Tierney, L., & Morse, C. E. (2024, April 4). America has legislated itself into competing red, blue versions of education. *Washington Post.* https://www.washingtonpost.com/education/2024/04/04/education-laws-red-blue-divide/

Newman, S. L. (2020). The politics of campus free speech in Canada and the United States. *Constitutional Forum, 29,* 19.

Opara, I. N. (2021, July 29). It's time to decolonize the decolonization movement. *PLOS.* https://speakingofmedicine.plos.org/2021/07/29/its-time-to-decolonize-the-decolonization-movement/

Osborne, E. (2001). Culture, development, and government: Reservations in India. *Economic Development and Cultural Change, 49*(3), 659–685.

Riley, J. L. (2023, September 5). The racial achievement gap and the war on meritocracy. *Wall Street Journal.* https://www.wsj.com/articles/the-racial-achievement-gap-and-the-war-on-meritocracy-education-race-reading-math-exams-medical-school-college-admissions-c2226334

Rosenfeld, B. (2020). *The autocratic middle class: How state dependency reduces the demand for democracy* (Vol. 26). Princeton University Press.

Silova, I., Rappleye, J., & Auld, E. (2020). Beyond the Western horizon: Rethinking education, values, and policy transfer. In G. Fan & T. S. Popkewitz (Eds.), *Handbook of education policy studies: Values, governance, globalization, and methodology, Volume 1* (pp. 3–29). Springer.

Spring, J. (2018). *Global impacts of the western school model: Corporatization, alienation, consumerism*. Routledge.

Tlostanova, M., & Mignolo, W. (2009). Global coloniality and the decolonial option. *Kult*, *6*(Special Issue), 130–147.

Tripathi, S. (2023). Modi's singular vision for India. *Index on Censorship*, *52*(1), 60–65.

Tuck, E., & Yang, K.W. (2012). Decolonization is not a metaphor. *Decolonization: Indigeneity, Education & Society*, *1*(1), 1–40.

Vaishnav, M. (2019). *The BJP in power: Indian democracy and religious nationalism*. Retrieved August, 21, 2022. https://carnegieendowment.org/research/2019/04/the-bjp-in-power-indian-democracy-and-religious-nationalism?lang=en

Vickers, E. (2020). Critiquing coloniality, 'epistemic violence' and western hegemony in comparative education – The dangers of ahistoricism and positionality. *Comparative Education*, *56*(2), 165–189.

Walsh, C. (2018). Decoloniality in/as praxis. In W. D. Mignolo & C. E. Walsh (Eds.), *On decoloniality: Concepts, analytics, praxis* (p. 17). Duke University Press.

Wojczewski, T. (2020). Populism, Hindu nationalism, and foreign policy in India: The politics of representing "the people." *International Studies Review*, *22*(3), 396–422.

QUANTCRIT IN COMPARATIVE EDUCATION RESEARCH: TACKLING METHODOLOGICAL NATIONALISM WHEN EXAMINING DIFFERENCES IN LEARNING OUTCOMES BETWEEN INDIGENOUS AND NON-INDIGENOUS CHILDREN IN PERU

Miriam Broeks

University of Cambridge, Germany

ABSTRACT

This paper aims to elucidate the opportunities that incorporating a Quantitative Critical Race Theory (QuantCrit) approach into Comparative Education brings to tackle Methodological Nationalism. It uses data from the Young Lives survey and Oaxaca-Blinder decompositions to examine the difference in mathematics scores at age 12 and educational attainment at age 20 between Indigenous and non-Indigenous children in Peru. Tackling Methodological Nationalism involves unpacking power relations linked to the nation-state. To do so, analyses incorporate QuantCrit by using a multidimensional and a binary operationalization of Indigeneity, by assessing potential biases in the outcome data, and by reflecting on the choice and categorization of explanatory factors. This helps ensure that this research is mindful of the historical power dynamics that have affected Indigenous populations in Peru. Results show that the differences in education outcomes are primarily attributable to differences in sample characteristics between groups and that the way Indigeneity is defined does matter for research conclusions. Only structural and educational opportunity variables make a significant contribution to close the outcome difference. Maternal education is the most important factor to close the score gap at age 12, while at age 20 it is wealth index. Using a multidimensional Indigeneity definition alongside a binary one allows distilling diversity in the experiences of children who can be considered Indigenous. Following a traditional nation-state approach whereby only language is used to determine Indigeneity would hinder doing so. This shows that a QuantCrit approach is helpful in providing new insights to address Methodological Nationalism.

Keywords: QuantCrit; Oaxaca-Blinder decomposition; education outcome difference; Indigenous; Peru; structural inequality

INTRODUCTION

National and international assessments have been used to examine the extent of inequalities in achievement between schools, regions, diverse groups, and countries. Results from these assessments have been used to inform policies. Yet, researchers in the field of Comparative Education seldomly question the research decisions underpinning quantitative survey studies that compare diverse groups, not only between but also within countries. Not reflecting on research decisions poses the risk of reinforcing unequal power relations through research. Shahjahan and Kezar (2013) seek to address Methodological Nationalism in education by encouraging researchers to "question their assumptions, discard artificial analytic boundaries, and extend their gaze" (p. 21). They highlight that the national container traditionally reinforces unequal power relationships and overlooks responsibility to historically oppressed groups, such as Indigenous groups, when they do not neatly fall into the nation-building project. Hence, tackling Methodological Nationalism entails unpacking power relations linked to the nation-state. This aligns with the principles of Quantitative Critical Race Theory (QuantCrit), which challenge any normalization of social inequity by critically engaging with statistical data and acknowledging that the categories used to collect and analyze statistical information shape research conclusions (Gillborn et al., 2018; Smith, 2021; Walter & Andersen, 2013). This paper aims to elucidate the opportunities that incorporating QuantCrit into Comparative Education brings to tackle Methodological Nationalism.

This paper provides a practical example of applying QuantCrit principles to comparatively study the learning outcomes of Indigenous children in Peru. It uses data from the Peru Young Lives survey (Young Lives, 2017)

and Oaxaca-Blinder decompositions (Jann, 2008) to examine the difference in mathematics scores and educational attainment between Indigenous and non-Indigenous children. The difference is decomposed to understand what factors drive it. The analysis incorporates QuantCrit principles in three main ways. Namely, by using a multidimensional operationalization of Indigeneity and a binary one, by assessing potential biases in the outcome data, and by reflecting on the choice and categorization of explanatory factors. This helps ensure that this research is mindful of the historical power dynamics that have affected Indigenous populations in Peru.

BACKGROUND
Quantitative Critical Race Theory

QuantCrit is an emerging but fast-growing approach. It takes insights from Critical Race Theory (CRT) to improve the use of statistical data in social science research (Castillo & Gilborn, 2022). CRT has traditionally been associated with qualitative methods. These are amenable to providing rich detail on the experiences of those affected by racism and have therefore been considered most appropriate to challenge deficit portrayals. Quantitative methods on the other hand have been criticized for their abstraction and for traditionally not examining the extent to which they may reproduce power imbalances (Covarrubias & Vélez, 2013). QuantCrit is established in an attempt to break this methodological silo. It takes lessons from CRT and applies them into quantitative enquiry. QuantCrit recognizes the subjectivity underlying statistics (Gillborn et al., 2018). Decisions around what issues should be researched, what questions are asked, how data are analyzed, and which findings are published are all influenced by researchers' belief systems.

CRT is a branch of Critical Theory that focuses on analyzing race inequalities. Critical Theory encourages looking at society through enquiring eyes to uncover and challenge power structures (Stage, 2007). It recognizes that our thinking is mediated by social and historically created power relations through which certain groups experience oppression (e.g., based on class, race, or gender). Therefore, research is influenced by historical, cultural, and social constraints that shape our thinking as researchers. Critical theorists are deeply aware of cultural differences and argue that mainstream research practices tend to reinforce different forms of oppression. They reject the idea of a detached scientist and instead acknowledge that individuals' belief systems will influence their subjectivity and how research is designed. Building on this and focusing on race issues, CRT assumes that racism is a normal and deeply ingrained part of daily life (López et al., 2018). It recognizes that race is not a scientific reality but rather a social construct underlying societal power relations (Gillborn et al., 2018; Ladson-Billings, 2021; Zuberi, 2000). CRT applied in education research has sought to understand and contest how racism structures change and reproduce inequalities within the education sphere over time (Garcia et al., 2018).

QuantCrit takes these notions and establishes five principles to guide quantitative social research. Gillborn and colleagues (Castillo & Gilborn, 2022; Gillborn et al., 2018) define them as follows:

(1) "The centrality of racism": Racism is deeply ingrained in society. QuantCrit commits to disrupt narratives that frame minoritized students as deficient or less able. It recognizes that attempts to measure race only provide approximations that can risk misinterpretations of the social dynamics behind it.
(2) "Numbers are not neutral": The way that data are collected and analyzed tends to reflect the worldview and values of the dominant elites. QuantCrit acknowledges that all data and analysis methods carry biases. It strives to minimize these biases and explicitly discuss them.
(3) "Categories are not natural": Race/ethnicity is a complex and evolving social construct. There is no scientific race distinction between humans. When used as a variable in analyses, the way it is operationalized will shape findings.
(4) "Data cannot speak for itself": Data are open to various interpretations. Analyses are guided by researchers' beliefs about key research problems and theories about the processes they are researching. QuantCrit gives importance to the experiential knowledge and insights coming from the marginalized groups under study to inform the interpretation of results.
(5) "A social justice orientation": Quantitative analyses can be used to critique official analyses and deficit assumptions.

Together these principles highlight the importance of incorporating reflexivity in quantitative research. Given the link between race/ethnicity and historical oppression of minority groups it is important to consider the historical context of the group under study to inform research decisions. Walter and Andersen (2013) problematize the use of statistics to describe lagged levels of educational achievement of Indigenous populations. They note that when little attention is placed on the way that these data are collected and analyzed, research conclusions may mask or exacerbate group differences. This can reinforce deficit narratives about Indigenous groups. However, when criticality and reflexivity are built into the research process, quantitative methods have the potential to enact transformation for greater equity. They urge researchers to invest more efforts in "exploring the interpretative limits of the very categories from which they draw information" (Walter & Andersen, 2013, p. 28). By and large, statistics on Indigenous peoples have produced views and understandings on them that are narrow, drive deficit portrayals but that are widely accepted.

The Peruvian Context and Operationalizing Indigeneity Quantitatively

Historical inequalities affecting Indigenous populations persist across the world. While they make up 5% of the global population, 15% account for the extremely poor (World Bank, 2021). The disparity is steeper in Latin America, where 8% of the region's population is Indigenous, of which 14% live in poverty and 17% in extreme poverty (UNDP, 2020). Inequalities become apparent in education.

Often, Indigenous children attend schools lacking basic materials, are taught by teachers who do not speak their language, and are more likely to attend school hungry and experience racial discrimination (United Nations, 2019). The situation is no different in Peru, which has one of the largest Indigenous populations in Latin America (PAHO WHO, 2023). There, Indigenous children obtain on average lower scores on academic tests than their non-Indigenous peers and tend to achieve lower education levels (Arteaga & Glewwe, 2019; Kirby et al., 2020). These inequalities are rooted in the colonial history of the country (Mahoney, 2003).

The nation-state project brought about by the Spanish colonization in Peru has led to the marginalization of Indigenous populations. Spanish rule between the 16th and 19th centuries sought the subjugation of local cultures to assert its domination. Having a unifying language was considered central for the nation-state project and therefore Spanish was imposed (Freeland, 1996). Speaking Spanish was linked to the elites, ideals of progress and education, while the opposite to speaking an Indigenous language.

While these mechanisms behind building the nation-state led to the loss of Indigenous languages, it did not completely eradicate them (Bellido, 2021). To date, Peru is an ethnically and linguistically diverse country. According to the 2017 national census, six million people self-identified as Indigenous, and four million reported speaking an Indigenous language (Hospina, 2019).[1] However, this colonial history has left deeply ingrained prejudices toward Indigenous populations in Peruvian society. Despite ongoing efforts to tackle educational inequalities affecting Indigenous children in Peru and a growing consciousness that pejorative societal views toward Indigenous populations need to change, discrimination against these groups continues to be salient (Ministerio de Cultura, 2017, 2022). A deficit discourse surrounding indigeneity whereby Indigenous individuals are seen as less able or ignorant is still present (Félix Bautista, 2021; Ledesma Narváez, 2018; Zamora Huamán, 2020; Zavala, 2011). In addition, the historical neglect toward Indigenous groups in the country means that they continue to have poorer access to health and education services than the rest of the population.

These complex historical and social dynamics surrounding Indigeneity in Peru need to be considered when undertaking comparative survey research. The continued stigma attached to being Indigenous means that some individuals avoid speaking their native languages to evade discrimination even if they self-identify as Indigenous (Cánepa, 2008; Figueroa & Barrón, 2005; Paredes, 2007; Zarate, 2011). This results in the loss of Indigenous languages between generations. As such, the question of how to define Indigenous children to study their education outcomes using survey data arises. Opting for a language-based definition can underestimate the proportion of Indigenous individuals. However, this has been the most common approach taken in official government statistics in Peru (Alcázar, 2019; Telles, 2014). Using self-identification information may be preferable, but this information is less commonly available in survey data. A review by Broeks and Sabates (2022) identified great diversity in how Indigeneity is defined in quantitative studies researching the learning outcomes of Indigenous children in Peru. Although diverse approaches were found, the most common approach was to use a binary definition based only on information about the language of the mother. Fewer studies use self-identification information or a combination of language and self-identification to define Indigeneity.

The above shows the inherent complexity in trying to operationalize a complex social construct quantitatively. Indigeneity is multifaceted (Snipp, 2016), and there is no prespecified right or wrong way to operationalize it when undertaking quantitative analyses. Various aspects can constitute an Indigenous identity. The key markers, as synthesized by the United Nations (2004), include historical antecedence, occupation of ancestral land, ethnic identity, cultural distinctiveness (dress, lifestyle, community membership), language, self-identification, and non-dominance in relation to a colonial nation-state. However, the options to incorporate these aspects in quantitative research are limited by the information available in survey data. In line with QuantCrit principles it is therefore paramount that, when making analytic choices to identify Indigenous groups, researchers critically consider the available options and choose an approach that is mindful of the historical power dynamics linked to Indigeneity.

METHODOLOGY

Acknowledging that research is influenced by a researcher's world views, it is important to position myself. I write about Indigenous populations in Peru given my Peruvian roots and interest in promoting equity through education. I am mestiza, a Peruvian-Dutch born in the Andean highlands of Peru, but would be classified as "White, other" in Western contexts. While I acknowledge the place of privilege I write from, growing up in a middle-class family and working in UK academia, I am interested in making a contribution to encourage reflection in educational research.

Data

This study uses data from the Young Lives project. Young Lives is a longitudinal survey that has collected six rounds of data in Ethiopia, India, Peru, and Vietnam to investigate childhood poverty. It follows two cohorts of children in each country. This study uses data from Peru and focuses on the younger cohort (around 2,000 cases). Data from the fourth round collected in 2013 and sixth round collected between 2020 and 2021 are used. Participants were aged 12 and 20, respectively. Round four is chosen since at this time children are at an important point in their educational journey. It marks the end of primary education and the start of secondary schooling. Round six is chosen since it contains the most recent information on educational attainment of participants from the younger cohort. It allows to explore factors explaining Indigenous to non-Indigenous group differences in educational attainment in early adulthood after basic compulsory schooling.

Young Lives is one of the most complete sources of social research data collected in Peru. It contains several indicators on children's characteristics, their families, communities, and school contexts, as well as on their education outcomes

(Young Lives, 2017a). Children were selected for the study using a multistage, cluster-stratified, random sampling approach, with oversampling for poor areas (Young Lives, 2017b). The richest 5% of Peruvian households were excluded.

Handling Missing Data

A common problem in survey research is the lack of complete data across all variables of interest for all participants and participant attrition especially in longitudinal studies (Biering et al., 2015; Brick & Kalton, 1996). In both cases, not only do sample sizes become affected but bias can be introduced when the data loss is greater among one group of participants. It is therefore important to assess the extent of missing data in the dataset used for analyses.

The missing data pattern across the variables of interest for this study was examined. It was identified that more than 10% of cases had some missing information and that the missingness was more pronounced for children in the Indigenous groups. After using Little's (1988) test to gauge whether the data may be missing completely at random it was not possible to conclude this was the case. Therefore, complete case analyses were deemed unsuitable, although this is an approach often taken in past studies. Instead, analyses are run with imputed data using multivariate imputation by chained equations (i.e., predicting the missing value based on other variables in the dataset) (McKnight et al., 2007). Five datasets were imputed and Rubin's Rules (1976) applied to pool parameter estimates and account for within and between variance imputation for the Oaxaca-Blinder decomposition analyses. Doing so seeks to minimize biases that could be introduced from ignoring missing data problems and to safeguard the applicability of research conclusions to Indigenous children.

Empirical Strategy

This paper seeks to contribute to the literature by investigating, through a QuantCrit lens, what factors may be most important to focus policy efforts on to close the educational outcome differences between Indigenous and non-Indigenous children. More specifically, it seeks to answer the following questions:

(1) How much of the mathematics score gap between Indigenous and non-Indigenous children at age 12 is attributable to:
   (a) differences in sample characteristics between groups?
   (b) differences in experience due to being Indigenous?
(2) Which factors account for a larger portion of the score gap?
(3) Do the same factors explain the group difference in educational attainment at age 20?

To investigate the drivers behind the average difference in mathematics scores and educational attainment between Indigenous and non-Indigenous children the technique known as Oaxaca-Blinder decomposition is used (Hlavac, 2014; Jann, 2008). The raw average difference in outcome between the two groups represents the overall disparity between them. In the literature this is referred to as the score

106   MIRIAM BROEKS

gap or difference (here both terms are used interchangeably). The Oaxaca-Blinder technique allows to decompose this difference into two elements with the aim to understand why it exists.

The score difference is broken down into an explained and unexplained portion. The explained portion represents the amount of the gap that is due to average differences in the *composition* of children in the sample, for example, differences between the two groups in the proportion of children who attended pre-primary education or who come from wealthier families. This is explored through question 1a.

The unexplained portion represents the amount of the score gap that is attributable to *differences in the effects* that explanatory variables have on each group. In other words, there may be differences in the returns or gains on mathematics scores that children obtain from having a particular characteristic or being exposed to a particular factor (Heckert, 2010). The role of gender or maternal characteristics could be different for each group. For example, it may be that girls obtain greater improvements in their mathematics score (e.g., 3 points) from having a mother with 5 years of education, than boys (scores improving by 1 point from having a mother with 5 years of education). The reasons why one group may benefit more or less from a particular variable is unknown. It could be due to unobserved factors such as discrimination or variables not included in the model (Słoczyński, 2020). Hence the term unexplained is coined. This is the focus of question 1b.

To implement the Oaxaca-Blinder decomposition, two groups need to be defined. In this study groups are defined according to children's Indigeneity. We start with the mathematics outcome, but the same applies with the educational attainment outcome. For each group of children, there is a measure of their mathematics score (ms) (or educational attainment), as well as information on a number of explanatory variables defined as X. The variables included in the model are described in detail in the next section. The sample mean mathematics scores can be estimated for each group of children separately using the following linear regression formula:

$$\overline{ms_{Gi}} = x'_{Gi}\beta_G + e_{Gi} \tag{1}$$

where G equals "group" with the values of 1 for Indigenous children and 0 for non-Indigenous children; i represents the ith child in the group; x'_{Gi} is a matrix of explanatory variables for a given individual; β_G is the vector of unknown coefficients that includes an intercept as its first value; and e_{Gi} represents the residuals. It is assumed that the residuals satisfy the assumptions of Ordinary Least Squares (OLS) estimation, namely, that in each group the residuals are identically independently distributed and have a normal distribution. Therefore, it is assumed that on average they equate to zero and the e_{Gi} term can be dropped from the equation. The same assumptions apply for the i term. To calculate the mean mathematics score difference between the non-Indigenous and Indigenous groups, the mean mathematics scores for each group are subtracted. This is represented in formula 3. After, some manipulation we arrive at the twofold Oaxaca-Blinder decomposition (formula 4).

$$\text{Average mathematics score gap } = \overline{ms_0} - \overline{ms_1} \tag{2}$$

$$= \overline{x_0'}\,\widehat{\beta_0} - \overline{x_1'}\,\widehat{\beta_1} \tag{3}$$

$$= \underbrace{\left(\overline{x_0'} - \overline{x_1'}\right)\widehat{\beta_0}}_{} + \underbrace{\overline{x_1'}\left(\widehat{\beta_0} - \widehat{\beta_1}\right)}_{} \tag{4}$$

$$= \text{'explained'} + \text{'unexplained'}$$

The sum of the "explained" and "unexplained" portions will always equal to the total gap. As such, it is possible for either the explained or unexplained portion to be greater in value than the total gap, and to be either positive or negative in sign. In this way they counterbalance each other to equal the total score gap when added together. A negative sign on a portion can indicate that when group characteristics or returns are equalized, the gap is not only closed but may mean that the Indigenous group average outcome may be higher than that of the non-Indigenous group. To determine the right interpretation each result needs careful examination by checking sample sizes (x) and beta coefficients (β).

Formula 4 is helpful in interpreting the meaning of the explained and unexplained portions of the Oaxaca-Blinder decomposition. The explained element captures *how the total score gap would change* if the reference group, in this case the non-Indigenous group,[2] would have the same covariate distribution (i.e., the same characteristics on the observed variables) as the Indigenous group. The "explained" term $\left(\overline{x_0'} - \overline{x_1'}\right)\widehat{\beta_0}$ can be re-written as $\overline{x_0'}\widehat{\beta_0} - \overline{x_1'}\widehat{\beta_0}$. As it can be seen, here what is observed for the non-Indigenous group $(\overline{x_0'}\widehat{\beta_0})$ is compared to what would happen if the non-Indigenous group had the sample characteristics of the Indigenous group $(\overline{x_1'}\,\widehat{\beta_0})$.

The unexplained portion, as specified in formula 5, represents a different hypothetical scenario where the sample characteristics of the Indigenous group is assumed for both groups, but the estimated coefficients for each group are maintained. As such, this element of the decomposition captures *how the score gap would change* due to differential returns from variables for the Indigenous group. The unexplained portion of the decomposition can be reformulated from $\overline{x_1'}\left(\widehat{\beta_0} - \widehat{\beta_1}\right)$ to $\overline{x_1'}\widehat{\beta_0} - \overline{x_1'}\widehat{\beta_1}$. Here what is observed for the Indigenous group $(\overline{x_1'}\widehat{\beta_1})$ is compared to what would happen if the Indigenous group had the returns (i.e., beta coefficient) of the non-Indigenous group $(\overline{x_1'}\widehat{\beta_0})$.

When computing the decomposition, the researcher decides which group is the reference. Namely, which group is placed first on the left-hand side of equation 4. There is no right or wrong way to do this, and researchers have the freedom to choose the group according to what is most relevant to their research question. However, it is known that there can be an "index number problem" related to the selection of the reference group (see Jann, 2008, for details). To avoid distorting the calculation of the unexplained portion, and following Jann's (2008) recommendation, a group indicator is included in the pooled model as an additional covariate. In addition, to meaningfully interpret the results, bootstrapped standard errors are reported based on 1,000 bootstrapping replicates. This provides an indication of the reliability of the values estimated for each decomposition element. The *oaxaca* package in R developed by Hlavac (2014) is used for the analyses.

Finally, it is important to interpret the Oaxaca-Blinder decomposition results as an indication of what would happen to the outcome gap if the hypothesized scenarios for each portion apply. The results provide pointers around the variables that can help address the gap. By breaking down the mean difference into two components, the Oaxaca-Blinder decomposition helps researchers and policymakers gain insights into plausible sources of inequality between the groups that affect their outcomes. However, this should not be interpreted as factors that cause the difference. An important limitation of the Oaxaca-Blinder decomposition is that it is not suitable for causal inference (Słoczyński, 2020).

Variables Used

Indigeneity

Considering the previously described complexity surrounding Indigeneity in Peru, a multidimensional variable is defined to operationalize Indigeneity. It combines language and ethnic identification information of the child and their parents. This choice is constrained by the information collected in the Young Lives survey. However, using it seeks to maximize covering as many aspects of Indigenous identity as possible. Therefore, the established categories aim to capture in as much as possible the inherent diversity among children that can be considered Indigenous. Specifically, it distinguishes groups based on having an Indigenous language, ethnicity, and ancestry since children with these characteristics may have different educational experiences.

The variable consists of five mutually exclusive categories as follows:

(1) Indigenous Family: All family members (child, mother, and father) speak an Indigenous language *and* are ethnically Indigenous.
(2) Indigenous Language: Children speak an Indigenous language *but* are ethnically non-Indigenous or have at least one parent who is linguistically or ethnically non-Indigenous.
(3) Indigenous Ethnicity: Children are ethnically Indigenous but do *not* speak an Indigenous language.
(4) Indigenous Ancestry: Children are linguistically and ethnically non-Indigenous but have at least one parent who is linguistically or ethnically Indigenous.
(5) Non-Indigenous: All family members speak a non-Indigenous language *and* are ethnically non-Indigenous.

This categorization takes into consideration the historical processes that have driven racial discrimination in Peru and the loss of Indigenous languages. Furthermore, although the Family and Language groups both include children that speak an Indigenous language these are considered conceptually distinct. The Family group may be the group experiencing the greatest levels of disadvantage or discrimination given the intersectionality between linguistic and

QuantCrit in Comparative Education Research 109

ethnic Indigeneity. Therefore, children in the Family group may have different experiences than the children in the Language or Ethnicity groups. By using this multidimensional Indigeneity definition this research moves away from conceptualizing the Indigenous population in Peru as a homogenous group, and instead acknowledges the diversity inherent in it.

To exemplify how research decisions may influence results, sensitivity analyses are undertaken using a binary Indigeneity definition. As previously noted, past research investigating the learning outcomes of Indigenous children in Peru primarily uses a binary operationalization of Indigeneity based on language information. This approach is often justified by arguing that it allows increasing the sample size of the Indigenous group. This study considers it paramount to consider more than one marker, and therefore when defining the binary variable the same information considered to establish the multidimensional variable is used. However, to replicate past research approaches a binary definition is established such that the sample size of the Indigenous group is maximized. This binary operationalization is labeled the 'Liberal definition' and combines all four Indigenous groups into one. Fig. 1 shows how the two Indigeneity operationalizations compare.

Education Outcomes

Mathematics Score at Age 12
The Young Lives survey includes various learning outcomes. For Round 4, data on three tests are available: a vocabulary, a mathematics, and a reading comprehension test. In line with QuantCrit, the selection of the outcome measure was informed by an assessment of potential biases in the available test data. Fig. 2 shows the distribution of the standardized test scores by Indigeneity. The mean of the non-Indigenous group is set to 0 to facilitate comparing it to the mean of the Indigenous groups in standard deviations. It shows that the difference in means scores is smallest for the mathematics test, around half a standard deviation. The score difference is most pronounced for the vocabulary test. Indigenous children in the Family group score on average more than one standard deviation lower than non-Indigenous children on this test.

Differential Item Functioning (DIF) analyses were undertaken to assess whether questions in these tests were easier or more difficult to answer for one group over another (Martinková et al., 2017). These analyses were carried for the mathematics and vocabulary tests only. These were chosen as these showed the

Multidimensional Definition	Liberal Definition
Indigenous Family	
Indigenous Language	Indigenous Liberal
Indigenous Ethnicity	
Indigenous Ancestry	
Non-Indigenous	Non-Indigenous

Fig. 1. Overview of How the Categories of the Indigeneity Definitions Compare.

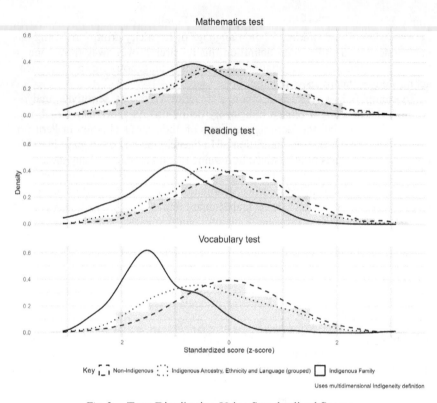

Fig. 2. Tests Distribution Using Standardized Scores.

greatest divergence in group differences. In addition, it was decided to exclude the reading test since its administration relies much more on language proficiency than the mathematics test and on reading skills compared to the vocabulary test. To assess bias, focus was placed on potential cross-cultural biases in the formulation of questions (Hambleton, 2006). These analyses provided evidence suggesting the presence of bias in the vocabulary test. The vocabulary test consists of questions containing four images from which the child needs to select the image that best represents the word the test administrator says. One-third of the questions from the vocabulary test were found to have DIF, meaning that children in the Indigenous groups were more likely to answer them wrong. Upon qualitatively inspecting the content of the questions showing DIF, it was concluded that the likely reason for this was the cultural inapplicability of the images used, and not a lower vocabulary ability of Indigenous children. In the case of the mathematics test none of the questions were flagged as having DIF.

Informed by this analysis, the mathematics test is chosen as the outcome measure. The mathematics test consists of 29 items. These are based on questions from national and international tests that are freely available. The test includes questions from the 2003 Trends in International Mathematics and Science Study for fourth grade. In addition, some questions were developed by the Young Lives team from existing measures that are commonly used to assess Mathematics skills (Cueto & León, 2012). The first 19 items included questions requiring addition, multiplication and division using both whole numbers and fractions. The last 10 items focused on Mathematics problem solving. Children were given 40 minutes to complete the test.

Using the mathematics data over the other available tests helps minimize carrying biases into the Oaxaca-Blinder decomposition analyses that are due to the design of the data collection tools used. Furthermore, this choice differentiates from past studies. After reviewing the literature, it was identified that the vocabulary test is the outcome data most commonly used in studies focusing on Peruvian children's learning outcomes. Research conclusions from such studies should be interpreted considering that the vocabulary test data likely carries bias that disadvantages Indigenous children and which potentially magnifies group differences.

Educational Attainment at Age 20
Additionally, educational attainment at age 20 is used as a secondary outcome measure. Specifically, this indicator captures the number of years of education the child attained at the time of the survey.[3] Higher levels of education have been linked not only to economic benefits such as better employability prospects and the reduction of poverty but also to better health and increased social mobility (World Bank, 2018). While some may argue that this is a more 'objective' measure that is less impacted by data collection biases (e.g., related to the formulation of questions) it is important to recognize some of its limitations.

While many low- and middle-income countries have increased the coverage of schooling, this does not guarantee quality education is provided and that children learn basic skills. International organizations have identified a learning crisis. Research shows that many children in low- and middle- income countries leave schooling without foundational literacy and numeracy skills (Pritchett & Viarengo, 2021). Therefore, comparing attained years of education could be misleading if for some groups of students (e.g., from richer households, non-Indigenous) one year of education provides better skills than for others. The choice of this outcome is limited by the availability of indicators in the Young Lives survey. There is no measure of skills knowledge after completing secondary education. As such, educational attainment measured by years of education is considered the best option for this study while acknowledging its constraints. Therefore, these analyses are exploratory and aim to provide pointers about the factors that may explain educational Indigenous to non-Indigenous differences after completing basic compulsory education, which in Peru includes early childhood, primary, and secondary education.

Explanatory Variables
Education entails complex processes and various factors have been shown to influence learning outcomes. The literature identifies child, family and structural factors. Child and family factors encompass inherent individual characteristics (e.g., sex, age, or health), and aspects that can be considered to be driven by personal choice or effort (e.g., number of members in the household, educational

attainment, wealth). Structural factors are considered external environmental or societal features that influence how a person lives and the opportunities they have (e.g., urban–rural or regional differences).

A QuantCrit conscious approach recognizes that certain factors do not exist independent from racism (Castillo & Gilborn, 2022). Therefore, while socio-economic status and parental education are usually considered family characteristics, it is argued that these do not solely capture individual choice or effort but are limited by societal structures influenced by racial discrimination. Smith (2013) criticizes inequality research that takes a victim-blaming stance, whereby lower educational outcomes or poverty is attributed to the choices of individuals in marginalized Indigenous groups. Instead, Smith notes the importance of focusing on structural factors that limit their opportunities. In the context of Peru, the colonial subjugation of Indigenous groups has forced them into a marginalized position where they lack good access to quality education and face discrimination that hinders their job and earning prospects (Moreno et al., 2004).

Therefore, the common categorization of explanatory variables into child, family, and structural factors is carefully considered. Upon reflection, the categorization is reconceptualized into two groups: *personal attributes* (of the child and family) and *structural and educational opportunity factors*. While this is primarily a conceptual change it allows to interpret results in a racism conscious way. As such, personal attributes are considered the child's sex, age and birth order, the mother's age, and the sex of the household head. Information on language and ethnicity is not included since they are accounted for in the Indigeneity definition.

Eight variables are included as structural and educational opportunity factors. These are the child's health (Height-for-Age z-Score, HAZ), maternal education, household size, wealth index, whether the child attended pre-primary, whether the child is grade-on-age, rural location, and region. Rurality and region[4] are used as proxy measures to capture aspects related to access to services and community-related influences. For the decomposition using the educational attainment outcome, the mathematics score at age 12 is added to the model to investigate whether prior achievement may limit later attainment. The first four variables are traditionally not considered structural or educational opportunity factors. In this study, HAZ is included as a measure of nutrition, but it is considered to not only capture the health of the child (a child characteristic) but also to represent structural inequalities that hinder a child's chances to access food. In the case of maternal education, household size, and wealth index, these are considered structural opportunity factors because for these variables it is not possible to disentangle personal choice or effort from the impact of discrimination that Indigenous populations have historically experienced.

This study does not include information on school factors such as infrastructure or teaching quality. This information was collected through a school survey in the Young Lives project. However, this was done only for a subsample. Hence, rich information on school characteristics is only available for around 600 of the 1,902 children included in this analysis. While not including school factors in the model ignores an important aspect that influences educational outcomes, this is an accepted limitation.

QuantCrit in Comparative Education Research 113

Finally, it was not possible to include information on school type and language of instruction in the model because there was a perfect separation in the sample across these characteristics by Indigeneity group. All Indigenous children attended public schools, while all non-Indigenous children in the sample received instruction in their mother tongue. Hence, while it was of interest to capture aspects around education quality and learning access through these variables, perfect sample separation makes comparing the two groups along these characteristics meaningless.

RESULTS

Descriptive Statistics

Table 1 provides an overview of the outcome differences between groups. The outcome gap is most pronounced when using the multidimensional definition for the Language and Family groups. For these groups the Indigenous to non-Indigenous difference (gap) is more than twice as large the difference between the groups defined using the Liberal definition. It further stands out that for the Ancestry and Ethnicity groups (multidimensional definition) the difference compared to the non-Indigenous group is not statistically significant. These results are consistent for both the mathematics score and educational attainment outcomes. The Oaxaca-Blinder decomposition analyses are only undertaken for groups that have a statistically significant outcome difference. Hence, the difference between the non-Indigenous group and the Ancestry and Ethnicity groups (multidimensional definition) is not examined.

Furthermore, Table AI in the Appendix provides information on the characteristics of children in the sample. In terms of personal attributes, across the groups approximately half are girls and have a similar average age. Only in the Language group are there more girls than boys (53%) and in the Family group children are slightly older. In both the Language and Family groups children tend to be later born compared to children in the other groups. In the Indigenous groups fewer children live in a female-led household (10%–15%) than non-Indigenous children (17%), with the only exception of the Ethnicity group (17%). Children in the Indigenous groups tend to have older mothers than those in the non-Indigenous group.

In terms of structural and educational opportunity factors, Indigenous children live in larger and poorer households and have a worse health status (HAZ) than non-Indigenous children. Further, fewer Indigenous children attended pre-primary, are enrolled in a grade expected for their age, and receive instruction in their mother tongue compared to non-Indigenous children. In terms of location, more Indigenous children live in rural areas and in the mountain region than non-Indigenous children.

Oaxaca-Blinder Decomposition Results

Overall Results
First, the outcome gap is decomposed into the overall explained and unexplained portions. The results for both the mathematics and educational attainment

Table 1. Overview of Between Group Outcome Differences.

Group		Sample Size	Mathematics Score				Educational Attainment			
			Average Score (%)	Gap	SE	*p*-value	Average Years of Education (Years)	Gap	SE	*p*-value
Non-Indigenous		1,131	58.33				12.54			
			Multidimensional definition							
Indigenous	Ancestry	276	57.96	0.67	1.21	0.583	12.18	0.26	0.14	0.074
	Ethnicity	149	55.31	3.17	1.65	0.055	12.51	0.07	0.15	0.618
	Language	122	41.69	16.51	1.66	<0.001	11.58	0.91	0.17	<0.001
	Family	127	42.00	16.26	1.82	<0.001	11.52	0.97	0.18	<0.001
			Liberal definition							
	Liberal	674	51.39	7.05	0.92	<0.001	12.03	0.47	0.09	<0.001

Notes: Gap captures the outcome difference of the Indigenous group compared to the non-Indigenous group. *p*-value calculated using *z*-test to determine if the mean difference between groups is significant. SE: Standard Errors.

outcomes are presented in Table 2. Scores are standardized to z-scores so that both outcomes use the same unit. This facilitates making comparisons between them. For both outcomes nearly all of the gap is attributable to the explained portion. This is consistent across Indigeneity definitions.

In the case of the mathematics score at age 12, between 79% and 118% of the outcome difference is attributable to the explained portion. For the Family and Language groups, the score difference between groups would close by more than half a standard deviation. The improvement is larger for the Indigenous Family group. In the case of the Liberal definition, the score gap would completely close. In fact, all of the differences between groups when using the Liberal definition can be explained by differences in sample composition between the Indigenous and non-Indigenous groups. The fact that the estimate covers more than the total gap suggests that if the non-Indigenous group would have the same sample characteristics as the Indigenous group the gap would change by 0.43 standard deviations. This means that not only would Indigenous children improve their mathematics scores, but the gap would revert. Indigenous children would obtain a slightly higher average score than non-Indigenous children.

The unexplained portions for the mathematics outcome are statistically insignificant. This suggests that the estimate is likely zero. The unexplained portion captures how the gap would change if Indigenous children would obtain the same gains or returns from a factor as the non-Indigenous group. The results suggest that none of the score gap can be attributed to differences in returns, or at least not based on the variables included in the model.

The results of the decomposition using the educational attainment outcome are similar. The only difference is that a slightly larger proportion (between 86% and 94%) of the difference in educational attainment is attributable to the explained portion. In this case too, none of the unexplained estimates are statistically significant indicating that these are likely zero. Hence, none of the outcome differences at age 20 can be confidently attributed to differences in returns between groups.

By Variable Decomposition Results
Breaking down the results at the variable level is helpful to better understand which variables contribute significantly to the explained or unexplained portions. Examining the share of the portion they cover provides a sense of the relative importance of these variables in closing the outcome difference between groups. First, the results for the mathematics score outcome are examined, followed by the results using the educational attainment outcome.

Mathematics Scores at Age 12. Table 3 presents the by-variable decomposition results for the explained portion for the mathematics outcome. It is only the structural and educational opportunity variables that significantly contribute to this portion. None of the personal attribute variables make a statistically significant contribution. From the opportunity variables, mother's years of education are the most important ones. It covers nearly half of the explained gap,

Table 2. Overall Decomposition Results by Outcome (Standardized Scores).

Group	Outcome gap	Explained				Unexplained			
		Estimate	SE	*p*-value	% gap	Estimate	SE	*p*-value	% gap
Mathematics score at age 12									
Indigenous Family	0.87	0.73	0.08	<0.001***	84.3	0.14	0.10	0.181	15.8
Indigenous Language	0.84	0.67	0.08	<0.001***	78.9	0.18	0.10	0.067	20.9
Indigenous Liberal	0.36	0.43	0.04	<0.001***	117.9	−0.06	0.05	0.190	−17.3
Educational attainment at age 20									
Indigenous Family	0.52	0.49	0.09	<0.001***	94.2	0.03	0.12	0.794	5.9
Indigenous Language	0.50	0.46	0.09	<0.001***	92.7	0.04	0.12	0.758	7.2
Indigenous Liberal	0.26	0.23	0.04	<0.001***	86.6	0.03	0.05	0.495	12.7

Significance levels: ***$p < 0.001$, **$p < 0.01$ and *$p < 0.05$.

Notes: Unit of mathematics score and attainment outcomes standardized to *z*-scores. The standardized scores have a mean of 0 and standard deviation of 1. "% gap" captures the proportion of the total outcome gap that is covered by each portion. SE: Standard Errors. Mathematics score is in percentage points out of 100%. Educational attainment in years of education.

Table 3. By Variable Breakdown of Explained Portion (Standardized Mathematics Outcome at Age 12).

Variable	Indigenous Family				Indigenous Language				Indigenous Liberal			
	Estimate	SE	p-value	Share	Estimate	SE	p-value	Share	Estimate	SE	p-value	Share
Personal attributes												
Child is female	0.00	0.00	0.974	-0.0%	0.00	0.00	0.677	0.2%	0.00	0.00	0.756	0.1%
Child age	-0.02	0.01	0.088	-2.2%	-0.01	0.01	0.219	-1.2%	0.00	0.00	0.305	-0.6%
Child birth order	-0.01	0.04	0.828	-1.0%	-0.01	0.03	0.845	-0.8%	0.00	0.01	0.922	-0.3%
Household head is female	0.00	0.00	0.709	-0.2%	0.00	0.00	0.698	-0.3%	0.00	0.00	0.300	-0.5%
Mother's age	0.00	0.01	0.495	-0.6%	-0.01	0.01	0.478	-0.9%	-0.01	0.01	0.088	-2.1%
			Total	*-4.0%*			*Total*	*-3.0%*			*Total*	*-3.4%*
Structural and educational opportunity												
Household size	0.03	0.01	0.049*	3.9%	0.03	0.01	0.037*	4.1%	0.02	0.01	0.011*	3.5%
Wealth Index	0.05	0.05	0.335	6.8%	0.10	0.04	0.021*	14.7%	0.05	0.02	0.011*	12.0%
Mother's years of education	0.34	0.06	<0.001***	47.0%	0.28	0.05	<0.001***	42.0%	0.21	0.03	<0.001***	48.1%
Child HAZ	0.01	0.04	0.809	1.2%	0.01	0.03	0.819	1.1%	0.01	0.02	0.695	1.4%
Child attended pre-primary	0.01	0.01	0.291	1.6%	0.02	0.01	0.247	2.5%	0.01	0.01	0.306	1.5%
Child is grade-on-age	0.22	0.04	<0.001***	30.3%	0.26	0.04	<0.001***	38.4%	0.12	0.02	<0.001***	28.6%
Rural area	0.22	0.05	<0.001***	29.8%	0.13	0.05	0.004**	20.1%	0.08	0.02	<0.001***	18.8%
Mountain region	-0.12	0.04	0.001**	-16.5%	-0.13	0.04	<0.001***	-20.0%	-0.04	0.02	0.021*	-10.5%
			Total	*104.0%*			*Total*	*103.0%*			*Total*	*103.4%*

Significance levels: ***$p < 0.001$, **$p < 0.01$ and *$p < 0.05$.

Notes: Mathematics score unit in standardized to z-scores with a mean of 0 and standard deviation of 1. Estimate refers to the amount of the outcome gap that is covered by variable. The unit of the estimate is in standardized to z-scores with a mean of 0 and standard deviation of 1. Share is the percentage of the explained portion covered by each variable. SE: Standard Errors. Child age is in months, mother's age in years. Child HAZ: Height-for-Age z-Score, in standard deviations from the mean height of children in their age group using a standard sample. Wealth Index includes values from 0 to 1. Household size captures number of members in house. Dummy variables are coded as follows: Child is female, yes = 1; Household head is female, yes = 1; Child attended pre-primary, yes = 1; Child is grade-on-age, yes = 1; Rural area, yes = 1; Mountain region, yes = 1.

118   MIRIAM BROEKS

between 42% and 48% depending on the Indigeneity definition. Being grade-on-age is also an important variable since it covers about a third of the explained gap (28%–38%). This is followed by living in a rural area, living in the mountain region, and wealth index. Some variation in the relative contribution these variables make to the explained portion is observed between Indigeneity groups. This suggests that children in these groups may have different experiences. For example, wealth index is not an important factor to close the explained gap for the Indigenous Family group while it is for the Family and Liberal Indigenous groups. We also see that the contribution of living in the mountain region is negative. This suggests that if there would be more non-Indigenous children living in the mountain region (i.e., the same amount as Indigenous children), the gap would become bigger. This indicates that non-Indigenous children benefit more from living in the mountain region than Indigenous children, but it is unclear why (see Table AII in the Appendix). Finally, household size also yields statistically significant estimates but the share of the gap covered by it is negligible.

Table 4 presents the by-variable results for the unexplained portion. These are reported for reference. However, since the overall decomposition results were unreliably estimated (these were not statistically significant), this indicates that the by-variable results are likely inaccurate. Most estimates are statistically insignificant. In four instances, however, a significant estimate is obtained. Nonetheless, there is great inconsistency across Indigeneity definitions. This alongside the statistically insignificant overall unexplained portion results is taken as an indication that these results are unreliable. This corroborates the finding that the group differences are primarily attributable to differences in sample composition (explained portion) rather than to differences in returns (unexplained portion).

Educational Attainment at Age 20 Table 5 presents the by-variable decomposition results for the explained portion using the educational attainment outcome. We see a similar pattern as with the mathematics outcome in that only the structural and educational opportunity variables make a statistically significant contribution to this portion. However, we see that the relative contribution of wealth index in closing the explained gap is the largest and substantially increases at age 20 compared to at age 12. The relative contribution of mother's years of education reduces in comparison. Wealth index covers half or more of the explained gap (between 48% and 56%). For the Family group the attainment gap would close by one-third (0.28) of a standard deviation of years of education if children in this group would obtain the same benefits from wealth index as non-Indigenous children. Mother's years of education on the other hand cover a smaller share, around a third, of the explained gap (31%–36%). This is smaller than the relative contribution that being grade-on-age and mathematics scores (both at age 12) make to the explained portion. For grade-on-age this ranges between 39% and 46% while mathematics scores at age 12 cover between 31% and 38% of the explained portion. This shows that progress during basic compulsory education can have lasting consequences for later attainment.

Table 4. By Variable Unexplained Portion (Standardized Mathematics Outcome at Age 12).

Variable	Indigenous Family			Indigenous Language			Indigenous Liberal		
	Estimate	SE	p-value	Estimate	SE	p-value	Estimate	SE	p-value
Personal attributes									
Child is female	0.10	0.09	0.267	−0.04	0.09	0.661	−0.01	0.04	0.879
Child age	0.33	3.67	0.929	2.90	3.13	0.355	1.18	1.70	0.487
Child birth order	−0.13	0.24	0.573	−0.18	0.19	0.348	−0.03	0.09	0.705
Household head is female	0.08	0.04	0.075	0.08	0.03	0.014*	0.06	0.02	0.001**
Mother's age	−0.22	0.72	0.762	−0.05	0.64	0.942	−0.40	0.26	0.129
Structural and educational opportunity									
Household size	0.36	0.33	0.270	0.42	0.34	0.219	0.12	0.13	0.351
Wealth Index	1.02	0.31	0.001**	0.01	0.33	0.972	0.00	0.18	0.991
Mother's years of education	−0.04	0.10	0.654	0.04	0.10	0.673	−0.14	0.08	0.103
Child HAZ	0.13	0.17	0.438	0.31	0.19	0.102	0.06	0.06	0.329
Child attended pre-primary	−0.14	0.26	0.595	0.09	0.22	0.687	0.10	0.16	0.502
Child is grade-on-age	0.00	0.13	0.971	0.00	0.11	0.983	0.01	0.10	0.928
Rural area	0.25	0.17	0.130	−0.24	0.15	0.110	−0.05	0.04	0.189
Mountain region	−0.06	0.27	0.827	0.44	0.23	0.053	0.13	0.05	0.005**

Significance levels: ***$p < 0.001$, **$p < 0.01$ and *$p < 0.05$.

Notes: Estimate refers to the amount of the outcome gap that is covered by variable. The unit of the estimate is in percentage points of the mathematics test score. SE: Standard Errors. See notes in Table 3 for details on variables.

Table 5. By Variable Explained Portion (Standardized Educational Attainment Outcome at Age 20).

Variable	Indigenous Family				Indigenous Language				Indigenous Liberal			
	Estimate	SE	*p*-value	Share	Estimate	SE	*p*-value	Share	Estimate	SE	*p*-value	Share
Personal attributes												
Child is female	0.00	0.01	0.976	0.0%	−0.01	0.01	0.236	−2.0%	0.00	0.00	0.651	−0.6%
Child age	0.01	0.01	0.284	2.1%	0.00	0.01	0.683	0.6%	0.00	0.00	0.439	0.7%
Child birth order	0.01	0.03	0.809	1.6%	0.00	0.03	0.888	−1.0%	0.01	0.01	0.636	3.1%
Household head is female	0.00	0.00	0.782	−0.2%	0.00	0.01	0.402	−1.0%	0.00	0.00	0.466	−0.6%
Mother's age	0.00	0.01	0.933	−0.1%	0.00	0.01	0.866	0.3%	0.00	0.00	0.763	−0.6%
			Total	3.4%			*Total*	−3.1%			*Total*	2.0%
Structural and educational opportunity												
Household size	0.02	0.01	0.120	4.6%	0.02	0.01	0.118	4.5%	0.01	0.01	0.129	4.0%
Wealth Index	0.28	0.06	<0.001***	56.4%	0.22	0.05	<0.001***	48.1%	0.11	0.03	<0.001***	50.1%
Mother's years of education	0.15	0.06	0.019*	31.1%	0.16	0.06	0.009**	34.3%	0.08	0.03	0.004**	36.2%
Child HAZ	0.00	0.02	0.936	0.4%	0.00	0.02	0.835	1.0%	0.01	0.02	0.720	2.6%
Child attended pre-primary	0.00	0.01	0.929	−0.3%	0.00	0.02	0.989	−0.1%	0.01	0.01	0.238	4.7%
Child is grade-on-age	0.19	0.04	<0.001***	39.6%	0.20	0.04	<0.001***	43.7%	0.10	0.02	<0.001***	45.8%
Mathematics score age 12	0.18	0.04	<0.001***	35.8%	0.18	0.04	<0.001***	38.4%	0.07	0.01	<0.001***	30.5%
Rural area	−0.14	0.06	0.014*	−29.4%	−0.08	0.05	0.098	−17.9%	−0.04	0.02	0.054	−18.0%
Mountain region	−0.20	0.04	<0.001***	−41.6%	−0.23	0.04	<0.001***	−49.0%	−0.13	0.02	<0.001***	−57.9%
			Total	96.6%			*Total*	103.0%			*Total*	98.0%

Significance levels: ***$p < 0.001$, **$p < 0.01$ and *$p < 0.05$.

Notes: Estimate refers to the amount of the outcome gap that is covered by variable. The unit of the estimate is in standardized z-scores of the years of education attained. Share is the percentage of the unexplained portion covered by each variable. SE: Standard Errors. The model for this decomposition includes the same variables as the decomposition for the mathematics outcome. See notes in Table 3. Hence, the data for the explanatory variables are taken from round 4 (age 12). This allows to gauge the influence of having these characteristics or conditions at an earlier age on educational attainment at age 20.

In terms of the location variables, we see that living in the mountain region continues to make a statistically significant but negative contribution to the explained portion (the score difference would increase). This is particularly notable for the Indigenous Language group for which one-fifth of the explained gap is covered by this variable. Finally, the contribution of living in a rural area is only statistically significant for the Family group and in this instance is negative. This means that if the same number of Indigenous children would live in rural areas as non-Indigenous children (i.e., if there were fewer Indigenous children in rural areas), the score gap would in fact increase. This is because children in the Family group obtain better gains in educational attainment from having lived in a rural area at age 12 than non-Indigenous children (see Table AIII in the Appendix). These results are different to the results obtained for the outcome at age 12. This variable made a positive and statistically significant contribution across all definitions in those analyses.

In terms of the by-variables results for the unexplained portion none of the estimates are statistically significant (Table 6). These estimates could not be reliably estimated. Hence, there is little certainty around these results.

CONCLUSIONS

This paper sought to elucidate how implementing a QuantCrit approach into Comparative Education research can help to tackle Methodological Nationalism. Shahjahan and Kezar (2013) note that Comparative Education researchers should think beyond traditional categorizations of groups as defined by the nation-state. Tackling Methodological Nationalism entails unpacking power relations linked to the nation-state that cause the marginalization of minority groups. This paper provides a practical example of how QuantCrit principles can be implemented in Comparative Education research. Indigenous to non-Indigenous education outcome differences of children in Peru are examined by taking analytic steps that are conscious of the historical oppression that Indigenous populations have experienced. In practice, this translates into using a multidimensional Indigeneity definition, carefully selecting the outcome measures, and reflecting on the categorization of explanatory variables. Furthermore, sensitivity analyses using a binary Indigeneity definition are undertaken to gauge whether the way Indigenous children are identified influences research conclusions.

Following QuantCrit principles, children are categorized using a multidimensional definition. The definition not only considers language but also ethnicity and ancestry as important markers of Indigeneity. As part of the nation-state building project in colonial times Spanish was imposed. This led to the marginalization of Indigenous individuals and the loss of Indigenous languages. In addition, traditionally government statistics in Peru have identified the Indigenous population based only on language. Therefore, using a multidimensional Indigeneity definition takes into account the historical marginalization that Indigenous populations suffered and the fact that speaking an Indigenous language is not the only aspect that constitutes Indigenous identity. Furthermore, the outcome measures

Table 6. By Variable Unexplained Portion (Standardized Educational Attainment Outcome at Age 20).

Variable	Indigenous Family			Indigenous Language			Indigenous Liberal		
	Estimate	SE	p-value	Estimate	SE	**p-value**	Estimate	SE	p-value
Personal attributes									
Child is female	0.15	0.09	0.106	0.00	0.10	0.998	0.02	0.04	0.589
Child age	2.39	3.86	0.539	−5.55	3.88	0.159	−0.24	1.78	0.893
Child birth order	0.13	0.22	0.548	−0.07	0.21	0.746	0.02	0.09	0.791
Household head is female	−0.04	0.04	0.314	0.00	0.04	0.967	0.00	0.02	0.987
Mother's age	0.15	0.09	0.106	0.00	0.10	0.998	−0.12	0.28	0.666
Structural and educational opportunity									
Household size	−0.09	0.30	0.773	−0.29	0.37	0.443	−0.10	0.16	0.527
Wealth Index	0.26	0.30	0.389	0.34	0.35	0.331	0.38	0.21	0.067
Mother's years of education	0.01	0.09	0.937	−0.05	0.13	0.697	0.01	0.09	0.941
Child HAZ	−0.20	0.18	0.268	0.12	0.22	0.585	0.10	0.07	0.173
Child attended pre-primary	−0.24	0.31	0.449	−0.22	0.37	0.547	−0.31	0.26	0.241
Child is grade-on-age	−0.05	0.15	0.760	0.17	0.15	0.273	0.04	0.13	0.784
Mathematics score age 12	0.27	0.24	0.257	0.02	0.26	0.948	0.18	0.18	0.316
Rural area	0.00	0.20	0.984	0.23	0.15	0.146	0.06	0.04	0.176
Mountain region	0.30	0.30	0.313	−0.18	0.48	0.714	0.05	0.06	0.397

Significance levels: ***$p < 0.001$, **$p < 0.01$ and *$p < 0.05$. Notes: Estimate refers to the amount of the outcome gap that is covered by variable. The unit of the estimate is in standardized z-scores of educational attainment years. SE: Standard Errors. See notes in Tables 3 and 5.

were carefully selected to avoid carrying biases from the data collection into analyses. Specifically, the mathematics test was chosen over data from a vocabulary test since the former did not show bias that disadvantaged Indigenous children. Finally, the explanatory variables were grouped into two categories: personal attributes, and structural and educational opportunity factors. This allows to acknowledge that maternal education and a families' wealth index are influenced by societal constraints and racial discrimination. Traditionally, these factors are considered family characteristics influenced by personal choice or effort. By grouping them differently this research moves away from taking a victim-blaming stance when interpreting results.

The Oaxaca-Blinder decomposition showed that differences are attributable primarily to structural and educational opportunity factors. At age 12, all of the outcome difference is covered by the explained portion. This means that the score difference is mainly due to differences in the sample composition between the Indigenous and non-Indigenous groups. Maternal education is the most important factor and covers half of the explained gap. In terms of the unexplained portion, estimates could not be reliably estimated. At age 20, the difference in educational attainment is also largely covered by the explained portion. However, in this case wealth index is the most important factor, covering over half of the explained gap. This suggests that as Indigenous children progress through education, socio-economic disparities become more important than maternal education or other educational opportunity factors. It indicates that wealth is a notable limiting factor to the educational attainment of Indigenous children in post-secondary education.

The analyses also show some variation in the results depending on how Indigenous children are identified. This shows that the way Indigeneity is defined does matter for research conclusions and that there is diversity within the group of children that can be considered Indigenous. More research is needed to understand why wealth index may not be associated with closing the explained mathematics scores gap at age 12 for children who are Indigenous in the Family group, while it is for all other Indigenous groups. It is also of interest to better understand why rurality for the Family group contributes to closing the explained educational attainment gap at age 20, while it does not for all other Indigenous groups. It is worth noting, that using the multidimensional Indigeneity definition alongside the binary liberal definition have allowed to identify the presence of variation in the explained portion results. This level of detail would have been lost if the analyses had followed the traditional nation-state approach of solely using language to determine Indigeneity. This provides a clear example of the new insights that incorporating a QuantCrit perspective in Comparative Education can bring to tackle Methodological Nationalism.

All in all, these findings emphasize the importance of framing the identified education outcome differences as educational *debts* society owes these groups, instead of an educational gap attached to Indigenous children. Efforts should be invested in breaking intergenerational inequalities that affect Indigenous children. Therefore, addressing structural and educational inequalities that affect Indigenous children early on has the potential to improve their long-term educational prospects. Supporting Indigenous children throughout their educational journey, promoting school completion, and providing financial support in post-secondary education have the potential to equalize outcomes.

NOTES

1. While most of the Indigenous population speaks Quechua (83%), other Indigenous languages include Aymara (11%) and native languages from the amazon (6%) (Guerrero et al., 2012; International Work Group on Indigenous Affairs, 2021).

2. This is a practical decision. In this way the score gap will have a positive sign, which makes the interpretation of results simpler. It is in the researcher's discretion which group is set as the reference group.

3. It combines information on the education level participants are enrolled in and the highest level of education achieved for those not pursuing further education at the time of the survey. Being enrolled in a program does not guarantee its completion. Hence, this measure may inflate attainment for those in postsecondary education. This is an acknowledged limitation.

4. Peru has three regions: coast, mountain, and jungle. However, focus is placed on whether children live in the mountain region because of the historical links of Indigenous peoples to this region. This was the cradle of the Inca empire and where the Indigenous population was concentrated. It could be expected that Indigenous communities have a better support network there which may positively impact educational outcomes. However, Peru's wealthiest region is the coast where the capital is located.

REFERENCES

Alcázar, L. (2019). *Brechas que perduran: Una radiografía de la exclusión social en Perú* | GRADE. BID. http://www.grade.org.pe/publicaciones/brechas-que-perduran-una-radiografia-de-la-exclusion-social-en-peru/

Arteaga, I., & Glewwe, P. (2019). Do community factors matter? An analysis of the achievement gap between indigenous and non-indigenous children in Peru. *International Journal of Educational Development, 65*, 80–91. https://doi.org/10.1016/j.ijedudev.2017.08.003

Bellido, G. (2021). *Race and indigenous language rights in Peru.* https://othersociologist.com/2021/09/20/race-and-indigenous-language-rights-in-peru/

Biering, K., Hjollund, N. H., & Frydenberg, M. (2015). Using multiple imputation to deal with missing data and attrition in longitudinal studies with repeated measures of patient-reported outcomes. *Clinical Epidemiology, 7*, 91–106. https://doi.org/10.2147/CLEP.S72247

Brick, J., & Kalton, G. (1996). Handling missing data in survey research. *Statistical Methods in Medical Research, 5*(3), 215–238. https://doi.org/10.1177/096228029600500302

Broeks, M., & Sabates Aysa, R. (2022). Influential choices: Deconstructing operationalisations of Indigeneity in survey-based education research using an example from Peru. *International Journal of Critical Indigenous Studies, 15*(1), 1–21.

Cánepa, G. (2008). *The fluidity of ethnic identities in Peru.* Working paper No. 46, 50. Centre for Research on Inequality, Human Security and Ethnicity, CRISE.

Castillo, W., & Gilborn, D. (2022). *How to "QuantCrit:" Practices and questions for education data researchers and users.* https://doi.org/10.26300/V5KH-DD65

Covarrubias, A., & Vélez, V. (2013). Critical race quantitative intersectionality: An anti-racist research paradigm that refuses to "let the numbers speak for themselves". In M. Lynn & A. D. Dixson (Eds.), *Handbook of critical race theory in education* (pp. 290–306). Routledge.

Cueto, S., & León, J. (2012). *Psychometric characteristics of cognitive development and achievement instruments in round 3 of young lives.* https://www.younglives.org.uk/content/psychometric-characteristics-cognitive-development-and-achievement-instruments-round-3-young

Félix Bautista, G. X. (2021). *Análisis del Discurso Periodístico sobre la discriminación de pueblos originarios de la Amazonía Peruana, En los diarios online: La República, El Comercio, RPP y Ojo*. http://repositorio.bausate.edu.pe/handle/bausate/213

Figueroa, A., & Barrón, M. (2005). *Inequality, ethnicity and social disorder in Peru*. Working paper no. 77. Department for International Development.

Freeland, J. (1996). The global, the national and the local: Forces in the development of education for indigenous peoples -- The case of Peru. *Compare: A Journal of Comparative and International Education*, 26(2), 167–195. https://doi.org/10.1080/0305792960260204

Garcia, N. M., López, N., & Vélez, V. N. (2018). QuantCrit: Rectifying quantitative methods through critical race theory. *Race Ethnicity and Education*, 21(2), 149–157.

Gillborn, D., Warmington, P., & Demack, S. (2018). QuantCrit: Education, policy, 'Big Data' and principles for a critical race theory of statistics. *Race Ethnicity and Education*, 21(2), 158–179. https://doi.org/10.1080/13613324.2017.1377417

Guerrero, G., Leon, J., Rosales, E., Zapata, M., Freire, S., Saldarriaga, V., & Cueto, S. (2012). *Young Lives school survey in Peru: Design and initial findings*. Young Lives.

Hambleton, R. K. (2006). Good practices for identifying differential item functioning. *Medical Care*, 44(11), S182. https://doi.org/10.1097/01.mlr.0000245443.86671.c4

Heckert, J. M. (2010). *Ethnic group disparities in academic achievement across four low-income countries*. https://etda.libraries.psu.edu/catalog/10743

Hlavac, M. (2014). *Oaxaca: Blinder-Oaxaca decomposition in R*. Available at SSRN 2528391.

Hospina, A. (2019, August 9). *Los Pueblos Indígenas en el Perú | El PNUD en Perú*. UNDP. https://www.pe.undp.org/content/peru/es/home/presscenter/articles/2019/los-pueblos-indigenas-en-el-peru.html

International Work Group on Indigenous Affairs. (2021, March 18). El Mundo Indígena 2021: Perú. *IWGIA – International Work Group for Indigenous Affairs*. https://www.iwgia.org/es/peru/4159-mi-2021-peru.html

Jann, B. (2008). The Blinder–Oaxaca decomposition for linear regression models. *The Stata Journal*, 8(4), 453–479.

Kirby, E., Tolstikov-Mast, Y., & Walker, J. L. (2020). Retention challenges for indigenous Peruvian college students on Beca 18 scholarship and strategies to improve their experiences and academic success. *Diaspora, Indigenous, and Minority Education*, 14(3), 162–176. https://doi.org/10.1080/15595692.2020.1740980

Ladson-Billings, G. (2021). Critical race theory—What it is not! In M. Lynn & A. D. Dixson (Eds.), *Handbook of critical race theory in education* (pp. 32–43). Routledge.

Ledesma Narváez, M. (Ed.). (2018). *Justicia e interculturalidad: Análisis y pensamiento plural en América y Europa*. Centro de Estudios Constitucionales.

Little, R. J. A. (1988). A test of missing completely at random for multivariate data with missing values. *Journal of the American Statistical Association*, 83(404), 1198–1202. https://doi.org/10.1080/01621459.1988.10478722

López, N., Erwin, C., Binder, M., & Chavez, M. J. (2018). Making the invisible visible: Advancing quantitative methods in higher education using critical race theory and intersectionality. *Race Ethnicity and Education*, 21(2), 180–207.

Mahoney, J. (2003). Long-run development and the legacy of colonialism in Spanish America. *American Journal of Sociology*, 109(1), 50–106. https://doi.org/10.1086/378454

Martinková, P., Drabinová, A., Liaw, Y.-L., Sanders, E. A., McFarland, J. L., & Price, R. M. (2017). Checking equity: Why differential item functioning analysis should be a routine part of developing conceptual assessments. *CBE Life Sciences Education*, 16(2), rm2. https://doi.org/10.1187/cbe.16-10-0307

McKnight, P. E., McKnight, K. M., Sidani, S., & Figueredo, A. J. (2007). *Missing data: A gentle introduction*. Guilford Publications. http://ebookcentral.proquest.com/lib/cam/detail.action?docID=362568

Ministerio de Cultura. (2017). *"Alerta Contra el Racismo" se renueva*. https://www.gob.pe/institucion/cultura/noticias/5109-alerta-contra-el-racismo-se-renueva

Ministerio de Cultura. (2022). *Intervención nacional contra el racismo: Alerta contra el racismo*. https://alertacontraelracismo.pe/intervencion-nacional-contra-el-racismo

Moreno, M., Nopo, H., Saavedra, J., & Torero, M. (2004). *Gender and racial discrimination in hiring: A pseudo audit study for three selected occupations in metropolitan Lima* (SSRN Scholarly Paper ID 491623). Social Science Research Network. https://papers.ssrn.com/abstract=491623

PAHO WHO. (2023). *The sociodemographic situation of indigenous peoples in Latin America and the Caribbean. Analysis in the context of aging and COVID-19*. Pan American Health Organization. https://doi.org/10.37774/9789275126479

Paredes, M. (2007). Fluid identities: Exploring ethnicity in Peru. *Centre for Research on Inequality, Human Security and Ethnicity, 40*, 1–35.

Pritchett, L., & Viarengo, M. (2021). *Learning outcomes in developing countries: Four hard lessons from PISA-D*. RISE Working Paper Series. 21/069. https://doi.org/10.35489/BSG-RISE-WP_2021/069

Rubin, D. B. (1976). Inference and missing data. *Biometrika, 63*(3), 581–592. https://doi.org/10.2307/2335739

Shahjahan, R. A., & Kezar, A. J. (2013). Beyond the "national container": Addressing methodological nationalism in higher education research. *Educational Researcher, 42*(1), 20–29. https://doi.org/10.3102/0013189X12463050

Słoczyński, T. (2020). Average gaps and Oaxaca–Blinder decompositions: A cautionary tale about regression estimates of racial differences in labor market outcomes. *ILR Review, 73*(3), 705–729.

Smith, L. T. (2013). The future is now. In *Inequality: A New Zealand crisis* (pp. 228–235). Bridget Williams Books Wellington.

Smith, L. T. (2021). *Decolonizing methodologies: Research and indigenous peoples/Linda Tuhiwai Smith* (3rd ed.). Zed Books.

Snipp, M. (2016). What does data sovereignty imply: What does it look like? In T. Kukutai & J. Taylor (Eds.), *Indigenous data sovereignty toward an agenda* (pp. 39–56). ANU Press. https://library.oapen.org/bitstream/handle/20.500.12657/31875/624262.pdf?seq#page=63

Stage, F. K. (2007). Answering critical questions using quantitative data. *New Directions for Institutional Research, 2007*(133), 5–16. https://doi.org/10.1002/ir.200

Telles, E. (2014). *Pigmentocracies: Ethnicity, race, and color in Latin America*. UNC Press Books.

UNDP. (2020, May 4). *The situation of Latin America's indigenous population and the impact of COVID-19*. UNDP. https://www.latinamerica.undp.org/content/rblac/en/home/blog/2020/impacto-y-situacion-de-la-poblacion-indigena-latinoamericana-ant.html

United Nations. (2004). *Martínez Cobo study* | United Nations for Indigenous Peoples. https://www.un.org/development/desa/indigenouspeoples/publications/2014/09/martinez-cobo-study/

United Nations. (2019). *Education* | United Nations for Indigenous Peoples. https://www.un.org/development/desa/indigenouspeoples/mandated-areas1/education.html

Walter, M., & Andersen, C. (2013). *Indigenous statistics: A quantitative research methodology/Maggie Walter and Chris Andersen*. Left Coast Press.

World Bank. (2018). *World development report 2018: Learning to realize education's promise*. The World Bank.

World Bank. (2021). *Indigenous peoples* [Text/HTML]. World Bank. https://www.worldbank.org/en/topic/indigenouspeoples

Young Lives. (2017). *A guide to Young Lives research*. https://www.younglives.org.uk/sites/www.younglives.org.uk/files/GuidetoYLResearch_0.pdf

Young Lives. (2017a). *A guide to Young Lives research*. Young Lives.

Young Lives. (2017b). *Young Lives survey design and sampling (Round 5): United Andhra Pradesh*. Young Lives.

Zamora Huamán, M. A. (2020). Breve evolución histórica de la discriminación lingüística en el Perú. *Lengua y Sociedad, 19*(1), Article 1.

Zarate, A. (2011). Las representaciones sobre los indígenas en los libros de texto de Ciencias Sociales en el Perú. *Discurso & Sociedad, 5*(2), 333–375.

Zavala, V. (2011). Racialization of the bilingual student in higher education: A case from the Peruvian Andes. *Linguistics and Education, 22*(4), 393–405. https://doi.org/10.1016/j.linged.2011.08.004

Zuberi, T. (2000). Deracializing social statistics: Problems in the quantification of race. *The ANNALS of the American Academy of Political and Social Science, 568*(1), 172–185. https://doi.org/10.1177/000271620056800113

APPENDIX

Table A1. Descriptive Statistics.

Variable	Statistic	Overall Sample	Non-Indigenous	Indigenous Ancestry	Indigenous Ethnicity	Indigenous Language	Indigenous Family	Indigenous Liberal	Missing Indigeneity Information
Child is female	Count	1,902	1,131	276	149	122	127	674	97
	Mean	0.50	0.49	0.49	0.49	0.53	0.49	0.50	0.57
	SD	0.50	0.50	0.50	0.50	0.50	0.50	0.50	0.50
	Missing	0	0	0	0	0	0	0	0
Age round 4 (months)	Count	1,879	1,121	273	146	120	124	663	95
	Mean	143.01	142.89	142.53	142.97	143.74	144.04	143.13	143.6
	SD	3.74	3.71	3.63	3.79	3.79	3.83	3.77	3.86
	Missing	23	10	3	3	2	3	11	2
Birth order	Count	1,902	1,131	276	149	122	127	674	97
	Mean	2.59	2.27	2.84	2.74	3.66	3.92	3.17	2.27
	SD	1.94	1.63	2.03	2.02	2.49	2.62	2.28	1.80
	Missing	0	0	0	0	0	0	0	0
Head of household is female	Count	1,893	1,127	274	148	121	127	670	96
	Mean	0.17	0.17	0.15	0.17	0.10	0.11	0.14	0.39
	SD	0.38	0.38	0.36	0.38	0.30	0.31	0.35	0.49
	Missing	9	4	2	1	1	0	4	1
Mother's age (years)	Count	1,893	1,127	274	148	121	127	670	96
	Mean	38.36	37.87	39.04	38.83	39.56	38.97	39.07	38.99
	SD	7.72	7.34	7.28	8.28	8.03	7.89	7.75	10.83
	Missing	9	4	2	1	1	0	4	1
Household size	Count	1,893	1,127	274	148	121	127	670	96
	Mean	5.23	5.06	5.23	5.27	5.96	6.08	5.53	5.05
	SD	1.81	1.76	1.69	1.84	1.85	1.78	1.81	2.15
	Missing	9	4	2	1	1	0	4	1

(*Continued*)

Table AI. *(Continued)*

Variable	Statistic	Overall Sample	Non-Indigenous	Indigenous Ancestry	Indigenous Ethnicity	Indigenous Language	Indigenous Family	Indigenous Liberal	Missing Indigeneity Information
Wealth Index	Count	1,893	1,127	274	148	121	127	670	96
	Mean	0.59	0.65	0.60	0.53	0.43	0.38	0.51	0.50
	SD	0.19	0.17	0.19	0.20	0.14	0.13	0.19	0.20
	Missing	9	4	2	1	1	0	4	1
Mother education	Count	1,893	1,127	274	148	121	127	670	96
(years)	Mean	7.26	8.79	7.05	6.11	2.35	1.84	5.01	5.00
	SD	4.39	3.76	4.24	4.15	2.56	2.29	4.30	4.17
	Missing	9	4	2	1	1	0	4	1
Child HAZ	Count	1,879	1,121	273	146	120	124	663	95
	Mean	−1.00	−0.73	−1.11	−1.18	−1.8	−1.95	−1.41	−1.36
	SD	2.36	2.89	1.16	0.96	0.81	1.09	1.10	1.11
	Missing	23	10	3	3	2	3	11	2
Child attended	Count	1,895	1,129	274	149	122	127	672	94
pre-primary	Mean	0.92	0.96	0.91	0.89	0.82	0.87	0.88	0.84
	SD	0.27	0.21	0.29	0.32	0.39	0.33	0.32	0.37
	Missing	7	2	2	0	0	0	2	3
Child is grade-on-age	Count	1,902	1,131	276	149	122	127	674	97
	Mean	0.80	0.87	0.82	0.77	0.55	0.58	0.72	0.66
	SD	0.40	0.34	0.38	0.42	0.50	0.50	0.45	0.48
	Missing	0	0	0	0	0	0	0	0
Language of instruction	Count	1,835	1,112	266	144	121	120	651	72
is in mother tongue	Mean	0.86	1.00	0.95	0.90	0.19	0.11	0.64	0.71
	SD	0.35	0.07	0.22	0.31	0.39	0.31	0.48	0.46
	Missing	67	19	10	5	1	7	23	25
Child lives in rural area	Count	1,902	1,131	276	149	122	127	674	97
	Mean	0.27	0.14	0.21	0.41	0.73	0.80	0.46	0.39
	SD	0.44	0.35	0.41	0.49	0.45	0.40	0.50	0.49
	Missing	0	0	0	0	0	0	0	0

Child lives in mountain region	Count	1,902	1,131	276	149	122	127	674	97
	Mean	0.44	0.26	0.50	0.74	0.93	0.91	0.71	0.58
	SD	0.50	0.44	0.50	0.44	0.25	0.29	0.46	0.50
	Missing	0	0	0	0	0	0	0	0
Mathematics score	Count	1,871	1,120	267	147	121	123	658	93
	Mean	55.62	58.33	57.96	55.31	41.69	42	51.39	52.91
	SD	18.95	17.52	18.78	19.56	18.32	19.65	20.39	19.24
	Missing	31	11	9	2	1	4	16	4
Educational attainment in round 6 (years)	Count	1,711	1,018	249	141	110	107	607	86
	Mean	12.32	12.54	12.18	12.51	11.58	11.52	12.03	11.70
	SD	1.82	1.71	2.07	1.52	1.81	1.75	1.89	2.10
	Missing	191	113	27	8	12	20	67	11
Age in round 6 (years)	Count	1,712	1,018	250	141	110	107	608	86
	Mean	19.51	19.56	19.44	19.46	19.4	19.48	19.44	19.51
	SD	0.54	0.52	0.53	0.55	0.62	0.56	0.56	0.53
	Missing	190	113	26	8	12	20	66	11

Notes: SD: Standard Deviation. Child HAZ: Height-for-Age *z*-Score, in standard deviations from the mean height of children in their age group using a standard sample. Wealth Index includes values from 0 to 1. Household size captures number of members in house. Dummy variables are coded as follows: Child is female, yes = 1; Household head is female, yes = 1; Child attended pre-primary, yes = 1; Child is grade-on-age, yes = 1; LoI (Language of Instruction) is in mother tongue, yes = 1; Rural area, yes = 1; Mountain region, yes = 1.

Table AII. Linear Regression Output (Standardized Mathematics Score Outcome at Age 12).

Variable	Non-indigenous			Indigenous								
				Family			Language			Liberal		
	Estimate	SE	p-value	Estimate	SE	p-value	Estimate	SE	p-value	Estimate	SE	p-value
Child is female	−0.04	0.05	0.451	−0.23	0.17	0.169	0.04	0.15	0.811	−0.02	0.06	0.712
Child age	0.01	0.01	0.033*	0.01	0.02	0.619	−0.01	0.02	0.769	0.01	0.01	0.505
Child birth order	−0.01	0.02	0.754	0.03	0.05	0.526	0.05	0.04	0.236	0.01	0.02	0.743
Household head is female	0.02	0.07	0.758	−0.53	0.27	0.048*	−0.63	0.25	0.012*	−0.33	0.09	<0.001***
Mother's age	0.00	0.00	0.435	0.01	0.02	0.586	0.00	0.01	0.728	0.01	0.00	0.006**
Household size	−0.03	0.01	0.085	−0.09	0.05	0.092	−0.10	0.05	0.039*	−0.05	0.02	0.013**
Wealth Index	0.39	0.19	0.039*	−2.14	0.74	0.004**	0.34	0.69	0.625	0.40	0.24	0.092
Mother's years of education	0.05	0.01	<0.001***	0.05	0.04	0.216	0.03	0.04	0.392	0.06	0.01	<0.001***
Child HAZ	0.00	0.01	0.649	0.07	0.09	0.390	0.18	0.10	0.064	0.05	0.04	0.187
Child attended pre-primary	0.16	0.12	0.207	0.32	0.26	0.228	0.05	0.20	0.798	0.04	0.11	0.694
Child is grade-on-age	0.78	0.08	<0.001***	0.78	0.19	<0.001***	0.76	0.16	<0.001***	0.76	0.08	<0.001***
Rural area	−0.28	0.08	0.001**	−0.63	0.23	0.007**	0.09	0.21	0.647	−0.15	0.09	0.093
Mountain region	0.21	0.06	<0.001***	0.26	0.30	0.391	−0.28	0.31	0.375	−0.05	0.07	0.506

Significance levels: ***$p < 0.001$, **$p < 0.01$ and *$p < 0.05$.

Notes: Average adjusted R-squared: Non-Indigenous group: 0.242. Indigenous groups Family: 0.211; Language: 0.251; Liberal: 0.371. SE: Standard Errors. Child age is in months, mother's age in years. Child HAZ: Height-for-Age z-Score, in standard deviations from the mean height of children in their age group using a standard sample. Wealth Index includes values from 0 to 1. Household size captures number of members in house. Dummy variables are coded as follows: Child is female, yes = 1; Household head is female, yes = 1; Child attended pre-primary, yes = 1; Child is grade-on-age, yes = 1; Rural area, yes = 1; Mountain region, yes = 1.

Table AIII. Linear Regression Output (Standardized Educational Attainment Outcome at Age 20).

Variable	Non-indigenous			Indigenous								
				Family			Language			Liberal		
	Estimate	SE	p-value	Estimate	SE	p-value	Estimate	SE	p-value	Estimate	SE	p-value
Child is female	0.14	0.05	0.007**	−0.16	0.17	0.349	0.14	0.17	0.410	0.10	0.07	0.148
Child age	−0.01	0.01	0.264	−0.02	0.02	0.323	0.03	0.03	0.248	−0.01	0.01	0.480
Child birth order	0.00	0.02	0.910	−0.04	0.05	0.475	0.02	0.06	0.738	−0.01	0.02	0.598
Household head is female	−0.07	0.07	0.360	0.25	0.32	0.443	−0.08	0.31	0.798	−0.07	0.10	0.489
Mother's age	0.00	0.00	0.937	0.01	0.02	0.517	0.00	0.02	0.885	0.00	0.01	0.609
Household size	−0.03	0.02	0.073	−0.01	0.05	0.803	0.02	0.06	0.723	−0.01	0.02	0.682
Wealth Index	1.07	0.21	<0.001***	0.41	0.75	0.584	0.30	0.73	0.679	0.40	0.27	0.143
Mother's years of education	0.02	0.01	0.028	0.01	0.04	0.740	0.03	0.04	0.451	0.02	0.01	0.092
Child HAZ	0.00	0.01	0.651	−0.10	0.10	0.313	0.07	0.12	0.545	0.08	0.04	0.033*
Child attended pre-primary	−0.06	0.19	0.750	0.21	0.29	0.471	0.20	0.30	0.519	0.28	0.14	0.065
Child is grade-on-age	0.68	0.09	<0.001***	0.76	0.19	<0.001***	0.40	0.20	0.051	0.63	0.09	<0.001***
Mathematics score age 12	0.01	0.00	<0.001***	0.01	0.00	0.285	0.01	0.01	0.046*	0.01	0.00	0.001**
Rural area	0.20	0.09	0.020*	0.22	0.24	0.374	−0.16	0.26	0.539	0.03	0.10	0.791
Mountain region	0.33	0.06	<0.001***	−0.01	0.28	0.959	0.52	0.36	0.142	0.24	0.08	0.003**

Significance levels: ***$p < 0.001$, **$p < 0.01$ and *$p < 0.05$.

Notes: Average adjusted R-squared: Non-Indigenous group: 0.272. Indigenous groups Family: 0.164; Language: 0.158; Liberal: 0.272. Child age is in months, mother's age in years. Child HAZ: Height-for-Age z-Score, in standard deviations from the mean height of children in their age group using a standard sample. Wealth Index includes values from 0 to 1. Household size captures number of members in house. Dummy variables are coded as follows: Child is female, yes = 1; Household head is female, yes = 1; Child attended pre-primary, yes = 1; Child is grade-on-age, yes = 1; Rural area, yes = 1; Mountain region, yes = 1.

PART 3

RESEARCH-TO-PRACTICE

INTO THE VOID: TEACHERS' EXPERIENCES WITH STUDENT WELL-BEING, PROGRAM (IN)CONSISTENCY, AND COMMUNICATION AT INTERNATIONAL SCHOOLS

Rebecca Stroud[a] and Shamiga Arumuhathas[b]

[a]Queen's University, Canada
[b]Western University of Ontario (UWO), Canada

ABSTRACT

The international education sector has seen significant growth, offering K-12 schooling options beyond national borders. However, this expansion presents equity challenges, with limited data available to assess their extent. International schools, predominantly English-medium K-12 institutions following externally set curricula, play a central role in this landscape. Our study examines unintended consequences of policy and practice within international schools, particularly regarding student well-being. Despite efforts to promote global citizenship by transnational organizational actors, oversight and gaps in inclusion can create adverse conditions for vulnerable students, identified by their mental or emotional fragility or concerns of neglect or abuse. As an acculturation study, participants were delimited to expatriate teachers counselors, and school leaders in international schools, who are known as sojourners, and who encounter diverse policies and pedagogies, forming a complex "policyscape" environment. While this offers opportunities for innovation, it also poses challenges, especially in supporting students' cultural and mental

---

Annual Review of Comparative and International Education 2023
International Perspectives on Education and Society, Volume 48, 135–155
Copyright © 2025 by Emerald Publishing Limited
All rights of reproduction in any form reserved
ISSN: 1479-3679/doi:10.1108/S1479-367920240000048008

health needs. This study identifies four policyscape manifestations including challenges in supporting students with mental health issues and special needs. Teachers faced greater stress and limited agency compared to school leaders, who benefited from structural support and resources. Policyscape implications on student well-being underscore the urgency of addressing these challenges in line with global education goals for inclusivity and quality education for all.

Keywords: International schools; policyscapes; acculturation; well-being; student mental health; student advocacy; program (in)consistencies; inclusive education; global citizenship education; international teachers

INTRODUCTION

The internationalization of K-12 education as a phenomenon continues to grow (Ingersoll et al., 2018; ISC Research, n.d.-b). Amid this growth, the world needs more teachers (UNESCO, 2016). With widespread variance in economies from country to country, and with different school structures (e.g., publicly funded; privately run), some regions can offer incentives to attract teachers; however, this may result in growing equity gaps in education requiring consideration. Of the United Nations' (UN) 17 Sustainable Development Goals (SDGs), two pertain directly to education. The UN's SGD 4 aims for quality education for all by 2030 and our analysis of a study of a sample of 17 educators at 11 private international schools (including both for- and non-profit models) in Southeast and East Asia is presented in this paper. Parts of this paper have been previously published (see Stroud Stasel, 2021; Stroud, 2024), and a cursory analysis of early data was addressed in Stroud Stasel (2022a). International schools are a diverse group of organizations with varying definitions. We define an international school as a K-12 school where English is the predominant language (50% or more) in a country where it is not the primary language. It is worth noting that countries that have increased the usage of English following colonialism are not classified as having English as their primary language. International schools generally serve more privileged populations, and their ability to recruit educators internationally means that equity issues must be addressed in the pursuit of SDG 4.

Many international schools' websites promote a pedagogy of inclusion and global citizenship, often monikered *international mindedness*. These schools are entrusted to educate 7.3 million students (ISC Research, n.d.-a). The growing transnational mobility necessitates a deeper examination of sojourner acculturation processes. For a definition of "sojourner" and other terms, see the Appendix. Despite the extensive literature on acculturation, few studies have specifically explored the experiences of teachers in this context. Our paper draws from a qualitative study involving 17 sojourning educators, including teachers, school counselors, and leaders, conducted over 18 months in five regions of Southeast and East Asia. The study aimed to elucidate the acculturation dynamics, including triggers for acculturative stress and adaptive strategies employed by educators to flourish in their overseas roles.

Acculturation refers to the process of social integration experienced by new-comers to a place to better understand their identity, origin, and how they can live authentically in the host country. It involves the process of adopting new com-munication methods (Pearce, 2015). Processes differ depending on whether one is a long-term immigrant or a temporary sojourner who eventually returns home, which could require re-acculturation (Safdar & Berno, 2016). Acculturation affects both individuals and host cultures in a bi-directional manner (Berry, 2006a). Understanding policy impacts from transnational perspectives is crucial in a professional setting, especially when it comes to navigating complex policy landscapes that could lead to either innovative approaches or cultural clashes in international schools with diverse student backgrounds (Berry, 2006b). The complexity of this situation is embodied in the metaphor of "policyscape," which considers policy accompanied by cultural nuances.

Contextualizing International School as Policyscape

In this paper, we conceptualize the international school as a policyscape where policies and practices are influenced by various actors, leading to unpredictable outcomes. Policyscape manifestations include positive and negative effects, such as the development of cultural competencies and unexpected legal issues resulting in teacher dismissal and program disruption.

We aim to critically confront certain cultural challenges that are to be expected in the policyscaped world of international schools, which are transnational spaces, amid the looming SDG targets and the ensuing challenges of how to operationalize responses in service of SDG 4. According to Hák et al. (2016, p. 565), "in practice users cannot often be sure how adequately the indicators measure the monitored phenomena" and argued that decision-makers, including policymakers, lack needed specificity upon which to act. We focus on defining, responding to, and integrating acceptable measures into policy and practice to address the needs of students who have disclosed self-harm or harm to others and to advocate for those who may be experiencing neglect or abuse.

The Broader Study and Subset

The term "midnight run" refers to educators abruptly breaking their contracts and leaving the host country. Studies suggest a significant percentage of expatri-ates terminate their contracts prematurely, highlighting the complexities of inter-national employment (von Kirchenheim & Richardson, 2005). We posited that *midnight runs* are linked with policyscape and acculturation difficulties, and that successful acculturation optimizes teachers' thriving, self-efficacy, and ultimately retention. For these reasons, research on the acculturation of sojourning educa-tors makes a valuable contribution to acculturation research.

Teaching overseas is believed to enhance educators' cultural competencies (Savva, 2013), although studies have yielded varied and nuanced findings. This underscores the importance of investigating the acculturation experiences of sojourning edu-cators, as acculturation intersects with well-being and identity formation (Berry & Hou, 2016). Despite extensive research on acculturation, studies focusing on sojourning educators have been limited. Yet, educators at international schools play a crucial role in the acculturation process of students from diverse backgrounds, the former assuming significant responsibilities akin to *in loco parentis*.

This study unpacked and examined the impact of policy on participants' experiences, revealing four manifestations. One was positive, reflecting enhanced cultural competency through interactions with diverse individuals. The other three manifestations were concerning, and they included: (1) how to support students with known or probable special education needs, (2) how to support students with mental health issues, and (3) how to advocate for student safety in cases of possible neglect or abuse. We analyze a subset of findings related to policyscape manifestations, particularly concerning the support of students with mental health issues and effective advocacy for child protection in transnational organizations.

REVIEW OF THE LITERATURE

We offer an overview of international schools, focusing on their underlying values and principles. Subsequently, we delve into the concept of policyscape, examining its relevance within the unique context of international school environments. We explore how policyscape manifests in schools, emphasizing its leadership implications. We contend to understand the manifestations of policyscape in schools as phenomena to comprehend the leadership implications of these manifestations. In turn, leadership is seen as a process rather than a position or a policy actor, although the nature of this process and the level of the agency involved may vary depending on the individual's role within the school (e.g., teacher, school counselor, or school principal).

International Schools

The growth of K-12 international schools, of students attending international schools, and of staff at international schools have each increased between 50% and 60% in the past 10 years (ISC Research, n.d.-b). This growth gives rise to diverse and potentially exciting opportunities for globally minded teachers, especially those who completed their training at Anglo-Western institutions due to the salience of English as a lingua franca as an advancement strategy for upwardly mobile students in non-English-speaking countries. One such possibility is the opportunities for rich professional growth, including early-career leadership opportunities for sojourning educators (Stroud Stasel, 2022b).

International schools overseas have experienced dramatic philosophical and structural changes since the 1950s (Heyward, 2002). From the founding of the United Nations Educational, Scientific, and Cultural Organization (UNESCO) in 1946 and the International Baccalaureate Organization (IBO, now called IB) in 1968, followed by the development of for-profit education hubs, high-level leaders in international schools have a lot to ponder as they strive to continue to deliver top-notch education to their growing student bodies.

Each of the above-named tensions features in the unique and vastly differing profile of any given international school. Allen (2004, p. 131) created a metaphor for international schools as "atolls in a coral sea. They have links, but different ways of life – different cultures." This metaphor is salient, not just because of the endless possibilities of permutations, but also because this metaphor is ecological, suggesting constant changes and adaptations, which is a feature of transnational spaces.

In contrast with the expected wide variances of international school culture, an idea that many international schools have embraced and feature in their marketing promotion strategy is that of global- or international-mindedness, which has acquired a certain currency in international schools. This construct featured prominently in the initial international schooling movement and remains in popular use today. However, some scholars have critically questioned what "international" refers to since philosophical discourse and decision-making have continued to reflect Western values (e.g., Roberts, 2013; Tarc, 2018). Roberts (2013) highlighted a paradox of international-mindedness, noting its rise and its potential downfall both originate from globalization. One of many effects of such a narrow scope of international-mindedness would be policies that do not accurately reflect the local values of where the international schools are located.

Transnational Flows and the Policyscaped Environment

In considering how the transnational space of the international school becomes a policyscape, it is helpful to consider the work of Appadurai (2013, p. 66) who explained that,

> histories produce geographies and not vice versa. versa. We must get away from the notion that there is some kind of spatial landscape against which time writes its story. Instead, it is historical agents, institutions, actors, and powers that make the geography.

Appadurai highlighted critical questions that policy actors in transnational contexts need to ask, such as, "How can [transnational movements] organize transnationally without sacrificing their local projects?" (p. 171) and how can "the mobility of capital and new information technologies be contained by, and made accountable to, the ethos and purpose of local democratic projects?" (p. 172). He pointed to horizontal learning as a means of sharing knowledge, understandings, and possibilities transnationally, or across cultures. Of course, the international school will always be subject to vertical policy (e.g., local, state, national) as well.

In conceptualizing the policyscape, Appadurai (1996, p. 33) coined a few *scapes*, such as *ethnoscape, mediascape, technoscape,* and *ideoscape,* to "look at the relationship among five dimensions of global cultural flows," noting that the "suffix -scape allows us to point to the fluid, irregular shapes of these landscapes, shapes that characterize international capital." Key in understanding scapes, such as the policyscape, is that these are not objectively given relations that look the same from every angle of vision but, rather, that they are deeply perspectival constructs, inflected by the historical, linguistic, and political situatedness of different sorts of actors: nation-states, multinationals, diasporic communities, as well as subnational groupings and movements (whether religious, political, or economic), and even intimate face-to-face groups, such as villages, neighborhoods, and families.

The policies and practices of an international school are shaped by the irregularity of cultural flows, making each school's policyscape unique. Policies are often perceived as tedious, but they provide specific guidelines for required or suggested actions, resulting in sanctioned operational frameworks that drive organizational behavior and management. While policy implementation can be complex and subject to varying interpretations and translations, following relevant policies provides individuals with professional security.

The UN's SDGs provide crucial policy guidance for schools, particularly SDG 4 with its 10 targets, many of which are already attained by international schools. Despite their access and privilege, achieving all targets may be challenging, suggesting even greater difficulties for schools with fewer resources. While SDGs are broadly defined to accommodate cultural variations and foster global betterment, their broadness leaves room for ambiguity and uncertainty in policy implementation (Hák et al., 2016).

METHODOLOGY

Participants, consisting of 17 educators, were selected based on their teacher training origins in Canada, the USA, or the UK, and their current sojourning employment in international schools across mainland China, Macau, Malaysia, Singapore, or Thailand. The study aimed to investigate educators' acculturation experiences and their impact on well-being and professional growth (Stroud Stasel, 2021). Research questions were formulated to explore these experiences, driving semi-structured and discussion interviews in two rounds. A lexicon of study terms was shared with participants, including a prompt asking for narratives on encountering "policyscapes." We focus on data derived from these interviews, supplemented by researcher field notes and participant reflexive journals.

All 17 participants resided and worked in host countries that they did not identify as belonging to. The participants occupied various roles within international schools, including teachers, counselors, and leaders, some with blended responsibilities. We adopted a modified narrative inquiry framework based on Clandinin's (2013) work, involving three phases of data collection.

Data collection comprised in-person semi-structured interviews, followed by virtual discussions. Initial interview data were coded using both predetermined and emergent and patterned codes (Saldaña, 2013), with subsequent interviews informed by initial analysis. Supplementary data collection methods included researcher and participant reflex journals, photovoice, artifacts, and field logs. Inductive data analysis employed a phronetic approach (Tracy, 2020), with three member-checking stages enhancing the study's trustworthiness.

FINDINGS

In sharing their experiences with policyscapes, most participants understood the policyscape as a complex intermingling of policies and practices. This

Into the Void 141

convergence often involved tensions related to how the issues that the policies and practices aimed to address were perceived, interpreted, or translated from policy-to-practice. The complications arose from taking a policy or practice that was initially framed in one local context but became embroiled in conflicting values and interpretations once in the transnational sphere. The participants thus viewed the policyscape manifestations as unplanned or unintended consequences of being implemented within a transnational and intercultural organization.

The manifestations were framed as causing professional tensions and personal stress. These manifestations were initially coded into broad categories, such as organizational behavior, pedagogy/practice, and policy gap/clash, and later were thematically analyzed into categorical propositions. That the responses to this question consistently yielded evidence of conflicting views or understandings about policy or practice suggests that the policyscape definition provided to participants invited a deficit-oriented translation, or that participants interpreted the policyscape manifestation in such an orientation. In the first interview, the following definition of policyscape was provided:

> A policyscape is like a landscape of policies that have originated from different theoretical, practical and pedagogical foundations. International schools may draw upon policies from a variety of countries. The practical implications for teachers may be confusing, especially when teachers are unfamiliar with the policies in their host country. (Interview #1 protocol)

The term policyscape left some participants uncertain about its meaning. To illustrate, we recounted an incident from the first author's experience teaching in an international school, where inadvertently, a local law was violated during a class discussion on a news story involving high-ranking political figures. Reflecting on this example, we recognize that it may have inadvertently steered participants toward dwelling on negative experiences rather than acknowledging the positive aspects of working in culturally diverse environments.

Following the analysis of interview data and subsequent reflective inquiry, a myriad of positive outcomes associated with policyscape were identified. Namely, there was a notable improvement in cultural competencies among younger educators. Even though one of the educators had set out to develop cultural competencies as a professional goal, she did not recognize that the conditions that allowed her to do so were a policyscape manifestation. These educators were excited about their learning and attributed it to their experiences of intercultural contact and their decision to teach abroad.

When asked if they had any experiences to share about policyscapes, participants readily responded to this question, sharing their experiences with similar policyscape manifestations despite participants being located at different international schools and presumably without knowing one another. Some policyscape manifestations were not immediately analyzed because they were isolated to one or two participants; however, both a secondary data analysis and a future study, currently being carried out shall seek to explore the policyscaped environment of international schools. Some manifestations encompassed more than one category, during which time, participants spoke fluidly across the categories. This is to be expected, as both codes and thematic categories were derived later when the data were being analyzed. In our preliminary analysis of the emergent findings, four policyscape manifestations manifested:

1. Working in a transnational educational setting develops cultural competencies;
2. Differences in policies and practices for students with special education needs creates tension for educators that can challenge their self-efficacy but can also lead to courageous actions;
3. International schools lack clear mental health policies. Educators must address diverse students' well-being, from anxiety to severe issues;
4. Ensuring safety in international schools is complex due to the need to balance host country laws with the needs of the transnational student body.

Participants shared demographic information during the interview, and additional details were collected later for comparison. See Table 1.

As previously noted, one of the policyscape manifestations signifies a positive outcome, which is being analyzed for another manuscript. The second manifestation "Special Education," which was the most prevalent, was analyzed for a journal manuscript (Stroud, 2024). In the subsequent sections, we delve into the findings related to the remaining two manifestations: "Student Mental Health" and "Student Protection." These findings demonstrate a myriad of nuances and complexities.

Table 1. Participant Information ($N = 17$).

Pseudonym	Languages[a]	Previous Sojourning as Teacher	# Years Teaching	Educative Role[b]
Bria	B/M, E	No	10–20	Teacher/Leader
Charlotte	E	Pre-Service	2–5	Teacher
Claire	B/M, L2+	Yes	20 +	Teacher
Frédéric	B/M	Yes	20 +	Teacher
Harry	E	Yes	10–20	Leader
Hayley	E	Yes	5–10	Teacher
Jake	E	No	10–20	Teacher
Jayna	E	Yes	10–20	Leader/Teacher
Joon-Ho	B/M, L2+	No	5–10	Leader
Lily	B/M, L2+	Yes	5–10	Teacher
Mandy	E	Yes	2–5	Teacher
May	B/M, L2+	Yes	10–20	Leader
Pat	B/M	No	5–10	Teacher/Leader
Ron	E	Yes	20+	Teacher
Rowan	E	Yes	10–20	Teacher/Leader
Sean	E	No	5–10	Teacher
Victoria	B/M, L2+	No	10–20	Teacher/Leader

[a]Bi- or multi-lingual – B/M; Mother tongue English – E; Mother tongue other than English/English as an additional language spoken – L2 + (not all participants disclosed their mother tongue).
[b]Where two roles are listed, the primary duties are listed first. A teacher whose primary duties are school leadership (e.g., principal, CEO, leadership consultant) is labeled Leader/Teacher; a teacher whose primary duties are teaching, with added leadership roles (e.g., lead teacher, division head, school counselor, etc.), is labeled Teacher/Leader.

Into the Void   143

Student Mental Health

Most participants reported concerns about student mental health, while fewer participants reported concerns about student safety. It is pertinent to acknowledge that data collection commenced prior to the onset of the COVID-19 pandemic. However, during the second phase of data collection, the pandemic unfolded, necessitating two adjustments to the study's design. Consequently, investigating the pandemic's effects became an additional research focus. As a result, a substantial volume of data emerged regarding mental health concerns, encompassing issues pertinent to teachers, educators' apprehensions regarding students' mental well-being, and the concerns of school leaders for both students and staff. Thus, these findings are delineated into two distinct periods of data collection: pre-pandemic and during the pandemic.

Before the COVID-19 Pandemic

The first phase of data collection, predating the pandemic, yielded ample evidence of policyscape manifestations on student mental health, indicating that this issue was not caused by the pandemic, although there was evidence that this event exacerbated mental health concerns. Some of the early data showed experiences of dissonance about what shall be described as a privilege spectrum. During the study, many educators discussed their realization of their privileged positionality globally as educators trained at Anglo-Western universities and living affluent lifestyles as expatriates. Participants unpacked some of their own identities when considering their privilege. For instance, one-quarter of the participants identified as being racialized in North America (4), while two of these participants enjoyed a newfound anonymity of "blending in" while sojourning overseas. One-quarter of participants indicated that their mother tongues were not English (5) and many participants were introduced to teaching English as an additional language (EAL) while sojourning either formally or embedding language supports and experimenting with translanguaging while teaching. A few educators extended their musing to the experiences of their students, and in this regard, students at international schools were often assumed to be privileged. Some assumed their students' privilege because these students were attending fee-paying schools in neighborhoods where government-run schools were also options, and some students flew in from other parts of the world to board at the school and host country. One participant became keenly aware of inequities that affected her own experiences as well as those of her students, conveying: "I didn't really realize before coming here, how privileged I actually am" (Hayley). Hayley got involved in various initiatives to enhance mental health, initially for her fellow teachers and then for the students. She also participated in two community-based initiatives; one focused on helping refugee youth who had been relocated near her school, while the other supported youth who were socioeconomically disadvantaged. However, these initiatives were not directly related to her work at the international school.

While less common than the policyscape manifestation related to supporting students with special education needs, the issue of how to support students disclosing mental health concerns was still notable across all five regions in this study. Educators recounted instances of students confiding in them about various mental health issues, including anxiety, depression, self-harm, and even delusions or suspected hallucinations. Guidance counselors were the most vocal about these issues, but school principals and teachers also engaged in discussions about them.

Counseling support was available in some schools but was intermittent. For instance, at two schools, students could reportedly book appointments with counselors, but there was no availability during holidays. These schools had two one-month-long breaks each year and other extended holidays like the Lunar New Year, resulting in hiatus periods. One participant, Victoria, expressed concern for students who might require assistance during these times. Participants also discussed how mental health problems are often viewed as shameful in their culture, which could prevent students from seeking help from their parents. No schools according to the participants, had a high capacity for being the primary support in this regard, although participants felt that in most cases, the school supports were the only supports available. The shortcomings became noticeable during prolonged student holidays, where there would be no support or outreach whatsoever, which was reported to distress students.

The Quagmire of Advocating for Supporting Student Mental Health

Cultural differences in addressing students' needs were apparent, with staff supporting methods that parents did not endorse. One participant, Rowan, shared:

> there's a big difference between the ones we have identified and their families as to the actual follow through. And again, we're in a culture where [the] same thing about mental health as it applies to special educational needs. Parents do not want a diagnosis. Parents do not want their child labelled. They will not. (Rowan)

Rowan had worked at other international schools prior to this one and she compared her experiences with other experiences in other countries. Furthermore, in her current school, which was new with physical and policy infrastructure still in development, she learned that the school leaders received guidance from an education hub in another city, yet this school was not part of that education hub. Rowan had met teachers and counselors working at other international schools and observed that the other educators:

> have a visiting psychiatrist, psychologist, access to all kinds of medical, help and, and support, where we are that is completely non-existent [here]. I had to try and quickly orientate myself to what services are available, where are they available, how do you access them? How do I recommend this?... I quickly also figured out that our, the culture here is not okay with admitting that people need mental health care. It's very taboo. It's not talked about. It's not acceptable. It's not as accepted as it is in North America. If you are involving parents and family members, sometimes they are quite reluctant to get help, get that kind of mental health support. I have often come across families and situations where it's almost a complete refusal to get help. There's some direct examples, but I guess I'll not go quite into the context, but I had one student who clearly said he was hearing voices, I'm not a doctor, but I'm thinking like emergent schizophrenia, who knows, you know. I wanted to have him assessed and mum felt that essential oils would be good and has gone with a different route and we still don't have an assessment on this child. And I'd been working with this family now since January.

Into the Void 145

Rowan acknowledged that her views on how to support students with disclosures of mental health concerns were culturally situated. She remarked:

> I have to really struggle sometimes to put away my preconceived notions, but I also need to have conversations with families around the fact that mental health and getting help for that is as normal as taking blood pressure if you need them. If you need a tablet, if you need medications, the same as if you have diabetes or if you have high blood pressure, why wouldn't you? I keep talking with families, like, when did you want to get your child the help that they need?

While Rowan's reference to the student hearing voices represents the seemingly most dire need for guidance and support to effectively support the students, several participants yearned for additional support and direction. In some cases, the support was elusive, and in some cases, there were evident gaps with silence from the school leadership.

Rowan was hired as a school counselor but after arriving found that she would also be fulfilling teaching and leadership duties in addition to her counseling duties. Since this international school was new and received guidance from an education hub, she found that leadership messaging was confusing. She often believed policy and leadership decisions were copied from another international school with different contexts and students that were poorly reflected in her context. She asserted:

> We're lacking policies and procedures at this school. It's pretty much how we act in leaps of faith, and we hope that our colleagues are doing the same, but there's no clear directions, no clear procedures, no clear policies at our school ... the invisible policies are around, they send us 16-page contracts, and yes, of course I've read it, but you know, that's still doesn't, that still doesn't mandate my day-to-day. That still doesn't give me ideas of like, again, what's acceptable, what is it, those kinds of things. So policyscapes. I like that term. (Rowan)

The ambiguity and vagueness of policies governing the daily operations in the international school resulted in feelings of uncertainty among Rowan and her colleagues who struggled to navigate what was deemed acceptable and unacceptable.

During the COVID-19 Pandemic

At the onset of the COVID-19 pandemic, schools in these five regions were among the first in the world to close even before the pandemic was declared globally. When schools' activities had to abruptly halt, it caused a lot of disruptions for teachers, leaders, counselors, and students. They had to switch to virtual learning models, which later turned into a hybrid of in-person and virtual learning. Many ancillary services provided by schools, such as cafeteria offerings and counseling support, suffered a significant decline. Harry, a school leader, explained that his school's cafeteria services were outsourced to dozens of individual caterers due to the diverse dietary needs of the global student body, comprising local students, expatriates' children, and boarding students. However, the pandemic caused distress among students as restrictions were imposed on food and preparation methods that correlated with their cultural habits. Additionally, many students liked to meet, eat, and work in the vast, open-aired cafeteria. As such, the cafeteria represented an open commons area that served substantial social well-being opportunities for belonging and for collaborating on work. However, with the crowd restrictions, new regulations came into effect at the cafeteria, impacting students' well-being directly which deteriorated over time. Some caterers struggled to sustain their businesses due to limited student patronage, resulting in diminished service options and offerings.

Upon revisiting the counseling support system provided to students by the school counselors and leaders, it was revealed that the school closures due to the pandemic caused a significant disruption in the continuity of counseling services. Victoria pointed out that there were no alternative measures in place for students in a state of mental distress. Two participants shared their concerns about the impact of these service disruptions on students, as they were left vulnerable to the deterioration of their mental health, ultimately increasing the risk of self-harm.

School leaders and counselors discussed challenges with supporting students with suicide ideations. Teachers, counselors, and principals lamented the school's capacity shortcomings in this area, which were numerous, and diverse, and the variation from school to school was a source of frustration, especially with educators who had prior sojourning experiences at other international schools that they believed to be better equipped to support students in this area. During the pandemic, work intensification was reported by participants at all schools. The nature of the intensification was as varied as the number of participants. Rowan reflected:

> I have all these random sorts of jobs that are undefined. Like it would be really fascinating to me right now. If you were in your next question was could you write out your job description? That would be such a joke. First of all, it would take me seven hours cause I'm not really clear. There's no definition, there's no defined boundaries, there's no defined duties. But yet I'm supposed to meet the, again, these random expectations that are unstated and unclear.

Rowan expressed her concern about feeling unsafe within her organization due to the lack of clarity in her job description. She found it difficult to understand her responsibilities and duties, which made her feel uncertain about her role in the company. She expressed:

> You hope they have your back and it seems quite arbitrary or as to whether whose back they will have and how and in what way. So it's a bit of a crap shoot ... the lack of policies and procedures leaves everybody feeling quite like that. If you have a discipline problem in your class, you don't know what to do about it ... it's a continual round of trying to figure out the policies and procedures do not exist and we don't even know what to do about that and where to move. Since January I have been trying to continually have discussions with our leadership about [how] we need these policies and procedures in place.

Student Protection

The issue of student protection within a policyscape was far less prominent than that of supporting student mental health. Participants in this study raised concerns about student protection in most regions. These concerns varied from macro-level issues like laws affecting student safety, meso-level concerns like

Into the Void 147

school-wide policies or behaviors impacting student safety, to micro-level concerns like individual student safety. Most of the participants were motivated to ensure that a specific student was not in danger as early evidence of this possibility emerged. These were concerns at the micro-level, but they also intersected with meso-level, such as the absence of substantive policy to direct professional actions to advocate for the student's safety, and in some cases at the macro-level. Despite this, supporting student mental health remained a prominent issue. However, it caused intense anxiety in some participants when it emerged in multiple regions. One teacher participant even decided not to renew her contract due to this unresolved issue, despite initially planning to fulfill her contract before moving on. This participant later became a midnight runner.

Examples Show Micro–Meso-Level and Micro–Meso–Macro-Level Issues
A variety of ideas connecting concerns for individual students' safety with school policies were expressed. Rowan and Victoria, both educators and school counselors at different international schools in different cities, spoke of concerns about students' reports of intention to self-harm, linking student mental health with student safety. Rowan also described several other concerns that included a desire to see greater supports developed at the school and including ancillary supports. Ron, a former correctional services worker, occasionally handled administrative duties enforcing school policy. He suspended students for vaping, viewing it as self-destructive and a threat to the student body. This contrasts with Jayna's belief in proactive measures for student flourishing. Worried about school policies, she advocated for greater protection for students and staff. In each of these cases, Rowan, Victoria, Ron, and Jayna, their responses reflect individual convictions and approaches to addressing concerns. They also linked their responses to their understanding of their professional roles, which were informed by their teacher training in Canada (Rowan, Victoria, and Ron) and the UK (Jayna). It should be noted that majority were trained in Canada, as the study was launched from a Canadian university and the initial snowballing participant recruiting methods began with Canadian-accredited international schools. By the end of participant recruiting, there were 14 whose professional training was completed in Canada, one whose professional training was completed in the UK with continuing education globally, one whose professional training was completed in the Philippines and the USA, and one whose training was completed in the UK and the USA, with continuing education globally.

Student Protection and Special Education Intersection
Jayna is a career international educator who has worked as a teacher and leader in several countries across six continents. She was responsible for overseeing the intake process of potential future students in the elementary division of her school. As part of this process, potential students spend one or more days in a classroom setting on a trial basis. During this time, Jayna observed the student's interactions with other students and teachers and made recommendations.

However, this work would have benefited from a specialist in special education, which was not in Jayna's area of expertise. She worked with an Information Communications Technology (ICT) coordinator who was also not trained in special needs. According to Jayna, the ICT coordinator was "really proactive" with the students.

One time, a young child came in with their guardian, and there were language barriers. Jayna only had a basic understanding of the language of the host country, while the guardian did not speak English. She shared that she and the ICT coordinator were "relying on the parent liaison officer to translate what we were saying. And because we don't speak [local language], we're not a hundred percent sure what she's saying."

Jayna observed the first day of the trial period and was concerned with what she saw. She requested two extra days of trial school time. However, parents were billed for these trial days, which she found unfair because there was no commitment from the school to admit the child during these days. Despite the issue, they proceeded with the two extra days. On the first day back, the child showed some improvement. Yet on the third day, he had a complete "meltdown" and threw things around the room.

Jayna opted against admitting the child, deeming the school ill-prepared to cater to students with complex special education needs. She cited the necessity for diagnostics, individualized support, and additional resources beyond the school's capacity. Despite the school's claim of serving special needs students on its website, Jayna clarified that it could only accommodate those with mild learning disabilities, lacking adequate teacher training and resources for more extensive support. Despite Jayna's decision, the school owner overrode it, and the child was formally admitted and began attending school. The child responded positively to Jayna, who was called in on numerous occasions. However, she felt unable to provide the support that he needed. Jayna disclosed:

> It got worse and worse. And he was a danger to himself, a danger to the children. And I was the only person for some stuff. And I'm not very good at special [education]. I mean, give me EAL, give me, you know, I'm not special needs is not my thing.

Jayna discovered that a student had significant communication and cognitive impairments due to a complex syndrome. The school was unable to provide the level of support needed and the child posed a danger to himself and others. After much damage had been done, the child was transferred to a specialized school. This incident ended up in court, and the school owner reprimanded the leadership team for admitting the child in the first place.

Student Protection and "Duty to Report"

Educators, especially those in K-12 settings, often face the challenging task of intervening to protect children from potential abuse, including neglect, physical, and sexual abuse, even in the absence of conclusive evidence. This responsibility can exacerbate stress, particularly for new educators who fear the consequences of acting on circumstantial evidence. In Ontario, Canada, educators are governed by the Duty to Report law, mandating the reporting of suspected abuse

Into the Void 149

to the Children's Aid Society. Such legal requirements supersede any internal reporting procedures within educational institutions. However, participants in this study, predominantly educators in international settings displayed varying levels of awareness regarding reporting procedures in their respective host countries. While educational leaders tended to have a better grasp of local laws, teachers often relied on guidance departments or principals to address their concerns, indicating a need for greater clarity and understanding of legal obligations across diverse contexts.

Harry explained the duty to report the law in his host country. He said that the nuts and bolts of the law were similar to laws in Canada, on suspicions of abuse or neglect. However, the leader explained how the law translated to practice would help an abusive parent or guardian to evade any investigation as a letter informing the parent or guardian would be sent by official governmental correspondence, which was perceived as a sort of FYI. In a conversation with the principal, a student voiced a poignant concern: "If you report this, you'll never see me again." This underscored the ease with which parents could relocate students to another international school in another country, potentially severing communication. The principal favored transformative leadership that sought to address the situation in a way that honored local culture but advocated for the student, which he said, required creative problem-solving and a lot of patience. To aid him in his decision-making, Harry sought the advice of a senior leader who was a host country national. He referred to her as a cultural mentor and believed that the extensive time he had spent living in the host country (10 + years), and his relationships with local people infused his professional behavior with confidence, boosting his agency.

Teachers in the study displayed a noticeable divergence in perspectives compared to leaders when it came to deviating from policy or protocol adherence. While leaders felt confident and empowered to respond flexibly to students' individual needs, influenced significantly by local culture, teachers appeared to lack the confidence or agency to adopt a transformative leadership approach. Their concerns about job security and a perceived lack of professional agency hindered their ability to respond courageously. Many participants reported explicit instructions to avoid certain discussions at work, including topics related to special education and mental health, due to their perceived politicization and associated risks of reprisal. Consequently, teachers felt constrained in their ability to act in alignment with their training and ethical obligations.

CONCLUSIONS

The two types of policyscape manifestations, involving how educators approached the difficult topics of supporting students with mental health concerns and the protection of students, were not always clear-cut categories. Rather, the manifestations were often messy and intersected with other types of policyscape manifestations, such as that of special education and work intensification. While work intensification represents a significant policy issue, and became exacerbated by the pandemic, findings of work intensification ubiquity across most work sectors indicate that this topic ought to be addressed separately and is not discussed in this paper. Policy manifestations in the policyscape often revealed gaps or contrasts in addressing vulnerabilities among students. The absence of infrastructure to aid students with mental health issues and the dearth of guidelines for culturally responsive support highlight crucial areas for improvement in international schools.

Addressing the complexities of providing mental health support within an international school setting amidst divergent perspectives poses significant challenges. Carney (2009) underscores the challenge of navigating local context and cultural dynamics within the broader framework of international influences. This challenge resonated with participants, who grappled with the tension between adhering to policies and the imperative to support students effectively.

While teachers often prioritized policy fidelity due to fear of reprisal, individuals in leadership roles, such as Harry, Jayna, and Rowan, demonstrated a greater willingness to take courageous principled action (Worline & Quinn, 2003). Embracing transformative leadership principles, they were more inclined to adapt organizational rules to support students in culturally responsive ways. Transformative leadership entails moral reflection and the courage to act accordingly (Shields, 2019).

In transnational educational spaces like international schools, understanding one's positionality in moral dilemmas is crucial. Harry's decision to seek guidance from local cultural experts and engage in ongoing reflection on cultural responsiveness highlights the importance of critically examining one's actions. While this approach may not guarantee culturally responsive outcomes, it represents a commitment to prioritizing cultural sensitivity over adherence to norms from a different context.

While not elaborated on in this paper, one of the data collection phases was purely reflective. During this time, participants confronted and questioned the plural identities that they carried with them. Individual identities are complex and multifaceted. For educators, personal and professional identities conjoin (Bukor, 2011), and for students in international schools, the construct of the third space that third culture kids experience (Pollock & Van Reken, 2009) can be informative. The participants in this study all showed an interest in centering their students and validating their diverse experiences.

Rowan and Jayna encountered challenges advocating for students' mental health and protection due to a cultural clash that stigmatized acknowledging special education or mental health needs. Despite their belief in the necessity of advocacy, they faced a cultural taboo and a lack of policy infrastructure, leading to feelings of isolation. Transformative leadership could have offered a solution, yet it risked exacerbating tensions with the host culture and exacerbating their sense of isolation. Mettler (2016) highlights how policies can evolve unpredictably over time due to their inherent dynamics, often leading to unintended consequences. In Rowan's case, the absence of articulated policies at her new school heightened her apprehension as evidence of students' precarious mental health accumulated.

Into the Void

Moreover, considering one's positionality is essential in understanding complex policy and practice issues. Rowan's cultural backlash against mental health and special education aligns with documented struggles in cultural integration and detachment from Western ideals among educators (Savva, 2017). Professionals' insufficient knowledge and training in cultural responsiveness further compound these challenges (Tarry & Cox, 2014). Kopish (2016) advocates for greater reflexivity and critical self-inquiry, particularly in pre-service education programs.

The COVID-19 pandemic has brought trauma to students, teachers, and school leaders, leading to emerging literature (Gurr & Drysdale, 2020; Harris, 2020), including studies on international schools (Bailey, 2021; Barker & Ramaka, 2022; Stroud Stasel, 2020, 2023). Weaknesses in school systems pre-pandemic have come to light, emphasizing mental health's importance and the need for global mobility in international schools. Research clusters may address issues like mental health understanding, identification, and policy implementation. The absence of continuous support during breaks highlights the necessity for consistent student care, as depression doesn't stop when school does.

Over 20 years ago, Bradley (2000) argued that international schools failed to support students with diverse identities. While participants noted special education teachers and ancillary supports were either advertised on school websites or employed at their schools, the continuity of programs was very much a precarious one, as Jayna and Lily had observed that when a special education teacher left, the replacement teacher was either unqualified or no replacement occurred.

These policyscape manifestations of student protection, although a lesser finding across the data, caused significant stress to educators. There was a divergent trend within the teachers' and the leaders' stakeholder groups, with the leaders feeling more confident to override policy by using courageous principled action which reflected culturally responsive leadership.

International schools, accredited by foreign bodies, adopt policies from their accrediting regions. Yet, applying these policies across diverse contexts pose risks, as seen in a principal's account of repercussions for reporting students. Policymakers should craft flexible policies for transnational students, promoting professional growth beyond leadership roles. It's vital to note that culturally biased policy reactions can backfire in the international school setting.

Significance and Implications for Practice

These findings underscore the need for a comprehensive response. This entails crafting school-specific policies prioritizing student welfare and providing guidance for educators navigating these complex practice landscapes. While the UN's SDGs were not explicitly discussed, they serve as a pertinent framework for emphasizing the imperative of ensuring equitable access to quality education. Bakhshi et al. (2017) shed light on the persistent stigma intersecting with this topic and highlighted epistemological disparities between Western and South

Asian special education approaches. They advocate for embracing complexity, transitioning from rhetoric to action, and critically analyzing policy implementation challenges. We outline six actions that can help to address these issues, which would be optimized by engaging in collective knowledge and multi-actor groups:

1. *Establish Mental Health Counseling Support Services*: Ensuring that there is a task force consisting of internal and external stakeholders (both organizational and non-organization actors) to develop and integrate a protocol to support teachers and students during regular operations and in the event of an emergency crisis.
2. *Cultivate an Affinity Between International Teachers*: Establishing networks including working groups comprising international teachers to facilitate peer support, knowledge-sharing, and collaboration. These communities could serve as a platform for sharing experiences, resources, and best practices, thereby enhancing professional development and promoting a sense of belonging and support among international educators.
3. *Utilize International Oversight*: Implementing a comprehensive assessment system that aligns with governance systems that include local education frameworks, frameworks used by accreditors, and international policymaking actors, and led by qualified educational inspectors, to assess policy comprehensiveness, policy-to-practice resolutions, and with a specific focus on the well-being of both domestic and international teachers as well as students. Additionally, establishing regular (expected and unexpected) check-ins and support structures to safeguard teachers' mental health, such as providing access to counseling services without extended blockout times would enhance consistency.
4. *Develop Teacher Agency and Voice*: To protect teachers considering policy-scape clashes, efforts should be taken to enhance their agency by establishing anonymous channels for resolving issues, including reporting. Using existing support structures along with new ones through collaborative partnerships with community actors.
5. *Evaluate and Re-evaluate School Policies*: There is a need for ongoing research and evaluation to assess the effectiveness of policies and practices in promoting student and teacher well-being within international school settings. This may involve conducting longitudinal studies, evaluating the impact of interventions, and sharing best practices across educational institutions globally.
6. *Prioritize Special Education in International Context*: The UN, in collaboration with multi-state actors, articulates inclusion as a human right and this extends to students with disabilities. The necessity for further research into the realm of special education within the international context and its corresponding policies. This research could focus on examining the efficacy and implementation of existing policies, identifying gaps or inconsistencies in support for students with special needs, and exploring best practices for inclusive education in diverse cultural settings.

Into the Void 153

ACKNOWLEDGMENTS

This study was supported by the SSHRC in Canada. A companion manuscript unpacking the policyscape manifestation of "special education" can be found at: https://doi.org/10.5206/eei.v34i1.16826

REFERENCES

Allen, K. (2004). Atolls, seas of culture and global nets. In M. Hayden, J. J. Thompson, & G. R. Walker (Eds.), *International education in practice: Dimensions for national & international schools* (pp. 129–144). Routledge Falmer.

Appadurai, A. (1996). *Modernity at large cultural dimensions of globalization.* University of Minnesota Press

Appadurai, A. (2013). *The future as cultural fact: Essays on the global condition.* Verso.

Bailey, L. (2021). International school teachers: Precarity during the COVID-19 pandemic. *Journal of Global Mobility: The Home of Expatriate Management Research, 9*(1), 31–43.

Bakhshi, P., Babulal, G. M., & Trani, J.-F. (2017). Education of children with disabilities in New Delhi: When does exclusion occur? *PloS one, 12*(9), e0183885. https://doi.org/10.1371/journal.pone.0183885

Barker, M. R., & Ramaka, S. B. (2022). Understanding middle-level leaders' empowerment during the Covid-19 pandemic: The context of international schools. In A-M. Wilmot & C. S. Thompson (Eds.), *Handbook of research on activating middle executives' agency to lead and manage during times of crisis* (pp. 134–160). IGI Global.

Berry, J. W. (2006a). Contexts of acculturation. In D. L. Sam & J. W. Berry (Eds.), *The Cambridge handbook of acculturation psychology* (pp. 27–42). Cambridge University Press.

Berry, J. W. (2006b). *Immigrant youth in cultural transition: acculturation, identity, and adaptation across national contexts.* Erlbaum.

Berry, J. W., & Hou, F. (2016). Immigrant acculturation and wellbeing in Canada. *Canadian Psychology [Psychologie canadienne], 57*(4), 254–264. https://doi.org/10.1037/cap0000064

Bradley, G. (2000). Inclusive education in international schools: A case study from Singapore. In M. Hayden, & J. Thompson (Eds.), *International schools & international education: Improving teaching, management & quality* (pp. 29–41). Kogan Page.

Bukor, E. (2011). *Exploring teacher identity: Teachers' transformative experiences of re-constructing and re-connecting personal and professional selves* [Doctoral dissertation, OISE University of Toronto].

Carney, S. (2009). Negotiating policy in an age of globalization: Exploring educational "policyscapes" in Denmark, Nepal, and China. *Comparative Education Review, 53*(1), 63–88.

Clandinin, D. J. (2013). *Engaging in narrative inquiry.* Left Coast Press.

Gurr, D., & Drysdale, L. (2020). Leadership for challenging times. *International Studies in Educational Administration (Commonwealth Council for Educational Administration & Management (CCEAM)), 48*(1), 24–30.

Hák, T., Janoušková, S., & Moldan, B. (2016). Sustainable Development Goals: A need for relevant indicators. *Ecological Indicators, 60*, 565–573. https://doi.org/10.1016/j.ecolind.2015.08.003

Harris, A. (2020). COVID-19 – School leadership in crisis? *Journal of Professional Capital and Community, 5*(3/4), 321–326. https://doi.org/10.1108/JPCC-06-2020-0045

Heyward, M. (2002). From international to intercultural: Redefining the international school for a globalized world. *Journal of Research in International Education, 1*(1), 9–32. https://doi.org/10.1177/147524090211002

Ingersoll, M., Hirschkorn, M., Landine, J., & Sears, A. (2018). Recruiting international educators in a global teacher shortage: Research for practice. *The International Schools Journal, 37*(2), 92–102.

ISC Research. (n.d.-a). *Data on international schools.* Retrieved August 5, 2024, from https://iscresearch.com/data/

ISC Research (n.d.-b). *International schools market growth: 10 year comparison.* Retrieved December 4, 2023, from https://iscresearch.com/data/

Kopish, M. A. (2016). Preparing globally competent teacher candidates through cross-cultural experiential learning. *Journal of Social Studies Education Research, 7*(2), 75–108.

Mettler, S. (2016). The policyscape and the challenges of contemporary politics to policy maintenance. *Perspectives on Politics 14*(2), 369–390. https://doi.org/10.1017/S1537592716000074

Pearce, R. (2015). Culture and identity: A method for exploring individuals within groups. In M. Hayden, J. Levy, & J. Thompson (Eds.), *The SAGE handbook of research in international education* (2nd ed., pp. 185–199). SAGE.

Pollock, D. C., & Van Reken, R. E. (2009). *Third culture kids: Growing up among worlds.* Nicholas Brealey.

Roberts, B. (2013). International education and global engagement: Education for a better world? In R. Pearce (Ed.). *International education and schools: Moving beyond the first 40 years* (pp. 119–145). Bloomsbury Academic.

Safdar, S., & Berno, T. (2016). Sojourners. In D. L. Sam & J. W. Berry (Eds.), *The Cambridge handbook of acculturation psychology* (2nd ed., pp. 173–195). Cambridge University Press. https://doi.org/10.1017/CBO9781316219218

Saldaña, J. (2013). *The coding manual for qualitative researchers* (2nd ed.). SAGE.

Savva, M. (2013). International schools as gateways to the intercultural development of North-American teachers. *Journal of Research in International Education, 12*(3), 214–227. https://doi.org/10.1177/1475240913512589

Savva, M. (2017). The personal struggles of 'national' educators working in 'international' schools: An intercultural perspective. *Globalisation, Societies and Education, 15*(5), 576–589. https://doi.org/10.1080/14767724.2016.1195728

Shields, C. M. (2019). *Becoming a transformative leader: A guide to creating equitable schools.* Routledge.

Stroud, R. (2024). "We need structures in place": Educators' experiences with special education at international schools. *Exceptionality Education International, 34*(1), 112–130. https://doi.org/10.5206/eei.v34i1.16826

Stroud Stasel, R. (2020). Learning to walk all over again: Insights from some international school educators and school leaders in South, Southeast and East Asia during the COVID crisis. *International Studies in Educational Administration (Commonwealth Council for Educational Administration & Management (CCEAM)), 48*(3), 95–101.

Stroud Stasel, R. (2021). *Educator acculturation while living and working overseas: Stories from seventeen sojourning teachers and school leaders at international schools* [Doctoral dissertation, Queen's University].

Stroud Stasel, R. (2022a). Beyond the hue and cry: Exploring the challenges and benefits of educator acculturation in overseas international schools. In A. Wiseman (Ed.), *Annual review of comparative and international education 2021 international perspectives on education and society* (Vol. 42B, pp. 225–246). Emerald. https://doi.org/https://doi.org/10.1108/S1479-36792022000042B012

Stroud Stasel, R. (2022b). The experiences of four women providing leadership at international schools in Southeast Asia. In H. S. Kim (Ed.), *Rethinking Asia: Women's leadership retold* (pp. 127–147). Acumen.

Stroud Stasel, R. (2023). Sojourning educators at international schools overseas and the Covid-19 pandemic. *The Canadian Journal of Action Research, 23*(2), 107–129.

Tarc, P. (2018). "Walking the Talk": A conceptualization of international mindedness to inform leadership in international schools. *Peabody Journal of Education, 93*(5), 486–499.

Tarry, E., & Cox, A. (2014). Professional development in international schools; issues of inclusion identified by a group of international school teaching assistants. *Journal of Research in Special Educational Needs, 14*(4), 248–254. https://doi.org/10.1111/1471-3802.12024

Tracy, S. J. (2020). *Qualitative research methods: Collecting evidence, crafting analysis, communicating impact* (2nd ed.). Wiley.

UNESCO. (2016). *The world needs almost 69 million new teachers to reach the 2030 education goals.* UNESCO Institute for Statistics.

von Kirchenheim, C., & Richardson, W. (2005). Teachers and their international relocation: The effect of self-efficacy and flexibility on adjustment and outcome variables. *International Education Journal, 6*(3), 407–416.

Ward, C., Bochner, S., & Furnham, A. (2005). *The psychology of culture shock* (2nd ed.). Routledge.

Worline, M. C., & Quinn, R. W. (2003). Courageous principled action. In K. S. Cameron, J. E. Dutton, & R. E. Quinn (Eds.), *Positive organizational scholarship: Foundations of a new discipline* (pp. 138–157). Berrett-Koehler.

APPENDIX: TERMINOLOGY DEFINITIONS

Educators: teachers, school counselors, and school leaders.

English as an Additional Language (EAL) refers to teaching students who are acquiring English as a secondary or subsequent language, regardless of their proficiency level. This includes learners for whom English is not their first language and maybe a secondary official language.

International school: a K-12 majority English-medium school (50%+) in a country with another primary language.

International student: attends an international school, residing either with family, boarding with a host family or at the school, either as a host country national or a sojourner.

International teacher: employed at an international school, they can be a host country national or an expatriate sojourning teacher.

Policyscape: a landscape of policies that have originated from different theoretical, practical, and pedagogical foundations. International schools adopt policies from diverse countries, which can be perplexing for teachers, particularly if they are unfamiliar with the policies in their host nation. This landscape is "deeply perspectival constructs, inflected by the historical, linguistic, and political situatedness of different sorts of actors" (Appadurai, 1996, p. 33).

Sojourner: a temporary acculturating group of people who are "between-society culture traveller[s]" (Ward et al., 2005, p. 6).

CAN TEACHING OVERCOME SOCIOECONOMIC INEQUALITY IN LATIN AMERICA? A TREND ANALYSIS USING ERCE DATA

Pablo Fraser, Fabián Fuentealba, Francisco Gatica, Alvaro Otaegui and Carlos Henríquez Calderón

UNESCO Santiago Offices, Chile

ABSTRACT

This paper seeks to contribute to the area studies and development of the 2023 Annual Review of Comparative and International Education by doing a trend analysis on the amount of variance of student achievement explained by socio-economic differences between 2013 and 2019 using the ERCE database in Latin America and the Caribbean. It also seeks to contrast these results with the amount of variance explained by a number of teacher characteristics, which the literature has identified as effective. In doing these analyses, we seek to assess on whether the region has made any progress on reducing the impact of socioeconomic differences on student achievement and increasing the levels of teacher efficiency.

Keywords: Student achievement; teacher effectiveness; trend analyses; Latin America and the Caribbean; variance decomposition; equity in education

---

Annual Review of Comparative and International Education 2023
International Perspectives on Education and Society, Volume 48, 157–174
Copyright © 2025 by Emerald Publishing Limited
All rights of reproduction in any form reserved
ISSN: 1479-3679/doi:10.1108/S1479-367920240000048009

INTRODUCTION

The paper seeks to contribute to the *area studies and development* of the 2023 Annual Review of Comparative and International Education by doing a trend analysis on the amount of variance of student achievement explained by socio-economic differences between 2013 and 2019 using the ERCE database in Latin America and the Caribbean. It also seeks to contrast these results with the amount of variance explained by teacher scales, which the literature has identified as effective. In doing these analyses, we seek to assess on whether the region has made any progress on reducing the impact of socioeconomic differences on student achievement and increasing the levels of teacher efficiency.

LITERATURE REVIEW

The acquisition of foundational learning is crucial steppingstone for more advanced skills that support the development and integration of societies. The United Nations' Transforming Education Summit called to increase support for foundational learning to ensure all children engage in early activities and learn basic reading, writing, and mathematics (United Nations, 2023). As such, the monitoring of foundational learning its embedded in the Sustainable Development Goals (SDGs) 4, which establish a series of indicators covering the access, trajectory, completion, and levels of achievement around the world.

Decades of research have shown that learning levels are conditioned by a series of factors, some corresponding to individual factors (abilities, previous performance, motivation, etc.) while others are external (social context, family characteristics, urban or rural settings, etc.). Probably the most studied external factor and the most sensitive for policymaking has been the association of socioeconomic levels and learning. Indeed, a strong association between a student socioeconomic status and performance has been conceptualized as a detriment to fairness and equity (Willms, 2006). Results from the recent Programme for International Student Assessment (PISA) 2022, the world's largest international assessment of 15 year olds, found that socio-economically advantaged students scored 93 points more in mathematics than disadvantaged students on average across OECD countries (OECD, 2023). Furthermore, the performance gap attributed to students' socio-economic status was greater than 93 score points. To this day, socio-economic inequalities in educational performance remains persistent (Chmielewski, 2019). PISA also showed that the socio-economic gap in mathematics performance did not change between 2018 and 2022 in 51 out of 68 systems with available PISA data (OECD, 2023).

Although the impact of socio-economic factors can be determinant for student achievement, school and classroom factors are also associated with learning outcomes and might even counteract the negative impact of socio-economic differences (Creemers & Kyriakides, 2010). In particular, teacher quality is the most important school-level predictor of student achievement (Hattie, 2009; Wayne & Youngs, 2003). Indeed a "teacher effect" (or a teacher's value-added) accounts for significant variation in student achievement (Chetty et al., 2014). The estimated magnitude of teacher effect is relatively large compared to other school variables (Jackson et al., 2014).

The context-situated nature of teacher's work makes it difficult to be conclusive about what teacher characteristics matter for student achievement. A strand of literature focusing on teacher effectiveness has highlighted on classroom practices relation of student achievement (Blazar & Kraft, 2017; Muijs et al., 2014). Other strands of literature have pointed to more "indirect effects" pointing out to school factors such as school climate, collaboration, and working conditions (Scheerens, 2001).

Educational systems in Latin American present interesting case studies to explore the association between socio-economic variables, teacher-related factors, and student outcomes. In terms of monitoring the SDGs have relied in ERCE – Estudio Regional Comparativo y Explicativo (Regional Comparative and Explanatory Study) – an international standardize test measuring achievements in reading, mathematics and science in third and sixth graders over a dozen countries in the region. Results from ERCE show that Latin American and Caribbean is a region of special focus as it is far from reaching the objectives of SDG 4, not only due to the low levels of proficiency but also due to an important stagnation of results for the last years. A primary factor behind the low achievement are the high levels of inequality in the region, which is anchored in the sharp socio-economic differences between students. Nevertheless, effective school systems have a potential margin to counteract the weight of socio-economic differences through quality teachers and teaching.

Results from ERCE 2019 have shown that there have been no significant changes in the levels of achievements between 2013 (TERCE)[1] and 2019 across participants in Latin America and the Caribbean. Furthermore, around half of the students in the third grade reached the required minimum levels of proficiency in the math and reading tests while in sixth grade less than a third reach these required minimum levels. The results are mostly driven by socioeconomic considerations. For example, ERCE 2019 results showed that only 40% of students from the lower socioeconomic quintile are able to meet the minimum competency level in third grades in contrast to 70% from the upper socioeconomic levels (UNESCO–UNICEF–CEPAL, 2022).

In contexts such as Latin America and the Caribbean where social inequalities are high, and resources are limited it is to be expected that the socio-economic conditions have a stronger hold than teacher factors on student achievement. However, the region has shown a steady increase in the resources allocated to the education sectors. If that is the case, it can be expected that school resources, such as teacher efficacy, could have a greater impact across the years.

The ERCE study has developed a series of items and scales that sought to capture the association of teacher characteristics and learning achievement. One of the teacher scales that shown a robust result with student outcomes was teacher punctuality. Students who are prepared by teachers who are usually present from the beginning of classes tend to show better results. This reveals the importance of valuing and using time at school, since the absence and lack of punctuality of the teacher means that students have fewer hours of activities directed to learning, which negatively affects performance.

However, whether the teacher is in the classroom is the bare minimum to achieve quality instruction. Even more important is what happens in the classroom – the interaction with the student, the pacing of the class, the level and quality of feedback, and quality provided (Muijs et al., 2014; Teddlie & Reynolds, 2000). Research has pointed out that effective teaching includes constructive and immediate feedback (Hattie, 2009; Muijs & Reynolds, 2001). The results from the most recent ERCE study showed that being attentive to student learning, encourage them to do their homework, recognize when students respond correctly, and appropriately correct errors when appropriate showed a positive association with student learning in most systems in the region.

The quality of teacher interactions with management staff, their peers, parents, and students is another crucial area of consideration for creating a learning inducing environment. Thus, school climate, understood as teacher's perception of the quality of their relationship in the workplace, is another factor that has shown a strong association with learning outcomes (OECD, 2021).

In light of the advancement done in the region regarding education investment, this paper set out to explore how the association of these three teacher variables with learning outcomes stand vis-á-vis the impact of socio-economic variables. A decrease in the strength of the association between socio-economic variables and learning outcomes over time can be interpreted to an increase in equity and fairness.

For Latin America and the Caribbean reach, the 2030 SDG 4 goals is of utmost importance to have quality monitoring of its educational performance based on robust indicators. ERCE 2019 database allows this due to its comprehensive coverage of educational systems as well of key achievement indicators and associated factors. Other international studies, such as PISA or TIMSS, given their international coverage and the heterogeneity of populations they encompass, present serious challenges for a uniform, consistent and relevant measurement of learning. However, ERCE being a regional study and with a methodology based on the close involvement of participating countries in the definition of its indicators, can do better in measuring learning for Latin American countries (Carrasco et al., 2023). The aim of the study is to showcase to the international community the usefulness of the ERCE database to conduct research in Latin America and the Caribbean that focus on achievement inequality and the role of the school to address these challenges.

RESEARCH OBJECTIVES

The paper will seek to answer the following research objectives:

- Provide a trend analysis on the amount of variance of student achievement in ERCE explained by socio-economic differences.
- Provide a trend analysis on the amount of variance of student achievement explained by the teacher characteristics of the ERCE students.
- Analyze and contrast the relative weight socio-economic variables and teacher characteristics variables have on student achievement for each participating country in ERCE.

METHODS

Database

This paper is based on the results of the Third Regional Comparative and Explanatory Study (TERCE) 2013 and the Regional Comparative and Explanatory Study (ERCE) 2019, from the UNESCO Santiago. The ERCE is an international large-scale assessment designed and implemented in Latin America primary education assesses the academic performance of third and sixth grade students in reading, writing, mathematics, and science (the latter only in sixth grade). It uses a stratified conglomerates and a two-stage sample design which is representative of the participating countries' school systems. The last two rounds of the study are comparable (with a mean of 700 and standard deviation of 100 set in TERCE).

The ERCE is a curricular-based study where the assessment framework is built from an analysis which considers the curricula of all the participating countries of the evaluated grades and domains. In addition, the study focuses on where learning takes place including a set of background questionnaires for students (both grades), their families, teachers, and school principals. With this approach, the study allows to identify the main associated factors to learning achievement and it aims to provide information of the school systems of Latin American countries (UNESCO, 2016, 2022).

Sample

In the 2013 round, a total of 114,255 students from 15 countries participated, whereas in the 2019 a total of 161,139 students from 16 countries of the region participated (UNESCO, 2016, 2022). This study considers only the countries that participate in both rounds.[2] Our analytic sample thus consists of 2,719 school and 40,530 students in 14 countries.

Scales

The associated factors are useful to describe the context of the school systems in the region and to identify latent variables that may be related to students' academic performance. Taking into consideration the purpose of this study, the literature review described in the previous sections, and the comparability of the associated factors of both rounds of the ERCE, four scales were considered: socioeconomic status of the students and their families (Socioeconomic scale), perception of sixth-grade students of the punctuality of their teachers (Punctuality scale), perception of the sixth-grade students of teacher support (Support scale), and the perception of teachers of the school environment climate (Climate scale).

The Socioeconomic scale includes three sets of variables that describe the educational level and occupation of students' parents, household goods and possessions, and the number of books at home. The scale is a continuous measure that indicates, from lower to higher, the relative status of families in the socioeconomic dimension. Students with higher scores on this attribute come from families with higher socioeconomic status, relative to their peers with lower scores.

The Punctuality scale includes a total of three items, referring to student's perception of the frequency with their teachers are absent, arrive late, or leave before the end of the class. Each item has three possible responses: Never or almost never; Sometimes; and Always or almost always, where responses associated with less frequency are related to greater attendance and punctuality by the teachers, thereby a lower score of the scale.

The Support scale includes seven items, through which students indicate the frequency with which their teachers perform different actions that are indicative of this dimension. For each item, there are four response categories: Never or almost never; Sometimes; Often; and Always or almost always. A higher score on this scale implies that students perceive a greater frequency of supportive practices from their teachers.

The Climate scale consist of five items, with which teachers rate the interpersonal relationships among the different members of the school. The scale consists of five alternatives: Very poor, Poor; Fair; Good; and Very good. A higher score on this scale indicates that teachers report better interpersonal relationships, while a lower score on this scale indicates a lower quality of relationships among the members of the educational unit.

Regression Model

The study conducted regression models to explore the association between student achievement, the socio-economic scale and teacher scales in 2013 and 2019. The dependent variable will be the achievement levels of sixth graders in reading and mathematics. As the independent variable, the study will use the student's family socioeconomic level, which is developed from the parents' questionnaire and teacher scales derived from the student questionnaire.

A hierarchical linear regression model was used, considering the nested structure of the data by school. The following multilevel linear regression model with random intercepts and slopes (Snijders & Bosker, 2012) was applied for each of the outcomes of the evaluations:

$$Y_{ij} = \beta_{0j} + \beta_{1j}X_{1ij} + \beta_2 X_{2j} + \beta_3 X_{3j} + \beta_4 X_{4j} + \varepsilon_{ij},$$
$$\beta_{0j} = \gamma_{00} + U_{0j},$$
$$\beta_{1j} = \gamma_{10} + U_{1j};$$

(1)

where Y corresponds to the learning achievement outcome of student i in school j. According to the literature and the research objectives of this study, the analysis includes the following sets of factors:

- Family socioeconomic status index, ISECF (represented by X_1 in equation (1)).
- Teacher support according to students, SUPPORT (represented by X_2 in equation (1)).
- School climate according to teachers, CLIMATE (X_3 in equation (1)).
- Perceived teacher punctuality by students, PUNCTUALITY (X_4 in equation (1)).

Can Teaching Overcome Socioeconomic Inequality in Latin America? 163

For the hierarchical linear model, the BIFIEsurvey package for R (BIFIE et al., 2022) was used, specifically the BIFIE.twolevelreg function for two-level multiple regression models. Plausible values methodology and balanced repli-cated weights were used for model estimates.

Oaxaca–Blinder Decomposition

Variance decomposition methods can reveal the relative importance of teacher scales in contrast to socioeconomic scales in explaining the differences. To ana-lyze the differences between each cycle we used an Oaxaca–Blinder (OB) decom-position of variance. This methodology was originally employed to analyze the wage differentials between high-wage and low-wage groups, such female and male differences as well as different ethnic's groups (Blinder, 1973; Oaxaca, 1973). In the field of education, this technique has been used to understand differences in academic performance between students from public and private schools (Oreiro & Valenzuela, 2012; Parvez & Laxminarayana, 2022; Romuald, 2023), gender (Gevrek et al., 2020), indigenous groups (Arteaga & Glewwe, 2019; Blanco, 2019), urban and rural schools (Lounkaew, 2013), among others.

The methodological approach is based on a threefold OB decomposition to analyze the difference in the ERCE test scores between the two last rounds of the study: ERCE 2019 and TERCE 2013. Following Parvez and Laxminarayana (2022) and Jann (2008), a simple version of the OB decomposition equation can be written as follows:

$$\hat{D} = \bar{Y}_t - \bar{Y}_{t'} = \left(\bar{X}_t - \bar{X}_{t'} \right)' \widehat{\beta_{t'}} + \bar{X}'_{t'} \left(\widehat{\beta_t} - \widehat{\beta_{t'}} \right) + \left(\bar{X}_t - \bar{X}_{t'} \right)' \left(\widehat{\beta_t} - \widehat{\beta_{t'}} \right)$$

where D is the mean difference between both groups $\bar{Y}_t - \bar{Y}_{t'}$, where $\bar{Y}_t$ is the mean of the ERCE 2019 group and $\bar{Y}_{t'}$ the mean of the 2013 group. The first compo-nent, $\left(\bar{X}_t - \bar{X}_{t'} \right)' \widehat{\beta_{t'}}$, the endowment effect, is the proportion of the difference attributable to the difference between the characteristics of each group. In other words, this could explain if the 2013 students had similar average features to 2019 students, this is how much their score would have increased. The second compo-nent, $\bar{X}'_{t'} \left(\widehat{\beta_t} - \widehat{\beta_{t'}} \right)$, the coefficient effect, corresponding to the portion of the differential attributable to differing coefficients, or how much of the 2013 stu-dents score would have increased if they had similar average returns to the 2019 students. Finally, $\left(\bar{X}_t - \bar{X}_{t'} \right)' \left(\widehat{\beta_t} - \widehat{\beta_{t'}} \right)$, the interaction between endowment and coefficient effect accounts for the fact that differences in endowments and coef-ficients exist simultaneously between the two groups. Both X and β are provided in the previous section.

RESULTS

Descriptive Analysis

This section presents descriptive analyses of the main variables of our study. We start presenting the descriptive results of the scales support, school climate,

164 PABLO FRASER ET AL.

teacher punctuality, and socioeconomic status between 2013 and 2019. Table 1 shows the mean and standard deviation of each index, which are disaggregated by subject.

In the support dimension, a slight decrease in averages is observed between 2013 and 2019 in all areas. In 2013, the averages were 0.059 (SD = 0.936) for reading, 0.061 (SD = 0.937) for mathematics, and 0.074 (SD = 0.932) for science. In 2019, the averages decreased to −0.008 (SD = 0.980), −0.010 (SD = 0.981), and −0.010 (SD = 0.981), respectively. This shift, shown in Fig. 1, suggests a decrease in the level of support provided in the educational context across the years.

Regarding the school environment climate, the results show a decline in the quality of the school environment across all three subjects between 2013 and 2019. In 2013, the averages were around −0.10 for all subjects. In 2019, they further declined to around −0.28 for reading and math, and around −0.26 for science. This significant decline in averages suggests a worsening school environment over the years (see Fig. 1).

In the dimension of teacher punctuality, the averages in 2013 were all around 0.01, which slightly decreased to around 0.007 in 2019 for all three subjects. This small change suggests a generally consistent level of teacher punctuality over time.

Finally, in the dimension of socioeconomic status, notable changes in averages were observed between 2013 and 2019. In 2013, the averages were around −0.12 in all three subjects, while in 2019, they improved to around −0.02 in all three

Table 1. Descriptive Statistics of Study Variables by Subject (2013–2019).

	TERCE 2013		ERCE 2019	
	Mean	Std. Dev.	Mean	Std. Dev.
Support				
Reading	0.059	0.936	−0.008	0.980
Math	0.061	0.937	−0.010	0.981
Science	0.074	0.932	−0.010	0.981
School environment climate				
Reading	−0.099	1.022	−0.276	0.995
Math	−0.089	1.014	−0.275	0.983
Science	−0.081	1.016	−0.264	0.977
Teacher punctuality				
Reading	0.011	0.999	0.008	0.994
Math	0.018	0.998	0.007	0.993
Science	0.022	1.000	0.007	0.993
Socioeconomic status				
Reading	−0.119	0.927	−0.024	0.894
Math	−0.116	0.926	−0.021	0.892
Science	−0.127	0.928	−0.024	0.892

Notes: This table shows descriptive statistics of the main scales considered in this analysis. All information was obtained at the individual level (students, teachers, and families). Data were obtained from the Regional Comparative and Explanatory Study (TERCE 2013 and ERCE 2019). The means and standard deviations of each scale by subject are presented in this table. For analysis purposes, missing and missing values were eliminated.

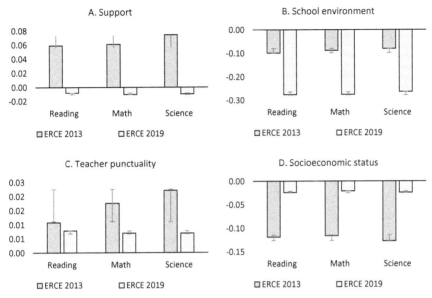

Fig. 1. Average of Main Indexes Between 2013 and 2019.
Notes: The plots were constructed following descriptive data of scales, using data from TERCE 2013 and ERCE 2019. Panel A shows average of Support scale, by subject. Panel B shows average of School environment climate scale, by subject. Panel C shows average of Teacher punctuality scale, by subject. Panel D shows average of Socioeconomic status scale, by subject.

subjects. This change indicates a moderate improvement in socioeconomic status, which may have positive implications for students' academic performance.

In summary, the ERCE results demonstrate a decrease in the averages of support and school environment climate between 2013 and 2019. Meanwhile, the averages in teacher punctuality remained relatively stable, and socioeconomic status experienced a moderate improvement. These changes may have various implications for academic performance, highlighting the importance of further research and potential interventions to enhance educational quality.

Multilevel Model Results

The results of the model are presented in Tables 2, 3, and 4 for language, mathematics, and science, respectively. Each column presents a model with each of the estimates for TERCE 2013 and ERCE 2019.

Language: In TERCE 2013, socioeconomic status has a significant positive association on language learning achievement, while school climate has a negative but not significant association. In ERCE 2019, socioeconomic status remains significant and positive, while teacher support and teacher punctuality have significant positive influences.

PABLO FRASER ET AL.

Table 2. Multilevel Model Results for Language in TERCE 2013 and ERCE 2019, Sixth Grade.

	Language			
	TERCE 2013		ERCE 2019	
Intercept	708.76***	(4.18)	692.98***	(1.49)
Socioeconomic Status	39.29***	(5.91)	29.21***	(0.85)
Teacher Scales				
APOYO	5.37***	(1.09)	10.12***	(0.52)
CLIMA	−3.37	(2.22)	−9.30***	(1.21)
PUNTUALIDAD	14.64***	(0.62)	−9.00***	(0.54)
Intraclass Correlation	0.1292		0.3026	
R2 level 1	0.2409		0.0836	
R2 level 2	0.6303		0.1188	
R2 total	0.3291		0.1188	
Number of Students	33,426		40,515	
Number of Schools	2,205		2,719	

Source: Own elaboration with data from UNESCO Santiago TERCE 2013 and ERCE 2019.
Notes: Senate sampling weights are used at the student level. *** indicates significance at the 1% level, ** indicates significance at the 5% level, and * at the 10% level. Random intercept and random slope are utilized for the variables.

Support (APOYO): In TERCE 2013, teacher support perceived by students shows a significant positive association with language learning achievement, and the association strengthens in ERCE 2019, suggesting a greater importance of teacher support over time.

School Climate (CLIMA): In TERCE 2013, school climate does not show a significant association with language learning achievement, but in ERCE 2019,

Table 3. Multilevel Model Results for Mathematics in TERCE 2013 and ERCE 2019, Sixth Grade.

	Mathematics			
	TERCE 2013		ERCE 2019	
Intercept	698.26***	(1.38)	695.65***	(1.48)
Socioeconomic Status	22.71***	(0.89)	17.42***	(0.97)
Teacher Scales				
APOYO	3.86***	(0.56)	6.04***	(0.53)
CLIMA	−4.32**	(1.45)	−5.79***	(1.31)
PUNTUALIDAD	11.36***	(0.55)	−7.59***	(0.58)
Intraclass Correlation	0.3685		0.4405	
R2 level 1	0.1096		0.0523	
R2 level 2	0.1390		0.0713	
R2 total	0.1207		0.0607	
Number of Students	33,260		40,530	
Number of Schools	2,213		2,710	

Source: Own elaboration with data from UNESCO Santiago TERCE 2013 and ERCE 2019.
Notes: Senate sampling weights are used at the student level. *** indicates significance at the 1% level, ** indicates significance at the 5% level, and * at the 10% level. Random intercept and random slope are utilized for the variables.

Can Teaching Overcome Socioeconomic Inequality in Latin America? 167

Table 4. Multilevel Model Results for Science in TERCE 2013 and ERCE 2019, Sixth Grade.

	Science			
	TERCE 2013		ERCE 2019	
Intercept	704.41***	(1.20)	696.49***	(1.28)
Socioeconomic Status	26.93***	(0.79)	21.56***	(0.70)
Teacher Scales				
APOYO	7.86***	(1.03)	8.36***	(0.53)
CLIMA	−1.06	(1.18)	−5.31***	(1.25)
PUNTUALIDAD	12.48***	(0.66)	−8.48***	(0.59)
Intraclass Correlation	0.2648		0.3513	
R2 level 1	0.1336		0.0742	
R2 level 2	0.2274		0.1257	
R2 total	0.1606		0.0930	
Number of Students	33,115		40,380	
Number of Schools	2,198		2,694	

Source: Own elaboration with data from UNESCO Santiago TERCE 2013 and ERCE 2019.
Note: Senate sampling weights are used at the student level. *** indicates significance at the 1% level, ** indicates significance at the 5% level, and * at the 10% level. Random intercept and random slope are utilized for the variables.

it has a significant negative association, indicating that a more negative school environment is associated with lower performance in language.

Teacher Punctuality (PUNTUALIDAD): The perceived punctuality of teachers by students shows a significant positive association in TERCE 2013, but in ERCE 2019, this association reverses and becomes negative, suggesting a change in the perception or effect of punctuality over time.

Mathematics: In TERCE 2013, socioeconomic status has a significant positive association, while school climate has a significant negative association on mathematics learning achievement. In ERCE 2019, socioeconomic status remains significant and positive, and both teacher support and teacher punctuality have significant positive qwwodiq5ion.

Support (APOYO): Both in TERCE 2013 and ERCE 2019, teacher support has a significant positive association with mathematics learning achievement, and this influence strengthens in ERCE 2019.

School Climate (CLIMA): In both measurements, school climate has a significant negative association with mathematics learning achievement, suggesting that a more negative school environment is associated with lower performance in this area.

Teacher Punctuality (PUNTUALIDAD): The perceived punctuality of teachers shows a significant positive association with TERCE 2013, but in ERCE 2019, this association reverses and becomes negative, indicating a change in its effect over time.

Science: In TERCE 2013, socioeconomic status has a significant positive association, while school climate is not significant. In ERCE 2019, socioeconomic status remains significant and positive, and both teacher support and teacher punctuality have significant positive association.

Support (APOYO): Both in TERCE 2013 and ERCE 2019, teacher support has a significant positive association on science learning achievement.

School Climate (CLIMA): In TERCE 2013, school climate does not show a significant association on science learning achievement, but in ERCE 2019, it has a significant negative association.

Teacher Punctuality (PUNTUALIDAD): The perceived punctuality of teachers shows a significant positive association TERCE 2013, but in ERCE 2019, this association reverses and becomes negative.

The R^2 values indicate how effectively the model accounts for variability in student outcomes at both the individual and school levels, offering insights into the model's efficacy in capturing the intricacies of the data over time.

In the context of ERCE 2019, there is a decrease in R^2 values compared to TERCE 2013, and this trend holds consistently across all application areas. This decline suggests that as time progresses, the model's ability to explain variability in scores appears to diminish. This, in turn, may imply a decrease in the perceived effectiveness of teaching practices and their impact on student outcomes.

Variance Decomposition

The coefficient and regressors from the regression analysis described above are used as an input for the OB decomposition. The results of three models, one for reading, math, and science, are presented in Table 5. The model indicates that the academic performance in Latin America decreased between 2013 and 2019, a total of 14.7 in math, 12.29 in reading and 5.2 in science. Although this only accounts for approximately 10% of a standard deviation of the ERCE scale (5% in science), it reveals in the best case, a stagnation phase of the region when it comes to learning achievement. Thus, in order to understand the current picture of Latin American countries, the results of the model share light of how the observed variables on teachers are playing a role in the present scenario. Normally, the OB decomposition would help us understand how different variables explain part of the gap between two groups. However, in this case, the decomposition allows us to understand if these factors have a role on the stagnation or setback on academic performance in the region.

The last column of every table test (the total column) is the sum of the endowments or characteristics, coefficients, and interactions, and it can be interpreted as the total contribution of each variable to the difference between the 2019 and 2013 results. Whereas the socioeconomic status of the students and their families, and teacher support have a positive contribution, on the contrary climate, and punctuality have negative contribution overall.

On the other hand, the last row summarizes the total effect attributable to the difference of the characteristics, the total effect of the coefficients and the interaction. On three cases, the endowment effect is positive, suggesting an improvement in the effect of the characteristics in the 2019 group of students. In terms of the ERCE scale, 5 points of the reading test results can be attributable to the difference of the features between the two groups of students, whereas 3.5 and 4 points in math and science, respectively. Another way to interpretate these results

Table 5. OB Variance Decomposition.

	Reading				Math				Science			
	Endow. effect	Coef. effect	Inter.	Total	Endow. effect	Coef. effect	Inter.	Total	Endow. effect	Coef. effect	Inter.	Total
media_APOYO	−0.69	−0.22	−0.32	−1.23	−0.42	−0.10	−0.15	−0.67	−0.58	−0.02	−0.03	−0.63
media_CLIMA	1.37	1.65	0.87	3.89	0.93	0.41	0.24	1.58	0.82	1.13	0.65	2.60
media_ISECF_2	5.71	−0.01	−1.97	3.73	3.43	−0.01	−1.04	2.38	4.26	−0.01	1.06	3.19
media_PUNTUALIDAD	−0.58	−0.81	−1.51	−2.90	−0.44	−0.65	−1.11	−2.21	−0.50	−0.72	−1.22	−2.44
Intercept		−15.78		−15.78		−15.78		−15.78		−7.92		−7.92
Total	5.82	−15.18	−2.93	**−12.29**	3.50	−16.13	−2.06	**−14.70**	4.00	−7.54	−1.66	**−5.20**

would be considering if the students of the 2013 round had the same features of the students of round 2019, it would be expected an increase between 3.50 and 5.82 in their results depending on the test. However, this variability is almost completely concentrated in the socioeconomic status of the students, suggesting that the positive socioeconomic changes concentrated almost all variability. Very little or no changes can be attributed to differences on the perception of the students on teachers support, punctuality, and school environment climate.

Despite the fact some incrementation of the ERCE 2019 results should have been expected doe to socioeconomical changes, the complete endowment effect is counterbalanced by the portion of differential attributable to differing coefficients (or coefficient effect). Under the consideration of the endowments as the inputs and the coefficients as the returns of the characteristics, the negative value of the latter could suggest an increase of the school systems inefficiency. This could explain a lower academic performance in the region compared to the 2013 round. Nevertheless, the negative effect is concentrated almost entirely in the intercept, which accounts for the unobservable part of the model. The latter could suggest, at least, that the perception of teachers has not play a negative role in the explanation of the decreasing of students' performance in the region between two rounds. In fact, the perception on environment climate has a better return, although modest, on the 2019 round.

CONCLUSIONS

Achieving proficient levels in foundational learning is an imperative for any system seeking to raise the quality of life of their citizens. Thus, a cornerstone of the SDG 4 has been the monitoring of foundational learnings across the world. Raising proficiency levels in developing regions like Latin America has been particularly challenging due to structural inequalities, low resources, and investment into the education system. Results from the ERCE study and its predecessor TERCE have shown that performance of most educational systems is low and has been stagnant across time. Results from international assessments showed that socioeconomic differences have a strong association with the gaps in performance. However, research has also showed that school and teachers can also have an important association with student outcomes.

We used the ERCE 2019 and TERCE 2013 database to analyze to what extent the relative association of socioeconomic variables with student outcomes shifted through time in comparison with a set of teacher characteristics (school climate, student support, punctuality) in 14 countries in Latin America. For this purpose, we conducted using a series of hierarchical regressions and a variance decomposition method (OB) for the subjects of reading, mathematics, and science.

In our descriptive results of the means of teacher scales across time, we observed that teacher punctuality remains consistent, but the values for teacher support and school climate have diminished. The decline in support can potentially impact student learning and overall educational outcomes. This change in trend is a significant finding, pointing to a need for further investigation into the causes and potential interventions to reverse the decline. Regarding school climate, results also showed an average decrease in the positive perception between 2013 and 2019. This trend points to potential issues with the educational setting, such as inadequate facilities, resources, or support systems for students and teachers. A decline in the school environment climate can have far-reaching implications for student engagement, learning outcomes, and overall academic success. This finding underscores the importance of addressing school environment factors to improve educational quality and equity.

As expected, one consistent result from the regression analysis is that socioeconomic status has a positive and significant association with student outcomes in all subjects. The findings show the inescapable power of socioeconomic factors on student outcomes and the need to develop sound school strategies to compensate for these potential inequalities. Teacher support and teacher punctuality show a significant positive influence on learning achievement in all areas, while school climate has a significant negative influence. The coefficients of influence of these factors may vary between measurements, suggesting changes in the importance of these factors over time. Our study is aligned with the research showing consistent results on the importance of the support and classroom interactions on student outcomes. Policy and research should invest efforts in identifying what are the effective interactions and support dynamics that contribute to student outcomes. As the scale takes into consideration perceptions of the students, they should be taken into account when assessing the effectiveness of the teaching strategy.

We note the contra intuitive result concerning the association between school climate and student outcomes, the higher the positive perception of school climate the lower the performance of students. This finding goes against what is usually found in the literature, which is the higher the positive perception of school climate the higher the student outcome. We believe that this result is actually a product of the regression model specification. The model was not controlled by countries fixed effects, and thus the negative significance level might be attributing to "noise" derived from the random specification. We conducted the same analyses country by country and our results showed that the association between school climate and student outcomes was positive significant for four systems and not significant for the rest. For future iterations, it would be ideal to run the model again with fixed effect specification.

OB variance decomposition method provides us additional insight about how much of the results can be attributed to the socio-economic background of the students and how much to teacher-related factors. Our results showed that the amount of the variation explained by socio-economic factors increased from one cycle to another in all tests for sixth grade. However, the proportion of the variance explained by the indexes related to teachers work only explained a small percentage of this variance and this has barely changed over time. As such, the results are disappointing since contrary to our expectation teacher scales have not been able to explain a higher degree of the variance across years. On the contrary, the power of socioeconomic factors has increased. These findings showed a worrisome scenario where variables susceptible of policy interventions such as teacher policies might been having little influence on student outcomes. Attention should be put on the overall effectiveness of school systems and the quality of current educational policies in Latin America to assess their impact for student learning.

LIMITATIONS

The limitation encountered by the study is mainly methodological. We were limited to the variables that were comparable between the two cycles of the ERCE study. Although, from the existing literature it would have been convenient to select teacher variables more grounded in the classroom practices, we were severely limited by the available indicators in these studies.

We also sought to run the analysis under the fixed effect model approach. The advantages of a fixed effect model are that it can account for unobservable country parameters and provide more robust estimates. However, the model proved to be too restrictive and limited the interpretability of the model. For a fixed effect model to be pursued, it is advisable to explore other model parameters or explore different sample sizes.

Also, we attempted to standardize the scales across the cycles to improve the comparability of the scales. However, since the standardization process was not able to converge for some countries, it would have meant to reduce the sample size. Thus, we made the decision to prioritize the sample size and left the scales not standardized across the cycles.

Finally, it would be advisable to continue the exploration between student outcomes and teacher variables at a country level rather than using averages, as we expect to be considerable heterogeneity on the significance and type of effects across these variables.

NOTES

1. In 2013, ERCE acronym was TERCE, which stood for Third Regional Comparative and Explanatory Study.
2. A total of 14 countries participated in round 2013 and 2019: Argentina, Brazil, Colombia, Costa Rica, Dominican Republic, Ecuador, Guatemala, Honduras, Mexico, Nicaragua, Panama, Paraguay, Peru, and Uruguay.

REFERENCES

Arteaga, I., & Glewwe, P. (2019). Do community factors matter? An analysis of the achievement gap between indigenous and non-indigenous children in Peru. *International Journal of Educational Development, 65*, 80–91. https://doi.org/10.1016/j.ijedudev.2017.08.003

BIFIE, Robitzsch, C., & Oberwimmer, K. (2022). *Tools for survey statistics in educational assessment. R package version 3.4-15*. https://CRcN.R-project.org/package=BIFIEsurvey

Blanco, E. (2019). Análisis de la brecha de aprendizaje entre indígenas y no indígenas en la enseñanza primaria en México. *Revista Electrónica de Investigación Educativa, 21*, 1–15. https://doi.org/10.24320/redie.2019.21.e16.1941

Blazar, D. & Kraft, M. (2017). Teacher and teaching effects on students' attitudes and behaviors. *Educational Evaluation and Policy Analysis, 39*(1), 146–170. http://dx.doi.org/10.3102/0162373716670260

Can Teaching Overcome Socioeconomic Inequality in Latin America? 173

Blinder, A. S. (1973). Wage discrimination: Reduced form and structural estimates. *The Journal of Human Resources, 8*(4), 436–455. https://doi.org/10.2307/144855

Carrasco, D., Rutkowski, D., & Rutkowski, L. (2023). The advantages of regional large-scale assessments: Evidence from the ERCE learning survey. *International Journal of Educational Development, 102*. https://doi.org/10.1016/j.ijedudev.2023.102867

Chetty, R., Friedman, J., & Rockoff, J. (2014). Measuring the impacts of teachers I: Evaluating bias in teacher value-added estimates. *American Economic Review, 104*(9), 2593–2632. http://dx.doi.org/10.1257/aer.104.9.2593

Chmielewski, A. (2019). The global increase in the socioeconomic achievement gap, 1964 to 2015. *American Sociological Review, 84*(3), 517–544. https://doi.org/10.1177/0003122419847165

Creemers, B., & Kyriakides, L. (2010). School factors explaining achievement on cognitive and affective outcomes: Establishing a dynamic model of educational effectiveness. *Scandinavian Journal of Educational Research, 54*(3), 263–294, http://dx.doi.org/10.1080/00313831003764529

Gevrek, Z. E., Gevrek, D., & Neumeier, C. (2020). Explaining the gender gaps in mathematics achievement and attitudes: The role of societal gender equality. *Economics of Education Review, 76*. https://doi.org/10.1016/j.econedurev.2020.101978

Hattie, J. (2009). *Visible learning: A synthesis of over 800 meta-analyses relating to achievement.* Routledge.

Jackson, C., Rockoff, J., & Staiger, D. (2014). Teacher effects and teacher-related policies. *Annual Review of Economics, 6*, 801–825. http://dx.doi.org/10.1146/annureveconomics-080213-040845

Jann, B. (2008). *The Blinder–Oaxaca decomposition for linear regression models.* https://doi.org/10.1177/1536867X0800800401

Lounkaew, K. (2013). Explaining urban–rural differences in educational achievement in Thailand: Evidence from PISA literacy data. *Economics of Education Review, 37*, 213–225. https://doi.org/10.1016/j.econedurev.2013.09.003

Muijs, D., Kyriakides, L., van der Werf, G., Creemers, B., Timperley, H., & Earl, L. (2014). State of the art: Teacher effectiveness and professional learning. *School Effectiveness and School Improvement, 25*(2), 231–256, http://dx.doi.org/10.1080/09243453.2014.885451.

Muijs, D., & Reynolds, D. (2001). *Effective teaching: Evidence and practice.* Sage Publications.

Oaxaca, R. (1973). Male-female wage differentials in urban labor markets. *International Economic Review, 14*(3), 693–709. https://doi.org/10.2307/2525981

OECD. (2021). *Positive, high-achieving students?: What schools and teachers can do.* TALIS, OECD Publishing. https://doi.org/10.1787/3b9551db-en

OECD. (2023). *PISA 2022 results (Volume I): The state of learning and equity in education.* PISA, OECD Publishing. https://doi.org/10.1787/53f23881-en

Oreiro, C., & Valenzuela, J. P. (2012). *Factores que determinan el desempeño educativo en el Uruguay, 2003–2006.* https://hdl.handle.net/11362/11549

Parvez, A., & Laxminarayana, K. (2022). Mathematics learning inequality among children of private and public schools. *Asia Pacific Education Review, 23*(2), 257–269. https://doi.org/10.1007/s12564-021-09733-6.

Romuald, N. K. (2023). An analysis of inequalities in school performance between public and private students in sub-Saharan Africa. *International Journal of Educational Development, 100*, 102802. https://doi.org/10.1016/j.ijedudev.2023.102802

Scheerens, J. (2001). School effectiveness research. In N. Smelser and P. Baltes (Eds.), *International encyclopedia of the social & behavioral sciences.* Elsevier. http://dx.doi.org/10.1016/b0-08-043076-7/02438-4

Snijders, T. C. B., & Bosker, R. J. (2012). *Multilevel analysis: An introduction to basic and advanced multilevel modeling.* SAGE Publications.

Teddlie, C., & Reynolds, D. (Eds.). (2000). *The international handbook of school effectiveness research.* Routledge.

UNESCO. (2016). *Tercer Estudio Regional Comparativo y Explicativo: Reporte técnico.* https://unesdoc.unesco.org/ark:/48223/pf0000247123

UNESCO. (2022). *Los aprendizajes fundamentales en América Latina y el Caribe: Informe de resultados del Estudio Regional Comparativo y Explicativo – ERCE 2019.* https://unesdoc.unesco.org/ark:/48223/pf0000380257

UNESCO-UNICEF-CEPAL (2022). *La encrucijada de la educación en América Latina y el Caribe. Informe regional de monitoreo ODS4-Educación.* https://unesdoc.unesco.org/ark:/48223/pf0000382636

United Nations. (2023). *Report on the 2022 Transforming Education Summit, New York.* https://transformingeducationsummit.sdg4education2030.org/report2022

Wayne, A. & Youngs, P. (2003). Teacher characteristics and student achievement gains: A review. *Review of Educational Research, 73*(1), 89–122, https://doi.org/10.3102/00346543073001089.

Willms, J. (2006). *Learning divides: Ten policy questions about the performance and equity of schools and schooling systems.* UNESCO Institute for Statistics.

CONTEXTUALIZING THE CIVIC ROLES OF POSTSECONDARY INSTITUTIONS WITH INSIGHTS FROM DIFFERENT TRADITIONS

Jakob Kost[a], Leping Mou[b] and Michael O'Shea[c]

[a]Bern University of Teacher Education, Switzerland
[b]University of Glasgow, UK
[c]University of Toronto, Canada

ABSTRACT

This paper explores the profound philosophical and conceptual foundations that underpin comparative international education research, particularly concerning the evolving roles of universities and colleges that transcend mere skills training or human capital development in contemporary times. Universities and colleges have predominantly focused on measuring their success through criteria such as research excellence and their ability to adapt to the ever-evolving demands of the job market. It is imperative to recognize that the diversity of postsecondary institutions is not only providers of human capital with curriculum shaped by labor market needs; rather, they should be recognized as institutions dedicated to human development, community anchors, the promotion of the public good, democratic education, the cultivation of civil society, and global citizenship. Relying on an extensive review of selected literature pertaining to the mission, goals, aims, and roles of the postsecondary sector in three regions (East Asia, Germanic Europe, and North America), this paper considers the question, "How do different approaches and traditions in different social contexts contribute to our understanding of the civic roles of postsecondary education institutions in shaping future global citizens, transcending the confines of national boundaries?" Throughout the paper, the unique contexts

---

Annual Review of Comparative and International Education 2023
International Perspectives on Education and Society, Volume 48, 175–196
Copyright © 2025 by Emerald Publishing Limited
All rights of reproduction in any form reserved
ISSN: 1479-3679/doi:10.1108/S1479-367920240000048010

and traditions of these regions are meticulously examined alongside thematic discussions, culminating in comprehensive analyses on what factors are considered as the civic roles of institutions and what challenges are there for them to realize their goals.

Keywords: Comparative education; international education; civic education; contextualization; tradition; democracy

INTRODUCTION

In an era of globalization and prevailing neoliberalism, postsecondary institutions such as universities and colleges have predominantly focused on measuring their success through criteria such as research excellence and their ability to adapt to the ever-evolving demands of the job market (Harvey, 2000; Marginson, 2009). However, this myopic approach often neglects other vital dimensions of their mission (Marginson, 2023). These institutions play a pivotal role not only in equipping individuals with job-specific skills but also in cultivating responsible citizenship and nurturing the capacity for lifelong learning. It is imperative to recognize that the diversity of postsecondary institutions is not only providers of human capital (Marginson, 2019; Moodie et al., 2019) with curriculum shaped by labor market needs; rather, they should be esteemed as institutions dedicated to human development, community anchors, the promotion of the public good (Marginson & Yang, 2022), democratic education (Molnar, 2010), the cultivation of civil society, and global citizenship (Franco, 2002). This perspective is especially critical in our current age, marked by geopolitical conflicts and the resurgence of nationalism.

We have yet to see studies examining regional differences in understanding of the civic role of postsecondary education institutions including universities and vocational institutions (e.g., TVET; Rojewski, 2009). Furthermore, the prevailing global higher education (HE) model has heavily been influenced by the Anglo-American paradigm (Marginson, 2022). The discourse on decolonization in HE underscores the need for a reevaluation of the future trajectory of HE (Stein & Andreotti, 2016), one that draws insights from diverse traditions and values. Such an approach is integral to our aspiration for a future characterized by inclusivity, diversity, and sustainability. Consequently, this paper is centered on a key research question: How do different approaches and traditions in different social contexts contribute to our understanding of the civic roles of postsecondary education institutions in shaping future global citizens, transcending the confines of national boundaries?

The paper delves into a comprehensive examination of selected literature elucidating the multifaceted roles of postsecondary education within diverse social landscapes across regions in East Asia, Europe, and North America. Employing the conceptual framework of "beyond national containers" (Shahjahan & Kezar, 2013), the discussion navigates through specific social and cultural traditions and values, shedding light on both the ideals of postsecondary education and the challenges encountered within contemporary societies due to various social and political factors. It extends the discussion of the civic roles of postsecondary institutions situated within a broader context of the social roles, encompassing aspects such as economic and social development, self-formation, knowledge dissemination, scientific advancement, health and environmental considerations, as well as the dynamics of politics and power. Throughout the paper, the unique contexts and traditions of these regions are meticulously examined alongside thematic discussions, culminating in comprehensive analyses on what factors are considered as the civic roles of institutions and what challenges are there for them to realize their goals. Throughout the paper, given the diverse contexts, we use postsecondary education or institutions to encompass the range of educational systems or pathways in various regional contexts, which include higher education, universities, and colleges.

SOCIAL ROLES OF POSTSECONDARY INSTITUTIONS: HISTORY AND CONTEXT

In this section, we briefly review the history and evolution of higher learning and postsecondary institutions by examining their relationship to social contexts, traditions, and values from which they emerged, together with the broader social roles they have played and their contributions to our globalized world. Higher learning and HE institutions (HEIs) (broadly defined) have existed and been highly developed in many ancient civilizations such as in European, Indian, Islamic, and Chinese contexts, although contemporary postsecondary education models are primarily influenced by Anglo-American models (Sam & Van der Sijde, 2014). These institutions, formed within and being influenced by their social political context and cultural tradition and values, have played important roles in the social, economic, scientific, and knowledge development.

The European model of postsecondary/HEIs or the prototype of modern HEIs, exemplified by the Medieval universities (Bologna, Salerno, and Paris), emerged from guild structures and attained a status equivalent to that of the Church and empire, constituting a third power as a legal corporation or juristic person (Rashdall, 1895). These medieval universities functioned as communities of scholars, their identity and structure safeguarded by papal or imperial authority, thus operating outside of local political jurisdiction. This autonomy allowed for action based on scholarly knowledge and afforded intellectual freedom within these institutions. The universities of the Middle Ages were seen as a significant intellectual accomplishment, shaping the progress and intellectual growth of Europe more profoundly than any future educational institutions, through their structure, traditions, studies, and activities.

Compared with the European tradition, there was less independence in the higher learning and institutional traditions of China (Hayhoe, 2001). The higher learning institutions in the Chinese context can trace their origins back to the 12th century, with institutions as the Chinese Academy: Hanlin Academy and Shuyuan. Unlike the European tradition, the Chinese academy was not a singular institution with autonomy and academic freedom, but rather comprised two contrasting poles: one emphasizing intellectual authority through civil service exams as in Hanlin Academy, and the other emphasizing intellectual freedom, particularly evident in Shuyuan located in remote areas and associated with the Buddhist traditions of India (Hayhoe, 2001). While the Hanlin Academy focused on grooming officials for the government, emphasizing intellectual authority with scholars' capacity to serve as officials, the Shuyuan lacked the protection of a charter, leading to exhibited fragile intellectual freedom and fragmented local autonomy.

In the Chinese Academy, there is less independence for knowledge but an emphasis on application to society and its advancements. Moreover, in higher learning institutions, a strong emphasis on personal development as an all-around scholar or person was evident (De Bary, 2014). This emphasis was not only for personal perfection but also for serving the country with social responsibility, underpinning the mission of education. This tradition leads to a model of Chinese higher learning academy which is different from the European model characterized by institutional autonomy and academic freedom. The tradition from these institutions continues to influence intellectual and higher learning traditions within Chinese contexts and beyond, extending to East Asian societies that also share the cultural tradition of Confucianism.

Modern HE, influenced by the colonial process, transitioned to the North American context, where early colleges and universities like Harvard and Yale primarily served the church and trained clergy. Rapid development occurred in the 18th and 19th centuries, drawing inspiration from the German model of research universities based on Humboldt's vision for the University of Berlin, leading to the establishment of institutions like the University of Chicago and Johns Hopkins University, which aimed to serve society and advance scientific development (Fallis, 2016). As universities evolved, they shifted from being outside society to integral parts of it, needing to balance meeting societal needs by occasionally providing not only what society desires but also what it truly requires, while scholars and scientists remain attentive to significant societal issues (Flexner, 1930/1968).

Subsequent to the massification of HE, the modern university underwent a transformation into a multiversity, characterized by a systemic rather than organic structure, which impacts governance, faculty dynamics, public authority, and the role and quality of leadership. This transformation results in a diverse array of communities within the university, encompassing undergraduates, graduates, humanists, social scientists, scientists, professional schools, and administrators, with blurred boundaries extending to alumni, legislators, farmers, and businessmen (Kerr, 1982/2001).

In its evolution into the contemporary multiversity, modern postsecondary institutions play a crucial role in shaping today's rationalized and globalized world, serving as a cornerstone for global integration and the modern service economy (Schofer et al., 2021). These institutions drive societal change by expanding professions, rationalizing state and societal organizations, establishing common global frameworks, and fostering new societal movements (Schofer et al., 2021). However, amidst these societal implications, the intrinsic value of

Contextualizing the Civic Roles 179

HE in personal development and self-formation often gets overlooked in policy and implementation. Thus, Robson (2023) shifts the focus from human capital employment concerns to a broader scope of factors relating to employability, highlighting the importance of student and graduate agencies and their complex interactions with economic, social, and policy structures. Similarly, Mok (2023) emphasizes the role of liberal arts education in nurturing excellence, humanities, holistic development, and societal care beyond economic pursuits. Marginson (2023) argues that HE is a reflective process that fosters ongoing self-making and self-aware agency throughout life. Considering these backgrounds and the current social challenges regarding citizens' development for an uncertain and complex world, the civic roles of postsecondary education institutions, along with their implementation and implications, need examination for future development and addressing social problems. This examination should involve fostering future citizenship toward shared values of inclusion, equity, and diversity by drawing insights from various social traditions and values of HE development in different contexts.

CONCEPTUAL FRAMEWORK, METHODS, AND DATA SOURCES

The method for this paper primarily relies on an extensive review of selected literature pertaining to the mission, goals, aims, and roles of the postsecondary sector in three regions: East Asia (Mainland China, Japan, and Taiwan), Europe (Switzerland and German speaking regions), and North America (Canada and USA). In reflecting on civic roles of postsecondary education we also drew on our experiences as scholar practitioners in the three study contexts. Direct translations of "civic" role (an English term with Latin political roots) led to varying search results in the different languages and had to be adapted linguistically and culturally in some cases. As we move through our discussion of "civic" roles of postsecondary education, we are aware of the limitations the word and framing of this word, as described in the Tractatus logico-philosphicus by Ludwig Wittgenstein "the limits of my language mean the limits of my world" (Wittgenstein, 1922/1998).

Civic is a Latin word with origins in the Ancient Roman political structure. It means: of or relating to a citizen, a city, citizenship, or community affairs and derived from Latin for citizen, or civis (Civic, 2024). Thus it will necessitate a different meaning in translation or relationship to other contexts. To a certain degree, this obscures international differences, among different languages, nation states, and nations. For example, a translation in a Germanic context might be *zivilgesellschaftlich* "regarding civil society"; in the Chinese context, it might be *gōngmín*. However, each translation will necessarily be imperfect as language reflects social and political realities.

The approach involves an in-depth examination of existing scholarship to elucidate current trends, via mapping conceptions of postsecondary institutions' civic roles. We recognize the rich diversity of institutional forms of postsecondary

180   JAKOB KOST ET AL.

institutions in our three study regions and admit that the features and themes might not cover all the institutions of the whole region due to the limitation of selected and available literature.

Literature review started with search terms "civic," "higher education," and the respective region. This yielded widely varying results depending on the context, which had to be adapted in a context-sensitive way. For example, during the research process, descriptions of "civic universities" (Goddard et al., 2016, p. 10) from the European context were used, to which various dimensions are attributed, such as a pronounced sense of place, active engagement with the wider world or a holistic approach to engagement (Goddard et al., 2016).

DISCUSSION ON CIVIC ROLES: COMPARING CONTEXTS AND TRADITIONS

In the following, we describe the civic role of postsecondary institutions in the three regions East Asia (Mainland China, Japan, Taiwan), Europe (Switzerland and German-speaking countries), and North America (USA and Canada). In today's global landscape, postsecondary institutions play a multifaceted civic role, transcending mere academic pursuits. Across nations, they shape societal values and foster community engagement. These institutions prepare students for active participation in society, emphasizing personal development and self-formation alongside academic achievement. Drawing from Confucian ideals and the principles of experiential learning, they offer a holistic approach to student growth and emphasize the sense of social responsibility and community engagement, and collective good. Echoing the Humboldtian tradition of "Bildung," they cultivate individuals capable of critical thinking and societal contribution. While job training remains vital, the focus extends to personal, social, and economic mobility. Moreover, postsecondary institutions provide spaces for deliberation and the pursuit of pure knowledge, fostering research generation and intellectual curiosity. They serve as dynamic hubs for societal advancement, embodying the intersection of academia, community, and civic responsibility.

East Asia: Japan, Taiwan, Mainland China

Asian Civic Values
In East Asian societies, civic values are deeply rooted in a sense of community or collective identity (Cho & Kim, 2012). Thus, the role of individuals is closely related to communal harmony and collective well-being, drawing from Confucian principles of morality and responsibility toward family and community. In these cultures, the notion of citizenship extends beyond individual rights to encompass the greater good and moral education, reflecting a commitment to shared values of civics (Print, 2000). Citizenship education emphasizes on morality rather than politics, leading to the common term "civic and moral education" instead of "civics education." Many Asian countries prioritize the development of individuality (centered on the self) and societal relations within citizenship education

(Lee, 2004). Despite the traditional underpinnings of East Asian civic identity, there exists a dynamic interplay between traditional civic values and democratic orientations of Western ideas with the influence of globalization and mobility (Cho & Kim, 2012; Kennedy, 2021). This hybridity allows for the integration of democratic values while retaining cultural roots, demonstrating an adaptation to evolving societal norms. Thus, East Asian civic identities navigate a delicate balance, incorporating both traditional (with undemocratic orientations) and democratic ideals to foster a sense of community and collective responsibility.

Influence of Confucianism on Postsecondary/Higher Education
The influence of Confucianism on HE in East Asia permeates various aspects of the system, including governance, participation, and cultural perceptions on the outcomes of HE. Marginson (2011) argued that the Confucian model of HE shapes governance structures and funding mechanisms, portraying education as a private duty intertwined with familial and societal obligations. The emphasis on high-stake exams and the pursuit of world-class universities reflects a hierarchical sense ingrained in Confucian values, often entwined with public funding priorities in research science. Choi and Nieminen (2013) highlight the cultural significance attached to successful entry into university, not merely as a personal achievement but as a victory for the entire family, underscoring the enduring influence of Confucian traditions on educational aspirations. Furthermore, Marginson and Yang (2022) elucidate how the Confucian concept of the public good, collective welfare (*Gong*), underpins the understanding of HE outcomes, emphasizing social values and communal benefits. In essence, Confucianism shapes HE in East Asia by intertwining familial duties, societal expectations, and a collective ethos, thereby influencing governance structures, perceptions of success, and the broader societal role of HE.

Considering the tradition and its strong influence, scholars envisioned a model of Chinese postsecondary institutions. For example, the Chinese model of HE, as envisioned in the concept of Chinese University 3.0, is distinguished by its inclusive nature, drawing from both Chinese cultural traditions and Western models, rather than simply hybridizing the two (Li, 2019). Central to this model is the incorporation of Confucian ethics, particularly exemplified by the concept of *Zhi-Xing*, which emphasizes ethical knowing and doing in alignment with Confucian humanism. *Zhi-Xing* underscores the mission of HE to cultivate innate virtue, promote societal renewal, and strive for the highest good, reflecting the profound influence of Confucian epistemology on Chinese approaches to learning and education.

Thus, the Chinese model of HE combines cultural heritage with modern innovation to foster a holistic and ethically grounded approach to teaching and learning. Specifically, normal universities in China represent a distinctive manifestation of the envisioned Chinese model of HE, blending traditional Confucian cultural values with influences from French and Anglo-American educational paradigms (Wu & Hayhoe, 2023). The term "normal" (*shifan*) itself conveys the idea of being a model in both teaching and morality, reflecting the ethical underpinnings deeply ingrained in these institutions. Through their integration of Confucian, Christian, and socialist values, normal universities play a pivotal role in cultivating responsible citizenship and fostering a cosmopolitan outlook that emphasizes human agency. This synthesis of diverse philosophical traditions underscores the unique position of normal universities as embodiments of the evolving Chinese model of HE, bridging tradition and modernity while shaping the ethical and intellectual landscape of society.

Civic and Citizenship Education in Universities: Implementation and Challenge
Research has identified the implementation of the civic roles of HEIs through social responsibility and community engagement. In a study on the public roles of universities in Japan, Takagi (2024) examined the significance of these roles as perceived by faculty members and whether universities actively fulfilled them. Regression analysis revealed the influence of individual and organizational factors on two distinct modes of perception: one emphasizing the economic-social responsibilities of universities and the other highlighting their civic-democratic duties.

Through the notion of "engaged universities," Chan (2022) argued that the social and civic mission of HE should be emphasized in this age, facing the dominance of economic and financial returns of HE. Specifically, he proposed that the Confucian influence on the understanding of intellectuals/educated persons with contributions to their society, should be reflected in the reconstructing of engaged universities for nurturing students as active citizens meeting social challenges, in fulfilling the function of universities with social responsibilities. He examined the case of Japan and Taiwan for their policy and initiatives in advancing the engaged universities with social responsibilities. In Japan, the government launched initiatives of the Center of Community Project (CCP) and the Program for Promoting Regional Revitalization by Universities as Centers of Community. The initiatives were intended to have universities taking greater responsibility for revitalizing the local community and rural development. Similarly, in Taiwan, the government initiated the policy of University Social Responsibility (USR) to urge universities to serve as think tanks for local development through cultivating students with innovation and locality in meeting local needs. The strategy for the university's role also focused on a few themes of development, such as local care, industrial linkage and economic sustainability, health promotion and food security, cultural sustainability, and sustainable environment. Moreover, universities are advised to integrate the Sustainable Development Goals (SDGs) of the UN agenda into their missions. In Japan and Taiwan, state-led initiatives aim to strengthen social and civic development within universities (Chan, 2022). However, challenges arise from the dominance of neoliberal policies for materialistic, instrumental, and utilitarian perspectives of the function of HE and the constricting environment of academic freedom, which may hinder the advancement of social and civic development agendas.

Through a nationwide survey of college students in China in the period of moving from elite to mass HE, Li (2009) examined the university experience and factors that influence students political orientations and socializations toward citizenship and civil society. The study found that generally students have a positive evaluative orientation toward civil society, which could trace its origin to the influence of Confucian values about the civil rights and responsibility of intellectuals.

Contextualizing the Civic Roles

Also, the study found that students' political orientation plays a significant role in the process of their political socialization. The findings highlight the need for policymakers and administrators of HE for a reevaluation of the purpose and role of HE in cultivating students as citizens. It is implied that universities could open more opportunities such as service learning and community-based programs for students to develop more fully engaged citizens. This reevaluation is suggested to be based on both Confucian values, emphasizing moral self-cultivation and public engagement, and Deweyan principles, promoting education as a civic function and fostering associated living (Li, 2009).

Furthermore, citizenship education in universities in China is dominated by an unbalanced curriculum on political matters and current affairs, with a strong motivation to maintain and promote a sense of national identity and patriotism in students (Tu, 2011). Thus, university students tend toward thin citizenship, demonstrating positive civic attitudes but lacking strong evidence of participatory citizenship. Tu's study revealed that universities in China have a paradoxical role in promoting active citizenry among students, with findings indicating both a significant impact on civic engagement attributed to the university environment and a perceived lack of support, particularly in terms of citizenship education curriculum. The study suggests the need for citizenship education curricula to incorporate experiential learning approaches (Tu, 2011).

While citizenship education and school curricula have been dominated by the political ideology under Xi's administration, research also found that in the implementation process, institutional actors and faculty members have different understandings and illustrations of the meaning of citizenship education and what an ideal citizen in China should include (Zhao, 2023). Zhao's research found that, from the perspective of university faculty members, current citizenship education for university students is rooted in the ideological commitment of socialist core values, which include the prosperity of the nation, the rule of law, professional dedication, and embracing traditional Chinese cultural values such as harmony. Ideal citizenship also includes the ability to contribute to social responsibility and extend to a broader worldview of cosmopolitanism.

In addition, spiritual development rooted in traditional Chinese culture could be used to contribute to the understanding of core citizenship values, such as social justice, ideals, humanity, morality, and identity (Zhao, 2023). Despite the fact that traditional culture is manipulated by the state's ideological hegemony of producing patriotic, logical, and passive citizen subjects, traditional culture could still be valuable in empowering the meaning of citizenship, transcending national and cultural boundaries, drawing from an Asian context, which differs from the Western citizenship focusing on rights and responsibilities. The study argues that a bottom-up perspective could bring us different angles in looking into the understanding and nuances of citizenship education in universities and the institutional actors' role in the universally dominated political ideology of citizenship curriculum and education.

To sum up, influenced by the shared values of Confucianism, civic values in East Asia emphasize a strong sense of community or collective identity, reflecting the educational focus on fostering individuals with social responsibility and

184 JAKOB KOST ET AL.

a commitment to community well being. Universities are increasingly recognizing their role in promoting civic education and integrating the goal of social responsibility through engagement with local communities. However, challenges stemming from top-down political regimes impact the implementation of civic education, often emphasizing patriotism and nationalism. These challenges hinder universities' full engagement in their mission of community development, as they may prioritize global rankings and adopt a utilitarian focus on economic development.

Europe: Switzerland and German-Speaking Countries

Universities and Universities of Applied Sciences

In Switzerland and the surrounding German-speaking countries, postsecondary education is organized into various educational pathways, which primarily differ in their classification as vocational or general education. Higher vocational schools and training courses typically require prior vocational training qualifications at the secondary level, whereas general education institutions such as universities require general education qualifications obtained at the secondary level, commonly referred to as grammar schools (Gymnasium).

Universities still have aspects of the Humboldtian university (Anderson, 2004), in that they systematically combine teaching and research and offer study programs that are closely oriented toward scientific disciplines. Ideally, they are committed to scientific progress and the education of young scientists, but questions of the usefulness of knowledge (e.g., on the labor market) or topicality (in the sense of political discussions) only play a role in certain areas. Due to their focus on disciplines and international orientation, their civic role is difficult to determine, especially in a local or regional context.

Universities stand in contrast to universities of applied sciences (UAS) in the tertiary sector, which have emerged in Switzerland over the past 30 years (Böckelmann et al., 2021). Similar institutions exist in the surrounding German-speaking countries. UAS prepares students for professional activities through practical studies and applied research. Due to their practical orientation in education and research, they are more directly linked to local and regional actors in politics, business and society (SERI, 2022). In terms of their orientation and standards, they are comparable to institutions referred to as community colleges in the North American (Canada and the USA) context (Weber et al., 2010). Given their relatively recent establishment, it is pertinent to inquire specifically into the extent to which they assume a distinct civic role.

Civic Role of UAS

Previous studies have primarily focused on analyzing the content, strategic direction, and funding of research conducted by UAS (Lepori & Kyvik, 2010). Furthermore, several projects have explored the significance of UAS for local labor markets, with particular emphasis on their role as catalysts for innovation within regional industries (Pfister et al, 2021; Schlegel et al., 2022). But there is

Contextualizing the Civic Roles 185

no research that attempts to describe the ways in which they take on a specific civic role.

As Swiss research to date has not dealt with the civic role of UAS, the publicly available information on the nine public UAS in Switzerland, in particular their self-presentation and newspaper reports, had to be evaluated for this study. This revealed a diverse picture.

In abstract form, the civic role of UAS is evidenced through their mission statements and strategic priorities. These statements often emphasize commitments to sustainable development, frequently aligning with the United Nations SDGs, as well as to care work. Moreover, UAS demonstrates a consistent dedication to addressing regional needs stemming from both business and societal sectors. This focus is expected, given that universities in federally organized Switzerland rely on funding from the regional (cantonal) education administration.

For a more nuanced understanding of the civic role and engagement of UAS, the principle of subsidiarity, as articulated by Hega (2000), is pivotal. This principle emphasizes that decisions should be made at the lowest feasible level of authority and that policy functions ought to be carried out by the lowest level of government capable of effectively addressing the task at hand (Hega, 2000, p. 3). This principle is applicable not only to the administration of education in Switzerland in general but also to many aspects of decision-making and development within universities themselves.

Consequently, overt manifestations of civic engagement are often less apparent at the overarching university level. Instead, such engagement tends to manifest at lower levels, closer to the daily activities of educators, students, and external partners. This can be observed through various means, such as public outreach events, community service initiatives, research and development endeavors that tackle specific community challenges, or educational programs that incorporate service learning methodologies.

The civic role of UAS can therefore be seen externally, through their appearance, communication, and cooperation. However, it also manifests itself internally, in internal processes and, in particular, in their interaction with students.

Specifically, study programs reveal tangible understandings of education that go well beyond the teaching of specific skills – this is the case where aspects are implemented in which education is understood as reflection in the context of one's actions, where ethical questions of professional action are discussed, where transformational processes are triggered in the students themselves, but also where professionalism is not only addressed in the context of a particular work task, but also where the social and political involvement of individual action is taken into account at local, regional, national, and international levels.

Bildung
In this internal civic role, a specific understanding of education becomes clear, which in the German-speaking context (and not only at UAS, but in all branches of the education system) can be described with the concept of "Bildung" (Bauer, 2003). Even if "Bildung" is sometimes directly translated as education in everyday

language, it has an extended meaning in pedagogical discourse. "Bildung" is a process of self-cultivation that traditionally has two different dimensions: "Bildung as 'inner' self-formation, and Bildung as the acquisition of a comprehensive knowledge based on an institutionalized canon of cultural traditions transmitted through the educational system" (Bauer, 2003, p. 211).

Originally, from the 18th century onwards, the term "Bildung" also had a social-transformative meaning, that is, one that concerned people's civic role.

> Bildung was here conceptualized in its core as a creative reconstruction and transformation of cultural and social experiences [...]. This critical impetus [...] was directed toward a change of social structures as well as a search for new forms of possible self–world relationships. (Bauer, 2003, p. 211)

We can see from these explanations that the civic role that UAS assumes is not only manifested in externally visible actions. With an understanding of education that refers to the concept of "Bildung," a central pedagogical dimension is thus named, which shapes the internal structures, the organization of learning opportunities, curricula and thus the entire pedagogical understanding.

Civic Role as a Function of the Education System?

The specific civic role of educational institutions is thus manifested in various externally visible and internally tangible actions. Furthermore, the inquiry into the civic role of educational institutions prompts a broader consideration. It evokes contemplation on the overarching relationship between the education system and society, and the role played by the education system and its institutions within society.

Since educational credentials are frequently linked with rights of access to further education or entry into regulated professions in the German-speaking context, discussions regarding the role of educational institutions within society are strongly aligned with the principle of utility. Within the framework of the Varieties of Capitalism literature, Switzerland and Germany are conventionally categorized as coordinated market economies (Hall & Soskice, 2001), characterized by close coordination among labor organizations, regulatory state bodies, and educational institutions regarding the design and content of educational qualifications. If education is primarily discussed in terms of its utility within the education system and on the labor market, it's clear why the specific civic role of educational institutions is often overlooked. Furthermore, educational institutions are predominantly public and funded by taxpayers' money. Consequently, these institutions also serve society as a whole to a certain extent. In consequence, there is a notable absence of discussions concerning the role of educational institutions within civil society.

On a more abstract level, Helmut Fend presented a general theory of the relationship between educational institutions and society (Fend, 2001). He described from a structural-functionalist perspective that educational institutions perform three central functions: (1) the reproduction of cultural systems: "This involves mastering basic symbolic systems ranging from language and writing to acquiring specific professional qualifications. Accomplished by instruction, this function is referred to hereafter as the *qualifying function*" (Fend, 2001, p. 4263); (2) the selection function "By way of school-based learning of qualifications, verified by a detailed system of examinations, the young generation is allocated to stratified occupational positions *(allocation and selection)*" (Fend, 2001); and (3) the function of social integration "School systems are instruments of social integration. Reproduction of norms, values, and belief systems serve to reinforce prevailing power relationships" (Fend, 2001).

From this viewpoint, educational institutions serve as mediators of the skills necessary for engaging in civic processes, while also being pivotal and legitimate tools in shaping disparities within civil society – disparities that, in certain instances, may restrict opportunities for civic engagement. As a result, a multitude of questions have emerged in research concerning the reproduction of social inequality by educational institutions overall, and specifically UAS.

UAS offers a promising avenue for educational progression, especially for individuals commencing their careers with an initial vocational education. Despite prior critiques questioning the extent to which UAS can help effectively mitigate social disparities in educational achievement (Kost, 2013) on a societal level, a degree from such institutions can indeed serve as a catalyst for economic and social mobility, at least on an individual level.

In summary, the civic role of educational institutions in Switzerland and the surrounding German-speaking countries is founded on an understanding of education that fosters inner self-cultivation, imparts cultural techniques and norms, and aims to equip individuals with the skills to shape and advance their social environment. However, these underlying structures often remain obscured, possibly overshadowed by the prevailing discourse on the utility of education.

North America: USA and Canada

The USA and Canada, despite major differences in size, population, and governance, share similarities, especially in relation to the other countries of North America (e.g., Mexico). For this reason they are worth considering as an analytic unit in this paper. Both are capitalist, multicultural liberal democracies with national immigrant identifies. Both are former British colonies and Settler colonial states that occupy Indigenous homelands and whose prosperity was built through the labor of enslaved peoples, immigrants, and low-wage workers (Estes, 2019; Wilder, 2013).

It may also be difficult to generalize about both countries' HE systems. The U.S. system is famously decentralized and heterogeneous, combining elements of elitism and mass access (Labaree, 2007). There are many influences of U.S. HE (Labaree, 2017; Thelin, 2011), including the English collegiate tradition, religious institutions, American liberal arts, and German research universities. There is "no such thing as a Canadian 'system' of higher education" (Jones, 1997, p. 1), which is shaped by English, US, French, and Indigenous traditions. Its approximately 280 institutions are "large, public, and amalgamated or federated, incorporated corporations under provincial legislation" (Jones, 1997, p. 6). However, there are nonetheless some major characteristics that invite comparisons and contrasts to HE in other regions or countries – and major points of comparison around civic roles that will be explored in this section.

The USA also has a longer self-narrative about "democracy" that is historically missing in Canada's origins story (e.g., de Tocqueville, 1835–1840). Though Canada today brands itself as a multicultural liberal democracy, it emerged as a country conservatively, without a violent revolution and accompanying revolutionary language. Both national origin stories, as national stories do, gloss over histories of exclusion, slavery, and discrimination affiliated with Settler colonialism. This national narrative affects the stories HE tells about themselves, such as through their mission statements. Several US colleges or universities include democracy in their mission statements, including Denison, Dickinson, and Miami Dade College (e.g., "Mission, Vision, and Core Values," 2024).

Civic Roles of HE in Region

Generally, literature in the recent period (from the 1990s onward) about civic roles focus on the following areas: supporting democracy and democratic habits of students, community engagement, and service learning. In the background is a story of decline (e.g., Perna et al., 2011) democratic erosion and broader social isolation (Putnam, 2000), and student disengagement with society. Thomas (1998) references hand-wringing at the University of Chicago, for example, dating this narrative of civic disengagement and decline to at least the 1980s on college campuses. One professor described his students as "lost souls … in the basement" (Bloom, 1987, quoted in Thomas, 1998, p. 6).

Serving Society/State and Strengthening Democracy

Serving and strengthening democracy is a persistent theme in the literature, accelerated since the Trump era, COVID-19 era, and continued attacks on democratic institutions. A report from Carnevale et al. (2020) is one example, which spots the rising tide of authoritarianism and notes HE's civic role in taming it through student education, liberal arts, and critical citizenship. Reflecting on an earlier period, Checkoway (2001) emphasizes the historic civic role of a research university and drift away from faculty and administrators: in both contexts, there is a sense that HE must do more in response to democratic decline and social issues (such as rising income inequality), especially in light of challenges in K-12 public schooling and communities that surround. HEIs, such as the Democratic Knowledge Project at Harvard University are directing HE resources and scholarships to support elementary and high school civic teachers ("Reimagining Civic Education," 2024).

In emphasizing contemporary college's civic responsibilities, authors frequently point to foundational documents and or historic roles of HE. This includes community college scholars (Franco, 2002, p. 1). Community colleges were created to democratize both American HE and the students who came through their open doors (Franco, 2002, p. 1). Scholars of American research universities strike a similar return-to-civic engagement tone, as they wrestle with HE's disengagement from this role:

Contextualizing the Civic Roles

> Many American research universities were established with a civic mission to prepare students for active participation in a diverse democracy and to develop knowledge for the improvement of communities ... it is hard to find top administrators with consistent commitment to this mission, few faculty members consider it central to their role, and community groups that approach the university for assistance often find it difficult to get what they need. (Checkoway, 2001, p. 125)

Preparing students for participation in a democratic society may compete with other goals of US HE, however, such as "social efficiency (training future employees) and local mobility (repairing individuals to compete for social positions" (Muñiz, 2024, p. 60). Such tension (Labaree, 1997) may explain various levels of engagement with this mission in US HE history.

Similar to the USA, there is concern about democratic disengagement in Canada. "In recent decades, Canada has witnessed a striking increase in political apathy among youth, mirroring trends in other parts of the Western world. The pressure for educators to cultivate civic participation among their students has thus mounted," note Bell and Lewis (2015, p. 1). In the Canadian context, there is a similar concern about democratic decline and how universities might respond in terms of community engagement, transmitting democratic values, citizenship, and service learning. Responding to this decline and flexing "civic responsibility is the contemporary version of higher education's historical outreach mission" (Thomas, 1998, p. 6).

Community Partnership, Service Learning, and Experiential Learning
Community partnerships – frequently connected to service and experiential learning – also occupy a large amount of the literature and also relate. "As noted, "there seems to be a proliferation of calls for creative pedagogical methods of fostering civic engagement and for the use of experiential learning in particular" (Bell & Lewis, 2015, p. 3). One salient example comes from Campus Compact, an organization of U.S. HEIs concerned about the state of U.S. demography. It was founded in 1985 by college presidents who "believed that higher education could be a more effective contributor to the sustainability of democracy with more robust support structures for community engagement" (About, 2023, para 12).

Foundational work and literature on university community partnership were carried out by Ira Harkavy at the University of Pennsylvania (e.g., Harkavy, 1996) and continues today through the university's Netter Center and Civic House. Benson and Harkavy (2000) put forth a necessary, "radical" proposal for US HE: "All higher-eds should explicitly make solving the problem of the American schooling system their highest institutional priority" (p. 48). They ask why the "great age" of American universities (writing in 2000) was also the period of crisis in US cities: mass deindustrialization, white flight, depopulation, racial conflict, and the effects of government segregation (Rothstein, 2017). The surest way for universities to support civic renewal is to invest and partner with K-12 school districts, thereby reinvigorating research universities' historic civic responsibility as part of a third revolution in HE toward a "democratic cosmopolitan civic university" (Benson & Harkavy, 2000, p. 47).[1] Such an approach draws upon the philosophies of Harper and Dewey (McCaul, 1959) who "placed schooling and education at the center of the American Progressive intellectual and institution-building agendas" (p. 49).

190   JAKOB KOST ET AL.

While appreciating the benefits of such partnerships, scholars of university-engagement urge caution, questioning the structures and impacts of community investment. Ratsoy (2016), for example, considers how neoliberalism creates the structural social economic conditions that create a space for such partnership to enter in the first place (Ratsoy, 2016, p. 77). Ehlenz (2016) considers to what extent university investment in West Philadelphia improved or gentrified (and displaced) the historically working-class black neighborhood surrounding the University of Pennsylvania.

Finally, community engagement has a deeper historical connection in the history of U.S. HE, namely the "booster" role of colleges in fledgling American (Settler) towns (Labaree, 2017; Thelin, 2011). A town of only a few hundred Settlers may seek to build a college, attracting only a handful of students as a way of boosting town pride and location of investment and further settlement. This legacy of universities as economic engines and community assets appears again in the "eds and meds" (e.g., Harkavy & Zuckerman, 1999) and literature around the turn of the last century and in the notion of urban colleges as "anchor institutions" (Birch et al., 2013).

In the same literature, amidst uptick in concern about democratic engagement is a concern about neoliberalism's eroding effect on HE's civic role. "Universities," he states, are being increasingly perceived as "institutions of the economy" – a role that "threatens to overwhelm their role as an institution of democracy," notes Ratsoy (2016, pp. 77–78). Giroux (2014) points to neoliberalism as a primary drive of democratic decline and erosion of education as a public good: "…the consequence of such dramatic transformations is the near-death of the university as a democratic public sphere" (p. 16).

There is a similar history of service learning in Canada that we see in the USA. Writing in 2016, for example, Thomas notes that "Many institutions profiled else-where in this paper have established and thriving programs in service-learning" (Thomas, p. 17). More recently, writing in 2018, King observed the growth in community engaged learning at Canadian universities including McMaster University, University of Toronto, and Cape Breton University in Newfoundland (King, 2018, p. 96).

There is also an acknowledgment that service learning and civic life have a longer history in the USA, and is "is a fairly recent experience in Canada." (Chambers, 2009, p. 78). Canadian universities are playing catchup: "it would appear that Canadian universities are increasingly recognizing the benefits of eroding barriers between the 'ivory tower' and the community surrounding them" (Bell & Lewis, 2015, p. 3). Service learning appears fairly widespread (Chambers, 2009) and may fit the university's mission of the preparation of responsible and engaged citizens (Chambers, 2009, p. 78). Work placements and project-based service learning at Canadian universities such as Cape Breton University, project a sense of university citizenship while fulfilling the university's historic commitment to social and economic development of the region.

Whose Civics in North America?
So far we have focused on the civic role of HE in these two contexts as they relate to the *civic* of the state, which are Settler states. Both states occupy or

Contextualizing the Civic Roles 191

have boundaries that encompass other sovereign Indigenous states. In those contexts HE plays a community-building role and is tied to tribal sovereignty and Native nation building (Brayboy, 2005; Nelson, 2015). The Tribal college movement is an example of this: locally controlled schools celebrate local culture and language, and connect Indigenous students to careers and community-uplifting employment.

Conversely focusing on single civic may obscure, universities are places of resistance and self-determination, born of necessity in response to oppression and segregation but also places of pride, achievement, mobility for the populations they serve. They serve their own community role. HBCUs (Historically Black Colleges and Universities), for example, founded when Black students were barred from attending white institutions, continue to their essential role in supporting Black achievement especially in the contemporary U.S. socio-political climate. Albritton (2012) notes that "HBCU history is deeply rooted in the Black community's commitment to racial uplift and community empowerment" (p. 312).

Civic is thus related to being citizens of a state, and in the particular state and in North American context means the Settler nation states of Canada and the USA. For this reason it's essential to disambiguate what kind of civil role we are referring to. If HE fails to advance social mobility for Indigenous students, for example, HE may fail in its social role but carry out its precisely civic role as intended – serving and strengthening the Settler colonial state and reproduction of power relations (Fend, 2001).

With an eye to these civic goals and idealism, we are cognizant of Canadian HE's shortfalls, and who has been excluded by design. While Canadian HE may be ostensibly founded on, and perceived as based on the "pursuit of knowledge, avant-garde in thinking, and fair in practice" (Henry et al., 2017, p. 3), the system has "consistently promised but persistently denied [social justice] for racialized and Indigenous scholars (p. 3)."

CONCLUSION

This paper explores the profound philosophical and conceptual foundations that underpin comparative international education research, particularly concerning the evolving roles of universities and colleges that transcend mere skills training or human capital development in contemporary times, as highlighted by Wheelahan et al. (2022). The paper goes one step further in exploring these conceptual foundations in a comparative educational context with a particular focus on East Asia (Mainland China, Taiwan, and Japan), Germanic Europe, and North America (Canada and USA). The paper addresses pressing questions that are integral to shaping our shared values in the civic roles of universities and colleges in the era of globalization, transcending the limitations of the "national container" (Shahjahan & Kezar, 2013). By moving beyond the "national container" and the dominant framework of the Anglo-American higher education model, the study explores the civic roles of postsecondary education institutions by taking into account traditions, values, and nuances in the context of different regions and how these factors influence and are reflected in current education systems and policies. Our vision is guided by a commitment to equity, diversity, and sustainability, while also emphasizing universities' role in nurturing global citizens. By cultivating these ideals, we aim to address the evolving challenges and opportunities that educational institutions face in our ever-changing world.

Across different regions, we discussed related themes regarding the civic role of postsecondary institutions. In East Asia, influenced by the Confucian value on the role of education and individual development, the focus lies on the public good, collective welfare, social responsibilities, and community engagement although these ideals have often been impacted by political regimes and neoliberal purposes. In the Germanic region, themes revolve around ideals of self-cultivation (Bildung), structural-functionalist perspectives on the role of HE within society and the importance of subsidiarity as a governance strategy, transcending national boundaries. In North America, emphasis is placed on serving society and strengthening democracy through community partnerships, service learning, and civic development. These regional themes coalesce into broader categories, such as serving society and local communities, preparing students for societal participation, fostering student self-formation, facilitating job training and economic mobility, promoting research, and providing spaces for deliberation.

Cross-nationally, the civic role of postsecondary institutions is underscored by various themes, reflecting its global significance. Institutions serve society and local communities by aligning initiatives with SDGs, emphasizing service learning, fostering university–community partnerships, and engaging in environmental projects. Through these efforts, students not only contribute directly to societal well-being but may also grasp the importance of active citizenship and collective responsibility.

Postsecondary education plays a pivotal role in preparing students for meaningful engagement in society by transmitting social norms and values. With the potential to serve as an incubator for civic development, postsecondary institutions introduce students to democratic principles, ethical behavior, and civic duties. This transmission of social norms lays the groundwork for students to become responsible citizens who embrace diversity, uphold justice, and actively participate in civic life. Additionally, the concept of student self-formation is central, drawing from Confucian ideals of self-cultivation, experiential learning, the liberal arts, or the German notion of "Bildung." Through these diverse approaches, students not only acquire knowledge but also cultivate critical thinking skills, empathy, and a profound sense of social responsibility crucial for effective civic engagement and making contributions to their community and beyond.

NOTE

1. The first two revolutions in the American (research) university is the German model at Johns Hopkins and the post-war research boom and expansion fueled by Cold War defense spending (Benson & Harkavy, 2000; Thelin, 2011).

REFERENCES

Albritton, T. J. (2012). Educating our own: The historical legacy of HBCUs and their relevance for educating a new generation of leaders. *The Urban Review*, *44*(3), 311–331. https://doi.org/10.1007/s11256-012-0202-9

Anderson, R. D. (2004). *European universities from the Enlightenment to 1914*. Oxford Academic Press.

Bauer, W. (2003). On the relevance of Bildung for democracy. *Educational Philosophy and Theory*, *35*(2), 211–225.

Bell, S., & Lewis, J. (2015). A survey of civic engagement education in introductory Canadian politics courses. *The Canadian Journal for the Scholarship of Teaching and Learning*, *6*(1). https://doi.org/10.5206/cjsotl-rcacea.2015.1.2

Benson, L., & Harkavy, I. (2000). Higher education's third revolution: The emergence of the democratic cosmopolitan civic university. *Cityscape*, *5*(1), 47–57.

Birch, E., Perry, D. C., & Taylor Jr, H. L. (2013). Universities as anchor institutions. *Journal of Higher Education Outreach and Engagement*, *17*(3), 7–16.

Böckelmann, C., Probst, C., Wassmer, C., & Baumann, S. (2021). Lecturers' qualifications and activities as indicators of convergence and differentiation in the Swiss higher education system. *European Journal of Higher Education*, *12*(3), 229–254. https://doi.org/10.1080/21568235.2021.1923547

Brayboy, B. M. J. (2005). Toward a tribal critical race theory in education. *The Urban Review*, *37*(5), 425–446. https://doi.org/10.1007/s11256-005-0018-y

Carnevale, A., Smith, N., Dražanová, L., Gulish, A., & Peltier Campbell, K. (2020). *The role of education in taming authoritarian attitudes* [Technical Report]. Georgetown University Center on Education and the Workforce. https://cadmus.eui.eu//handle/1814/68515

Chambers, T. (2009). A continuum of approaches to service-learning within Canadian post-secondary education. *Canadian Journal of Higher Education*, *39*(2), 77–100. https://doi.org/10.47678/cjhe.v39i2.486

Chan, S. J. (2022). Higher education and social and civic development: The experiences of engaged universities and social responsibility in the Asia-Pacific region. In W. O. Lee, P. Brown, A. L. Goodwin, & A. Green (Eds.), *International handbook on education development in Asia-Pacific* (pp. 1–17). Springer Nature.

Checkoway, B. (2001). Renewing the civic mission of the American research university. *The Journal of Higher Education*, *72*(2), 125–147. https://doi.org/10.1080/00221546.2001.11778875

Cho, Y. H., & Kim, T. J. (2012). Asian civic values: A cross-cultural comparison of three East Asian societies. *The Asia-Pacific Education Researcher*, *22*, 21–31.

Civic. (2024). In *Merriam-Webster dictionary*. https://www.merriam-webster.com/dictionary/civic

Choi, S. H. J., & Nieminen, T. A. (2013). Factors influencing the higher education of international students from Confucian East Asia. *Higher Education Research & Development*, *32*(2), 161–173.

De Bary, W. T. (2014). *The great civilized conversation: Education for a world community*. Columbia University Press.

de Tocqueville, A. (1835–1840). *De la démocratie en Amérique*. Saunders and Otley.

Ehlenz, M. M. (2016). Neighborhood revitalization and the anchor institution: Assessing the impact of the University of Pennsylvania's West Philadelphia initiatives on university city. *Urban Affairs Review*, *52*(5), 714–750. https://doi.org/10.1177/1078087415601220

Estes, N. (2019). *Our history is the future: Standing rock versus the Dakota access pipeline, and the long tradition of indigenous resistance*. Verso.

Fallis, G. (2016). *Multiversities, ideas, and democracy. Chapter 2: The idea of a university* University of Toronto Press.

Fend, H. (2001). Educational Institutions and Society. In N. Smelser & P. Baltes (Eds.), *International encyclopedia of the social & behavioral sciences* (pp. 4262–4266). Elsevier.

Flexner, A. (1930/1968). *Universities: American, English, German* (pp. 3–36). Oxford University Press.

Franco, R. W. (2002). The civic role of community colleges: Preparing students for the work of democracy. *The Journal of Public Affairs*, *6*(1), 119–136.

Giroux, H. A. (2014). *Neoliberalism's war on higher education*. Haymarket Books.

Goddard, J., Hazelkorn, E., Kempton, L., & Vallance, P. (Eds.). (2016). Chapter 1: Introduction: why the civic university? In *The Civic university*. Edward Elgar Publishing. Retrieved August 16, 2024, from https://doi.org/10.4337/9781784717728.00008

Hall, P. & Soskice, D. (2001). *Varieties of capitalism. The foundations of comparative advantage*. Oxford University Press.

Harkavy, I. R., & Zuckerman, H. (Eds.). (1999). *Eds and meds: Cities' hidden assets*. Brookings Institution, Center on Urban and Metropolitan Policy.

Harvey, L. (2000). New realities: The relationship between higher education and employment. *Tertiary Education & Management, 6*(1), 3–17.

Hayhoe, R. (2001). Lessons from the Chinese academy. In R. Hayhoe & J. Pan (Eds.), *Knowledge across cultures: A contribution to dialogue among civilizations* (pp. 323–347). Comparative Education Research Centre (CERC), University of Hong Kong.

Hega, G. M. (2000). Federalism, subsidiarity and education policy in Switzerland. *Regional & Federal Studies, 10*(1), 1–35. https://doi.org/10.1080/13597560008421107

Henry, F., Dua, E., James, C. E., Kobayashi, A., Li, P., Ramos, H., & Smith, M. S. (2017). *The equity myth: Racialization and indigeneity at Canadian universities*. UBC Press.

Jones, G. A. (1997). *Higher education in Canada: Different systems, different perspectives*. Garland Pub.

Kennedy, K. J. (2021). Asian students' citizenship values: Exploring theory by reviewing secondary data analysis. In B. Malak-Minkiewicz & J. Torney-Purta (Eds.), *Influences of the IEA civic and citizenship education studies: Practice, policy, and research across countries and regions* (pp. 233–245). Springer International Publishing.

Kerr, C. (1982/2001). *The uses of the university* (3rd ed., pp. 1–45). Harvard University Press.

King, S. (2018). *Have not no more'-Educating for civic engagement at Atlantic Canadian universities* [Doctoral dissertation]. The University of New Brunswick. UNB Scholar Research Repository.

Kost, J. (2013). Does promoting permeability decreases social inequality in VET? Promises and pitfalls of a widespread idea. In S. Akoojee & Ph. Gonon (Eds.) *Apprenticeship in a globalised world: Premises, promises and pitfalls* (S. 195–198). LIT.

Labaree, D. F. (1997). Public goods, private goods: The American struggle over educational goals. *American Educational Research Journal, 34*(1), 39–81.

Labaree, D. F. (2017). *A perfect mess: The unlikely ascendancy of American higher education*. University of Chicago Press.

Lee, W. O. (2004). Emerging concepts of citizenship in Asian contexts. In D. Grossman, W.O. Lee, & K. Kennedy (Eds.), *Citizenship education in Asia – Concepts and issues* (pp. 25–35). Comparative Education Research Centre/Kluwer Academic Publishers.

Lepori, B., & Kyvik, S. (2010). The research mission of universities of applied sciences and the future configuration of higher education systems in Europe. *Higher Education Policy, 23*, 295–316.

Li, J. (2009). Fostering citizenship in China's move from elite to mass higher education: An analysis of students' political socialization and civic participation. *International Journal of Educational Development, 29*(4), 382–398.

Li, J. (2019). Chinese model of higher education. In M. Peters (Ed.), *Encyclopedia of educational philosophy and theory* (pp. 1–8). Springer.

Marginson, S. (2009). The knowledge economy and higher education: Rankings and classifications, research metrics and learning outcomes measures as a system for regulating the value of knowledge. *Higher Education Management and Policy, 21*(1), 1–15.

Marginson, S. (2011). Higher education in East Asia and Singapore: Rise of the Confucian model. *Higher Education, 61*, 587–611.

Marginson, S. (2019). Limitations of human capital theory. *Studies in Higher Education, 44*(2), 287–301.

Marginson, S. (2022). What is global higher education?. *Oxford Review of Education, 48*(4), 492–517.

Marginson, S. (2023). Is employability displacing higher education?. *International Higher Education, 116*, 3–5.

Marginson, S., & Yang, L. (2022) Individual and collective outcomes of higher education: A comparison of Anglo-American and Chinese approaches. *Globalisation, Societies and Education, 20*(1), 1–31. https://doi.org/10.1080/14767724.2021.1932436

McCaul, R. L. (1959). Dewey's Chicago. *The School Review, 67*(2), 258–280.

Mission, Vision and Core Values. (2024). *Miami Dade College*. https://www.mdc.edu/media/mdc/institutional-research/documents/Mission_Vision_and_Core_Values.pdf

Mok, K. H. (2023). *Repurposing university education: The role of liberal arts education in Asia*. CGHE, University of Oxford/UCL. https://www.researchcghe.org/events/cghe-seminar/repurposing-university-education-the-role-of-liberal-arts-education-in-asia/

Molnar, C. J. (2010). *Democratic postsecondary vocational education*. Fielding Graduate University.

Moodie, G., Wheelahan, L., & Lavigne, E. (2019). *Technical and vocational education and training as a framework for social justice*. Education International.

Muñiz, R. (2024). The need for educational research engagement with courts, public policy, and practice in a post-Dobbs Era. *Educational Researcher*, *53*(1), 59–65. https://doi.org/10.3102/0013189X231209969

Nelson, C. A. (2015). *American Indian college students as native nation builders: Tribal financial aid as a lens for understanding college-going paradoxes*. https://repository.arizona.edu/handle/10150/556872

Perna, L., Finney, J., & Callan, P. (2011). *A story of decline: Performance and policy in Illinois higher education*. Institute for Research on Higher Education, University of Pennsylvania.

Pfister, C., Koomen, M., Harhoff, D., & Backes-Gellner, U. (2021). Regional innovation effects of applied research institutions. *Research Policy*, *50*(4). https://doi.org/10.1016/j.respol.2021.104197

Print, M. (2000). Civics and values in the Asia-Pacific region. *Asia Pacific Journal of Education*, *20*(1), 7–20.

Putnam, R. D. (2000). *Bowling alone: The collapse and revival of American community*. Simon and Schuster.

Rashdall, H. (1895). Chapter 1: What is a university? *The universities of Europe in the Middle Ages: Salerno. Bologna. Paris* (Vol. 1). Clarendon Press.

Ratsoy, G. R. (2016). The Roles of Canadian Universities in Heterogeneous Third-Age Learning: A Call for Transformation. *Canadian Journal of Higher Education*, *46*(1), 76–90. https://doi.org/10.47678/cjhe.v46i1.185319

Reimagining Civic Education. (2024). *Democratic knowledge project*. https://www.democraticknowledgeproject.org/

Robson, J. (2023). Graduate employability and employment. In S. Marginson, B. Cantwell, D. Platonova, & A. Smolentseva (Eds.), *Assessing the contributions of higher education* (pp. 177–196). Edward Elgar Publishing.

Rojewski, J. W. (2009). A conceptual framework for technical and vocational education and training. In R. Maclean & D. Wilson (Eds.), *International handbook of education for the changing world of work: Bridging academic and vocational learning* (pp. 19–39). Springer Netherlands.

Rothstein, R. (2017). *The color of law: A forgotten history of how our government segregated America*. Liveright Publishing.

Sam, C., & Van der Sijde, P. (2014). Understanding the concept of the entrepreneurial university from the perspective of higher education models. *Higher Education*, *68*, 891–908.

Schlegel, T., Pfister, C., & Backes-Gellner, U. (2022). Tertiary education expansion and regional firm development. *Regional Studies*, *50*(11), 1874–1887. https://doi.org/10.1080/00343404.2021.2010695

Schofer, E., Ramirez, F. O., & Meyer, J. W. (2021). The societal consequences of higher education. *Sociology of Education*, *94*(1), 1–19.

SERI State Secretariat for Education, Research and Education. (2022). *Vocational and professional education and training in Switzerland – Facts and figures*. SERI. https://www.sbfi.admin.ch/dam/sbfi/en/dokumente/webshop/2020/bb-f-z-2020.pdf.download.pdf/fakten_zahlen_bb_e.pdf

Shahjahan, R. A., & Kezar, A. J. (2013). Beyond the "national container" addressing methodological nationalism in higher education research. *Educational Researcher*, *42*(1), 20–29.

Stein, S., & Andreotti, V. D. O. (2016). Decolonization and higher education. In M. A. Peters (Ed.), *Encyclopedia of educational philosophy and theory*. Springer Science+ Business Media.

Takagi, K. (2024). Faculty perceptions of public roles of the university in Japan. *Global Higher Education Webinar*. The Education University of Hong Kong.

Thelin, J. R. (2011). *A history of American higher education*. Johns Hopkins University Press.

Thomas, N. L. (1998). *The institution as a citizen: How colleges and universities enhance their civic roles*. New England Resource Center for Higher Education (NERCHE). https://scholarworks.umb.edu/nerche_pubs/20

Tu, Y. (2011). Citizenship with Chinese characteristics? An investigation into Chinese university students' civic perceptions and civic participation. *Frontiers of Education in China*, 6, 426–448.

Weber, K., Tremel, P. & Balthasar, A. (2010). Die Fachhochschulen in der Schweiz: Pfadabhängigkeit und Profilbildung. *Swiss Political Science Review 16*(4), 687–713.

Wheelahan, L., Moodie, G., & Doughney, J. (2022). Challenging the skills fetish. *British Journal of Sociology of Education*, 43(3), 475–494.

Wilder, C. (2013) *Ebony and ivy: Race, slavery, and the troubled history of America's universities*: Bloomsbury Publishing. https://www.bloomsbury.com/us/ebony-and-ivy-9781608193837/

Wittgenstein, L. (1922/1998). *Tractatus logico-philosophicus*. Suhrkamp.

Wu, H., & Hayhoe, R. (2023). China's normal universities and their ethical engagement in social transformation: Philosophical traditions, historical evolution, and social influence. In E. Basio & G. Gregorutti (Eds.), *The emergence of the ethically-engaged university* (pp. 161–184). Springer International Publishing.

Zhao, Z. (2023). What does the ideal citizen look like in China's new era? A bottom-up view. *Citizenship Studies*, 27(6), 744–760.

PART 4

AREA STUDIES AND REGIONAL DEVELOPMENTS

EDUCATION AND ECONOMIC DEVELOPMENT IN SOUTH ASIA

Amrit Thapa, Mary Khan, Will L. H. Zemp and James Gazawie

Graduate School of Education, University of Pennsylvania, USA

ABSTRACT

This paper provides a snapshot of educational and economic trends across South Asia with an exploratory and comparative approach. Before COVID-19, South Asia was the world's fastest-growing regional economy, concurrently achieving major strides in poverty reduction and access to education. Despite the region's economic and educational accomplishments, the countries of South Asia fall short of international benchmarks in public education expenditure, resulting in a persistent lag in educational quality that hampers individuals, the workforce, and overall economic productivity. The paper highlights themes in the literature, including context-specific evidence for the various theories of economic growth, the returns to education, and educational inputs (e.g., teachers and private schools) that highlight how spending can be leveraged to increase educational outcomes. In addition, it examines the relationship between education, poverty, and marginalization factors that explain why some populations are deprived of education and its benefits. We provide a broad perspective of the dynamics of the economics of education and the related challenges in this region. This discussion aims to enhance the understanding of the inefficiencies in South Asia's educational systems and, ultimately, in the development of the region's human capacities.

Keywords: Education; economic development; economic growth; South Asia; education attainment; education expenditure; education inequality

---

Annual Review of Comparative and International Education 2023
International Perspectives on Education and Society, Volume 48, 199–217
Copyright © 2025 by Emerald Publishing Limited
All rights of reproduction in any form reserved
ISSN: 1479-3679/doi:10.1108/S1479-367920240000048011

INTRODUCTION

This paper provides a review of research on the relationship between education and economic growth in South Asia with a focus on India, Pakistan, Bangladesh, and Nepal (IPBN). Acknowledging the reciprocal impact between education and economic development and their collective influence on enhancing quality of life, this paper focuses on the burgeoning developments observed in South Asia over the past few decades. This region was the fastest-growing in the world prior to COVID-19, with a projected annual GDP growth rate of over 6% and making concurrent strides in poverty reduction (Richards et al., 2022). Nevertheless, many South Asian countries fall short of meeting international benchmarks in public education expenditure (Béteille et al., 2020). This disjuncture raises questions about such topics in the region. This paper will provide a comparative snapshot of educational and economic trends across the countries of interest. By spotlighting the dynamics between education and economics, our analysis aims to enhance the global education community's understanding of the interactions shaping South Asia's ongoing development.

Since Schultz (1961), Becker (1962), and Mincer (1970) popularized the role of "human capital" for the economic growth of a nation, education economists have widely embraced the human capital approach (see Barro, 2013; Hall, 2002; Hanushek, 2013). Despite this, there remains a relative scarcity of studies on this topic, particularly around South Asia, which is projected to boast the world's largest youth labor force by 2040 (UNICEF, 2019). However, around 30% of South Asians between the ages of 15–24 are not in employment, education, or training (Generalao, 2022). Of the youth engaged in schooling, education data highlight substantial deficiencies in the overall quality of learning. UNICEF estimates show that 75% of children are affected by learning poverty, lacking basic literacy and numeracy skills (UNICEF, 2022). A report published in collaboration between Global Business Coalition for Education and the Education Commission (2019) posits that only 26% of South Asian youth are on track to complete secondary schooling and acquire skills essential to workforce participation. The World Bank's Human Capital Index indicates that the average future productivity of a South Asian child is considerably lower than expected if they had complete access to health and education (World Bank, 2021). The inadequacies of educational systems in South Asia for equipping youth with the necessary skills to thrive in the modern economy not only means a significant loss of human capital but also has the potential to exacerbate challenges related to the well-being of the people and the development of South Asia.

The findings in this paper highlight results from our study of the body of literature on the economics of education in South Asia. The paper progresses through themes developed from inductive coding of primary and quantitative research on the region, with a focus on the IPBN countries, during the 50-year span of 1973–2023. The five databases searched are: ERIC, Scopus, Web of Science, PubMed, ProQuest Dissertation & Theses Global using keywords relating to economics of education in IPBN countries. The first section covers education spending and the returns to education. The second section delves into the influence of demographics or marginalization factors on educational and economic outcomes.

Education and Economic Development in South Asia 201

Through our analysis of the literature, we provide a broad perspective of the dynamics of the economics of education and the related challenges in this region. Our goal is to foster new insights and encourage further research into the complex relationship between education and development and thereafter improve the practices of policymakers in education.

RESULTS

Education's Impact on Gross Domestic Product (GDP)

Understanding the relationship between education investment and economic development is crucial for efficiently allocating limited resources, especially in the context of low and middle-income countries. Evidence from South Asia indicates public expenditure on education has a positive association with economic growth in the long term. Across a large sample of Asian countries, including India, Pakistan, Bangladesh, Sri Lanka, and Nepal between 1973 and 2012, educational expenditure seems to have positive association with GDP (Mallick et al., 2016). A country-specific analysis by Maitra and Mukhopadhyay (2012) finds that educational expenditure is positively associated with GDP in Bangladesh, Sri Lanka, and Nepal. These results are corroborated by numerous regression analyses that reveal a positive and significant relationship between the two variables in the region and in some individual countries (Ali et al., 2012; Jalil & Idrees, 2013; Muhammad Al & Kameyama, 2019; Qadri & Waheed, 2011). However, educational expenditure had no significant relationship or a negative relationship with GDP in other Asia and Pacific countries not covered in this literature review (Maitra & Mukhopadhyay, 2012). Thus, the evidence underscores the potential of education to foster economic growth in South Asia and supports the position that education spending is a sound public investment.

Analysis of education by primary, secondary, and tertiary levels is one way of examining the complexities and contextual factors that impact the economic returns of education. In India, from 1970 to 1994, only primary education had a significant positive impact on economic growth in a state-by-state analysis, despite large differences in social infrastructure indicators such as literacy rates and secondary schooling between states (Nagaraj et al., 2000). In Pakistan, results are mixed: Jalil and Idrees (2013) find that primary education surpasses secondary and tertiary education in its contribution to growth; from 1960 to 2010, while all levels of education had a significant positive effect on GDP, primary education's effect was the largest with a 2% growth effect on GDP. Conversely, some studies show secondary education has the largest positive and statistically significant impact on long-term economic growth (Abbas & Foreman-Peck, 2008a; Qadri & Waheed, 2017), and another study (Afzal et al., 2011) shows higher education has generated more GDP growth in Pakistan than the other levels of education. Results from different countries are likely to vary due to contextual factors and the dynamic nature of education and growth. Within a country like Pakistan, results of studies may vary due to data quality or methodological differences. Research on the returns to education worldwide shows that primary education is the most publicly profitable level of education (Psacharopoulos & Patrinos, 2018).

How large are the gains from educational investments? A 1% increase in educational expenditure in the Indian subcontinent between 1973 and 2012 is associated with an annual increase in economic growth (GDP) ranging from 0.45% to 0.71% over the long term (Mallick et al., 2016). Looking specifically at India, where the growth rate was 0.71%, every additional dollar invested in education, in present day dollars, would translate to an additional US$20 in GDP per year (UIS, 2020–2023).

Most of the countries in South Asia spend less on education than the 4%–6% of GDP recommended by members of UNESCO in order to make progress toward the Sustainable Development Goals 2030 (UNESCO, 2015). The average education spending in the IPBN countries was 2.8% of GDP from 2016 to 2021 (UIS, 2020–2023). Qadri and Waheed (2014) explored three different scenarios of education spending in Pakistan: 5% for five years, 3% for the first year with a 0.5% increase for four years, and 5% followed by four years at 3% and predicted that subsequent increases in GDP would range from 3.18% to 3.45%.

In a creative proxy analysis, Castelló-Climent et al. (2017) find that districts with higher education levels, as indicated by the location of Catholic missionaries in the early 20th century, had higher levels of development, as measured by light density at night in 2001. This alternative study of the long-term effects of education on development controls for factors like infrastructure and population, and the relationship holds using consumption per capita and district-level GDP per capita. The use of Catholic missionaries as an instrumental variable addresses the issue of endogeneity between education and development. Interestingly, primary education is not a significant factor in explaining development through the lens of light density and the other measures used.

In a different perspective on the value of education as an investment, Bleakley and Gupta (2023) examine whether the government of Nepal recoups the costs of education from future tax payments. By employing a Mincer-like model, they estimate the fiscal externality of primary, secondary, and higher education, considering both the opportunity cost to the individual and the government subsidy. At the primary level, the fiscal marginal benefits are slightly less than fiscal marginal costs, but do not quite zero out the fiscal marginal costs. Each year of schooling is associated with a median tax payment of an additional US$ 8.47. Secondary education also does not fully cover its costs, but tertiary education yields a substantial fiscal benefit of US$ 75 a year at the mean.

Reverse Causality

The idea that education contributes to economic growth and development appears as a universal truth in popular consciousness. Economists, however, also study the possibility that the opposite may be true: economic growth is an important precursor to increased educational spending and, ultimately, educational outcomes. Findings from South Asian countries show influence in both directions, suggesting a simultaneous relationship between the two variables. The adult literacy rate

Education and Economic Development in South Asia

and GDP growth in South Asia exhibits a bidirectional relationship (Islam, 2020). Evidence from Pakistan and Bangladesh also supports two-way causality (Afzal et al., 2011; Islam et al., 2007). However, when the analysis of Bangladesh narrows the time frame from 1976–1984 to 2003, when rates of inputs started to take off, there is no relationship between education and growth (Islam et al., 2007). Despite these differing findings, both studies conclude with weak support for a bidirectional relationship between education and economic growth. Note that these studies use different models: Islam (2020) employs the adult literacy rate and life expectancy at birth as determinants, while Islam et al. (2007) utilize labor, capital, and government educational expenditure. In the context of Pakistan, results are also complicated: Afzal et al. (2011) find that the relationship between GDP growth does not bring more educational expenditure or higher education, but Chaudhary et al. (2009) find reverse causality: growth does increase higher education attainment. The relationship between education and economic growth remains an unresolved issue in the larger context and is the subject of many studies (e.g., see Bils & Klenow, 2000; Pritchett, 2006).

Human capital emphasizes the education and health of individuals and the resulting effect on economic growth, and because of the importance attributed to these two factors, studies often consider both. As the previous paragraph about uni- or bidirectional relationships between education and economic growth demonstrates, there is mixed evidence for an endogenous relationship between human capital and growth. Nonetheless, the endogenous growth model is the most popular model of economic growth. According to the endogenous growth theory, there exists a positive feedback loop between human capital and economic growth (Lucas, 1988). Several studies in our review support this theory (e.g., see Afzal et al., 2011; Islam, 2020; Islam et al., 2007). The Granger causal relationship finding between the adult literacy rate and GDP growth in South Asia is one example (Islam, 2020). Conversely, findings like those of Qadri and Waheed (2011) and Abbas and Foreman-Peck (2008a) in Pakistan suggest that human capital increases GDP but not the other way around, lending support to the exogenous growth theory. Regardless of whether there is a feedback loop, the returns from human capital in Pakistan are enormous: human capital accounts for an estimated 40% of the increase in GDP per capita in Pakistan (Abbas & Foreman-Peck, 2008a).

Returns to Education

In addition to examining the connection between education and economic growth, researchers have also explored the relationship between an individual's years of education and their income. For each additional year of schooling, the average global return to an individual's wages is 9%–10% (Montenegro & Patrinos, 2021; Patrinos & Psacharopoulos, 2020). In Pakistan, returns for each additional year of schooling for men in paid employment, self-employment, and agriculture average 9.2%, 8.3%, and 7.1%, respectively. For women, the returns average 14%, 10.3%, and 4.3% in these respective sectors. From primary to tertiary, the estimated returns range from 1.1% to 23.6%; in other words, as years of education increase, there is a progressive rise in income for both men and women (Abbas & Foreman-Peck, 2008b). Interestingly, the difference in the results between employed and self-employed individuals in this data lends support to the idea that employers offer additional wages not for actual knowledge and skills but for the perceived value and skills that educational credentials signal. This is known as signaling theory because educational credentials serve as a shortcut, or signal, to employers that a job applicant possesses the necessary qualifications to succeed (Spence, 1973).

Inputs and Outputs

What we have presented thus far is focused on the distal outputs of education, that is, economic growth and wages, but both inputs and outputs are important factors in the economics of education. In the broadest terms, the inputs are capital and labor, and proximal output is knowledge or student achievement; this function is known as the educational production function (Hanushek, 1979).

One of the most ubiquitous measures of the output of education is enrollment rates. In developing countries, ensuring enrollment, or access, and keeping students in school remains a significant challenge (Patrinos & Psacharopoulos, 2011). In 2018, the primary net enrollment rate in South Asia was 88%, with gender distribution at 89% for males and 87% for females. However, there is a sharp decline in secondary school enrollment, with a net rate of 61% (61% for males and 60% for females) (UIS, 2020–2023). This trend persists when examining enrollment by country and gender. Among the IPBN countries, Pakistan exhibits the lowest enrollment rates, with 82% of males and 71% of females enrolled at the primary level and with especially low rates at the secondary level, with only 49% and 40% enrolled, respectively. Nepal has the highest primary enrollment rates at 96% for males and 93% for females but experiences a significant drop in secondary enrollment to 57% for males and 53% for females. Notably, Bangladesh shows higher female than male enrollment rates at both primary and secondary levels, with 93% for females and 88% for males at the primary level, and 67% for females and 57% for males at the secondary level (EPDC, 2018). In 2022, India also had varying enrollment rates, with a drop from 88.6% at the primary level to 47.9% at the secondary level (Education For All, 2023). Moreover, students can be silently excluded from the system, attending irregularly, repeating grades, and displaying low academic achievement (Cameron, 2010). In developing contexts, it can be difficult to track these over-age and often absent students and obtain precise measures of gross and net enrollment rates.

School attainment by grade level, despite challenges, is an easier measure of human capital to obtain than student knowledge or achievement measured through a test. However, grade level is a less reliable measure because the quality of education can vary significantly across different countries. It provides a relative reflection of a person's skills or knowledge and a country's level of human capital. Well-designed tests are more precise impact measures and have demonstrated the effects of a wide array of relevant factors and interventions such as early

Education and Economic Development in South Asia

childhood education, maternal education, household chores (e.g., see Hamlet et al., 2021; Sekhri & Debnath, 2014; Vikram & Chindarkar, 2020).

Test scores are often seen as indicative of teachers, whether fairly or unfairly, who are a key educational input. Research from the region highlights how teachers can be employed for increased output, for example, teacher incentive programs have been found to raise students' test scores. In Rajasthan, India, for example, a program that tracked teacher attendance using cameras and offered small wage incentives resulted in a substantial reduction in teacher absenteeism and an increase in children's test scores (Duflo et al., 2012). Additionally, a program in Andhra Pradesh that provided small wage incentives for teachers led to an increase in test scores; schools with individual incentive programs, rather than group incentive programs, experienced greater gains (Muralidharan, 2012). Tutoring, or small group instruction, is another form of teaching that can be effective: a program involving young local women leading small breakout groups with the lowest performing children for two hours a day saw test scores increase. An alternative mode of instruction, using computer games to reinforce mathematical skills for two hours per week, also increased test scores (Banerjee et al., 2007). Teachers are an input of utmost importance because they are the largest educational expenditure for governments.

Another key subject in raising test scores and outputs is the argument over public versus private education. The private education sector is larger in South Asia than any other region in the world (UNESCO, 2022). In the context of Nepal, Thapa (2015) found private schools perform better than public schools; private school students scored almost 11 points more on the secondary school public examination, controlling for personal and family characteristics. In other words, even after considering selection bias, such as students with more socio-economic advantage being more likely to attend private schools, there was still a significant positive private school effect.

Private schooling results are mixed in the broader context. In India, a lottery voucher program for private schools in an urban slum area of Delhi found that, over the course of several years, private school attendance had a positive impact on English test scores for students who attended private schools compared to those who did not due to not being selected for the voucher program. However, there was no impact on mathematics test scores and a negative impact on Hindi test scores. Additionally, the lottery winners selected to attend private schools received vouchers for books, uniforms, and meals in addition to tuition, and students were allowed to change to other schools in the program. These additional acts control for, or mitigate, some of the downward biasing effects from non-school confounding factors like food insecurity and low-quality schools. The minimal test score gains seen in the treatment group attending private schools raise credible questions about low-quality private schools (Dixon et al., 2019). Likewise, another study using data from both rural and urban India finds no private-school benefit when selection issues were addressed with propensity score matching technique; children in low free private schools performed no better than their public school counterparts (Chudgar & Quin, 2012).

In Pakistan, the government subsidizes private schooling. Specifically, there is a subsidy program that provides low-cost private schools with per-student monthly payments. An analysis of schools just above the average test score threshold required for program participation compared to those that applied but did not meet the requirement revealed significant positive impacts on school inputs: additional teachers, additional classrooms, and fewer students. Cost-effectiveness analysis indicates that this intervention was highly cost-effective. When the program was introduced, the per-student subsidy was less than half of the estimated per-student expenditure in government schools (Barrera-Osorio & Raju, 2015). However, a subsidy program that supported low-income primary school students in attending rural government primary schools did not have positive effects on educational outcomes (Baulch, 2011).

In summary, increased spending alone is not sufficient; governments and policymakers should strategically allocate educational funds to maximize efficiency and improve education outcomes.

Poverty

A number of established approaches on human development such as the human capital approach (see Becker, 1964; Mincer, 1974; Schultz, 1961), Amartya Sen's (1999) capability approach, and the basic needs approach as outlined by Paul Streeten et al. (1981) posit that education decreases poverty. Previously, we presented evidence on the (bidirectional) relationship between education and economic growth. Now we examine poverty, acknowledging that education and economic growth present issues of equity and may not be equitably distributed among all segments of society. To what degree do increases in education benefit those who are socioeconomically or otherwise marginalized in South Asia?

Poverty poses a significant challenge in South Asia. The World Bank's *Poverty and Shared Prosperity Report* (2022b) reveals that, although poverty levels have been steadily declining, South Asia still maintains the second-highest percentage of the population living at or below the US$ 2.15 per day poverty line, with a rate of approximately 10% in 2018 (Fig. 1, p. 37). At higher poverty lines, the distribution of global poor is highest in South Asia (Fig. 2, p. 42). 41% of those living in poverty are children, although they make up only 34% of the population (p. 39). Among IPBN, the largest proportion living under extreme poverty are found in India, Bangladesh, and Pakistan (pp. 36). Furthermore, these measures, while useful for benchmarking purposes, do not account for heterogeneity along the dimensions of social exclusion. In the following section we look at the relationship between poverty and education both broadly and at its intersection with gender, geography, and by extension parental characteristics, ethnicity, and caste.

Several empirical studies in South Asia explore the link between poverty and education. Chaudhry et al. (2010) find that higher education significantly reduces poverty in Pakistan, with a clear inverse relationship between education and poverty levels. Similarly, in Nepal higher literacy rates are linked to lower household income poverty, and conversely, poverty is linked with lower enrollment rates

Education and Economic Development in South Asia

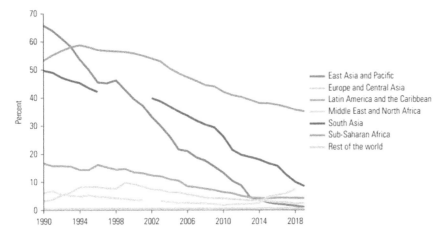

Source: World Bank, Poverty and Inequality Platform, https://pip.worldbank.org.
Note: The figure shows poverty trends at the US$2.15-a-day poverty line, by region, 1990–2019. Poverty estimates are not reported when regional population coverage is below 50 percent within a three-year period before and after the reference year (see online annex 1A).

Fig. 1. Poverty Trends at the US$2.15-a-Day Poverty Line, By Region, 1990–2019.

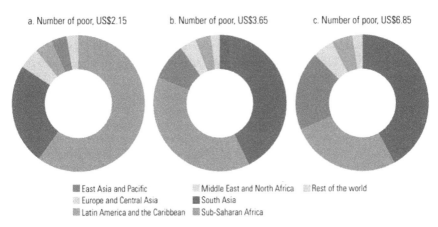

Source: World Bank, Poverty and Inequality Platform, https://pip.worldbank.org.
Note: The figure shows the distribution of the global poor at the US$2.15-a-day (panel a), US$3.65-a-day (panel b), and US$6.85-a-day (panel c) poverty lines, by region, in 2019.

Fig. 2. Distribution of the Global Poor at the US$ 2-a-day, US$ 3.65-a-day, and US$ 6.85-a-day Poverty Lines, By Region, in 2019.

(Thapa, 2013). When disaggregating analysis by geography, school, and household characteristics poverty remains a significant determinant of educational outcomes (Khan & Ahmed, 2020; Sajjad et al., 2022). These results demonstrate that education can increase the economic means of the poorest individuals, but students also need economic means in order to attend school.

Poverty's influence on educational attainment is mediated through factors such as child labor. Amin et al. (2006) show reduced school attendance and fewer overall years of schooling for working children in Bangladesh. In India, Hamlet et al. (2021) correlates increased time spent water-fetching, a form of child labor in the home, with lower test scores. Similarly, in Nepal household chores significantly hinder educational achievement, with each additional chore resulting in a 0.391 decrease in final exam scores (Neupane, 2017). Hafeez and Hussain (2019) find in Pakistan that school enrollment is associated with less child labor and also influenced by the household head's education levels.

Gender, Rurality, and Other Marginalization Factors

Lower female education rates and labor force participation outside the home are widely believed to be an economic detriment to a country. While gender equality in education has improved substantially in South Asia, larger gaps remain at higher schooling levels (Riboud et al., 2007).

Oztunc et al. (2015) conducted a macroeconomic study across 11 Asia-Pacific nations, including Bangladesh and India, revealing that higher primary school enrollment and female labor force participation (FLPR) led to increased GDP per capita. Shah and Haq (2022), focusing on FLPR in Pakistan, Bangladesh, India, and Nepal corroborate these results, noting a positive, albeit unidirectional, relationship between economic growth and FLPR, facilitated by female education. Both studies also find higher fertility rates are associated with lower economic growth and FLPR. Further, Munir and Shahid (2021) also find a significant positive relationship between lower fertility rates and economic growth in Bangladesh, India, Pakistan, and Sri Lanka.

However, despite the aforementioned results about the relationship between women's education or FLPR and economic growth, the relationship is not necessarily positive and linear. In the short term, a positive relationship between economic growth and FLPR is observed in South Asia, but Shah and Haq predict that in the long term it is U-shaped, meaning as the region moves through lower and middle levels of economic output, women's labor force participation will decrease. However, while the regional aggregated analysis shows a U-shaped relationship, separate analyses of Bangladesh, India, and Nepal, predict the opposite: an inverse U-shaped relationship, meaning women's labor force participation will continue to increase in the short term (Shah & Haq, 2022).

Within Pakistan gender equality, both in education and the economy, contributes to favorable economic outcomes. Time-series analysis from 1970 to 2005 shows that overall literacy rates, the ratio of literate females to males, and the ratio of female to male enrollment at the primary level, had a significant positive effect on economic growth (Chaudhry, 2007). In rural households, female–male enrollment ratio, female–male literacy ratio, female–male ratio of total years of schooling, and female–male ratio of earners are all significantly linked with poverty reduction (Chaudhry & Rahman, 2009). Riaz and Pervaize (2018) emphasize women's education and employment in enhancing women's empowerment as measured by household and health decision-making. However, findings from Aslam and Kingdon (2012) raise questions about the extent to which Pakistani women are able to fully benefit from the equality-promoting aspects of education and workforce participation. The authors find that women's education increases their chances of being in the labor force, but only beyond eight years of schooling. The Georgetown Institute for Women Peace and Security (2021) estimates that, in Pakistan, women complete an average 3.9 years of schooling, and that across provinces 10% or less of women complete secondary schooling. Aslam and Kingdon (2012) also find that, while women experience higher returns to education, men still earn substantially more. Abbas and Foreman-Peck (2008b) attributes high female returns to education in Pakistan to low labor market participation. Hossain and Tisdell (2005) posit that, although most women in the workforce are self-employed or employed in low-skill jobs, their participation in high skill and entrepreneurial jobs as well as policy-making bodies has increased and overall, female education positively correlates with workforce participation.

Results from India demonstrate how addressing gender disparities in education could narrow gender disparities later in life. Jain et al. (2022) find that female disparities in cognition scores in middle aged and older adults can be attributed (up to 74%) to early life socioeconomic conditions and education. Factors like caste, religion, father's education, urbanity, and region of residence correlate with average cognitive scores but do not explain that mid-aged and older women have cognitive deficits compared to men that, on average, are the equivalent of nine years of education. If gender disparities persist, this has troubling implications for India's future human capital. India has the largest number of out-of-school girls across South Asia (UNICEF, 2014 as cited in Mitra et al., 2023). Girls in India are 16% more likely than boys to be out of school, with those from lower wealth quintiles, rural conglomerates, and scheduled tribes being most vulnerable (Mitra et al., 2023). Bangladesh presents similar results both in terms of gender equality, economic outcomes, and the challenges faced by women in formally participating in the economy. Wei et al. (2021), in a study on the effect of women's empowerment on poverty reduction in northern Bangladesh found that women's education levels, and other measures of women's empowerment, were linked with decreases in poverty.

Child marriage presents a significant impediment to educational attainment among girls in South Asia. Paul (2019) finds that despite a 30% decline in child marriage rates over 25 years, roughly 285 million girls in the region were married before 18, accounting for 44% of global cases (UNICEF, 2018; as cited in Paul, 2019). Bangladesh has the highest prevalence at 59% (2014), followed by Nepal at 40% (2016), India at 27% (2015–2016), and Pakistan at 21% (2012–2013) (UNICEF Global Databases, 2018; as cited in Paul, 2019). Poverty has been shown to be an impetus of child marriage with girls belonging to the lowest wealth quintiles at the highest risk. Conversely, the completion of secondary schooling and higher education have been shown to delay marriage timing, a potential result of empowerment, increased autonomy, and workforce aspirations (Lee-Rife & Malhotra, 2012; Raj et al., 2014; UNICEF & UNFPA, 2018; as cited in Paul, 2019). Looking at the consequences of child marriage, Amir-ud-Din et al. (2021) find that married and lower and middle wealth quintile children were most likely to drop out, especially in secondary and higher education in Pakistan. Sekhri and Debnath's (2014) research in India, evaluating the intergenerational impact of child marriage on child development, found that a delay in a girl's marriage increases her child's achievement in reading and math; for each year of marriage delay, a child was 3.5 percentage points more likely to be able to read a short story, even after controlling for parental, household, and child characteristics.

Additionally, the research indicates that educational deprivation is concentrated in certain regions and communities. Rurality, for example, plays a central role in shaping educational and economic landscapes in South Asia, with implications for poverty and social dynamics. Studies from the literature we reviewed indicate a number of substantial barriers faced by rural communities including limited infrastructure, socio-economic disparities, and school characteristics, among others.

Research in Nepal underscores the impact of rurality, along with student and family factors, on limiting educational outcomes. For example, in a study on secondary school attainment in rural areas, Neupane (2017) finds notable disparities in exam scores, with girls, Dalit (lowest caste) and Janajati (indigenous, disadvantaged ethnic groups) lagging behind boys and higher-caste peers. Acharya et al. (2023) find a 5.2% higher prevalence of developmental delays among Nepalese children in rural regions.

In India, the probability of a child being out of school is 35% higher in rural areas, and higher still for girls, Muslims, and those belonging to backwards castes (Mitra et al., 2023). Examining family background in educational mobility among youth (16–17 years old) in pre/post-reform India, Emran and Shilpi (2015) find that despite moderate improvements in mobility among women, the gender gap in rural areas remains substantial. Azam (2019) posits that differential distribution of educational levels in urban and rural areas of India explain a significant part of the urban-rural welfare gap. The author notes that while primary school access is similar in rural and urban India, rural areas face significant disparities in accessing upper primary and secondary schools, with over 12% of rural households lacking secondary schools within 5 km, contrasting with negligible cases in urban areas (NSSO, 2015; as cited in Azam, 2019). Azam predicts a gap in living standards between urban and rural regions as countries urbanize. Nonetheless, this gap raises questions about the current status of rural human capital development.

In Pakistan, a rural–urban divide also persists: the province of Balochistan has a literacy rate of 40%, while the more urbanized Punjab Province has a rate of 64% (Sajjad et al., 2022). Alderman et al. (2003) find that urban schools may benefit from school and family-level characteristics not shared by their rural counterparts. Running a randomized control trial to gauge the effectiveness of private schools for underprivileged girls, findings indicate that the pilot schools situated in urban areas had a higher success rate than those in rural areas. Factors attributed to the success of urban schools include improved availability of teachers, experienced school operators, and parents with higher levels of education and income.

Likewise, urban slums often have poor levels of educational achievement. In Bangladesh, the proportion of children who never enrolled in school in the slums of Dhaka is double that of students in rural areas. Among the 300,000 primary school-age children in the slums of central Dhaka in 2008, 23% were out of school. Like in the rural areas, lack of access to government schools was a major reason for low enrollment in the slums. Many of these children were not enrolled in school, and few continued on to secondary school due to the reliance on NGOs for basic "unformalized" education (Cameron, 2010). Similarly, in the slums of Karachi, Pakistan, 51% of school-age children were found not attending school (Khan & Ahmed, 2020).

A consequential aspect of both rurality and poverty is work-related migration – both within and between countries – and remittances, or the transfer of money from the worker to the family. The number of migrants who secure work and send remittances back home can have a profound impact on socioeconomic and educational outcomes. Between 2012 and 2017, Bangladesh, India, Nepal, and Pakistan saw annual migration ranging from 46,000 to 71,000 workers (World Bank, 2022a). From 1990 to 2017, the total number of South Asian expatriates increased from 23.9 million to 38.4 million (ILO, 2018). Furthermore, these numbers do not account for intra-country migration flows which are likely to be substantial given ever increasing urbanization.

An essential question then is to what extent do migration and remittances impact poverty, education, and inequality within IPBN? Surprisingly, given the magnitude of migration from IPBN, regional literature on this subject is limited and findings are inconclusive. Bontch-Osmolovski (2009) analyzed data from the 1995–1996 and 2003–2004 Nepal Living Standards Survey (NLSS) and the 2001 national census to study familial migration's impact on children's education using logistic regression. The study finds that fathers' migration was associated with a 16% increase in the likelihood of their children enrolling in school, consistent across genders and ages. This effect was 28% higher for disadvantaged rural households. Challenging these findings, a more recent study using 2010 NLSS data by Karki (2016) finds that, despite increasing non-food and educational expenditures, remittances affect neither educational outcomes nor child labor in Nepal. The authors attribute this incongruence to factors such as the difficulty of switching from public to private schooling in the Nepalese school system. Cameron (2010) argues that rural-urban migration in Bangladesh intensifies educational difficulties within slum areas, compounding pressure on the limited number of government schools. Ultimately, this necessitates more focused research to better understand its impact on education-economic dynamics within IPBN.

SUMMARY AND DISCUSSION

Demand for more investment in education is seen in the Sustainable Development Goals 2030, specifically SDG 4, which aspires to education for all, and UNESCO member states urging 4%–6% of a country's GDP to be allocated toward education in public expenditures every year. This review of the literature on the economics of education in South Asia highlights the critical role that educational spending plays in promoting both human development and economic development of the region.

While numerous studies give insights into the dynamics between education and economic growth, there are significant limitations in the results. First, data accessibility and quality are severely limited in low and middle-income countries which can affect the robustness and reliability of empirical analyses like those seen in this paper. Second, estimation issues mean results are unreliable. Untangling the complexities of the education-economic growth relationship with advanced econometric methods inherently involves unobserved factors that influence both education and economic outcomes. For example, educational quality plays a substantial role in influencing a country's economic growth (Barro, 2013; Hanushek, 2013). Unfortunately, many studies only consider educational quantity in their analyses. The outcomes from educational investments are not realized immediately. There are lags before their effects are seen in economic development. In Bangladesh, for example, the gestation lag for the impact of education spending on GDP was four years, while the lag for the impact of healthcare spending on GDP was one year (Maitra & Mukhopadhyay, 2012). Likewise, economic development of a country is dependent on factors such as health, infrastructure, political stability, etc. Education alone cannot drive economic development, requiring a supportive institutional framework (Acemouglu et al., 2001; Pritchett, 2006). Finally, in addition to pecuniary benefits, education also yields non-pecuniary private and social benefits that are much harder to measure, often manifesting over generations.

These limitations notwithstanding, findings from the literature underscore the role of education in yielding benefits for individuals and broader economies in South Asia. Efforts over recent decades have been aimed at expanding access to primary and secondary education, resulting in a significant reduction in the number of out-of-school children (Béteille et al., 2020). This trend is particularly noteworthy in countries like India, which boasts a substantial and youthful population, prompting increased emphasis on skill development and higher education to meet the demands of a globalized economy (Patel & Annapoorna, 2019; Sekhri, 2020).

However, despite these efforts, significant challenges persist. Many children and adolescents remain excluded from educational opportunities, and the current system has yet to produce robust learning outcomes across all levels commensurate with the scale of investment (Béteille et al., 2020). South Asian countries are not upgrading the skills of their population at a pace sufficient to catch up to the rest of the world, slowing sustainable economic development (Riboud et al., 2007). To pick up the pace, these countries need additional educational expenditure and increased efficiencies. Inefficiencies hinder sustainable development, such as in a stipend program for children from low-income rural households in Bangladesh, which failed to improve the grade progression outcomes of primary school students. The program stipend was not large enough and the stipends were allocated by the school management committees subjectively allocating stipends to "deserving" students, rather than according to the program's criteria for targeting low-income students (Baulch, 2011). This illustrates how program design and program implementation are equally important for achieving results.

Education and Economic Development in South Asia

Global education challenges have been compounded in recent years by the disrupting effect of COVID-19 on education provision, the ever-increasing technologization of global labor markets, and the corollary shift in the skillsets demanded of the current students who will, one day, be participating in it (Graetz et al., 2022; UNICEF, 2022). The literature demonstrates that inefficiencies in the education-economy pipeline are shaped by a number of intersectional factors including gender disparities, rurality, caste/ethnicity-based inequalities, the overall quality of education, access to quality education, and teacher quality (Bétielle et al., 2020; Munir & Kanwal, 2020; Mottaleb & Pallegedara, 2018; Bairagya & Varughese, 2021). The labor market is a critical factor that can impact an individual's earning potential. This is demonstrated by the fact that overeducated workers in India faced a wage penalty of 7% on average (Bahl & Sharma, 2020). Overeducated workers possess more education than the mean years of education for workers in their particular occupation and their earnings decrease the average rate of return to education. To most effectively allocate resources, it is important for policymakers to consider the needs of the labor market.

Addressing these challenges will require holistic approaches that focus on expanding access, improving quality, assuaging systemic inequalities, and leveraging the potential of both public and private education sectors to create inclusive and sustainable educational ecosystems. Given South Asia's vast genetic, cultural, and environmental diversity there is a pressing need for focused, grassroots studies targeting the barriers faced by specific communities. Ensuring quality, accessible education, and equity-focused economic policies is critical for lifting populations and driving socio-economic mobility. Research provides a foundation to raise the floor and narrow gaps for marginalized communities in South Asia. However, truly impactful solutions must be developed with inclusivity in mind, built from the bottom-up, not vice-versa. This will require dialogue at all levels and across sectors, spotlighting the voices of those who have historically gone unheard. Robust, sensitive, and well-communicated data will be instrumental in aligning the aspirations of communities, implementers, and decision-makers toward policies that alleviate both internal and external constraints.

REFERENCES

Abbas, Q., & Foreman-Peck, J. (2008a). Human capital and economic growth: Pakistan, 1960–2003. *The Lahore Journal of Economics, 13*(1), 1–27. https://doi.org/10.35536/lje.2008.v13.i1.a1

Abbas, Q., & Foreman-Peck, J. (2008b). The Mincer human capital model in Pakistan: Implications for education policy. *South Asia Economic Journal, 9*(2), 435–462.

Acharya, K., Rahman, M. S., Islam, M. R., Gilmour, S., Dhungel, B., Parajuli, R. P., Nishimura, T., Senju, A., & Tsuchiya, K. J. (2023). Socioeconomic and education-based inequality in suspected developmental delays among Nepalese children: A subnational level assessment. *Scientific Reports, 13*(1), 4750.

Acemouglu, D., Johnson, S., & Robinson, J. A. (2001). The colonial origins of comparative development: An empirical investigation. *American Economic Review, 91*(5), 1369–1401.

Afzal, M., Rehman, H. U., Farooq, M. S., & Sarwar, K. (2011). Education and economic growth in Pakistan: A cointegration and causality analysis. *International Journal of Educational Research, 50*(5–6), 321–335.

Alderman, H., Kim, J., & Orazem, P. F. (2003). Design, evaluation, and sustainability of private schools for the poor: The Pakistan urban and rural fellowship school experiments. *Economics of Education Review, 22*(3), 265–274.

Ali, S., Chaudhry, I. S., & Farooq, F. (2012). Human capital formation and economic growth in Pakistan. *Pakistan Journal of Social Science*, *32*(1), 229–240.

Amartya Sen, K. (1999). *Development as freedom*. Oxford University Press.

Amin, S., Quayes, S., & Rives, J. M. (2006). Market work and household work as deterrents to schooling in Bangladesh. *World Development*, *34*(7), 1271–1286.

Amir-ud-Din, R., Mahmood, H. Z., Abbas, F., Salman, V., & Zafar, S. (2021). Leaving studies because of lack of interest: An analysis of the risk factors of school dropouts in Pakistan. *Quality & Quantity*, *56*, 3189–3214.

Aslam, M., & Kingdon, G. (2012). Can education be a path to gender equality in the labour market? An update on Pakistan. *Comparative Education*, *48*(2), 211–229.

Azam, M. (2019). Accounting for growing urban-rural welfare gaps in India. *World Development*, *122*, 410–432.

Bahl, S., & Sharma, A. (2020). Education–occupation mismatch and dispersion in returns to education: Evidence from India. *Social Indicators Research*, *153*(1), 251–298.

Bairagya, I., & Varughese, A. R. (2021). Interstate variation in household spending on education in India: Does it influence educational status? *Structural Change and Economic Dynamics*, *59*, 405–415.

Banerjee, A. V., Cole, S., Duflo, E., & Linden, L. (2007). Remedying education: Evidence from two randomized experiments in India. *The Quarterly Journal of Economics*, *122*(3), 1235–1264.

Barrera-Osorio, F., & Raju, D. (2015). Evaluating the impact of public student subsidies on low-cost private schools in Pakistan. *The Journal of Development Studies*, *51*(7), 808–825.

Barro, R. J. (2013). Education and economic growth. *Annals of Economics and Finance*, *14*(2), 301–328.

Baulch, B. (2011). The medium-term impact of the primary education stipend in rural Bangladesh. *Journal of Development Effectiveness*, *3*(2), 243–262.

Becker, G. S. (1962). Investment in human capital: A theoretical analysis. *Journal of Political Economy*, *70*(5, Part 2), 9–49.

Becker, G. S. (1964). *Human capital: A theoretical and empirical analysis with special reference to education* (1st ed.). National Bureau of Economic Research.

Béteille, T., Tognatta, N., Riboud, M., & Nomura, S. (2020). *Ready to learn: Before school, in school, and beyond school in South Asia*. World Bank Publications.

Bils, M., & Klenow, P. J. (2000). Does schooling cause growth? *American Economic Review*, *90*(5), 1160–1183.

Bleakley, H., & Gupta, B. (2023). Mind the gap: Schooling, informality, and fiscal externalities in Nepal. *The World Bank Economic Review*, *37*(4), 659–674.

Bontch-Osmolovski, M. (2009). *Essays in labor economics: Work-related migration and its effect on poverty reduction and educational attainment in Nepal* [Doctoral dissertation, The University of North Carolina at Chapel Hill].

Cameron, S. (2010). *Access to and exclusion from primary education in slums of Dhaka, Bangladesh*. (Create Research Monograph No. 45). http://www.create-rpc.org/pdf_documents/PTA45.pdf

Castelló-Climent, A., Chaudhary, L., & Mukhopadhyay, A. (2017). Higher education and prosperity: From Catholic missionaries to luminosity in India. *The Economic Journal*, *128*(616), 3039–3075.

Chaudhary, A., Iqbal, A., & Gilliani, S. (2009). The nexus between higher education and economic growth: An empirical investigation for Pakistan. *Pakistan Journal of Commerce and Social Sciences*, *3*, 1–10.

Chaudhry, I. S. (2007). Gender inequality in education and economic growth: Case study of Pakistan. *Pakistan Horizon*, *60*(4), 81–91.

Chaudhry, I. S., Malik, S., Hassan, A., & Faridi, M. Z. (2010). Does education alleviate poverty? Empirical evidence from Pakistan. *International Research Journal of Finance and Economics*, *52*, 134–141.

Chaudhry, I. S., & Rahman, S. (2009). The impact of gender inequality in education on rural poverty in Pakistan: An empirical analysis. European Journal of Economics, *Finance and Administrative Sciences*, *15*(1), 174–188.

Chudgar, A., & Quin, E. (2012). Relationship between private schooling and achievement: Results from rural and urban India. *Economics of Education Review*, *31*(4), 376–390.

Dixon, P., Egalite, A. J., Humble, S., & Wolf, P. J. (2019). Experimental results from a four-year targeted education voucher program in the slums of Delhi, India. *World Development*, *124*, 1–13.

Education and Economic Development in South Asia

Duflo, E., Hanna, R., & Ryan, S. P. (2012). Incentives work: Getting teachers to come to school. *American Economic Review, 102*(4), 1241–1278.

Education for All in India. (2023). *Decoding UDISE + 2021-22 enrolment ratios*. https://shorturl.at/jwyBJ

EPDC: Education Policy Data Center. (2018). *National education profiles*. https://www.epdc.org/taxonomy/term/90.html

Emran, M. S., & Shilpi, F. (2015). Gender, geography, and generations: Intergenerational educational mobility in post-reform India. *World Development, 72*, 362–380.

Generalao, I. N. (2022). *Youth not in employment, education or training in Asia and the Pacific: trends and policy considerations*. ILO Regional Office for Asia and the Pacific.

GIWPS: Georgetown Institute for Women Peace and Security. (2021). *Consistently low rates of women's inclusion across Pakistan's provinces*. https://shorturl.at/eAGOR

Global Business Coalition for Education & The Education Commission. (2019). *The 2030 skills scorecard*. https://gbc-education.org/resources/the-2030-skills-scorecard/

Graetz, G., Restrepo, P., & Skans, O. N. (2022). Technology and the labor market. *Labour Economics, 76*, 1–4.

Hafeez, A., & Hussain, S. (2019). An empirical analysis of child labor: Evidence from Pakistan. *Pakistan Economic Review, 2*(1), 48–64.

Hall, R. (2002). The value of education: Evidence from around the globe. In E. Lazear (Ed.), *Education in the twenty-first century* (pp. 25–40). Hoover Institution Press.

Hamlet, L. C., Chakrabarti, S., & Kaminsky, J. (2021). Reduced water collection time improves learning achievement among primary school children in India. *Water Research, 203*, 1–11.

Hanushek, E. (1979). Conceptual and empirical issues in the estimation of educational production functions. *The Journal of Human Resources, 14*(3), 351.

Hanushek, E. (2013). Economic growth in developing countries: The role of human capital. *Economics of Education Review, 37*, 204–212.

Hossain, M. A., & Tisdell, C. A. (2005). Closing the gender gap in Bangladesh: Inequality in education, employment, and earnings. *International Journal of Social Economics, 32*(5), 439–453.

ILO. (2018). *International labour migration statistics in South Asia: Establishing a sub-regional database and improving data collection for evidence-based policymaking*. International Labour Organization.

Islam, Md. S. (2020). Human capital and per capita income linkage in South Asia: A heterogeneous dynamic panel analysis. *Journal of the Knowledge Economy, 11*(4), 1614–1629.

Islam, T., Wadud, M. A., & Islam, Q. (2007). Relationship between education and GDP growth: A mutivariate causality analysis for Bangladesh. *Economics Bulletin, 3*(35), 1–7.

Jain, U., Angrisani, M., Langa, K. M., Sekher, T. V., & Lee, J. (2022). How much of the female disadvantage in late-life cognition in India can be explained by education and gender inequality. *Scientific Reports, 12*(1), 5684.

Jalil, A., & Idrees, M. (2013). Modeling the impact of education on the economic growth: Evidence from aggregated and disaggregated time series data of Pakistan. *Economic Modelling, 31*, 383–388.

Karki Nepal, A. (2016). The impact of international remittances on child outcomes and household expenditures in Nepal. *The Journal of Development Studies, 52*(6), 838–853.

Khan, A., & Ahmed, R. (2020). Empirical analysis of correlates of education in the slum population: An evidence from Karachi, Pakistan. *International Transaction Journal of Engineering, Management, & Applied Sciences & Technologies, Management, 11*, 1–9.

Lucas, R. E. (1988). On the mechanics of economic development. *Journal of Monetary Economics, 22*(1), 3–42.

Maitra, B., & Mukhopadhyay, C. K. (2012). Public spending on education, health care and economic growth in selected countries of Asia and the Pacific. *Asia-Pacific Development Journal, 19*(2), 19–48.

Mallick, L., Das, P., & Pradhan, K. (2016). Impact of educational expenditure on economic growth in major Asian countries: Evidence from econometric analysis. *Theoretical and Applied Economics, 2*(607), 173–186.

Mincer, J. (1970). The distribution of labor incomes: A survey with special reference to the human capital approach. *Journal of Economics Literature, 8*(1), 1–26.

Mincer, J. (1974). The human capital earnings function. In J. A. Mincer (Ed.), *Schooling, experience, and earnings* (pp. 83–96). NBER.

Mitra, S., Mishra, S. K., & Abhay, R. K. (2023). Out-of-school girls in India: A study of socioeconomic-spatial disparities. *GeoJournal*, *88*(1), 341–357.

Montenegro, C. E., & Patrinos, H. A. (2021, October 27). A data set of comparable estimates of the private rate of return to schooling in the world, 1970–2014. *International Journal of Manpower*, *44*(6), 1248–1268.

Mottaleb, K. A., & Pallegedara, A. (2018). Patterns and determinants of private tutoring: The case of Bangladesh households. *International Journal of Educational Development*, *59*, 43–50.

Muhammad Al, M., & Kameyama, Y. (2019). Education and economic growth in South Asia. *International Journal of Development and Economic Sustainability*, *7*(4), 49–59.

Munir, K., & Kanwal, A. (2020). Impact of educational and gender inequality on income and income inequality in South Asian countries. *International Journal of Social Economics*, *47*(8), 1043–1062.

Munir, K., & Shahid, F. S. U. (2021). Role of demographic factors in economic growth of South Asian countries. *Journal of Economic Studies*, *48*(3), 557–570.

Muralidharan, K. (2012). Long-term effects of teacher performance pay: Experimental evidence from India [Working Paper]. University of California San Diego. https://econweb.ucsd.edu/~kamurali/papers/Working%20Papers/Long%20Term%20Effects%20of%20Teacher%20Performance%20Pay.pdf

Nagaraj, R., Varoudakis, A., & Veganzones, M.-A. (2000). Long-run growth trends and convergence across Indian States. *Journal of International Development*, *12*(1), 45–70.

Neupane, P. (2017). Barriers to education and school attainment – Evidence from secondary schools in rural Nepal. *International Education Studies*, *10*(2), 68–83.

Oztunc, H., Oo, Z. C., & Serin, Z. V. (2015). Effects of female education on economic growth: A cross country empirical study. *Educational Sciences: Theory and Practice*, *15*(2), 349–357.

Patel, G., & Annapoorna, M. S. (2019). Public education expenditure and its impact on human resource development in India: An empirical analysis. *South Asian Journal of Human Resources Management*, *6*(1), 97–109.

Patrinos, H. A., & Psacharopoulos, G. (2011). *Education: Past, present, and future global challenges* [World Bank Policy Research Working Paper 5616]. World Bank.

Patrinos, H. A., & Psacharopoulos, G. (2020). Returns to education in developing countries. In S. Bradley & C. Green (Eds.), *The economics of education* (pp. 53–64). Elsevier.

Paul, P. (2019). Effects of education and poverty on the prevalence of girl child marriage in India: A district–level analysis. *Children and Youth Services Review*, *100*, 16–21.

Pritchett, L. (2006). Does learning to add up add up? The returns to schooling in aggregate data. In E.A. Hanushek & F. Welch (Eds.) *Handbook of the economics of education* (pp. 635–695). North-Holland.

Psacharopoulos, G., & Patrinos, H. A. (2018). Returns to investment in education: A decennial review of the global literature. *Education Economics*, *26*(5), 445–458.

Qadri, F. S., & Waheed, A. (2011). Human capital and economic growth: Time series evidence from Pakistan. *Pakistan Business Review*, *1*, 815–833.

Qadri, F. S., & Waheed, A. (2014). Human capital and economic growth: A macroeconomic model for Pakistan. *Economic Modelling*, *42*, 66–76.

Qadri, F. S., & Waheed, A. (2017). Human capital-economic growth relationship: Finding the most relevant level of education in Pakistan. *South Asian Journal of Management Sciences*, *11*(2), 140–152.

Riaz, S., & Pervaiz, Z. (2018). The impact of women's education and employment on their empower-ment: an empricical evidence from household level survey. *Quality & Quantity: International Journal of Methodology*, *52*(6), 2855–2870.

Riboud, M., Savchenko, Y., & Tan, H. (2007). *The knowledge economy and education and training in South Asia*. World Bank.

Richards, J., Ahmed, M., & Islam, S. (2022). *The political economy of education in South Asia*. University of Toronto Press.

Education and Economic Development in South Asia

217

Sajjad, M., Munir, H., Kanwal, S., & Naqvi, S. A. A. (2022). Spatial inequalities in education status and its determinants in Pakistan: A district-level modeling in the context of sustainable development Goal-4. *Applied Geography, 140*, 102665.

Schultz, T. W. (1961). Investment in human capital. *The American Economic Review, 51*(1), 1–17

Sekhri, S. (2020). Prestige matters: Wage premium and value addition in elite colleges. *American Economic Journal: Applied Economics, 12*(3), 207–225.

Sekhri, S., & Debnath, S. (2014). Intergenerational consequences of early age marriages of girls: Effect on children's human capital. *The Journal of Development Studies, 50*(12), 1670–1686.

Shah, I. A., & Haq, I. U. (2022). Female labor participation rate and economic growth in South Asian countries. *Population Review, 61*(1), 43–57.

Spence, M. (1973). Job market signaling. *The Quarterly Journal of Economics, 87*(3), 355–374.

Streeten, P., Burki, S. J., ul Haq, M., Hicks N., & Stewart, F. (1981). *First things first: Meeting basic human needs in developing countries*. Oxford University Press.

Thapa, A. (2015). Public and private school performance in Nepal: An analysis using the SLC examination. *Education Economics, 23*(1), 47–62.

Thapa, S. B. (2013). Relationship between education and poverty in Nepal. *Economic Journal of Development Issues, 15 & 16*(1–2), 148–161.

UNESCO. (2015). *Incheon declaration and framework for action*, ED-2016/WS/28. https://unesdoc.unesco.org/ark:/48223/pf 0000245656

UNESCO. (2022). *South Asia: Non-state actors in education: Who chooses? Who loses?* Global Education Monitoring Report 2022.

UNESCO Institute for Statistics (UIS). (2020–2023). UIS. Stat bulk data download service. Retrieved September 19, 2023, from apiportal.uis.unesco.org/bdds

United Nations Children Fund (UNICEF). (2019). *More than half of South Asian youth are not on track to have the education and skills necessary for employment in 2030*. https://www.unicef.org/press-releases/more-half-south-asian-youth-are-not-track-have-education-and-skills-necessary

United Nations Children Fund (UNICEF). (2022). *The state of global learning poverty: 2022 update*. UNICEF. https://www.unicef.org/media/122921/file/StateofLearningPoverty2022.pdf

Vikram, K., & Chindarkar, N. (2020). Bridging the gaps in cognitive achievement in India: The crucial role of the integrated child development services in early childhood. *World Development, 127*, 1–15.

Wei, W., Sarker, T., Żukiewicz-Sobczak, W., Roy, R., Alam, G. M., Rabbany, M. G., Hossain, M. S., & Aziz, N. (2021). The influence of women's empowerment on poverty reduction in the rural areas of Bangladesh: Focus on health, education and living standard. *International Journal of Environmental Research and Public Health, 18*(13), 6909.

World Bank. (2021). *The human capital index 2020 update: Human capital in the time of COVID-19*. World Bank.

World Bank. (2022a). *Coping with shocks: Migration and the road to resilience*. World Bank.

World Bank. (2022b). *Poverty and shared prosperity 2022: Correcting course*. World Bank. https://doi.org/10.1596/978-1-4648-1893-6

EDUCATIONAL SHIFT OR NEW AGE FOR TEACHING AND LEARNING: EXAMINING THE JOURNEY OF THE INDIAN EDUCATIONAL SYSTEM DURING THE COVID-19 PANDEMIC

Praveen K. Dubey

Montana State University Northern, USA

ABSTRACT

This paper provides an examination of the characteristics of educational shift in Indian education during COVID-19 based on the existing research published from March 2020 to December 2023. The paper examines the technological preparedness of all the stakeholders and how technological preparedness created digital equity and inclusivity for digital learning in Indian schools. Given the world-wide closure and shutdown during early 2020, schools were forced to switch their instructions to the newly adopted educational model; namely, digital learning which makes it important to examine two aspects in education: (1) measures taken to provide digital educational opportunities to all students and (2) steps taken to create digital equity and inclusivity in the Indian educational system. The results suggest that several initiatives were taken at national, state, and local level. However, issues of digital equity existed for underprivileged student populations.

Keywords: COVID-19; India; equity; digital preparedness; technology initiatives

---

Annual Review of Comparative and International Education 2023
International Perspectives on Education and Society, Volume 48, 219–233
Copyright © 2025 by Emerald Publishing Limited
All rights of reproduction in any form reserved
ISSN: 1479-3679/doi:10.1108/S1479-367920240000048012

INTRODUCTION

The globalization and open market in the early 1990s created an opportunity in Indian society that has helped the country grow economically and technologically, and provided technological advantages for education (Singh & Kaur, 2017). The significant technological advancements created an alternative form of teaching and learning but could not provide the same access as traditional ways of learning. Thus, to create human development, the Indian government needs to promote globalization of Information and Communication Technology (ICT) in the Indian education system wisely (Behera & Sahoo, 2022). The barriers exist in the Indian education system in the form of ICT scarcity, lack of ICT understanding, and missing opportunities in teacher preparation; however, there is an enormous possibility for India to address these issues constructively and innovatively (Byker, 2014). The 21st-century digital revolution helped improve India to overcome the issues of first-order barriers but the second-order barriers, especially teachers' beliefs remain the challenge in integrating technologies in education (Grover & Mathew, 2022).

The Indian Government reauthorized the National Education Policy (NEP) 2020 with the vision to promote digital technology as a way of transforming India into a global knowledge hub (Gilbertson et al., 2023; NEP, 2020). However, during the pandemic, the schools in India had been closed indefinitely despite the evidence that most children had no access to technology for online learning (Azim Premji Foundation, 2020). Even though there was technological advancement, the COVID-19 pandemic disrupted the teaching-learning process for both students as well as teachers (Singh & Meena, 2022). The second-order barriers hindered the successful implementation of the digitalization of the educational system in India during the pandemic (Grover & Mathew, 2022). The students were severely affected due to lockdown (UNESCO, 2023) which forced teachers and students to continue the teaching-learning process with the help of technology-driven digital platforms such as Skype, Google meet, Microsoft Team, and Google Classroom (Onyema, 2020). According to UNICEF 2020 report, in India, the school closure impacted 275 million students in preschool, elementary, and secondary schools which makes it extremely important to examine the impact of the COVID-19 pandemic on the Indian education system.

The worldwide closure forced schools to shut down during early 2020 which also affected Indian schools. The schools in India were forced to switch their instructions to the newly adopted educational model; namely, digital learning which raises tons of issues and concerns among all the stakeholders. Different state governments responded to combat the pandemic by using educational apps that were aligned with the NEP 2020 to create transparency and accountability among learners and provide extended learning opportunities (Hindustan Times, 2022; The Times of India, 2022). Online teaching stood out as the only option for learning during the pandemic (Gilbertson et al., 2023). Thus, this paper examines the characteristics of educational shift in Indian education during the COVID-19 pandemic based on the existing research published from March 2020 to December 2023. The literature review focuses on examining the technological preparedness of all the stakeholders and what initiatives

Educational Shift or New Age for Teaching and Learning

had been taken to provide the availability of resources and material for online learning. Additionally, I am examining how digital equity and inclusivity were presented in Indian schools for Indian teachers and students. Given the importance of digital learning in Indian schools, it is important to examine two aspects: (1) initiatives taken to provide digital educational opportunities for all students and (2) steps taken to create digital equity and inclusivity in the Indian education system. Interestingly, this study will provide insight into the Indian education system in creating a new landscape through technology for teaching and learning and how a new ecosystem would develop to address the future initiatives for educational policy.

HISTORY OF TECHNOLOGY USAGE IN INDIAN EDUCATION

The Indian education system is the prime example of both challenges and opportunities as cultural values are deep rooted in society and being a part of education is to bring the best practices to bridge the learning gaps (Brinkmann, 2018). In the last two decades, the Government of India has attempted to positively transform the school education system through programs such as the Sarva Shiksha Abhiyan (SSA) 2001, the National Curriculum Framework for School Education (NCF) 2023, the Right to Education Act (RTE) 2009, and the NEP 2020. These plans are based on developing the range of human capacities, values, and dispositions, improving curricular and pedagogical structure, and helping change the practices in education (NCF, 2023). In an attempt to streamline education, India is moving from "teacher-centered" learning to "learner-centered" classrooms (Brinkmann, 2018).

Equitable and inclusive learning for all is echoed to reduce the societal gaps in access, participation, and learning outcomes in school education (NEP, 2020). Under NEP, the "Digital India Campaign (DIC)" is initiated as "Technology Enabler" by creating the National Educational Technology Forum (NETF) to enhance learning, assessment, planning, and administration with the use of technology. The core principles of NETF are to ensure equity in quality access of education, thriving education ecosystem, mobility, integrating technology, and self-sustainability (NETF, n.a.). These principles entail steps to include technology in education but face enormous challenges as the general belief is that face-to-face teaching is the only way to shape the future. Adding technology to education is somehow motivated by "learner-centered" education reforms where students' learning is rooted in culturally shaped beliefs of teacher practices (Brinkmann, 2018).

THE NEP

The first NEP was formulated by the Government of India in 1968 as a result of Kothari Commission Report 1966 to provide vision for the national education system (Guhathakurta, 2020). Recently, the NEP was reauthorized by Prime

Minister Narendra Modi in 2020 to achieve the nation's full potential for human development while promoting equity, inclusivity, and just society. The goals of NEP 2020 are aligned with the Indian government's global agenda initiative as described in the United Nations Sustainable Development Goal (SDG) which states that by 2030 India will "ensure inclusive, equitable and quality education for all" (SDG India Index Baseline Report, 2018, p. 51).

The NEP 2020 defines new pedagogical and curricular structure into four stages of schooling defined as $5 + 3 + 3 + 4$ where foundational stage starts at the age of 3–6 (pre-school) and 6–8 (grades 1 and 2); preparatory stage from age 8–11 (grades 3–5); middle stage from age 11–14 (grades 6–8); and secondary stage from age 14–18 (grades 9–12) (NEP, 2020). The NEP addresses the issues of teacher quality through teacher-focused reforms where teacher employment is based on merit-based scholarships, incentives for relocation, teacher proficiency exams, and need-based regular professional development (NEP, 2020). The NEP also recognizes teachers who perform outstanding work and recognizes them with promotion and salary increases.

The NEP 2020 has a strong focus on the use of ICT as an integral part of classroom teaching and learning through the DIC. The goal of the DIC program 2015 was to build a digitally empowered society to enhance the knowledge economy which is centered in three areas: (1) digital infrastructure as a core utility to every citizen, (2) governance and services on demand, and (3) digital empowerment of citizens (Digital India, n.d.; NEP, 2020). The NEP 2020 uses similar principles and majors to promote the integration of technology in education and ensures the equitable use of technology (NEP, 2020).

In recent years, India started a movement to switch from "teacher-centered" to "learner-centered" classrooms through different reforms such as SSA program, the NCF 2005, and the RTE 2009 (Brinkmann, 2015). The NEP recognizes these efforts and reiterates that education is the foundational and fundamental to human development and ICT plays an inevitable role in acquiring knowledge, and information. Technology is described as a fundamental principle stated as "extensive use of technology in teaching and learning, removing language barriers, increasing access for Divyang students, and educational planning and management" (NEP 2020, p.5).

TEACHER BELIEF FOR TECHNOLOGY INTEGRATION IN CLASSROOM

The advancement in 21st-century technology and digital problem-solving skills has mandated its use in education (Ferrari, 2013; Siddiq et al., 2016; Van Laar et al., 2017). The diffusion of ICT has influenced the adoption of school technology policies around the globe (Siddiq et al., 2016). Similar efforts have been seen in India through the nationwide adoption of technology policy forums such as the NETF. To achieve the ambitious goals of technology-enabled classrooms, teachers should be the focus (Ertmer & Ottenbreit-Leftwich, 2013). However, to familiarize with using technology in classrooms, teachers need training on how to use digital devices for teaching and learning (Hashim & Vonkulluksn, 2018).

Interestingly, a meta-analysis study in low- and middle-income countries suggests that technology-driven professional development can support peer learning, leverage cultural differences, and improve the attitude and cognition of teachers (Hennessy et al., 2022). Before considering any digital devices or platforms for student learning, schools need to investigate whether these digital devices or platforms support students' easy access and train teachers how to make it useful for student learning (Sun et al., 2021). Additionally in developing countries, the facilitators or coaches play an extremely important role in technology-embedded professional development in improving teachers' skills and attitudes toward technology usage in teaching and learning (Hennessy et al., 2022).

The importance of integrating ICT in education is recognized but possesses challenges and barriers. Two types of barriers exist in technology usage in education: (1) external or first-order, which is associated with resources, training, and support, and (2) internal or second-order, which is associated with attitudes and beliefs, knowledge, and skills (Ertmer, 1999). Research suggests that first-order barriers can be removed by providing teachers ICT resources, professional development, and digital curriculum, and the second-order barriers with effective implementation of ICT policies (Prestridge, 2012). Interestingly, teachers agreed that professional development activities will help plan online learning effectively, and focus should be on personalized professional learning opportunities (Shin et al., 2022). On another note, the Technological Pedagogical Content Knowledge (TPACK) framework identifies what technological knowledge and skills teachers lack and what professional development is needed to improve the effective use of technology in teaching and learning (Koehler & Mishra, 2009; Mishra & Koehler, 2006). Thus, it is important to consider such a framework to provide professional learning opportunities to teachers' in improving teachers' use of technology for pedagogical purposes.

During the COVID-19 pandemic, students depend on educational apps for learning as a source which provides academic assistance by bridging the gap between classroom and home learning, and it recommends all stakeholders to increase the usage of educational apps in academics (Menon, 2022). Similar study in Singapore schools revealed that the substantial student population did not use digital devices for reading at all but used it for playing games as they lacked required skills for digital reading (Sun et al., 2021). Thus, it is evident that the emphasis should be on providing training and help while implementing digital technology for teaching and learning for a positive learning experience. Additionally, the importance lies in supporting teachers with using and troubleshooting technology along with best practices for teaching and learning (Shin et al., 2022).

For India, even though the entire Indian education system was switched to online learning, many teachers remained ignorant in the implementation of technology into their classrooms where their beliefs and attitudes contributed heavily (Grover & Mathew, 2022). The idea of ICT revolves around creating a rich, student-centered learning environment which promotes opportunities for learning (DenBeste, 2003), and technology can facilitate real-life learning experiences with an interesting classroom environment and better student attention (Pazilah et al., 2019). So, India as a developing country requires significant investment in education as a combating tool with poverty (Al-Zaidiyeen et al., 2010).

Content and pedagogical knowledge are mutually exclusive which helps teachers to integrate pedagogy and content to answer what and how of teaching (Shulman, 1986a). However, teachers' transformation of pedagogical content knowledge is influenced by their individual cultural and philosophical beliefs associated with their instructional strategies, students' previous content knowledge and learning difficulties (Deng, 2018). Thus, to achieve the goals of equity learning, transformation process should include content knowledge, pedagogical content, and curricular knowledge (Shulman, 1986b). To support such a claim, a study shows that the school closure during the COVID-19 pandemic did not affect students' reading preference as they still prioritize print reading over digital reading because of negative experiences such as difficulty obtaining materials or some physical constraints and years of training with print reading (Sun et al., 2021). Additionally, to fight such barriers, use of technology for professional development can reduce inequalities in remote areas with sufficient investment and strategic planning especially for situations such as created during COVID-19 (Hennessy et al., 2022).

The evidence presented here suggests that the future of the Indian education system is based on teachers' belief that the use of technology can provide high-quality education irrespective of sex, religion, location, and backgrounds. Most importantly, professional development can improve teachers' attitude and cultural beliefs toward technology usage for learning. This claim is supported by a meta-analysis study that suggests that the use of technology for providing professional development to preservice and in-service teachers in middle- and low-income countries is effective if it is designed involving teachers and for the teachers instead of being imposed (Hennessy et al., 2022). The NEP 2020 lays a similar vision with policy recommendation for the use of digital technology in providing online classes and e-learning resources to enhance digital equity in education. The policy emphasizes the need to develop digital infrastructure through significant investments from public and private sectors to integrate digital technology as a part of curriculum (NEP, 2020), which will eventually help teachers to improve their personal and cultural beliefs regarding use of technology for teaching and learning processes.

Elements of Teacher Quality and Pandemic

Teacher quality is the strongest factor in the student learning process (Hattie, 2003) and it has the most contribution in determining student achievement (Hanushek, 2011; Tyler et al., 2010). The importance of teacher quality in student achievement makes it an essential element for improvement. Previous research suggests that teacher quality can be improved through active-learning strategies, job-embedded practices, and sustained focus on improvement (Kraft & Blazar, 2016; Wiswall, 2011).

The classroom observation has elements that provide information regarding students' academic achievements which suggests that high-performing teachers are necessary for learning as well as for the nation's economy (Hanushek, 2011; Tyler et al., 2010). Schools lack a robust teacher-evaluation system which needs

Educational Shift or New Age for Teaching and Learning 225

to be overhauled so that effective teacher characteristics and best practices can be identified (Hanushek, 2011). So, robust teacher evaluation systems are important in identifying best practices and characteristics of effective teachers (Hanushek, 2011). There are several characteristics that are associated with higher student achievement and factors that most influential are effective classroom instructions with quality (Vagi et al., 2019). Similar results have been found on a meta-analysis which suggests classroom management, structured lessons, and appropriate learning outcomes influence student achievement (Hattie, 2008).

In particular, research on India suggests that teachers have a great influence on students' achievement, and they matter a lot (Azam & Kingdon, 2015). Teachers add value to student learning and teacher value-addition focuses directly on the relationship between teacher and student where a good teacher gets higher achievement from their students consistently (Hanushek & Rivkin, 2012). In other words, a teacher influences students to an extent where they constantly perform higher. The NEP recognizes the importance of teacher quality and puts teachers at the center of the education system. Thus, from a policy perspective, it is necessary to focus on the characteristics of teacher quality that matter most such as creating a pipeline to provide continuing professional development and relationship building exercises so that teachers' have value added services because the observed characteristics such as qualifications, training, years of experience does not matter for teacher quality (Azam & Kingdon, 2015).

To meet the goals of higher teacher quality, the NEP 2020 recommends integrating technology in education through support, adoption, interventions, and transparency. Under NEP 2020, the NETF is created to promote the use of technology to enhance learning, assessment, planning, and administration (NEP, 2020). Implementing such measures will not only improve teacher quality but ensure equitable use of technology in online and digital learning for students. Additionally, to ensure the teacher quality of teacher education programs and in-service teachers, the NEP 2020 recommends streamline recruitment and deployment, improved school environment and culture, continuous professional development, robust merit-based structure for tenure, promotion, and salary, and professional standard protocol for teachers (NEP, 2020). The goal is to motivate and empower teachers so that children have quality teachers who are building the future of the nation. Apart from all these initiatives and standardized definition of teacher quality in India, characteristics of teacher quality are vague and have no common understanding of what teacher quality is or should be (Kumar & Wiseman, 2021).

DATA AND METHODOLOGY

To examine the measures taken in providing educational opportunities and digital equity and inclusivity to all students in the Indian educational system during the COVID-19 pandemic, the comparative and international education research publication was analyzed from March 2020 to December 2023. The research articles were collected from international subscription journals, journals focused on Indian education, open access journals, reports published by different national and international organizations, and different state and national government websites. Additionally, research articles that focus only on the Indian education system were considered. The paper also reviewed articles and reports from the Ministry of Education, Government of India, Indira Gandhi National Open University (IGNOU), State Education Ministry, The United Nations Educational, Scientific and Cultural Organization (UNESCO), United Nations International Children's Emergency Fund (UNICEF), World Health Organization (WHO), and other available open sources.

The literature was reviewed in two categories. First, the research articles were reviewed for the technological preparedness in the Indian education system during COVID-19. Second, the articles were reviewed for the evidence of digital equity and inclusivity for learners. Finally, the articles were compared to examine how these two categories interact and overlap with each other. The research suggests a severe shortage of published literature on Indian education and analysis of situations of education during COVID-19 pandemic, and made it extremely difficult to examine the entire picture of the Indian education system.

RESULTS

ICT Initiatives in India During Pandemic

The Indian Government always preferred using ICT to meet the learning needs of its masses. In fact, India successfully initiated the Computer Literacy and Studies in Schools (CLASS) 1984 project to meet learning goals of nations schools' and become a role model for other developing countries (Nag, 1989). Such efforts continued throughout the pandemic. In fact, during the pandemic, the Indian education system witnessed several ICT-driven initiatives on national, state, and local levels. Some of these ICT programs already existed and the central government leveraged it to meet the educational needs created by the pandemic (Singh et al., 2021).

In this section, we will examine the initiatives taken at national, state, and local levels to revamp the teaching and learning needs of teachers as well as students.

National-level Initiatives

To fight the challenges of online learning, the Indian government initiated PM eVidya, a national campaign under the "Atma Nirbhar Bharat Abhiyaan" on May 17, 2020, to consolidate all the digital initiatives as one portal (India Report Digital Education, 2020). The goal was to unify all the efforts to enable equitable learning for 250 million school-going students. Additionally, the National Council for Educational Research & Training (NCERT) developed an alternative academic calendar for grades 1–12 to overcome the challenges created by the global pandemic (India Report Digital Education, 2020).

Digital Infrastructure for Knowledge Sharing (DIKSHA)

DIKSHA (Digital Infrastructure for Knowledge Sharing) was launched on September 5th, 2017 (Ministry of Education, Government of India, n.d.). The digital learning infrastructure for teachers and students is available in 18

Educational Shift or New Age for Teaching and Learning 227

different languages. The Diksha online portal tracks students' progress and monitors students' resource usage with their state affiliations.

National Repository of Open Educational Resources (NROER)
The NROER was launched on August 2013 as a collaborative initiative of the Department of School Education and Literacy, the Central Institute of Educational Technology (CIET), NCERT, and Homi Bhabha Centre for Science Education. The resources are available in different formats such as audios, videos, images, and documents for students to use for learning.

ePathshala
ePathshala is a learning portal developed in collaboration with CIET and the NCERT and launched in 2015 to provide educational resources for teachers, students, parents, and researchers. The contents are available through apps in three different languages such as English, Hindi, and Urdu. The platform offers Grades 1–12 NCERT books, periodicals, and teacher training materials (Pai, 2015).

Manodarpan
The outbreak of the COVID-19 pandemic created a challenging environment for students, teachers, and families. To fight for the well-being of all, the Indian government started an Initiative the "MANODARPAN" for psycho-social support for mental health and well-being of students (Manodarpan Initiatives, 2020). The program created a dedicated website, helpline, counseling support, webinars, interactive chat platform, and national-level database directory of health professionals to support well-being of all stakeholders.

Swayam Prabha TV Channels
Swayam Prabha TV Channels were inaugurated on July 7, 2017, to telecast high-quality educational programs 24 hours a day, 7 days a week through 12 dedicated TV channels (Swayam Prabha, n.d.). Under the Swayam Prabha program, at least 4 hours of educational content are presented and it gets repeated 5 more times throughout the day to allow students to choose a time which is convenient and works best for their learning needs (Singh et al., 2021).

All India Radio
During the lockdown, All India Radio (AIR) broadcasted educational content through their regional channels to help students continue their education and provided curriculum-based classes for all grade levels (The Economic Times, 2020). Additionally, these virtual classes include quizzes in several states.

State-level Initiatives
State governments also took an effort to e-Learning initiatives to meet the demands of teaching and learning during the pandemic (Sharma, 2021). Several states launched digital learning programs to meet the specific demands of their

228 PRAVEEN K. DUBEY

student populations. For example, Chhattisgarh – Education at your doorstep initiative, Kerala – KITE initiative, Madhya Pradesh – DigiLEP initiative, Delhi – Parenting in times of Corona, Punjab – iScuela Learn, Andhra Pradesh – Abhyasa APP, Bihar – eLearning portal, and Jammu and Kashmir – Samadhan AI-based educational Chatbot (Singh et al., 2021).

Individual Initiatives

To help meet the learning needs of students during the pandemic, the individual institutions for both profit and non-profit collaboratively participated in providing interactive learning opportunities through ICT resources, computers and laptops, and learning platforms. For example, Lenovo initiated SmarterED learning platforms in multiple languages for students and teachers, Digital Empowerment Foundation initiated Digital Daan to crowdsource digital technology devices from urban to rural areas, and several individual teachers created learning groups to meet the learning needs of teachers and students (Sharma, 2021).

Digital Equity and Inclusivity During Pandemic in Indian Education System

Equitable and inclusive education supports and welcomes diversity among all students with a purpose to eliminate social exclusion created due to attitudes and responses based on race, social class, ethnicity, religion, gender, and ability (Ainscow, 2020). Thus, to achieve the goals of equity and inclusion, academic assistance, convenience, entertainment, social influence, novelty, activity, and engagement are the motivations behind the use of digital technology resources such as apps (Menon, 2022). But the quick move to online learning highlighted inequalities in students' and teachers' preparation, access to digital devices, and high-speed internet for learning activities (Shin et al., 2022).

Technology enhances student-centered learning as it promotes the idea of digital equity and inclusivity. The meta-analysis suggests that educational apps embedded into school contexts and routines improved students' achievement in reading and math compared to schools with no such app usage (Kim et al., 2021). Thus, the success of the student-centered learning approach depends on bringing Indian teachers teaching practices aligned with their beliefs and providing them professional development based on their self-assessed commitments to achieve their own professional goals (Brinkmann, 2015).

Similar issues are common around the world (Atmojo & Nugroho, 2020), and it is recommended that schools should consider infrastructure issues carefully before designing and facilitating online learning activities (Shin et al., 2022). The report from September 2020 suggests that most children in India had no access to online education and recommended to open schools immediately (Azim Premji Foundation, 2020). Ashikali et al. (2020) suggest that students need to feel that they belong to the group and have enough opportunities to express themselves in inclusive classrooms. Another study suggests that a positive relationship between social influence and the intention to use educational apps for learning exists (Menon, 2022). Additionally, teachers' perception suggests that students' self-preparedness impacted their online learning and faced challenges due to the

Educational Shift or New Age for Teaching and Learning 229

modality of learning (Shin et al., 2022). It is recommended to consider the main challenges faced by teachers were keeping students engaged, learning progression, and issues associated with technology troubleshooting (Shin et al., 2022). Parents and students have different motives behind using educational apps and digital technology (Menon, 2022) so careful consideration is needed to assess the situations and opportunities of digital classrooms.

Even though India has transitioned to an advanced digital revolution the educational outcomes were decreased due to the digital divide affecting low-income groups during the pandemic (Grover & Mathew, 2022). The situations created by the pandemic prompted educational systems to adopt an emergency learning with quick transfer to meet the student learning. The teacher's competence and skills to use technology stand out as an important factor in online learning (Muthuprasad, 2021).

CONCLUSION

The Indian education system suffered with the COVID-19 pandemic crisis which created short-term learning losses, school closures, and loss in human capital; additionally, economic uncertainties widened the digital divide among masses (World Economic Forum, 2020). The results showed that during the time of sheer uncertainty and constant fear amid the COVID-19 pandemic, technology has been a source of hope and lifeline in many ways (Sharma, 2021). All the technological initiatives started at national, state, and local levels during the pandemic were aligned with the visions of NEP 2020 to implement digital technology in education.

The research findings of this study suggest that the government of India started several initiatives during the COVID-19 pandemic but a lot of the programs started way before and were streamlined during the pandemic to provide equitable learning opportunities for all students. In fact, the Indian government used a uniform approach to avail all the digital resources through PM eVidya's Atma Nirbhar Bharat Abhiyaan. Additionally, to create awareness, the Indian Government launched a week-long campaign "bharatpadhe online" to improve the online transfer of knowledge in schools (Bozkurt et al., 2020).

The benefits of online learning were evident, but teachers were not yet ready to handle online teaching during these times (Mahesh, 2020; Azevedo et al., 2020). E-learning became the new normal, but students and institutions had suffered with uncertainty imposed by untrained and underqualified teachers to use digital technology for educational purposes (World Economic Forum, 2020). The Indian educational system had opportunity gaps among different groups and the pandemic made it visible. Additionally, economic uncertainties created by the pandemic widen the digital divide among masses. More training and proper procedures were demanded by teachers in providing online learning.

The impact of COVID-19 on education drastically affected India's Human Development Index where India ranked lowest among BRICS countries (Grover & Mathew, 2022). In Singapore, during the COVID-19 school closure, reading was a preferred leisure activity for fun and relaxation because students had more time and supported students' mental well-being (Sun et al., 2021) but similar results were not visible in India. The National Sample Survey Organization (NSSO) 2017-2018 report suggests that less than 47% of households have more than 12 hours of electricity and more than 36% of schools have no access to electricity which impacts schools with lower SES (Ministry of Statistics and Program Implementation, 2019). Similar situations affected students with lower SES for technology usage during the pandemic. Many initiatives were taken but there was a large digital divide that existed and created the issues of social justice towards education because of missing teaching and learning opportunities (Sahni, 2020). In fact, the COVID-19 pandemic caused educational inequality and worsened the existing disparities (UNICEF, n.d.). The students from underprivileged backgrounds end up having inefficiency and lack of adaptation of technology for learning (World Economic Forum, 2020). In other words, underprivileged students suffered due to the pandemic even after multiple initiatives started at national, state, and local levels.

REFERENCES

Ainscow, M. (2020). Promoting inclusion and equity in education: Lessons from international experiences. *Nordic Journal of Studies in Educational Policy*, 6(1), 7–16. https://doi.org/10.1080/2002 0317.2020.1729587

Al-Zaidiyeen, N. J., Mei, L. L., & Fook, F. S. (2010). Teachers' attitudes and levels of technology use in classrooms: The case of Jordan schools. *International Education Studies*, 3(2). https://doi. org/10.5539/ies.v3n2p211

Ashikali, T., Groeneveld, S., & Kuipers, B. (2020). The role of inclusive leadership in supporting an inclusive climate in diverse public sector teams. *Review of Public Personnel Administration*, 41(3), 497–519. https://doi.org/10.1177/0734371x19899722

Atmojo, A. E., & Nugroho, A. (2020). EFL classes must go online! Teaching activities and challenges during COVID-19 pandemic in Indonesia. *Register Journal*, 13(1), 49–76. https://doi. org/10.18326/rgt.v13i1.49-76

Azam, M., & Kingdon, G. G. (2015). Assessing teacher quality in India. *Journal of Development Economics*, 117, 74–83. https://doi.org/10.1016/j.jdeveco.2015.07.001

Azevedo, J. P., Hasan, A., Goldemberg, D., Iqbal, S. A., & Geven, K. (2020). Simulating the potential impacts of covid-19 school closures on schooling and learning outcomes: A set of global estimates. The World Bank. https://reliefweb.int/report/world/simulating-potential-impacts-covid-19-school-closures-schooling-and-learning-outcomes

Azim Premji Foundation. (2020). Myths of online education. Field studies in education. Azim Premji Foundation. https://azimpremjiuniversity.edu.in/field-studies-in-education/myths-of-online-education

Behera, J., Sahoo, D. (2022). Asymmetric relationships between information and communication technology (ICT), globalization, and human development in India: evidence from non-linear ARDL analysis. *Economic Structures*, 11, 10. https://doi.org/10.1186/s40008-022-00269-5

Bozkurt, A., Jung, I., Xiao, J., Vladimirschi, V., Schuwer, R., Egorov, G., Lambert, S. R., Al Freih, M., Pete, J., Olcott, D., Jr., Rodes, V., Aranciaga, I., Bali, M., Alvarez, A. V., Jr., Roberts, J., Pazurek, A., Raffaghelli, J. E., Panagiotou, N., de Coëtlogon, P., ... Paskevicius, M. (2020). A global outlook to the interruption of education due to COVID-19 pandemic: Navigating in a time of uncertainty and crisis. *Asian Journal of Distance Education*, 15(1), 1–126. https://doi. org/10.5281/zenodo.3878572

Brinkmann, S. (2015). Learner-centred education reforms in India: The missing piece of teachers' beliefs. *Policy Futures in Education*, 13(3), 342–359. https://doi.org/10.1177/1478210315569038

Educational Shift or New Age for Teaching and Learning 231

Brinkmann, S. (2018). Teachers' beliefs and educational reform in India: From 'learner-centred' to 'learning-centred' education. *Comparative Education, 55*(1), 9–29. https://doi.org/10.1080/030 50068.2018.1541661

Byker, E. (2014). ICT in India's elementary schools: The vision and realities. *International Education Journal: Comparative Perspectives, 13*(2), 27–40.

DenBeste, M. (2003). Power point, technology, and the web: More than just an overhead projector for the new century? *The History Teacher, 36*(4), 491. https://doi.org/10.2307/1555576

Deng, Z. (2018). Pedagogical content knowledge reconceived: Bringing curriculum thinking into the conversation on teachers' content knowledge. *Teaching and Teacher Education, 72,* 155–164. https://doi.org/10.1016/j.tate.2017.11.021

Digital India. (n.d.). *Vision & vision areas.* https://digitalindia.gov.in/vision-vision-areas/

DIKSHA. (2017). *DIKSHA (Digital Infrastructure for Knowledge Sharing).* https://pmevidya.education.gov.in/diksha.html

Ertmer, P. A. (1999). Addressing first- and second-order barriers to change: Strategies for technology integration. *Educational Technology Research and Development, 47*(4), 47–61. https://doi.org/10.1007/bf02299597

Ertmer, P. A., & Ottenbreit-Leftwich, A. (2013). Removing obstacles to the pedagogical changes required by Jonassen's vision of authentic technology-enabled learning. *Computers & Education, 64,* 175–182. https://doi.org/10.1016/j.compedu.2012.10.008

Ferrari, A. (2013). *DIGCOMP: A framework for developing and understanding digital Competence in Europe.* No. 38. 3-17. http://www.openeducationeuropa.eu/nl/elearning_papers

Gilbertson, A., Dey, J., Singh, P., & Grills, N. (2023). The only option? Distance learning in North India during the COVID-19 pandemic. *Learning, Media and Technology,* 1–14. https://doi.org/10.1080/17439884.2023.2189734

Guhathakurta, A. (2020, August 24). India's New Education Policy 2020: Highlights and opportunities. British Council. https://education-services.britishcouncil.org/insights-blog/india%E2%80%99s-new-education-policy-2020-highlights-and-opportunities

Grover, S., & Mathew, L. (2022). Exploring the digital revolution in education in India during the COVID-19 pandemic. *The International Journal of Social Quality, 12*(2), 51–71. https://doi.org/10.3167/ijsq.2022.120204

Hanushek, E. (2011). Valuing teachers: How much is a good teacher worth? https://hanushek.stanford.edu/publications/valuing-teachers-how-much-good-teacher-worth

Hanushek, E. A., & Rivkin, S. G. (2012). The distribution of teacher quality and implications for policy. *Annual Review of Economics, 4*(1), 131–157. https://doi.org/10.1146/annurev-economics-080511-111001

Hashim, A. K., & Vonkulluksn, V. W. (2018). E-reader apps and reading engagement: A descriptive case study. *Computers & Education, 125,* 358–375. https://doi.org/10.1016/j.compedu.2018.06.021

Hattie, J. (2003). *Teachers make a difference, what is the research evidence?* ACER Research Repository. https://research.acer.edu.au/research_conference_2003/4/

Hattie, J. (2008). *Visible learning: A synthesis of over 800 meta-analyses relating to achievement.* Routledge.

Hennessy, S., D'Angelo, S., Kreimeia, A., Koomar, S., Cao, L., McIntyre, N., Brugha, M., & Zubairi, A. (2022). *Technology use for teacher professional development in low- and middle-income countries: Recommendations for policy from a systematic review.* https://doi.org/10.53832/edtechhub.0080

HindustanTimes.(2022,March24).*EdtechstartupTagHiveallsettodeployitsAI-poweredapp'ClassSaathi'.* https://www.hindustantimes.com/brand-stories/edtech-startup-taghive-all-set-to-deploy-its-ai-powered-app-class-saathi-101648122883812.html

India Report Digital Education. (2020). Major initiatives | Government of India, Ministry of Education. https://www.education.gov.in/sites/upload_files/mhrd/files/India_Report_Digital_Education_0.pdf

Kim, J., Gilbert, J., Yu, Q., & Gale, C. (2021). Measures matter: A meta-analysis of the effects of educational apps on preschool to grade 3 children's literacy and math skills. *AERA Open, 7,* 233285842110041. https://doi.org/10.1177/23328584211004183

Koehler, M., & Mishra, P. (2009). *What is technological pedagogical content knowledge (TPACK)?* Learning&Technology Library (LearnTechLib). https://www.learntechlib.org/primary/p/29544/

Kraft, M. A., & Blazar, D. (2016). Individualized coaching to improve teacher practice across grades and subjects. New experimental evidence. *Educational Policy*, *31*(7), 1033–1068. https://doi.org/10.1177/0895904816631099

Kumar, P., & Wiseman, A. W. (2021). *Teacher quality and education policy in India*. https://doi.org/10.4324/9781003054726

Mahesh, S. (2020, May). A need now but no replacement: Teachers share concerns about online classes during COVID-19. *The New Indian Express*. https://www.newindianexpress.com/education/2020/may/06/a-need-now-but-no-replacement-teachers-share-concerns-about-online-classes-during-covid-19-2139605.html

Manodarpan Initiatives. (2020). *Ministry of human resource development*. Covid Advisories. https://covidadvisories.iisc.ac.in/wp-content/uploads/2020/07/Manodarpan-initiative.pdf

Menon, D. (2022). Uses and gratifications of educational apps: A study during COVID-19 pandemic. *Computers and Education Open*, *3*, 100076. https://doi.org/10.1016/j.caeo.2022.100076

Mishra, P., & Koehler, M. J. (2006). Technological pedagogical content knowledge: A framework for teacher knowledge. *Teachers College Record*, *108*(6), 1017–1054. https://doi.org/10.1111/j.1467-9620.2006.00684.x

Ministry of Education, Government of India (n.d.). *Major initiatives*. https://www.education.gov.in/sites/upload_files/mhrd/files/India_Report_Digital_Education_0.pdf

Ministry of Statistics and Program Implementation, Government of India. (2019). *Periodic Labour Force Survey (PLFS)*. https://mospi.gov.in/sites/default/files/publication_reports/Annual%20Report%2C%20PLFS%202017-18_31052019.pdf?download=1

Muthuprasad, T., Aiswarya, S., Aditya, K., & Jha, G. K. (2021). Students' perception and preference for online education in India during COVID-19 pandemic. *Social Sciences & Humanities Open*, *3*(1).

Nag, B. (1989). Informatics education in India: The CLASS project for secondary students. *Higher Education Policy*, *2*(4), 71–72. https://doi.org/10.1057/hep.1989.76

National Education Policy. (2020). Major initiatives | Government of India, Ministry of Education. https://www.education.gov.in/sites/upload_files/mhrd/files/NEP_Final_English_0.pdf

National Repository of Open Educational Resources (NROER). (2013). *Major initiatives | Government of India*. Ministry of Education. https://www.education.gov.in/sites/upload_files/mhrd/files/upload_document/National%20Repository%20of%20Open%20Educational%20Resources.pdf

Onyema. (2020). Impact of coronavirus pandemic on education. *Journal of Education and Practice*, *11*(13), 108–121. https://www.iiste.org/Journals/index.php/JEP/article/view/52821/54575

Pai, V. (2015, November 9). *Government launches ePathshala & other initiatives for education*. MediaNama. https://www.medianama.com/2015/11/223-shalasiddhi-epathshala-saaransh/

Pazilah, F. N., Hashim, H., & Yunus, M. M. (2019). Using technology in ESL classroom: Highlights and challenges. *Creative Education*, *10*(12), 3205–3212. https://doi.org/10.4236/ce.2019.1012244

Prestridge, S. (2012). The beliefs behind the teacher that influences their ICT practices. *Computers & Education*, *58*(1), 449–458. https://doi.org/10.1016/j.compedu.2011.08.028

Sahni, U. (2020). *COVID-19 in India: Education disrupted and lessons learned* [Web log post]. https://www.brookings.edu/blog/education-plus-development/2020/05/14/covid-19-in-india-education-disrupted-and-lessons-learned/

SDG India Index Baseline Report. (2018). *NITI Aayog*. https://www.niti.gov.in/sites/default/files/2020-07/SDX_Index_India_Baseline_Report_21-12-2018.pdf

Sharma, A. (2021). *Center for sustainable development*. https://csd.columbia.edu/sites/default/files/content/docs/ICT%20India/Papers/ICT_India_Working_Paper_42.pdf

Shin, J. K., Borup, J., Barbour, M. K., & Quiroga Velasquez, R. V. (2022). Webinars for English language teachers during the pandemic: Global perspectives on transitioning to remote online teaching. *AERA Open*, *8*, 233285842210839. https://doi.org/10.1177/23328584221083976

Shulman, L. S. (1986a). Those who understand: Knowledge growth in teaching. *Educational Researcher*, *15*(2), 4–14. https://doi.org/10.3102/0013189X015002004

Shulman, L. (1986b). Paradigms and research programs in the study of teaching: A contemporary perspective. In M. C. Witrock (Ed.), *Handbook of research in teaching* (3rd ed., pp. 3–36). Macmillan.

Siddiq, F., Hatlevik, O. E., Olsen, R. V., Throndsen, I., & Scherer, R. (2016). Taking a future perspective by learning from the past – A systematic review of assessment instruments that aim to measure primary and secondary school students' ICT literacy. *Educational Research Review, 19*, 58–84.

Singh, A. K., & Meena, M. K. (2022). Challenges of virtual classroom during COVID-19 pandemic: An empirical analysis of Indian higher education. *International Journal of Evaluation and Research in Education (IJERE), 11*(1), 207. https://doi.org/10.11591/ijere.v11i1.21712

Singh, I., & Kaur, N. (2017). Contribution of information technology in growth of Indian economy. *International Journal of Research -GRANTHAALAYAH, 5*(6), 1–9. https://doi.org/10.29121/granthaalayah.v5.i6.2017.1986

Singh, M., Adebayo, S. O., Saini, M., & Singh, J. (2021). Indian government E-learning initiatives in response to COVID-19 crisis: A case study on online learning in Indian higher education system. *Education and Information Technologies, 26*(6), 7569–7607. https://doi.org/10.1007/s10639-021-10585-1

Sun, B., Loh, C. E., & Nie, Y. (2021). The COVID-19 school closure effect on students' print and digital leisure reading. *Computers and Education Open, 2*, 100033. https://doi.org/10.1016/j.caeo.2021.100033

Swayam Prabha. (n.d.). *Free educational DTH channels| Educational DTH channels | India.* https://www.swayamprabha.gov.in/index.php/about

The Economic Times. (2020, April 17). *Education in time of COVID-19: DD, AIR will broadcast virtual classes through regional channels.* https://economictimes.indiatimes.com/magazines/panache/education-in-time-of-covid-19-dd-air-will-broadcast-virtual-classes-through-regional-channels/articleshow/75200617.cms?from=mdr

The Times of India. (2022, April 21). *New chapter: Yogi 2.0 frames 100 days plan for reforms in educational sector in Uttar Pradesh|Lucknow news.* Times of India. https://timesofindia.indiatimes.com/city/lucknow/new-chapteryogi-2-0-frames-100-days-plan-for-reforms-in-educational-sector-in-uttar-pradesh/articleshow/90968614.cms

UNICEF. (n.d.). *Education.* https://www.unicef.org/india/what-we-do/education

UNICEF. (2020). *Lives upended: How COVID – 19 threatens the futures of 600 million South Asian Children.* https://www.unicef.org/rosa/sites/unicef.org.rosa/files/2020-06/UNICEF%20Upended%20Lives%20Report%20-%20June%202020.pdf

Tyler, J. H., Taylor, E. S., Kane, T. J., & Wooten, A. L. (2010). Using student performance data to identify effective classroom practices. *American Economic Review, 100*(2), 256–260. https://doi.org/10.1257/aer.100.2.256

UNESCO. (2023, March 16). *Education: From school closure to recovery. Building peace through education, science and culture, communication, and information.* https://en.unesco.org/covid19/educationresponse

Vagi, R., Pivovarova, M., & Barnard, W. (2019). Dynamics of preservice teacher quality. *Teaching and Teacher Education, 85*, 13–23. https://doi.org/10.1016/j.tate.2019.06.005

Van Laar, E., Van Deursen, A. J., Van Dijk, J. A., & De Haan, J. (2017). The relation between 21st-century skills and digital skills: A systematic literature review. *Computers in Human Behavior, 72*, 577–588. https://doi.org/10.1016/j.chb.2017.03.010

Wiswall, M. (2011). *The dynamics of teacher quality.* SSRN. https://doi.org/10.2139/ssrn.1911309

World Economic Forum. (2020). *The future of jobs report 2020.* https://www3.weforum.org/docs/WEF_Future_of_Jobs_2020.pdf

GLOBAL INJUSTICES OF COLONIAL SCHOOLS: EDUCATIONAL REPARATIONS AND REPRESENTATIONS OF THE HUMAN

Benjamin D. Scherrer[a], Brandon Folson[b], Chevy R. J. Eugene[c], Ellie Ernst[b], Tinesh Indrarajah[d], tavis d. jules[d], Madeleine Lutterman[b] and Anastasia Toland[b]*

[a]*State University of New York at Oswego, USA*
[b]*Loyola University Chicago, USA*
[c]*Dalhousie University, Canada*
[d]*Loyola University Chicago School of Education, USA*

ABSTRACT

Drawing connections between Indigenous boarding schools in North America and the expansion of colonial schooling worldwide, this chapter conceptualizes methods of re-engagement with the topic of reparations for communities who have been subjected to the consequences of colonial schooling. Models of colonial schooling instill education practices aimed at enforcing the assimilation of populations into dominant cultures while reinforcing globalized racializing hierarchies. The epistemic violence central to the conceptualization of the colonial school is a key component of this colonial technology and is reproduced within modern education systems throughout the Global South. Moving toward the interconnected articulation of reparative material and epistemic justice in education for American Indian and African American communities in the United States and post-colonial communities worldwide, the chapter aims to create openings in comparative and international education for addressing the colonial residues within modern education on local and global

---

Annual Review of Comparative and International Education 2023
International Perspectives on Education and Society, Volume 48, 235–248
Copyright © 2025 by Emerald Publishing Limited
All rights of reproduction in any form reserved
ISSN: 1479-3679/doi:10.1108/S1479-367920240000048013

levels, recentering the foundational terms by which schools function and the solidarities necessary for repair.

Keywords: Educational reparations; colonial schooling; epistemic violence; indigenous boarding schools; industrial education; comparative and international education

INTRODUCTION

Berlin of 1884 was effected through the sword and the bullet. But the night of the sword and the bullet was followed by the morning of the chalk and the blackboard. The physical violence of the battlefield was followed by the psychological violence of the classroom. But where the former was visibly brutal, the latter was visibly gentle .... The bullet was the means of physical subjugation. Language was the means of the spiritual subjugation. (Ngũgĩ wa Thiong'o, *Decolonizing the Mind*, 1986)

In [American] Indian civilization I am a Baptist, because I believe in immersing the Indian in our civilization and, when we get them under, holding them there until they are thoroughly soaked. (Richard Henry Pratt, *Battlefield and Classroom: Four Decades with the American Indian, 1867—1904* (1964))

Underemphasized in the field of comparative and international education (CIE), this chapter draws on connections between Indigenous boarding schools in North America and colonial schooling in different parts of the world. In particular, the authors examine the relationships between the histories of colonial schooling as a central technology of oppression and racialization within North America and the rise and reproduction of colonial schools in the Global South. Turning to the epigraphs, Kenyan literary scholar Ngũgĩ wa Thiong'o draws connections between the more obvious physicality of colonial violence enacted during the Berlin Conference of 1884 and the accompanying modes of psychological violence embedded within practices of re-education central to colonization and colonial schooling in particular. The more "visibly gentle" complexities of the erasure of language and accompanying elements of cultural and spiritual life in everyday policies within the classroom remain. Highlighted in the second epigraph, the founder of the United States' most notorious boarding school and global colonial school influencer Richard Henry Pratt's metaphorical narrative is a reminder of the "immersive" and suffocating nature of colonial schooling which was designed as a comprehensive method of pacification and induction into a racialized industrious labor force. Thinking in the wake of colonial school systems that emerged on a global level, the authors conceptualize methods of re-engagement with the topic of colonial boarding schools through an interconnected global lens. This chapter aims to create openings for renewed scholarship and practice, thinking together the enmeshed colonial residues within modern education on local and global levels. In doing so, the authors suggest that a turn to the study of connections between geographically distant colonial school systems might open

Global Injustices of Colonial Schools

opportunities to move toward actionable reparations and reparative material and epistemic justice in education for Indigenous communities in North America and post-colonial communities worldwide.

Colonial schooling was a unique intervention that emerged within missionary schools, refined within the context of the early American Indian and African American education, and spread within the Global South (Yang, 2017). The common characteristics of colonial schools that have metastasized through global systems include spiritual, linguistic, and cultural extermination; detachment from family and coming of age traditions/adulthood membership social status; temporal reorientation toward militarized obedience and violence (settler time); and the unique focus on the racialized economic being, in relation to the Western white economic human genre (Wynter, 2003), positioning the racialized other as a key category within the global labor market. The chapter presents evidence of how schools throughout the global south continue to rely on the set of educational interventions, now reproduced within post-colonial communities and nation-states as cultural norms. This chapter focuses on the question of how to identify, account for, and offer an approach to educational reparations for the harms related to the expansion of the colonial school.

Reparations, as a concept in international law, is defined as "the redressing of gross violations in international human rights law or serious violations of international humanitarian law" (United Nations) based on a set of principles that must be followed to qualify as reparatory justice: proportionality to the harm suffered, direct fault of the state or legal entity, and genuine effort to correct the past wrong committed. Within the context of this chapter, more specifically, educational reparations are defined as the redress of harm within colonial schools given the specific set of characteristics and forms of erasure, brutality, dehumanization, and racialization by which these systems are defined. In this case, reparations are not the same as decolonial projects that rely on the labor and resources of harmed communities, nor are they the forms of redress that are dictated by external (mostly Western) groups. For example, forms of international development in the form of educational aid are not considered reparations if not mutually agreed upon measures that are designed to address past harms. Inclusive of the field of CIE, the authors are interested in moving from the more abstract conceptual ideas toward admission of harm, forms of obligation, and practices of repair.

A critical distinction in terms of thinking about repair relates to how the struggle to build just social systems cannot be achieved through "universal" programs that address common problems because not all social problems are in fact common to everyone (Táíwò, 2022). From the point of view of education, it is not enough to provide access to compensate for unfair economic structures when socially constructed race-based discrimination continues to produce forms of value-based difference. Robin D. G. Kelley takes up a similar perspective on thinking about reparations in Black America, suggesting that it was never entirely, or even primarily, about money. The demand for reparations was about social justice, reconciliation, reconstructing the internal life ... eliminating institutional racism ... focusing less on individual payments than on securing funds to build autonomous black institutions, improving community life. (pp. 114–115)

In this sense, reparations are more about developing the political economy in different ways where the relationship between the racialized individual and the broader society is remade and shifted more toward collective needs than the emphasis on accumulation (Kelley, 2022). The projects of reparative justice are tied to financial compensation but are also much more, a project of world-making whereas commitments to building structural justice are recognized and articulated and interconnected on a global systems level with "redistribution of global wealth, from the First World (back) to the Third World" (Táíwò, 2022, p. 5). At the same time, reparative projects must address both the consequences of settler colonialism and racial capitalism, which are intimately tied to one another. For example, when thinking about land-back movements for Black, Black-Indigenous, and Indigenous communities, how is it possible to provide Black land without being in relation with Indigenous communities that were also dispossessed? Such complications suggest an interlinking between global colonial projects.

In what follows, first, the authors present a brief background on Indigenous boarding schools, a particular model of colonial boarding school originating within North America. The chapter uses "Indigenous" and "Indian" interchangeably at times, given scholarly citation and context. The section draws critical connections within specific colonial contexts globally and extends the examination of the topic and how the colonial school was transplanted. In the second section, the authors provide a framework to articulate specific modes of repair and justice through the conceptual lens of reparations, interconnected, in this case with the topic of colonial schools, concerning the concept of reparations, both martially and through shifts in ways of knowing and being. Third, the authors present examples of reparations for Indigenous and Colonial education. To conclude, the authors speculate on the questions: what might the field of CIE look like in the future, through reparative perspectives? What isolated examples are there today (or in the past) that can be used as guides? Thinking about the implications of material practices of decolonization and reparative justice in the field of education, the authors turn to co-author Brandon Folson's knowledge of and intimate connections with boarding schools with his Yankton Sioux Tribe and Oglala Lakota Sioux Tribe in South Dakota and ongoing efforts to address the injustices perpetrated within these institutions. Folson's personal knowledge informs the chapter and is woven within its sections.

BACKGROUND

The global transmission of colonial schooling modeled after the American Indian boarding school and later the industrial education school of African Americans

Global Injustices of Colonial Schools

which emerged shortly after the Civil War can be identified in colonial education systems throughout the Global South. Different from earlier missionary school models, this educational approach not only emphasized Christianity and the erasure of cultural traditions but also emphasized a militarized educational approach centering economic labor productivity (Yang, 2017). In this section, the authors address the question of what did the Indian boarding schools in the United States set out to do and how was it done. And in particular, how do we remain in the wake of these strategies, systems, and structures today?

According to scholars in the field, boarding schools have served as a systematic tool through which the US government employed education against American Indians (Treuer & Keenan, 2022). This policy first aimed to transfer the management of Indian reservations to Christian denominations and missionary societies (Smith, 2004). The American Indian boarding school system in the United States was formally established following the implementation of President Grant's "Peace Policy" in 1869/1870 (Smith, 2004). This policy aimed to end the Indian Wars and promote the assimilation of Native Americans through brutal educational initiatives (McKenzie, 1914). Influenced by the prevailing ideology of Manifest Destiny, which advocated for the expansion of white American culture across the continent, the policy disregarded the rights and well-being of Indigenous Nations. For example, the incursion by white settlers, driven in part by the gold rush, led to the incentivized decimation of the great buffalo herds, crucial to the culture and survival of the Oceti Sakowin – a union of the Lakota, Nakota, and Dakota Indigenous Nations. The devastation of the buffalo herds, coupled with pressures from the Northern Pacific Railroad and unstable American governmental and military policies, epitomized the destructive strategies of white settler colonialism (Murphy, 2022). These actions not only disrupted the physical environment but also systematically targeted the cultural foundations and identities of Native American communities, highlighting the extent of settler colonialism's impact (McKenzie, 1914).

In 1879, Richard Henry Pratt established the Carlisle Indian Industrial School in Carlisle, Pennsylvania, marking the creation of the first off-reservation boarding school (Brunhouse, 1939). Pratt, known for his controversial educational philosophy of "kill the Indian, save the man" (Pratt, 1973), aimed to assimilate Native American children into mainstream American society. This institution was part of a broader national agenda of cultural assimilation within a racialized global system. Over the next three decades, the number of similar off-reservation boarding schools expanded to 25, while by 1909, there were also 157 on-reservation boarding schools and 307 day schools operating across the United States (Adams, 1995; Brunhouse, 1939).

The particular strategies and policies of the US Government for colonial "Indian" schools aimed to supplant traditional American Indian family structures with "civilized" influences. These policies included providing academic and industrial training, enforcing proper behavior and gender-specific roles, creating surrogate home environments, and categorizing the schools into distinct types (Cahill, 2011). To further the goal of cultural assimilation, Indian boarding schools were structured into different categories: day schools, on-reservation boarding schools, and off-reservation boarding schools. This classification allowed for varying degrees of immersion into American culture, with off-reservation schools being particularly isolated from Native influences, thus enhancing assimilation (Cahill, 2011). Native American students were forcibly removed from their tribal communities and placed in off-reservation boarding schools, effectively isolating them from their families and cultural backgrounds (Harrington & Pavel, 2013). In addition, Indian schools implemented a standardized curriculum that emphasized Western education while largely neglecting Native American history, culture, and traditions.

This approach led to the cultural erasure of Native American identities and the subjugation of the people into a racialized labor force. The schools strategically replaced familial connections with bonds formed with school staff, portrayed as carriers of civilized values (Cahill, 2011) weakening ties to Indigenous culture. Furthermore, these institutions also functioned as homes, with staff assuming parental roles to foster the acceptance of what were identified as white Western "American" cultural norms (Cahill, 2011). Students were severely punished for engaging in their cultural traditions, penalized for speaking their native languages, and compelled to conform to Western customs (Harrington & Pavel, 2013). And in particular, the model strongly emphasized vocational/industrial training, providing Native American students with skills in Western modes of farming, building, and domestic work, delinked from the land and places they came from (Harrington & Pavel, 2013). The curriculum was designed to incorporate academic subjects including the English language and "practical skills" training to foster "economic self-sufficiency." This approach was intended to prepare students for life within the "American economic framework," aligning their education with the broader "economic goals" of the United States (Cahill, 2011, p. 54; McKenzie, 1914, p. 765).

Several key figures have profoundly influenced the history and operations of the Carlisle Indian Industrial School and the broader context of Indian boarding schools. Captain Henry L. Scott, who served as the superintendent from 1879 to 1882, played a pivotal role in the early development of the school and the implementation of its assimilation policies, helping shape the school's foundational approach to Native American education (Harrington & Pavel, 2013). Despite the efforts of Indian Schools, educational outcomes for Native American students have remained significantly lower than those of their non-Native peers, with lower graduation rates and ongoing educational disparities (Harrington & Pavel, 2013). Furthermore, many Native American students experienced trauma and abuse at Indian schools, including physical, emotional, sexual abuse, and even high rates of child death, with long-lasting effects on Native communities (Harrington & Pavel, 2013). By the time most countries in the Global South emerged independent from their colonizers, American Indian boarding schools numbered more than 523 (US Indian boarding school history). In many ways the complicated nature of post-colonial education and the education of American Indian and African American communities remains intact. The impacts on Indigenous communities resulted in lasting effects, encompassing intergenerational trauma, cultural detachment, and oppressive socio-economic conditions. The epistemic violence central to the conceptualization of the boarding school was a key component of this colonial technology. John Oberly, the commissioner of Indian affairs at the time, stated in an 1886 report that through schooling, the Indian "should be instilled with the elevating egotism of American civilization, encouraging him to use 'I' instead of 'We,' and declare 'This is mine' rather than 'This is ours'" (Treuer & Keenan, 2022). In 1896, Merrill Gates, who would later become the head of the Board of Indian Commissioners, expressed the idea: "We must encourage a more intelligently selfish attitude in the Indian .... Through property acquisition, individuals express their personality and exert control over material through their own thoughts and will" (Treuer & Keenan, 2022).

Along the same colonial school framework, the Virginia Hampton Normal and Industrial Institute was the first of the "Negro training schools" founded by northern philanthropy on the principle that "no education is complete which does not train the hand to work" (Du Bois, 1973). At Hampton, established in 1868 and located in Virginia, founder Gen. Samuel Armstrong of the Freedmen's Bureau popularized a "practical curriculum" of industrial and agricultural education. The approach of combining "traditional" learning with trade education to "showcase the possibilities of the Negro race" attracted significant attention in the late 1870s. Thinking within more recent practices of development and voluntourism, it was not unusual for several hundred northern white "tourists" a day to visit the school. Booker T. Washington was Hampton's most famous graduate and was the face of the industrial curriculum, establishing a second training school at Tuskegee, Alabama, in 1881. Washington was recommended for the position by his "mentor," Armstrong.

Models of colonial schooling trafficked around the world with colonial powers instill education practices aimed at enforcing the assimilation of populations into dominant cultures while reinforcing racialized hierarchies. The colonial schooling in Kenya, Black schooling in the post-Abolition US South, education for the pacification of Indigenous peoples in the Pacific, and Indian boarding schools in North America are entwined through a set of exchanges of people, ideas, models, and philosophies never more than a few degrees of separation from the US military apparatus (Yang, 2017). Kenya's Alliance High School was modeled on the 19th-century system for educating Native Americans and African Americans in the South (Wa Thiong'o, 2010). Wa Thiong'o describes how in 1924–1925, G. A. Grieves, the first principal of Alliance, visited and studied both at the Hampton Normal and Industrial Institute, Tuskegee Institute. Implemented throughout the world, colonial schooling was built and run by the US Army in the Philippines beginning in 1901, a military appropriation according to General Arthur MacArthur necessary "as an adjunct to military operations calculated to pacify the people" (MacArthur, 1966, p. 3). In this global context, colonial schools emerge as a map of the trafficking of colonial technologies (Yang, 2017). Similarly, links have been uncovered between historical and ongoing CIE research and practice emanating from the global North and colonial and imperial projects in the Global South (Sriprakash et al., 2020; Takayama, 2018).

THE LENS OF REPARATIONS

Reparations are written into international law as a means of "redressing of gross violations in international human rights law or serious violations of international humanitarian law" (UN) while at the same time in practice remains contested. The UN conception of humanitarian-based redress encompasses several principles to consider for a legitimate mode of reparatory justice: proportionality to the harm suffered, direct fault of the state or legal entity, and genuine effort to correct the past wrong committed. Reparations, viewed in this light, have been largely constructed as a moral objective, where correcting an injustice can only be done by, "acknowledgment on the part of the transgressor that what he is doing is required of him because of his prior error" (Boxill, 1972). Although the conception of reparations has been viewed as a "moral" requirement or transgression, reparations is a definitively legal concept, requiring that the wronged individual establish more than a general corrective duty to repair, but be able to illustrate a particularized breach of duty to which an individual can trace their experienced harm.

In the United States, the idea of reparations is most commonly associated with acknowledgment and redress for the past harm experienced through slavery, Jim Crow laws, and ongoing discrimination. This is a process that has been met with resistance because of the complexity of placing a value on the generational effects of harms not directly correlated to the individuals alive today. Several psychoanalytic theories of interpersonal relationships between social groups have supported the idea that repairing the rupture in a social bond and lack of a genuine effort toward apology can, "result in harmful consequences that can last generations, even centuries, where the silencing of the reparative human instinct yields a distorted, typically hostile, set of interactions between the injured parties and their descendants" (Volkan, 2014) in such a method that effective reparations must reach beyond the common notion of simple materialism, a feat that cannot be accomplished only through a purely legal-financial conception of reparations. The American legal system is one uniquely intertwined with the concept of punishment or compensation for harm, causing the misconception that reparations can only be given through compensatory means. Reparations can manifest as the restitution of civil and political rights, rehabilitation, access to land, healthcare, or education.

Reparations for Black, Indigenous, and Black-Indigenous communities underscore a complex and interwoven confrontation with historical injustices resulting from European colonization and imperialism. The experiences and systemic oppression encountered by each group necessitate tailored reparative measures to redress their distinct losses effectively. In contrast to the African American reparations, which primarily address the legacies of slavery and segregation, American Indian reparations include compensation for: land dispossession; cultural genocide, in particular through "enforced assimilation" policies in both on and off-reservation boarding schools: and ongoing violations of US Government treaty obligations toward Native Nations

Global Injustices of Colonial Schools 243

and peoples. Historically, American Indians have suffered from centuries of US governmental policies deliberately aimed at obliterating tribal cultural identities and ways of life, starkly highlighted by J. West Phippen's declaration, "Kill Every Buffalo You Can! Every Buffalo Dead Is an Indian Gone" (Phippen, 2021).

The interconnectedness of African American and American Indian reparative themes illustrates a common underlying framework of colonial and racial ideologies that drove both the transatlantic slave trade and the territorial displacement of American Indian peoples.

Land Reparation and Restitution: This entails ensuring the restitution of lands unjustly seized or the full honoring of extant land rights and treaties.

Cultural Reparation: This involves the revitalization of native languages and traditions and the accurate representation of Native histories and epistemologies within educational curricula.

Compensation: Financial reparations should be provided for the economic disenfranchisement brought about by centuries of marginalization and policy-driven impoverishment. This includes addressing challenges such as the isolation of reservation lands from predominant economic hubs and the appropriation of natural resources, exemplified by incidents like the seizure of the sacred lands.

Healing and Rehabilitation: Funding should be allocated for traditional American Indian mental health practices to address the intergenerational trauma caused by forced assimilation and cultural eradication.

The theoretical underpinnings of reparations acknowledge the unique sovereignty of Native tribes and the targeted colonial and federal policies they faced (Justia Law, n.d.). This perspective advocates for reparations beyond mere financial restitution, promoting a comprehensive approach to healing and reconciliation.

As part of broader educational and social justice reforms, representing a decolonial effort to remove colonial legacies from education systems and more, American Indian reparations initiatives are aligned with movements that aim to rectify the enduring damages caused by racial capitalism and settler colonialism, recognizing their profound effects on marginalized groups across the colonized world. American Indians attending US boarding schools assert, as per *The Truth Commission into Genocide in Canada* (2001), that severe offenses were documented. The report, along with the uncovering of more recent findings also emphasized the existence of mass unmarked graveyards on school grounds, particularly for children, indicating an even broader system of violence (Annett, 2001). Some churches and the Canadian government have taken limited steps to address their involvement through official statements and ceremonies, while the US Government has not addressed similar abuses (Smith, 2004). As an example, in light of South Dakota's problematic history with boarding schools, the state legislature must first prolong the statute of limitations on childhood sexual abuse claims (Healy & Peyton, 2019). Such a modification could facilitate claims and essentially serve as a form of reparation.

LINKING REPARATIONS IN EDUCATION AS A GLOBAL PROJECT

> When we got talking, 'cause we're not allowed to talk our tribal language, and then me and my cousin, we get together and we talk in Indian, we always hush up when we see a teacher or faculty coming. And then we always laughed and said, 'I think they're trying to make little white boys out of us.' (Charles Chibitty, Comanche Code Talker (smithsonian.org))

Concerning the field of CIE, the following section focuses on the need for moves toward both epistemic and material reparations for colonial schooling, addressing both the physical harm and violence done to communities and the epistemic erasure of language and culture, recentering the foundational terms by which schools function (Brissett & jules, 2023). Several critical scholars in the field have drawn already drawn attention to the ways in which CIE has been implicated in colonial projects (Shields & Paulson, 2024; Sobe, 2017; Takayama et al., 2017). The field remains connected with racist and colonial ideologies that are perpetuated in Eurocentric policy and everyday practice guided by "experts" in the Global North (jules & Scherrer, 2021; Strong et al., 2023; Takayama, 2018). This work invites "dialogue about the active colonial legacies in the field" and "a major rethinking of the norms and knowledge about difference, comparison and research that have been inherited from the field's history" (Takayama et al., 2017) seeking ways to acknowledge and repair the harms of coloniality in current and future research. More specifically, this chapter argues that thinking from the ongoing wake of the colonial school era holds the potential to significantly contribute to forms of critical engagements and repair. In particular, global reparations movement as related to education and schooling, necessitat the interlinking of national struggles (Smith, 2004). Turning to the section's epigraph, this section considers the ramifications of what it means to "make little white boys out of us" and extends his assertion that not only was this the intent of the colonial school, but it was also based on the fundamental epistemic disordering that reoriented the ideal racial subject as never fully human.

The striving for epistemic justice for victims of colonial schooling first requires the acceptance that the actions taken by administrators and policy-makers of the schooling project constitute grave human rights violations. Words are important, and the act of silencing justice-oriented vocabulary, whether in the past by preventing the speaking of "Indian" at the boarding schools as Chibitty notes or the watering down of harm and violence enacted upon American Indians, needs to be contested and resisted. The classification of the atrocities of the colonial schooling project as human rights violations will then necessitate the introduction of external, impartial, and authoritative global bodies to investigate the veracity of these claims. In the case of the American Indian, this would suggest a movement away from dealing directly with the United States government, and rather, a focus on developing a collective case to be filed at a global forum. Along these lines, Smith (2004) argues that "rather than seek redress primarily through the courts of the colonizer, it seems more appropriate to use bodies that adjudicate disputes between nations, such as the United Nations" (p. 97).

Global Injustices of Colonial Schools 245

Alongside the active push for adjudication on colonial school violations, Lajimodiere (2012) and Tencer (2022) also stress the importance of creating healing spaces within reparatory justice movements. The "soul wounds" suffered due to the imposition of colonial schooling on American Indians are still being explored, revealed, and processed by the community (see Lajimodiere, 2012; Tencer, 2022). The Boarding School Healing Project is an example of a community-driven effort to create safe and vulnerable spaces for victims of boarding schools and their descendants to share their stories and heal from the wounds imposed by their childhood experiences under violent colonial rule (Smith, 2004). Additionally, Tencer (2022) advocates for land-based healing programs for American Indians due to their deep history and relationship with the land, which is outside of the settler colonial extractivist understanding of land; "land-based healing programs, institutions, and interventions, through the decolonization of trauma work, are starkly contrasted with Western and colonial psychological and therapeutic philosophies which characterize Indigenous suffering as pathology rather than being brought on by settler colonialism" (p. 109). Thus, a reparatory justice movement about the effects of colonial schooling must cater and foster a healing space for stakeholders to broach their "soul wounds."

Chibitty's assessment of the boarding school administrators desire to "make little white boys out of us" was not restricted to just American Indian children, but to anyone who did not fit the White settler colonial definition of civilization and progress. A global educational reparations project requires contextualized understanding of how settler colonialism systematically undermined localized culture and tradition to assert colonial (usually European Christian) forms of knowledge. Though the colors of the tools used by the perpetrators of colonial violence may differ, the way the tools of division and dehumanization functioned were largely similar. To counter centuries of divide and rule, we need to develop closer global relationships built upon knowledge sharing. Eugene et al.'s (2024) recommendation of the Caribbean-Africa Knowledge Program, which intro-duces knowledge of the Caribbean and Africa to people from both regions, serves to bridge the knowledge gap between similarly afflicted populations and build momentum for a trans-regional call for reparations. The proactive sharing of knowledge and best practices to combat the residues of settled colonialism glob-ally needs to be prioritized by all stakeholders interested in justice and account-ability for the colonial schooling project and prevent the persisting efforts to mold us into "little white boys."

A global educational project that addresses the harms of colonial school-ing also requires settler colonialists and their descendants to acknowledge past actions and assess their current role in holding up unjust structures in the pre-sent. Tencer (2022) stresses that "further self reflection, learning, undoing, and re-learning, without actions that are performative, surface level, or increase one's own social capital are necessary" (p. 114). One way forward would be the recogni-tion of the persisting colonial relationship between settler colonists, Indigenous and Black peoples, and the nation-state. Doing so opens the doors for more critical conversations about land relations and non-monetary reparations – topics that American Indian nations are focused on advocating for as merely accepting financial payouts from the American government inadvertently presumes tacit agreement that the harms of coloniality have been appropriately accounted for (Smith, 2004). Education for settler colonialists about relations with land that is not centered on capitalistic extractivist practices but rather on regeneration, deglobalization, and reciprocity would also ideally influence an other valid ways of existing. Overall, global progress for educational reparations cannot happen without the accountability and buy-in from current beneficiaries of colonial schooling harms.

CONCLUSIONS

The impact of the American Indian boarding school policy continues to pro-foundly affect schooling around the globe. The repercussions span multiple gen-erations and reverberate today. The legacy of colonial schools is a deep-seated wound that marks the cultural uprooting and disruption of familial bonds. As we continue to confront and address these historical impacts, the journey of healing and reclaiming heritage remains a pivotal challenge. For instance, grandparents who did not attend an Indian boarding school retained vital connection to their cultural heritage. However, the situation for their children was starkly different. They were forced into on-reservation boarding schools, significantly diluting their linguistic and cultural ties. This divergence within a single-family gen-eration highlights the profound impacts of the boarding school system in eroding indigenous linguistic heritage and cultural identity, which left present generations searching for methods or reconnecting with places called home.

Interconnected with Ngũgĩ wa Thiong'o's concept of language as a means of accessing different mental universes, Indigenous elders emphasize that language is not just a tool for communication but a vessel that carries our worldview and the philosophical foundations of our civilization. In the boarding schools, children were systematically taught to abandon their heritage, disrupting cultural and famil-ial structures. This loss of language has left subsequent generations without the cultural resources necessary to live according to traditional values and norms, a loss that is difficult to comprehend fully.

As communities embark on the journey to reclaim lost cultural and lin-guistic heritage – epistemic ways of knowing and being in the world – they are confronted with a deep-seated legacy of distrust toward mainstream educational and institutional frameworks. The experiences of colonial schooling enabled and produced this legacy. To overcome these challenges, it is essential for the wider society – on local, national, and global levels – to acknowledge the harms and provide forms of repair – based in the frameworks defined under international law and applied within situated histories – to enable recovery, rec-onciliation, and the enactment of alternative justice-centered modes of education that decenter colonial objectives. In relation to the field of CIE, these efforts are essential for addressing injustices and moving toward reparations – accounting

Global Injustices of Colonial Schools 247

for the moral obligations to restore the integrity of our global communities who have undergone colonial schooling.

REFERENCES

Adams, D. W. (1995). *Education for extinction: American Indians and the boarding school experience, 1875–1928*. University Press of Kansas.

Annett, K. D. (2001). *Hidden from history: The Canadian Holocaust: The untold story of the genocide of Aboriginal peoples by church and state in Canada: A summary of an ongoing, independent inquiry into Canadian native "residential schools" and their legacy*. Truth Commission into Genocide in Canada.

Boxill, B. R. (1972). The morality of reparation. *Social Theory and Practice, 2*(1), 113–123.

Brissett, N. O., & jules, t. d. (2023). (Re) thinking material and epistemic futures: Caribbean reparations, development, and education. *Race Ethnicity and Education*, 1–17.

Brunhouse, R. L. (1939). *The founding of the Carlisle Indian School*. Pennsylvania History.

Cahill, C. (2011). *Federal fathers & mothers: A social history of the United States Indian Service, 1869–1933*. The University of North Carolina Press.

Du Bois, W. E. B. (1973). *The education of black people*. University of Massachusetts Press.

Eugene, C., jules, t. d., & Indrarajah, T. (2024). An African Union-Caribbean Community alliance in the global reparations movement: promises, perils, and pitfalls. *The Round Table, 113*(1), 29–42.

Harrington, B. G., & CHiXapkaid (D. Michael Pavel). (2013). Using Indigenous educational research to transform mainstream education: A guide for P–12 school leaders. *American Journal of Education, 119*(4), 487–511.

Healy, P. (2019) A change in South Dakota's child sexual ab use statute of limitations: An equal protection violations? *American Indian Law Journal, 7*(2), Article 4. https://digitalcommons.law.seattleu.edu/ailj/vol7/iss2/4

Jules, T. D., & Scherrer, B. D. (2021). Black lives matter in our syllabi: Another world is possible. *Comparative Education Review, 65*(1), 166–178. https://doi.org/10.1086/712782

Justia Law. (n.d.). *Cherokee Nation v. Georgia, 30 U.S. 1 (1831)*. https://supreme.justia.com/cases/federal/us/30/1/

Kelley, R. D. (2022). *Freedom dreams: The black radical imagination*. Beacon Press.

Lajimodiere, D. (2012). A healing journey. *Wicazo Sa Review, 27*(2), 5–19.

MacArthur, A. (1966, June 8). Cited in Renato Constantino, "The Miseducation of the Filipino". *Weekly Graphic*, 3 (Internet resource transcribed by Bert M. Drona, The Filipino Mind). http://thefilipinomind.blogspot.com/

McKenzie, F. A. (1914). The assimilation of the American Indian. *American Journal of Sociology, 19*, 761–772.

Murphy, J. D. (2022). *American Indian wars: The essential reference guide*. ABC-CLIO.

Phippen, J. W. (2021, June 7). Kill every buffalo you can! every buffalo dead is an Indian gone. *The Atlantic*. https://www.theatlantic.com/national/archive/2016/05/the-buffalo-killers/482349/

Pratt, R. H. (1973). The advantages of mingling Indians with whites. *Americanizing the American Indians, 35*, 260–271. https://doi.org/10.4159/harvard.9780674435056.c39

Shields, R., & Paulson, J. (2024). Toppling statues? Complicity, whiteness and reckoning in comparative and international education. *Compare: A Journal of Comparative and International Education*, 1–17. https://doi.org/10.1080/03057925.2024.2321851

Smith, A. (2004). Boarding school abuses, human rights, and reparations. *Social Justice, 31*(4), 89–102.

Sobe, N. W. (2017). Travelling researchers, colonial difference: Comparative education in an age of exploration. *Compare: A Journal of Comparative and International Education, 47*(3), 332–343.

Sriprakash, A., Tikly, L., & Walker, S. (2020). The erasures of racism in education and international development: Re-reading the 'global learning crisis'. *Compare: A Journal of Comparative and International Education, 50*(5), 676–692. https://doi.org/10.1080/03057925

Strong, K., Walker, S., Wallace, D., Sriprakash, A., Tikly, L., & Soudien, C. (2023). Learning from the movement for Black lives: Horizons of racial justice for comparative and international education. *Comparative Education Review, 67*(S1), S1–S24.

Takayama, K. (2018). Beyond comforting histories: The colonial/imperial entanglements of the International Institute, Paul Monroe, and Isaac L. Kandel at Teachers College, Columbia University. *Comparative Education Review, 62*(4), 459–481. https://doi.org/10.1086/699924

Táíwò, O. O. (2022). *Reconsidering reparations.* Oxford University Press.

Takayama, K., Sriprakash, A., & Connell, R. (2017). Toward a postcolonial comparative and international education. *Comparative Education Review, 61*(S1), S1–S24. https://doi.org/10.1086/690455

Tencer, O. N. (2022). *Healing intergenerational wounds: Land and memory as the site of Indian boarding school violences in the United States.* Senior Projects Spring 2022. 209. https://digitalcommons.bard.edu/senproj_s2022/209

Thiong'o, N. (2010) *Dreams in a time of war: A childhood memoir.* Pantheon Books.

Treuer, D., & Keenan, S. (2022). *The heartbeat of wounded knee: Life in Native America.* Viking.

Volkan, V. (2014). *Blind trust: Large groups and their leaders in times of crisis and terror.* Pitchstone Publishing.

Wynter, S. (2003). Unsettling the coloniality of being/power/truth/freedom: Toward the human, after Man, its overrepresentation—An argument. *CR: The New Centennial Review, 3*(3), 257–337. https://doi.org/10.1353/ncr.2004.0015

Yang, K. W. (2017). *A third university is possible.* University of Minnesota Press.

PART 5

DIVERSIFICATION OF THE FIELD

INTERNATIONAL SCHOOLS FOR LGBTQ+ YOUTH: A COMPARATIVE CASE STUDY OF THE EDUCATIONAL FUNCTION OF INTERNATIONAL SCHOOLS IN POLAND

Joanna Leek, Marcin Rojek and Elżbieta Szulewicz

University of Lodz, Poland

ABSTRACT

This study explores the role of international schools in creating safe and inclusive environments for lesbian, gay, transgender, bisexual, queer, and questioning (LGBTQ+) youth, particularly in light of the challenging political climate of the current prevailing authoritarian education policy in Poland. Drawing upon Merton's concept of "educational functions" influenced by socio-political and economic factors, we investigate how international schools navigate and subvert authoritarian policies to promote LGBTQ+ inclusion. Through a multi-faceted approach analyzing curricula, media discourse, and school law documents, we examine the potential of international schools as agents of change in fostering educational inclusivity for marginalized groups. By examining the interplay between planned educational functions and implementation, the study sheds light on the potential of international schools to serve as inclusive spaces for LGBTQ+ individuals in politically charged environments. Our findings highlight the positive impact of international education programs in supporting LGBTQ+ students and contributing valuable insights to ongoing discussions

Annual Review of Comparative and International Education 2023
International Perspectives on Education and Society, Volume 48, 251–272
Copyright © 2025 by Emerald Publishing Limited
All rights of reproduction in any form reserved
ISSN: 1479-3679/doi:10.1108/S1479-367920240000048014

on promoting diversity and acceptance in educational settings. Ultimately, the findings contribute to ongoing discussions about the challenges and possibilities of fostering educational inclusivity for marginalized groups in such politically charged environments as authoritarian systems of education.

Keywords: International schools; LGBTQ+ in Poland; LGBTQ+ youth; LGBTQ+ in schools; educational policy; marginalized groups; education in Poland

INTRODUCTION

While existing studies consistently demonstrate the positive impact of inclusive school environments on educational outcomes, retention, mental health, and overall well-being of lesbian, gay, transgender, bisexual, queer, and questioning (LGBTQ+)[1] students (Kosciw et al., 2013; Shannon, 2016), unfortunately, schools continue to be settings where physical and verbal abuse, discrimination, and social exclusion against these young people are prevalent (Ferfolja & Ullman, 2017; Hill, 2001; MacAulay et al., 2021; McBride & Neary, 2021). LGBTQ+ students are subject to victimization based on their sexual orientation, gender identity, or gender expression. As a result, these students more often report negative physical and mental health outcomes and negative emotions than their peers. In recent years, as documented by research literature and through observation of educational practices, many strategies and approaches have emerged that aim to prevent or minimize the oppression that faces the LGBTQ community. In our article, we have used the example of Polish international schools to argue that international education programs can play a positive role that is vital in this respect. Poland's post-communist transition once heralded as a beacon of democratic progress, has taken a concerning turn toward authoritarianism. This resurgence has had a profound impact on marginalized groups, including LGBTQ+ individuals, who face increasing discrimination and social exclusion. Within the education system, conservative policies implemented by the current government have perpetuated a climate of insecurity and neglect, further jeopardizing the rights and well-being of LGBTQ+ students (Ploszka, 2023).

This study delves into the precarious situation of LGBTQ+ youth in Polish education, exacerbated by discriminatory policies toward LGBTQ+ (Abreu & Kenny, 2018). Against this backdrop, the research explores the potential of international schools to act as "islands of resistance" (Leek, 2020) against the prevailing authoritarian tide. We examine how these schools, which in many cases, have chosen to adopt international programs, promote educational inclusivity for LGBTQ+ individuals through internal school law.

The paper was inspired by the ranking of LGBTQ+-friendly schools in Poland and the very high positions in the ranking of schools that have implemented international educational programs. Conducted between 2021 and 2023, during a period marked by oppressive educational policies, the study investigates the role of international schools in fostering a more inclusive learning environment for LGBTQ+ youth. Using media discourse, and analysis of school documents, our analysis focuses on the aspect of international schools as agents of change, and how international schools in Poland utilize their own legal frameworks to promote inclusivity for LGBTQ+ youth. We build upon Leek's (2020) work on international schools as agents of educational resistance against the authoritarian education policy by focusing on the specific "educational functions" of these schools toward LGBTQ+ inclusion, as defined by Merton (1968) understood as "the results of socio-political and economic influences on education" (p. 68). By exploring these themes, this research endeavors to provide valuable insights into the potential of international schools to serve as safe and inclusive environments for LGBTQ+ youth, especially in challenging political climates. We also aspire to inform policies and practices that foster greater inclusivity and support for LGBTQ+ individuals within the educational landscape of international schools in general. Ultimately, this research seeks to shed light on the complex interplay between authoritarian policies, international school frameworks, and the lived experiences of LGBTQ+ youth in Polish education. By employing a multi-faceted approach, analyzing both planned and implemented curricula and drawing upon media discourse and school law document analysis, we aim to gain a deeper understanding of how international schools navigate and sometimes subvert the prevailing authoritarian context. This knowledge will contribute to ongoing discussions about the challenges and possibilities of fostering educational inclusivity for marginalized groups in politically charged environments like authoritarian systems of education.

The situation in Poland briefly illustrated here also provides a detailed exemplification of the almost universal situation in schools in other countries that has been reported among others by Russell et al. (2021), McDermott et al. (2023), and Marshal et al. (2011). School students have a higher prevalence of depression, self-harm, suicidal tendencies, and problematic substance use than cis-hetero young people. They are more likely to suffer discrimination in schools compared with cisgender youth (Mackie et al., 2021; Martín-Castillo et al., 2020). Recent studies that have compared suicidality in youth have shown that trans youth were six times more likely to report a history of attempted suicide than cis-hetero youth, bisexual youth were five times more likely, and lesbian and gay youth were four times more likely (Di Giacomo et al., 2018).

Our research is in line with the trend of pedagogy of the oppressed (Freire, 2017), according to which specific population groups can be pushed to the margins of society. "Oppressed" groups are denied the right to vote and the right to decide freely about themselves and the world in which they live. Paul Fereiro, in the early stages of developing a pedagogy of the oppressed, paid particular attention to what he considered the two most important criteria for social exclusion, namely social class and race. At a later stage, he wrote about further criteria that can lead to social exclusion, or marginalization, such as gender, ethnicity, or sexual orientation. These are criteria that serve to control the lives of some groups in society by restricting their freedom of self-determination. According to

Fereiro, education should aim to nurture the capacity for critical consciousness in students that allows them to ask questions related to important aspects of the environment (Nweke & Owoh, 2020) and take action to bring about change. In Poland, an example of this can be found in international schools, where despite the discrimination-based policies that dominated in previous years, they were welcoming places for various minorities including LGBTQ+.

LGBTQ+ IN POLAND

According to the research conducted by the Public Opinion Research Center (Feliksiak, 2013) Poles' attitudes toward LGBTQ+ people have changed positively over the last 25 years. Despite this, Poland is still included on the list of countries with the lowest acceptance of homosexual people in the European Union and a high level of prejudice (Gorska & Mikolajczak, 2015; Štulhofer & Rimac, 2009; Van den Akker et al., 2013).

Every year in Poland, there are relatively high numbers of extremely homophobic incidents. The exact numbers are difficult to estimate because not all of them are reported. Particularly significant was the establishment of over a hundred "LGBT-free zones" in cities and municipalities that together constitute one-third of the territory of Poland. Paradoxically, this was a response to support the LGBTQ+ community by the Mayor of Warsaw. Some political and religious leaders and conservative media are even fueling hate speech against LGBTQ+ people, counting on political support and viewership. Aggression against LGBTQ+ people also occurs during equality marches, which manifests in burning rainbow flags and throwing smoke flares, bottles, and eggs at participants. It happens that protests by LGBTQ+ activists will also be met with increased police brutality when arrested.

These actions trigger negative psychological consequences among LGBT+ people who still struggle to deal with strong stigmatization, and are exposed to high levels of stress, depression, and overt homophobic behavior, which especially applies to people living in small towns and villages. In research on social distance, 25% of Polish respondents declared that they would not accept a homosexual person in their neighborhood or be willing to work with such a person (Stefaniak & Witkowska, 2015). As claims Feliksiak (2013), 44% of respondents believe that there are professions that should not allow gays, while 36% have a similar opinion about lesbians, with the greatest opposition to such people working with children and young people. According to CBOS research, 87% of Poles are also against the adoption of children by homosexual couples (Feliksiak, 2013). These social attitudes of Poles toward homosexuality are not just private declarations of a worldview, but they constitute a real base for shaping attitudes and developing experiences for students. In 2017, the first judgment in Poland was passed according to which one person from a school in Warsaw had to apologize to her former student for violating his rights personal: bodily integrity, dignity, and honor, due to the information disclosed by his homosexual orientation. These examples raise questions about the practical implementation of the assumed functions of Polish education in LGBTQ+ inclusion and their practical implementation.

School as an educational institution influences children's adaptation to life in society and promotes social and cultural inclusion. The study (Raport z badania, 2020) commissioned by the authorities in Krakow shows that counteracting LGBTQ+ discrimination in post-primary education is insufficient. Schools most often do not respond sufficiently to cases of homophobia or transphobia. Most of the students that were surveyed are aware of the presence of LGBTQ+ people and same-sex couples in their schools. A significant number of students completing the study survey declared that they had observed symbols associated with the LGBTQ+ community in schools. The study showed that the reactions of the teaching staff to the presence of these types of symbols were mostly described as neutral. There was little awareness among the teaching staff about respectful ways to address transgender people. Most pupils do not know if students are allowed to choose which changing room to use for physical education classes. At the same time, there are still many cases of symbols of hate speech against LGBTQ+ people.

This issue is presented in open statements as one of the primary areas in which LGBTQ+ people are met with a lack of acceptance and understanding. Despite growing recognition of sexual and gender diversity (SGD) identities, significant disparities persist in Poland, where schools remain a breeding ground for discrimination based on sexual orientation and gender identity. ILGA-Europe's 2023 report highlights Poland's status as having the lowest LGBTQ+ rights among European Union countries. The rationale for implementing anti-discrimination education in schools is bolstered by the widespread support for such initiatives, as evidenced by the findings of the Ombudsman for Citizen Rights (RPO). Over two-thirds of Polish citizens (70%) surveyed as part of the RPO's study on "Legal Awareness in the Context of Equal Treatment" in 2020, alongside 81% of students included in the same study, advocate the integration of anti-discrimination education within school curricula. Furthermore, the findings from the European Commission's report titled "Legal gender recognition in the EU: The journeys of trans people towards full equality" (2020) indicate that 69% of Polish students surveyed reported "always" or "often" experiencing or witnessing negative comments or actions toward LGBTQ+ individuals in school settings. Despite the growing interest in this issue, the situation of LGBTQ+ people in Polish schools is still largely uncharted territory. The Polish situation outlined here is a detailed exemplification of the European situation of students. According to Arjan Van Der Star and Danielle Jansen:

> the situation for sexual and gender minorities varies greatly within Europe. Stigma towards these groups is often deeply rooted in culture and history. Variations in discriminatory legislation and attitudes towards sexual and gender minorities create very different settings for youth growing up across countries in Europe. Many of these differences between European countries remain unexplored. (Van Der Star & Jansen, 2018, pp. 22–23)

Undoubtedly, social inclusion issues concerning LGBTQ+ people are universal, and researchers from all over the world are keeping a close eye on them to try to explain them and find practical ways to solve them. Therefore, constant and new research is necessary to design empowering bullying interventions and resilience strategies to create safer school and home environments for LGBTQ+ youth across Europe. In turn, a typical educational issue of the LGBTQ+ movement in Poland is organizing an event in schools called Rainbow Friday. KPH (Campaign against Homophobia) is a non-governmental organization, which promotes the inclusion of LGBTQ+ people and started to organize Rainbow Friday. According to information presented on the website, the KPH organization (2024) supports the LGBTQ+ community at both the national and the international level. They support the LGBTQ+ movement through legal proceedings and political advocacy. Their goal is to make Poland a friendly place for all people, regardless of their declared gender and sexual orientation.

KPH was also an organizer of the Rainbow Friday campaign, which is an annual celebration initiated to show solidarity with LGBTQ+ youth and support them in the school environment. The initiators of this year's Rainbow Friday are the GrowSPACE foundation. The aim of Rainbow Friday (2024) is to strengthen LGBTQ+ youth of school age. The first event was organized in 2016 and since then it has been held every year in October. In 2018, 216 schools took part. In 2022, there were about 70 due to the ministry's guidelines which limited this type of action in schools. After the parliamentary elections and the change of government in Poland, the number of schools participating in the campaign increased again to 120 in 2023. The Rainbow Friday campaign is an expression of resistance against homophobia and a way to build an inclusive educational environment.

INTERNATIONAL SCHOOLS IN POLAND

In Poland, the first schools to offer the International Baccalaureate (IB) program began to emerge in 1993. Before that, since Poland was a closed, communist country, there were no such schools. It was only after the socio-political changes that happened in Poland in the 1990s that the chance for schools to offer international curricula arose. This was also in response to emerging demands from parents and students for this type of institution (Rojek et al., 2023). For example, in 2005, 13 schools were offered the IB curriculum, whereas in 2007, there were 32 schools, and in 2014, this number rose to 55 (Leek, 2022). In 2024, according to the IB Organization (IBO, 2024), 67 schools were offering IB program curricula at various levels (see Table 1), including 33 public schools (49%) and 34 (51%) non-public schools. Public schools offer the opportunity to study the Diploma Programme (DP), which is a two-year program that prepares students to pass the IB.

Table 1. IB Schools in Poland (as of January 2024).

Level	Number of Schools in Total	Public Schools	Non-public Schools
Primary Years Programme (PYP)	9	–	9
Middle Years Programme (MYP)	16	9	7
Diploma Programme (DP)	42	24	18
Career-Related Programme (CP)	–	–	–

Source: Own study.

This program can be preceded by studying in bilingual classes. These are classes that follow the Polish core curriculum while introducing bilingualism in selected or all lessons. In addition to preparation for the IB, some non-public schools also offer learning at the Primary Years Programme (PYP) level for children aged 3–12; in 2024, there are nine schools. In the Middle Years Programme (MYP) level for children aged 11–16, in 2024, there are 16 schools. State schools at this point in time, that is, the end of 2023, do not offer learning opportunities at the PYP level. The exception is Primary School No. 108 in Wroclaw, which has candidate school status for the PYP. The school is on its way to being the first publicly authorized IB World School.

RESEARCH DESIGN

The purpose of the research was to identify the function of the IB program in international schools in Poland. The method used to conduct the study was the grounded theory method according to Kathy Charmaz (2015). Following this method, the collection of research material began, to gather rich data. To begin with, sensitizing concepts were identified and used to collect research material. These were international schools, the IB, DP, MYP, PYP, and the Cambridge International Curriculum.

For the study, a particular meaning is attributed to structural functionalism, with its assumption that the functions of education can be perceived from manifest or latent perspectives. These functions arise from the logic of modern society, influencing its organization through rational planning and as a result of education policy, the expectations of students and their parents (Merton, 1968). Educational functions concerning the educational functions of international schools in fostering LGBTQ+ inclusion can be considered from the perspective of plans, meaning the written expectations of education (Merton, 1968). Plans or intentions, as in any area of social life, can deviate from the final results. The ways a planned program (sometimes also called curriculum) is introduced in schools are called the implemented program, and the curriculum outcomes are called the attained program (Morris, 1998). In the study of educational functions, we understand after Merton (1968) as results of activities performed by an educational institution in the form of activities that are intended and unintended, anticipated and desired, unforeseen and undesirable.

In everyday educational practice, planned functions and assumed educational goals most often do not fully translate into attained functions and results. This happens mainly because schools and teachers do not function in a material and axiological vacuum, but their functioning is complicatedly conditioned. The conditions that cause difficulties in translating planned functions into attained ones can be divided into three parts (see Fig. 1): material (e.g., school architecture and equipment), socio-cultural (e.g., social relationships between teachers, students, parents, local, national, and global communities, value system, teachers' personal beliefs, and their "private educational theories"), and organizational (e.g., school organizational culture, educational law).

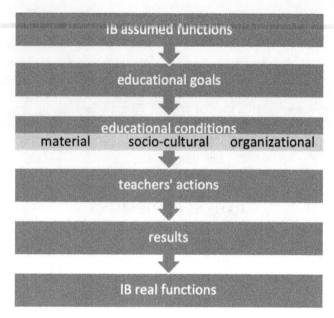

Fig. 1. Planned Versus Attained IB Functions. Deviation Condition. *Source*: Own study.

These three groups of conditions not only make it impossible to achieve attained functions but also bring into existence functions that were not planned at all. The latest proof of this thesis is the COVID-19 pandemic, during which the conditions for these three groups of conditions changed significantly, which caused many problems and challenges in achieving the assumed educational goals. Additionally, there were also results not intended by the school program (Campbell & Harris, 2021; Ismail et al., 2021).

In this context, what is interesting for us and important for educational practice is the relationship between IB planned and attained functions.

To study the educational functions of international schools in fostering LGBTQ+ inclusion in Poland, we formulated the following main research questions:

To what extent do the educational practices of international schools in Poland contribute to a more inclusive environment for LGBTQ+ individuals?

Our specific questions were:

- How do international schools in Poland encourage the development of talent and nurture social inclusion, particularly concerning the LGBTQ+ community?
- How do international schools in Poland shape a safe and inclusive school environment?
- In what ways do international schools in Poland contribute to building a more tolerant and accepting society toward LGBTQ+ individuals?

International Schools for LGBTQ+ Youth

Document Analysis

In the study, we analyzed school law documents of international schools in Poland and press articles. For studying in-school law, we used document analysis as a research method. Documents exist within social "fields of action," a term used to designate the environments within which individuals and groups interact. Documents are therefore not mere records of social life, but integral parts of it – and indeed can become agents in their own right (Prior, 2003). In line with the views of Mogalakwe (2009) and Prior (2003), we found that documents are a source of knowledge not only about the past but also about the present.

Document analysis can be used as a standalone method to analyze the contents of specific types of social practices as they evolve over time and differ across geographies, however, document analysis can also be powerfully combined with other types of methods to cross-validate (i.e., triangulate) and deepen the value of concurrent methods. Bardach and Patashnik (2015) suggest alternating between documents and interviews as sources of knowledge, as one tends to lead to the other. Depending on our research questions, document analysis was used in combination with different types of interviews (Berner-Rodoreda et al., 2018), observation (Harvey, 2018), and quantitative analyses.

As documents, we analyzed in-school-law documents, so-called School Statutes of 10 international schools in the year 2023 that were mentioned as being LGBT-friendly schools according to NGO LGBTPlusMe (https://lgbtplusme.com/en). All of the schools were secondary schools. Out of 10 schools, 6 were public schools and 4 – non-public schools. The School Statute is a legal act regulating tasks, the organizational structure, and the method of operation of the school (Paragraph 60 section 1 of the Act of September 7, 1991, Law on Education System). In the analysis of school statuses, data analysis was conducted utilizing a document analysis technique. The process comprised several sequential steps. Firstly, content identification was conducted, involving meticulous examination of each document to isolate passages germane to the benefits of the IB curriculum and the distinct characteristics of the constructivist approach in curriculum development and implementation.

Following content identification, a Case Study Development ensued. In this phase, case study narratives were meticulously constructed for each school. These narratives were crafted to delve into how schools, through their institutional policies (in-school law), incorporate inclusive practices. Subsequently, a cross-analysis was performed employing thematic analysis techniques. This entailed condensing voluminous document data into smaller analytical units, aligned with similar themes identified in the previous phase. These units were subsequently coded to facilitate systematic analysis. Lastly, the data underwent categorization and coding. Instances denoting "inclusive school spaces" were discerned through references to school activities reflective of concepts such as celebrating and representing diversity, utilizing inclusive language and communication, fostering student voice and empowerment, implementing anti-bullying policies and procedures, and providing opportunities for students to explore and express their gender identities.

Media Discourse

In addition to document analysis, we used media discourse. According to O'Keeffe (2013), media discourse refers to interactions that take place via a broadcast platform, in the case of our study of written texts, where the message is directed at an absent reader. The discourse itself is audience-oriented. That is, media discourse is a public, produced, and at the same time registered form of interaction (O'Keeffe, 2013). We made the assumption that publicly available press materials would be analyzed. Searching for press materials in both print and online media, terms related to international schools were used. 103 articles were collected in the first stage. After the initial analysis, the research material was supplemented by theoretical sampling (Charmaz, 2015; Charmaz & Thornberg, 2021), that is, looking for additional sources of research material that served to fill in the categories and enabled the creation of new ones. The research work consisted of constantly comparing the collected material, codes, and research notes to formulate a grounded theory on the media discourse on international schools.

Table 2 shows the number of articles in the given years, with a breakdown between national and regional texts.

As a result, 121 newspaper articles were collected on the subject of international schools in Poland. The first publication appeared in 2002, and the last articles are from the end of 2023 (see Table 2). In the initial period, there was little media interest in the topic of international schools, with only a few articles

Table 2. Number of Articles in 2002–2023.

Year of Publication	National Coverage	Regional Coverage	Total
2002	1	2	3
2003	–	1	1
2004	–	–	–
2005	–	2	2
2006	–	1	1
2007	–	–	–
2008	–	–	–
2009	–	2	2
2010	1	–	1
2011	2	2	4
2012	3	1	4
2013	1	1	2
2014	–	3	3
2015	3	1	4
2016	4	5	9
2017	1	4	5
2018	2	6	8
2019	4	6	10
2020	5	4	9
2021	5	4	9
2022	8	7	15
2023	13	16	29
Total	53	68	121

Source: Own study.

published annually. It can be seen that over time, this interest increased to 29 articles in 2023. Of the 121 articles, 53 (43.8%) went nationwide and 68 (56.2%) were regional. Most of the articles were published in regional media, but available to all readers. We assigned identification codes (DW, DGP) to individual media and subsequent numbers (DW1, DGP4) to articles.

The collected research material was subjected to content analysis (Krippendorff, 2018), which is used to study written material, in this case, newspaper articles (Rubin & Babbie, 2008). This method is used to study various forms of communication and involves coding and collating the types of content conveyed that appear. The units of analysis were individual articles. During repeated readings, codes were extracted to construct categories. In the study, we were interested in the qualitative, that is, we were not concerned with counting individual words or the frequency of their occurrence, but with the topics covered in the media discourse on international schools in Poland.

The codes we found related to the issues discussed in the articles are:

1. CODE – promoting multiculturalism,
2. CODE – following the values of tolerance and respect,
3. CODE – preventing homophobia,
4. CODE – organizing Rainbow Friday at international schools on the initiative of students,
5. CODE – schools bearing consequences for organizing Rainbow Friday, and
6. CODE – emphasizing awareness of discrimination issues.

The above codes were combined into a category we called caring for students' school welfare. The criterion for selection was the topics covered in newspaper articles. If a section of an article dealt with issues related to tolerance, safety, and/or equality, it was categorized as related to students' welfare. Due to the variety of topics covered related to building a safe and tolerant environment, subcategories concerning shaping a safe and friendly school environment, caring for minorities, and creating a welcoming environment for LGBTQ+ people were distinguished. The category we are interested in, which concerns caring for the well-being of students, including LGBTQ+ topics, was described in 20% of the articles collected, those with a nationwide reach, as well as those with a local reach. For each category we created subcategories, for example, the category we identified was what we called Caring for Students' School Welfare with the following sub-categories: "Shaping a Safe and Friendly School Environment," "Caring for Minorities," and "Creating a Welcoming Environment for LGBTQ+ People." The analysis of this category called "Caring for Students' Welfare" is what we want to focus on in this article. As defined by the Cambridge Dictionary, welfare means "physical and mental health and happiness, especially of a person" (Cambridge Dictionary, 2024). That is, we understand the category called "Caring for Students' School Welfare" as providing the best possible conditions for students' learning and development, regardless of biological and declared gender, sexual orientation, ethnicity, nationality, or skin color.

RESULTS

Shaping a Safe and Friendly School Environment

Media discourse accentuates that the international program emphasizes values such as freedom, tolerance, respect for human rights, and openness. Students are expected to develop these values in themselves so that they can live and work freely in a multicultural society. However, a balance is maintained between multiculturalism and the preservation of national identity and culture. Students participate in traditional school events, an example being the prom, the traditional ball held before high school graduation. Young people prepare costumes and learn to dance the Polonaise, a dance traditionally performed at proms.

> If anyone thought that with the end of the winter holidays, the prom season in Lublin also ended, they are mistaken. The fun of future high school graduates continues. This time, on Friday, the solemn countdown to the matriculation exam began with the students of Paderewski International High School. (DW3)

Classes working according to the international program emphasize the importance attached to learning and expect students to be involved in the learning process. Care is taken to foster climate-friendly knowledge acquisition and to emphasize that learning is important. Students are expected to take responsibility for their progress, be self-reliant in their actions, and be involved in the process of acquiring knowledge. Being a student in a class with an international profile is shown as a source of pride. Schools and classes are seen as prestigious. Moreover, students who achieve the best results and get into prestigious universities are role models worthy of emulation. A cult of learning and development is created. Students in the articles are portrayed as ambitious young people with crystallized plans for the future. They are supposed to be characterized by courage in achieving their goals.

> "Our IB graduates most often choose (and get in): in the UK: University College London, Imperial College, King's College London, London School of Economics, Oxford, Cambridge, St. Andrews in Scotland, Warwick, Edinburgh, Bristol and others. In the U.S.: New York University (or more recently, its Shanghai branch), they are applying to Harvard (one of this year's graduates, but not from the IB but from the Polish programme just got an offer as the only Pole), Yale (we have one graduate there), Stanford (there is also an offer this year) and others from the Ivy League and beyond. There was also interest in Denmark this year - I guess mainly because of the finances. In Poland, our graduates choose among others: UW, WUM, SGH, PW, SGGW and UJ," says the director. (DGP4)

Creating a learning community in schools and classrooms with an international program concerns both the students and teachers, and each is expected to appreciate the importance of development and education, which in the case of students allows them to continue their education at prestigious universities. Teachers, on the other hand, see working in an international program as developing and prompting them to prepare interesting, innovative activities for their students. The content of the articles combines the sphere of science, acquiring a prestigious education with multicultural education, and preparing students to study and work in international teams. Sensitization to otherness and diversity within the school environment is in progress. Safety and a good school atmosphere are being singled out in articles as factors associated with good academic performance.

International Schools for LGBTQ+ Youth   263

> "We focus first and foremost on being a student-friendly school because the student is the centre
> of our interest. Of course, it's all about didactics and good teaching results, but they don't exist
> when students feel bad. You have to look broadly. The important thing is that everyone feels
> safe here," the director stresses. (TVN1)

Teachers are obliged to take care of the "psychophysical development of students" (S2), and "adjust educational requirements to suit the special developmental needs of the student, creating conditions that support the student, providing conditions for the student's development and their preparation for life with others" (S2).

Fostering Multicultural Awareness and Social Openness

There is a substantial amount of information reported in the press about how international schools in Poland promote multiculturalism, are open to otherness, and teach sensitivity to people from other cultures. One international school is attended by children from about 50 different nationalities, and it is through this international environment that young people can learn how diverse the world is.

> "This school has been breathing diversity and multiculturalism for years. (...) Because of the
> diversity, the level of tolerance and understanding is very high. There is also a very high aware-
> ness of issues of discrimination or racism," says the director of the International School of
> Bydgoszcz (ISOB) in an interview. (RC1)

Surprisingly, references to multicultural school environments do not appear that often, and when they do, these mainly refer to non-public schools. In doing so, references to adapting to life in a multicultural environment focus on the school curriculum, for example:

> The school implements the goals and tasks set out by the International Baccalaureate
> Organization and those included in the Education Act that in particular, support and direct
> the development of children and youth in accordance with their potential in the context of
> multicultural social and axiological space. (S7)

> The school creates a "Discussion Club" within which students have the opportunity to organize
> various activities related to the implementation of the exchange programme with international
> students and establishing contacts with them within the programme promoting global and
> European multiculturalism. (S5)

Children who stay in such a group develop sensitivity and empathy toward each other, as well as an understanding of otherness. This prepares them for life in a multicultural society and teaches them openness to the world. Awareness of discrimination issues is emphasized by the management and teachers.

> "This institution was established for the families of foreigners who settled in Krakow. In recent
> years, more and more Poles have been sending their children here. I think people come to our
> school because they care about a multicultural, international educational experience for their
> children," says the new director of the institution, in an interview with our newspaper. (GK1)

Mixing students from different cultures is a practical opportunity for students to get to know each other, cooperate on a daily basis, and learn to work together in an international setting. Schools with fewer foreign students also focus on acceptance of otherness, tolerance, and learning about other cultures. Building students' social openness can be seen as contributing to building a worthwhile society. Students are expected to develop in themselves an openness to the needs of others.

> It is the promotion in education of the European values of respect for the human dignity, freedom, democracy, equality, the rule of law and respect for human rights, including the rights of persons who belong to minority groups. (GW28)

In contrast to press releases, school documents on this subject do not emphasize high degrees of tolerance for multicultural environments to such an extent. Instead when referring to tolerance, they refer to interpersonal relations, for example:

> Students show tolerance towards different views and attitudes; students need to be polite and respectful towards other people. Schools prohibit all aggressive actions and the use of vulgar words, phrases and gestures. (S06)

Creating an Unwritten Support for LGBTQ+

Surprisingly, in school law documents there are no direct references to LGBTQ+. Only in one school were references that indicated respect for a student's "sexual identity" found.

> The school allows students to maintain their national, ethnic, linguistic, religious, and sexual identity. (S10)

Information about schools that follow an international program is associated with the discourse on tolerance and acceptance that includes LGBTQ+ people. These schools rank highly in the ranking of LGBTQ+[2] Friendly Schools. They promote values such as equality and tolerance to emphasize human rights. As a result, LGBTQ+ youth can find a safe place for them to learn in these institutions.

> The action's website reads: As much as 30% of physical violence takes place at school, with as many as 70% of LGBT youth experiencing violence. Curricula do not explicitly indicate equality, anti-discrimination content or even reliable information about sexual orientations and gender identities. Misrepresentation of sexuality still occurs in textbooks. Rainbow Friday provides an opportunity to respond to the inadequacies of the Polish education system. (QU1)

Schools with an international program are portrayed as safe for students and stress that this does not just refer to physical, but also mental safety. The school is supposed to care not only about learning, but also the educational aspect is equally important, which in the international program refers to tolerance and respect for others.

> "Safe, means being open to diversity, teaching empathy and respect, where everyone feels cared for and understood. Where youth from the LGBTQ+ community are accepted, and where the backgrounds, abilities or special educational requirements of people from other minorities are also respectfully considered so that they too will also feel comfortable there," says the coordinator. (GW37)

High spots in the LGBTQ+-Friendly Schools Ranking are held by schools with an international program. The purpose of conducting the ranking is to raise the level of acceptance and encourage being an "inclusive" school in the region. News articles emphasize the importance of creating a school that is safe for all students.

International Schools for LGBTQ+ Youth 265

> "We are pleased that we once again ranked high in the ranking of LGBTQ+-Friendly Schools. We would like to see all schools from the Lublin region ranked first at the same time. It is important that every person attending the school feels safe and secure," stressed a teacher at the Paderewski International High School in Lublin. (KL1)

In their statements, the teachers link the school's high ranking in the LGBTQ+-Friendly Schools Ranking to students' sense of safety and to building an inclusive school climate. At the same time, pointing out that this should be the case in all schools, not just those that have received awards.

Because acceptance of LGBTQ+ people has stood in contradiction to the policy of the Ministry of Education and Science in Poland in previous years, schools have faced consequences for, for example, agreeing to hold "Rainbow Fridays"[3] at school. The consequence, for example, was an inspection by the Board of Education and recommendations handed down after the inspection. In one high school, students expressed support for the management, which allowed the organization of "Rainbow Fridays," thus expressing approval for the organization of such actions at school.

> According to the Olsztyn Board of Education, before any school again allows an action on LGBT tolerance within its walls, it must first ask the opinion of all parents of students. At the First High School, the youngsters in the case stood firmly behind their principal. (GW17)

The articles also described an issue related to the school's barrage of approvals for the IB, despite earlier declarations by the Ministry of Education and Science and obtaining IB accreditation. The following is the opinion of parents, which links the lack of permission to conduct the IB Baccalaureate to the school's organization of the "Rainbow Friday" campaign.

> "The Ministry of Education is taking revenge on our children for Rainbow Friday," claim the parents of students of the First High School in Olsztyn. The children were preparing for the International Baccalaureate. The Ministry of Education decided that they could not pass it. (GW22)

Students who learned that they would not be allowed to take the IB had to change their class profiles at short notice and start preparing to take the National Baccalaureate. Their junior classmates continued preparing to take the IB, with no guarantee that the school would receive approval from the Ministry of Education at the time. Press materials described the disappointment of students, parents and teachers that accompanied this situation.

CONCLUSIONS

The findings of this study illuminate the diverse roles played by international schools in Poland, with a specific emphasis on their impact on the inclusion and empowerment of LGBTQ+ individuals.

Firstly, talent development for social inclusion is a function that includes critical aspects in understanding the implementation of policies pertaining to the LGBT+ community and lies within the economic sphere, specifically examining the prevailing values within different socioeconomic contexts. Inglehart (1977), who is recognized for pioneering the concept of post-materialist values, proposes that in regions characterized by stable and advanced socio-economic conditions, such as those commonly found in Western societies, there is a notable shift away from prioritizing basic needs and physical security toward prioritizing quality of life. This shift in values is particularly significant when considering countries that belong to the Organization for Economic Cooperation and Development (OECD), where there tends to be a higher degree of social and political acceptance of LGBT+ rights compared to other nations (Valfort, 2017).

Recent research conducted by Badgett et al. (2019) further reinforces this idea, indicating a positive correlation between economic development and the social inclusion of the LGBT community. Poland is considered to be the country that benefited the most from European integration after joining the European Union and achieved the greatest success among European Central and Eastern countries. Strengthening industry (especially the ICT), industrial, and food sectors, allows it to compete with EU Member States and other countries. However, in the coming years, Poland will face many key economic developmental challenges. The most important of them is the reduction of the labor force and the loss of competitiveness due to an aging society. LGBTQ+ inclusion translates into better results economic, business, and individual.

The data show that openness, favorable inclusivity, and diverse societies are better for economic growth, whereas discrimination based on sexual orientation or gender identity may negatively impact long-term economic prospects. Enterprise capabilities supporting the inclusion of LGBTQ+ people to attract and retain talent, introduce innovations, and build customer loyalty and brand strength translate into better financial results. Moreover, people working in open, diverse, and inclusive environments usually perform better. Cultures based on inclusion and diversity may contribute to improving results individually – this applies to everyone, not only LGBTQ+ people (Open For Business. 2021, p. 13). International schools, although initially intended to fulfill an educational function, indirectly, also fulfill an economic function, in the sense that their graduates will be more open to diversity, which will help build a supportive atmosphere in the work environment.

Employees working in open, diverse, and inclusive environments have a higher level of motivation and are more attached to the values and culture of their workplace. The inclusion of LGBT+ people contributes to an increased level of entrepreneurship, creativity, and innovation, and cultivates a diverse and creative environment conducive to innovation. People working in diverse, inclusive environments achieve greater productivity rates, are more efficient, perform better, and are more willing to reflect constructively on the need to improve results. Currently, this function is socially very important because it responds to the needs of a growing part of society. People working in open, diverse, and inclusive environments are more satisfied with their work, are not exposed to discrimination that causes mental problems and physical violence, and are more willing to go beyond their duties and contribute to the well-being and culture of the company.

Companies that are more diverse and inclusive create an atmosphere of trust and better communication that is essential for effective teamwork. International schools perform this role well, but there are too few of these schools to significantly change the social position of LGBTQ+ employees in the work environment. As Maji et al. (2023) claim LGBTQ+ people encounter multiple negative workplace experiences and emotions, especially proximal (hiring discrimination, housing discrimination) and distal workplace discrimination (unsafe work climate, microaggressions, harassment). These aversive experiences lead to work stress while also mandating that people manage their sexual identity and style of dressing. This situation negatively impacts their work and family life, job satisfaction, and careers.

The second question that we posed in the study refers to the issue of how international schools cultivate inclusive environments for LGBTQ+ students. Our study showed the transformative role of schools with international programs in creating safe and welcoming environments for LGBTQ+ students. In authoritarian and oppressive political contexts, LGBT+ rights are conspicuously absent, often leading to the criminalization of LGBT+ behaviors within the legal framework (Tarrow, 2011). Additionally, under such repressive political regimes, avenues for traditional forms of political activism are severely constrained. In terms of the political aspect, Encarnación (2014, p. 1) underscores the pivotal role played by a nation's political structure in shaping LGBT+ rights, contending that "while gay rights may not be universally present in all democracies, they are notably absent in non-democratic regimes."

Transformative leadership is a style that fosters positive change in individuals and society through a shared vision, motivation, action, and social justice. It is based on Burns's (1978) idea of transforming leadership, which involves a "revolution" – "a complete and pervasive transformation of an entire social system" (p. 202). This is also aligned with Freire's (1970) "critical" or "problem-posing" approach in education, which enables learners to "come to see the world not as a static reality, but as a reality in the process of transformation" (p. 84). Transformative leadership aims to create leaders of social justice in education, who can balance academic excellence and social transformation (Shields, 2013, p. 3). Social justice education is defined as "full and equal participation of all groups in a [school] ... [through educational practices that are] democratic and participatory, inclusive and affirming of human agency and human capacities for working collaboratively to create change" (Adams et al., 2007, pp. 1–2).

It is also a philosophy and a practice that respects and values all people with fairness, respect, dignity, and generosity (Nieto, 2006, p. 2). Our study revealed the transformative role of international schools in Poland, emerging as havens that foster inclusive environments for LGBTQ+ individuals. Positioned as "islands of resistance" against prevailing authoritarian policies, these schools provide safe spaces where LGBTQ+ students can flourish and receive essential support. Through the adoption of international curricula like IB and Cambridge, these schools actively promote tolerance, acceptance, and human rights, cultivating a culture of inclusivity and respect for diversity. Inclusive education refers not only to general acceptance but also specifically to a welcoming and supportive environment in which LGBTQ+ students feel unafraid to express their diverse identities (Sadowski, 2016).

Our study showed that this inclusive environment within schools with international programs in Poland is developed by a supportive physical environment, an international curriculum recognized for its tolerance and openness to diversity, and discursive interactions between staff and students. Schools as safe spaces improve not only the well-being and mental health of LGBTQ+ students but also their educational outcomes and levels of retention (Shannon, 2016). The analysis of press materials underscores the significant impact of international schools in challenging discriminatory practices and creating institutional spaces that advance LGBTQ+ inclusion within the educational landscape. International schools not only challenge the existing norms but also actively engage in practices that support LGBTQ+ students. Initiatives such as Rainbow Friday and the establishment of policies that honor students' sexual identities illustrate their commitment to fostering a broader societal shift toward greater acceptance of sexual differences. Thus, the planned functions based on in-school laws that are inclusive for LGBTQ+ youth align with the attained curriculum, as evidenced by press releases highlighting the proactive stance of international schools in promoting LGBTQ+ inclusion and challenging discriminatory practices.

The last research question concerns the contributary role performed by international schools in building a valuable and tolerant society. The functions identified during the research relate to education in tolerance and respect. In international schools, one interacts with diversity and multiculturalism. Therefore, the level of tolerance and understanding is very high. Awareness is built on issues of discrimination or racism among teachers, students, and parents. By being in an international environment, students in a school setting have the opportunity to learn to cooperate with people from different cultures daily. In this way, they acquire abilities and prepare themselves to live and work in an open and diverse society. In international schools, students representing different cultures, and nationalities have the opportunity to get to know each other and cooperate also on a daily basis. Schools, stimulate socio-economic changes and development in their local environment (Benneworth & Cunha, 2015; Monteiro et al., 2021).

This can be considered a contribution to building a valuable society. International schools secure the opportunity for students to be in a tolerant environment. Because of the values promoted, such as respect for human dignity, equality, freedom, democracy, the rule of law, and respect for human rights, international schools provide a safe place for students who might fear an unfriendly reception at other schools because of their sexual orientation (e.g., Abreu & Kenny, 2018). As such, schools are arenas for critical understanding and taking action to eliminate inequalities (Apple, 2008). According to Erin B. Godfrey and Justina Kamiel Grayman (2014) critical consciousness is made up of three parts: critical reflection, understood as the ability to critically read social conditions, socio-political effectiveness, that is, the sense of effectiveness in bringing about changes, and critical action, which is actual participation. This is achieved by combining the promotion of values related to tolerance, recognizing the problems faced by LGBTQ+ youth, and actual activities related to organizing actions promoting an understanding of diversity. International schools carry out related tasks to build students' social openness by combining preferred values with actual

International Schools for LGBTQ+ Youth 269

participation. Because of the values promoted, in these schools, students who are LGBTQ+ can feel comfortable in an accepting and tolerant environment. This can reduce the possibility of victimization (Sterzing et al., 2017) related to sexual orientation or declared gender identity.

ACKNOWLEDGMENT

The inspiration to write this paper came from the research work we undertook as part of the project entitled Educational Functions of IB Programs in schools in Poland (Grant no. 27/IDUB/MLOD/2021).

NOTES

1. We acknowledge the dynamic nature of terminology concerning this demographic and the continuing discourse on the most suitable terms (Monro, 2020). In line with contemporary research in sexuality education (Helmer, 2016), we employ the acronym LGBTQ to encompass the array of identities and sexual orientations they represent. Additionally, we incorporate "queer" to acknowledge individuals who embrace identities divergent from societal norms, understanding the complexities and potential controversies associated with this term.

2. The ranking of LGBTQ+ Friendly Schools is organized in Poland within the framework of the projects "LGBTQ+ Friendly Schools" (October 2021 to July 2022) and "LGBTQ+ Friendly Schools 2.0" (October 2022 to July 2023) funded by Iceland, Liechtenstein and Norway from the EEA and Norwegian Funds under the Active Citizens - Regional Fund Programme. The ranking aims to help students choose a high school by identifying schools that are most open to diversity. https://lgbtplusme.com/pl/ranking/pl

3. Rainbow Friday is a holiday, held in Poland, every October, to support LGBTQ+ youth at school and show that every person is entitled to attend a school that is safe and welcoming regardless of psychosexual orientation, gender identity, or sexual characteristics. https://lgbtplusme.com/teczowy-piatek

REFERENCES

Abreu, R. L., & Kenny, M. C. (2018). Cyberbullying and LGBTQ youth: A systematic literature review and recommendations for prevention and intervention. *Journal of Child & Adolescent Trauma*, *11*(1), 81–97. https://doi.org/10.1007/s40653-017-0175-7

Adams, M., Bell, L. A., & Griffin, P. (2007). *Teaching for diversity and social justice*. Routledge.

Apple, M. W. (2008). Can schooling contribute to a more just society? *Education, Citizenship and Social Justice*, *3*(3), 239–261.

Badgett, M. V., Waaldijk, K., & Rodgers, Y. (2019). The relationship between LGBT inclusion and economic development: Macro-level evidence. *World Development*, *120*, 1–14.

Bardach, E, & Patashnik, E. M. (2015). *Practical guide for policy analysis: The eightfold path to more effective problem solving*. SAGE.

Benneworth, P., & Cunha, J. (2015). Universities' contributions to social innovation: Reflections in theory & practice. *European Journal of Innovation Management*, *18*(4), 508–527.

Berner-Rodoreda, A., Bärnighausen, T., Kennedy, C., Brinkmann, S., Sarker, M., Wikler, D., Eyal, N., & McMahon, S. (2018). From doxastic to epistemic: A typology and critique of qualitative interview styles. *Qualitative Inquiry*, *26*, 291–305.

Burns, J. M. (1978). *Leadership*. Harper & Row.Shields and Hesbol.

Cambridge Dictionary. (2024). Retrieved January 8, 2024, from https://dictionary.cambridge.org/pl/dictionary/english/well-being.

Campbell, K., & Harris, S. (2021). Teachers' perceptions of principals' supportive behavior during COVID-19. *Journal of Education and Human Development, 10*, 92–101. https://doi.org/10.15640/jehd.v10n1a8

Charmaz, K. (2015). *Constructing grounded theory*, SAGE Publications Ltd.

Charmaz, K., & Thornberg, R. (2021). The pursuit of quality in grounded theory. *Qualitative Research in Psychology, 18*(3), 305–327. https://doi.org/10.1080/14780887.2020.1780357

Di Giacomo, E., Krausz, M., Colmegna, F., Aspesi, F., & Clerici M. (2018). Estimating the risk of attempted suicide among sexual minority youths: A systematic review and meta-analysis. *JAMA Pediatrics, 172*, 1145–1152. https://doi.org/10.1001/jamapediatrics.2018.2731

Encarnación, O. G. (2014). Gay rights: Why democracy matters. *Journal of Democracy, 25*(3), 90. https://doi.org/10.1353/jod.2014.0044

Feliksiak, M. (2013). *Stosunek do praw gejów i lesbijek oraz związków partnerskich*. Centrum Badania Opinii Publicznej. Pobrane z: https://www.cbos.pl/SPISKOM.POL/2013/K_024_13.PDF

Ferfolja, T., & Ullman, J. (2017). Gender and sexuality diversity and schooling: Progressive mothers speak out. *Sex Education, 17*(3), 348–362. https://doi.org/10.1080/14681811.2017.12.85761

Freire, P. (1970). *Pedagogy of the oppressed*. Continuum.

Freire, P. (2017). *Pedagogy of the oppressed*. Penguin Classics.

Godfrey, E. B., & Grayman, J. K. (2014). Teaching citizens: The role of open classroom climate in fostering critical consciousness among youth. *Journal of Youth and Adolescence, 43*, 1801–1817.

Gorska, P., & Mikolajczak, M. (2015). Tradycyjne i nowoczesne uprzedzenia wobec osób homoseksualnych w Polsce [Traditional and modern homonegativity in Poland]. In A. Stefaniak, M. Bilewicz, & M. Winiewski (Eds.), *Uprzedzenia w Polsce* (pp. 179–206). Liberi & Libri.

Harvey, S. A. (2018). Observe before you leap: Why observation provides critical insights for formative research and intervention design that you'll never get from focus groups, interviews, or KAP surveys. *Global Health: Science and Practice, 6*, 299–316.

Helmer, K. (2016). Gay and lesbian literature disrupting the heteronormative space of the high school English classroom. *Sex Education, 16*(1), 35–48. https://doi.org/10.1080/14681811.2015.1042574.

Hill, I. (2001). Early stirrings: The beginnings of the international schools movement. *International Schools Journal, 23*(2), 11–22.

IBO. (2024). Retrieved January 31, 2024, from https://www.ibo.org/about-the-ib/the-ib-by-country-and-territory/p/poland/

Inglehart, R. (1977). Values, objective needs, and subjective satisfaction among western publics. *Comparative Political Studies, 9*(4), 429. https://doi.org/10.1177/001041407700900403

Ismail, F., Pawero, A. M. D., & Umar, M. (2021). Education planning and its implications for education policy during the COVID-19 pandemic. *International Journal of Vocational Education Studies, 3*, 110–115. https://doi.org/10.29103/ijevs.v3i2.4441

Kosciw, J., Palmer, N., Kull, R., & Greytak, E. (2013). The effect of negative school climate on academic outcomes for LGBT youth and the role of in-school supports. *Journal of School Violence, 12*(1), 45–63. https://doi.org/10.1080/15388220.2012.732546

KPH Organization. (2024). *Rainbow Friday hit the jackpot – campaign with 17.875 million hits in 24 hours*. Retrieved February 26, 2024, from https://kph.org.pl/teczowy-piatek-podsumowanie/

Krippendorff, K. (2018). *Content analysis: An introduction to its methodology*. Sage Publications.

Leek, J. (2020). From educational experiment to an alternative to the national programme. International Baccalaureate Programmes in Poland – policy and practice perspectives. Compare: *A Journal of Comparative and International Education, 52*(3), 475–491. https://doi.org/10.1080/03057925.2020.1777842

Leek, J. (2022). International Baccalaureate schools as islands of educational resistance. A case study of Poland. *Globalisation, Societies and Education, 22*(4), 625–637. https://doi.org/10.1080/147 67724.2022.2089976

LGBTPlusMe. (2024). https://lgbtplusme.com/pl

MacAulay, M., Ybarra, M. L., Saewyc, E. M., Sullivan, T. R., Jackson, L. A., & Millar, S. (2021). They talked completely about straight couples only: Schooling, sexual violence and sexual and gender minority youth. *Sex Education, 16*, 1–14. https://doi.org/10.1080/14681811.2021.1924142

Mackie, G., Lambert, K., Patlamazoglou, L. (2021). The mental health of transgender young people in secondary schools: A scoping review. *School Mental Health, 13*, 13–27. https://doi.org/10.1007/s12310-020-09403-9

International Schools for LGBTQ+ Youth 271

Maji, S., Yadav, N., & Gupta, P. (2023). LGBTQ+ in workplace: A systematic review and reconsideration. *Equality, Diversity and Inclusion, 43*(2), 313–360. https://doi.org/10.1108/EDI-02-2022-0049

Marshal, M. P., Dietz, L. J., Friedman, M. S., Stall, R., Smith, H. A., McGinley, J., Thoma, B. C., Murray, P. J., D'Augelli, A. R., & Brent, D. A. (2011). Suicidality and depression disparities between sexual minority and heterosexual youth: A meta-analytic review. *Journal of Adolescent Health, 49*, 115–123. https://doi.org/10.1016/j.jadohealth.2011.02.005

Martín-Castillo, D., Jiménez-Barbero, J. A., del Mar Pastor-Bravo, M., Sánchez-Muñoz, M., Fernández-Espín, M. E., & García-Arenas, J. J. (2020). School victimization in transgender people: A systematic review. *Children and Youth Services Review, 119*, 105480. https://doi.org/10.1016/j.childyouth.2020.105480

McBride, R. S., & Neary, A. (2021). Trans and gender diverse youth resisting cisnormativity in school. *Gender and Education, 33*(8), 1090–1107. https://doi.org/10.1080/09540253.2021.1884201

McDermott, E., Kaley, A., Kaner, E., Limmer, M., McGovern, R., McNulty, F., Nelson, R., Geijer-Simpson, E., & Spencer, L. (2023). Understanding how school-based interventions can tackle LGBTQ+ youth mental health inequality: A realist approach. *International Journal of Environmental Research and Public Health, 20*(5), 4274. https://doi.org/10.3390/ijerph20054274

Merton, R. K. (1968). *Social theory and social structure.* The Free Press.

Mogalakwe M. (2009). The documentary research method – Using documentary sources in social research. *Eastern Africa Social Science Research Review, 25*, 43–58.

Monro, S. (2020). Sexual and gender diversities: Implications for LGBTQ studies. *Journal of Homosexuality, 67*(3), 315–324. https://doi.org/10.1080/00918369.2018.1528079

Monteiro, S., Isusi-Fagoaga, R., Almeida, L., & García-Aracil, A. (2021). Contribution of higher education institutions to social innovation: Practices in two southern European universities. *Sustainability, 13*(7), 3594.

Morris P. (1998). *Curriculum: Development, issues and politics.* Kong University Press.

Nieto, S. (2006). *Teaching as political work: Learning from courageous and caring teachers* [The Longfellow Lecture at the Child Development Institute]. Sarah Lawrence College.

Nweke, C. C., & Owoh, A. T. (2020). On pedagogy of the oppressed: An appraisal of Paulo Freire's philosophy of education. *Ogirisi: A New Journal of African Studies, 16*, 62–75.

O'Keeffe, A. (2013). Media and discourse analysis. J. P. Gee, M. Handford (Eds.), *The Routledge handbook of discourse analysis* (1st ed., pp. 441–454). Routledge.

Open For Business. (2021). *Research series: The economic case for LGBT+ inclusion in Central and Eastern Europe (CEE) Hungary, Poland, Romania and Ukraine.* https://static1.squarespace.com/static/5bba53a8ab1a62771504d1dd/t/60d1b199e098bd3ca30df42b/1624355229493/The+Economic+Case+for+LGBT%2B+Inclusion+in+CEE+EN+July+2021.pdf

Ploszka, A. (2023). From human rights to human wrongs. How local government can negatively influence the situation of an individual. The case of Polish LGBT ideology-free zones. *The International Journal of Human Rights, 27*(2), 359–379. https://doi.org/10.1080/13642987.2022.2121708

Prior, L. (2003). *Using documents in social research.* SAGE.

Rainbow Friday. (2024). Retrieved February 26, 2024, from https://teczowypiatek.org.pl

Raport z badania. (2020). *Sytuacja osób LGBTQIA w krakowskich szkołach ponadpodstawowych.* Retrieved December 27, 2023, from https://www.queerowymaj.org/wp-content/uploads/2020/11/LGBTQIA-w-szkole.pdf

Rojek, M., Leek, J., & Kosiorek, M. (2023). Mutual learning community: teachers' opinions about their learning possibilities in schools implementing international programmes. *Annales Universitatis Mariae Curie-Skłodowska. Sectio J, Paedagogia-Psychologia, 36*(1), 27–43. https://doi.org/10.17951/j.2023.36.1.27-43

Rubin, A., & Babbie, E. (2008). *Research methods for social work* (6th ed.). Brookes/Cole.

Russell, S. T., Bishop, M. D., Saba, V. C., James, I., & Ioverno, S. (2021). Promoting school safety for LGBTQ and all students. *Policy Insights from the Behavioral and Brain Sciences, 8*(2), 160–166. https://doi.org/10.1177/23727322211031938.

Sadowski, M. (2016). *Safe is not enough: Better schools for LGBTQ students.* Harvard Education Press

Shannon, B. (2016). Comprehensive for who? Neoliberal directives in Australian 'Comprehensive' sexuality education and the erasure of GLBTIQ identity. *Sex Education, 16*(6), 573–585. https://doi.org/10.1080/14681811.2016.1141090

Shields, C. (2013). *Transformative leadership in education: Equitable change in an uncertain and complex world* (pp. 1–148). Eye on Education.

Stefaniak, A., & Witkowska, M. (2015). Społeczne kontakty Polaków, czyli czy znamy ludzi innych niż my sami i czy chcemy ich poznawać? In A. Stefaniak, M. Bilewicz, & M. Winiewski (red.) *Uprzedzenia w Polsce* (s. 99–124). Liberi Libri.

Sterzing, P. R., Ratliff, G. A., Gartner, R. E., McGeough, B. L., & Johnson, K. C. (2017). Social ecological correlates of polyvictimization among a national sample of transgender, genderqueer, and cisgender sexual minority adolescents. *Child Abuse & Neglect, 67*, 1–12.

Štulhofer, A., & Rimac, I. (2009). Determinants of homonegativity in Europe. *Journal of Sex Research, 46*(1), 24–32. https://doi.org/10.1080/00224490802398373.

Tarrow, S. (2011). *Power in movement: Social movements and contentious politics.* https://voidnetwork. gr/wp-content/uploads/2016/09/Power-in-Movement.-Social-movements-and-contentious-politics-by-Sidney-Tarrow.pdf

Valfort, M. A. (2017). *LGBTI in OECD countries: A review.* https://doi.org/10.1787/d5d49711-en

Van den Akker, H., van der Ploeg, R., & Scheepers, P. (2013). Disapproval of homosexuality: Comparative research on individual and national determinants of disapproval of homosexuality in 20 European countries. *International Journal of Public Opinion Research, 25*(1), 64–86. https://doi.org/10.1093/ijpor/edr058.

Van Der Star, A., & Jansen, D. (2018). Growing up being LGBT in Europe: the impact of bullying and parenting behavior on mental health. *European Journal of Public Health, 28*(4). https://doi.org/10.1093/eurpub/cky213.053

INDEX

Academic freedom, 49, 182
Academic knowledge, 44
Access to services, 112
Acculturation, 137
African American reparations, 242
All India Radio (AIR), 227
Allegiance, 93
American Association of University
    Professors (AAUP), 89
American Indian boarding school
    system, 238
American Indian reparations, 242
American legal system, 242
Analytical method, 74
Anchoring, 64–67
Anglo-American paradigm, 176
Anti-positivist breakthrough, 68
Artificial intelligence, 7
Asian civic values, 180–181
Assessments, 85–86
Atma Nirbhar Bharat Abhiyaan, 226
Authentic patriotism, 88
Authoritarian movements, 46
Authority of science, 40
Automatic processing, 64
Availability heuristic, 66–67

Basic needs approach, 206
Bildung, 185–186
Boarding School Healing Project,
    245
Boarding schools, 238
Boko Haram, 92–93
Bourgeois public space, 86–87
Brexit, 46, 49–50

Canada, 21
Canadian universities, 190
Capability approach, 206

Caribbean-Africa Knowledge
    Program, 245
Caring for Students' School
    Welfare, 261
Center of Community Project (CCP),
    182
Central Institute of Educational
    Technology (CIET), 227
ChatGTP, 7
Child marriage, 209
Chinese Academy, 177–178
Chinese University 3. 0, 181
Citizenship education in
    universities, 183
Citizenship rights, 40
Civic and citizenship education in
    universities, 182–184
Civic and moral education, 180
Civic education, 183
Civic responsibility, 189
Civil society, 182
Climate scale, 162
Co-option of public space, 86–88
College, 60
Colonial matrix of power, 87
Colonial schooling, 238
Colonial schools, 234 (*see also*
    International schools)
  background, 238, 240
  lens of reparations, 238, 242
  linking reparations in education as
    global project, 244–246
Color-blind admission
    policies, 50
Communication technologies, 30
Community colleges, 184
Community engagement, 190
Community Partnership, 189
Community-based programs, 183

274 INDEX

Comparative and international
education (CIE), 4, 20,
22–23, 28, 236
literature survey, 4–7
modes of education, 13–14
research methodology, 7–8
responsibilities of CIE researchers
and practitioners, 34
results, 8–13
Comparative and International
Education Society (CIES),
12, 29
Comparative education, 28, 58–59,
100
among other sub-disciplines of
pedagogical sciences, 60–64
field in Hong Kong, 23–24
functions, 70
impetus of SOMEC, 29–33
rationale, 28–29
responsibilities of CIE researchers
and practitioners, 34
the west and "the rest", 20–22
Comparative Education Review, 4–6,
9–10, 13
Comparative international research, 61
Comparative methods, 10
Comparative pedagogical studies, 58
Comparative research, 58
comparative education among
other sub-disciplines of
pedagogical sciences, 60–64
heuristic of availability, anchoring
and false accessibility, 64–67
qualitative research in comparative
studies, 74–76
selected methods in, 67–74
Comparative studies, 58
Compare, 61
Compensation, 242
Computer Literacy and Studies in
Schools (CLASS), 226
Confucian ethics, 181
Confucianism on postsecondary/HE,
181–182

Constellation of interests, 87
Constructivism, 62
Content analysis, 8
Cornell University, 89
Correlationism, 75–76
Corruption, 92
Cost-effectiveness analysis, 206
COVID-19 pandemic, 220
Creed of Human Rights, 12
Critical ethnography, 10
Critical Race Theory (CRT), 101
Criticality, 102
Cultural anthropology, 70
Cultural reparation, 243
Cultural variation, 22
Curriculum, 32

Data interpretation methods,
10–11
Decoloniality, challenge of, 83–86
Decolonization, 83
challenge of "western" curriculum,
92–93
challenge of decoloniality, 83–86
co-option of public space, 86–88
free speech, 89–90
hypothetical "war on merit",
90–92
neo-decolonial trap, 93–94
weaponization of progressive
educational practices, 88
Decolonizer, 86
Deficit narrative, 102
Definability, 63
Democracy, 187
Democratic engagement, 190
Descriptive method, 71
Determinism, 70
Development-industrial complex, 84
Deweyan principles, 183
Differential Item Functioning (DIF),
109–110
Digital equity, 221, 228–229
Digital inclusivity, 221, 228–229
Digital India Campaign (DIC), 221

Index 275

Digital Infrastructure for Knowledge Sharing (DIKSHA), 226–227
Digital learning, 220–221
Diploma Programme (DP), 256
Diversity, 41–42
Diversity, equity, and inclusion (DEI), 83
Document analysis, 259
Driving forces, 61
Due diligence, 71
Duty to report, 148–149

East Asian education, 21
Economic development, 200
Economic growth, 200, 202
Economic self-sufficiency, 240
Economically marginalized individuals, 47
Economics, 70
Education, 6, 40, 45, 200
    effect on gross domestic product, 201–202
    returns to, 203–204
Education as an institution, 41–45
Education attainment, 203
Education expenditure, 200
Education for All (EFA), 45
Education in Poland, 252
Education outcomes, 100
Education quality, 113
Educational attainment at age 20, 111
Educational contestations, 41
    areas for future inquiry, 50–52
    illiberal reaction to education, 45–50
    liberal world order and education as institution, 41–45
Educational deprivation, 210
Educational equity, 29
Educational institutions, 187
Educational opportunities, 49, 92, 212, 221, 225
Educational policies, 41, 85
Educational policy, 34, 44, 221

Educational practices, 73, 252
Educational production function, 204
Educational reforms, 47
Educational reparations, 237
Educational systems, 59, 82, 159
Educators, 155
Elisionism, 59
Empiricism, 70
Empowered individual, 41
Endogenous growth model, 203
"Enforced assimilation" policies, 242
Engaged universities, 182
English as an additional language (EAL), 143, 155
ePathshala, 227
Epistemic violence, 240
Equity, 29, 40, 91, 221
Equity in education, 11
Estudio Regional Comparativo y Explicativo (ERCE) study, 159
Ethnocentrism, 49
Ethnography, 10, 75
Ethnoscape, 139
Europe, 23, 177
Experiential Learning, 189
Explained portion, 106, 115
Explanatory variables, 111–113
Externalism, 75

Fair Admissions decision, 51
False accessibility, 64–67
False consensus effect, 67
Falsifiability, 63
Feature similarity, 64
Female labor force participation (FLPR), 208
Formal education, 6–7
Free speech, 89–90
Fundamental methodological error, 74

Galloping, 5
Gender, 208–211
    disparities in education, 209
    equality, 208–209

INDEX

Generality, 70
Generalizing science, 68
Germany, 72, 186
Girls, 47
Global citizenship, 51
Global research assessment
    frameworks, 21
Global testing culture, 44
Globalization, 220
Google Classroom, 220
Google meet, 220
Grade level, 204
Gross domestic product (GDP),
    201–202
    education's effect on, 201–202

Hard data, 69
Harmony, 183
Healing, 243
Healthcare industry, 85
Height-for-Age z-Score (HAZ), 112
Hermeneutic approaches, 75
Hermeneutics, 68
Heuristic of availability, 64–67
Hierarchical linear regression model,
    162
Higher education (HE), 44, 176, 179,
    206–207
Higher education institutions (HEIs),
    177
Higher learning, 177
Historical method, 59, 73
Hong Kong, 19–20
    field in, 23–24
Human capabilities theory, 12
Human capital, 40, 200, 203
    employment, 178–179
Human Development Index (HDI), 44
Human rights, 11, 40
Humanity, 183
Hypothetical "war on merit", 90–92

Ibero-American Society of
    Comparative Education, 28
Ideals, 183
Identity, 183

Ideoscape, 139
Illiberal narratives, 40
Illiberal reaction to education, 45–50
Illiberalism, 45, 49
    impacts, 52
Inclusion, 32, 50
Inclusive school spaces, 259
India, 220
India, Pakistan, Bangladesh, and
    Nepal (IPBN), 200
Indian education system, 221
    data and methodology, 225–226
    digital equity and inclusivity,
        228–229
    elements of teacher quality and
        pandemic, 224–225
    history of technology usage in, 221
    NEP, 221–222
    results, 226–229
    teacher belief for technology
        integration in classroom,
        222–225
Indian Government, 220
Indigeneity, 103–104, 108–109
Indigenous, 42, 100, 102–103, 108,
    121, 237, 241
Indigenous boarding schools, 238
Indigenous ethnicity, 108
Indigenous groups, 100
Indigenous language, 103, 108, 121
Indigenous peoples, 42, 102, 241
Indira Gandhi National Open
    University (IGNOU), 226
Indirect effects, 159
Individual human rights, 45
Individual initiatives, 228
Industrial education, 238
Inequality, 159
Informal education, 6–7
Information and Communication
    Technology (ICT), 220
    initiatives in India during
        pandemic, 226–228
Information Communications
    Technology (ICT), 148
Innovation, 28

Index

Inquiry, 75
Internalism, 75
International academic communities, 20
International assessments, 100
International Baccalaureate (IB) program, 256
International Baccalaureate Organization (IBO), 138
International cooperation, 45
International education, 191
International human rights regime, 43
International institutions, 44
International mindedness, 136
International organizations, 23
International research, 61–62
International schools, 136, 138–139, 155, 250 (*see also* Colonial schools)
  broader study and subset, 137–138
  contextualizing international school as policyscape, 137
  findings, 140–149
  fostering multicultural awareness and social openness, 263–264
  international schools in Poland, 256–257
  LGBTQ+ in Poland, 254–256
  methodology, 140
  in Poland, 256–257
  research design, 257–261
  results, 262–265
  review of the literature, 138–140
  shaping safe and friendly school environment, 262–263
  transnational flows and policyscaped environment, 139–140
  unwritten support for LGBTQ+, 264–265
International student, 155
International System for Observation and Feedback (ISTOF), 10
International teacher, 155
International test series, 14

Internationalization
  of higher education, 49
  of K-12 education, 136
Interpretative approaches, 75
Intersectionality, 108

Johns Hopkins University, 178
Justification, 63

KPH, 256

Labor relations, 87
Land reparation and restitution, 243
Latin America, 29–30
Latin America and the Caribbean, 158
"Learner-centered" education reforms, 221
Lebenswelt, 70
Left-wing populists, 46
Lesbian, gay, transgender, bisexual, queer, and questioning (LGBTQ+) students, 252
LGBTQ+ in Poland, 252, 254–256
LGBTQ+ in schools, 252
LGBTQ+ inclusion, 253–254
LGBTQ+ students, 90
LGBTQ+ youth, 252–253
Liberal arts education, 179
Liberal democracy, 45
Liberal world order and education as institution, 41–45
Liberal/illiberal culture, 52
Liberalism, 51
Lifelong learning, 41
Linear regression formula, 106
Local knowledges, 86
Location, 113

Manifest Destiny, 239
Manodarpan, 227
Marginalization factors, 208–211
Marginalized groups, 252
Mass online open courses (MOOCs), 14
Mathematics score at age 12, 109–111
Media discourse, 260–261
Mediascape, 139

Methodological individualism, 10
Methodological Nationalism, 100
Methodology contexts in comparative
research, 59
Mexican Society for Comparative
Education (SOMEC), 28
impetus of, 29–33
Micro–meso-level issues, 147
Micro–meso–macro-level issues, 147
Microsoft Team, 220
Middle Years Programme (MYP), 257
Middle-class voters, 87
Midnight run, 137
Möbius strip, 76
Morality, 183
Mother education, 128
Multiculturalism, 51
Multidimensional, 59, 101
Multilevel model results, 165–168

Narratives, 11–12
Nation-states, 40
National assessments, 100
National Council for Educational
Research & Training
(NCERT), 226
National Curriculum Framework for
School Education (NCF),
221
National Education Policy (NEP),
220–222
National Educational Technology
Forum (NETF), 221
National Repository of Open
Educational Resources
(NROER), 227
National-level initiatives, 226
Nationalism, 49, 92, 100
Nationalist political ideologies, 86
Nationalist sentiments, 49
Nationalists, 40
Negro training schools, 241
Neo-colonialism, 84, 88
Neo-decolonial trap, 93–94
Neo-liberal economics, 11
Neoliberal principles, 43

Nepal Living Standards Survey
(NLSS), 211
Nomothetic science, 68
Nonformal education, 6–7
Normative cascade, 52
North America, 21, 187

Oaxaca–Blinder (OB) decomposition,
105–108, 163
results, 113–121
Ombudsman for Citizen Rights
(RPO), 255
Online teaching, 220
"Oppressed" groups, 253
Oppression, 94
Ordinary Least Squares (OLS), 106
Organizational behavior, 141
Other backward communities
(OBC), 92

Parental education, 112
Patriarchy, 87
Peace Policy, 239
Pedagogy/practice, 141
Peru, 100
Phenomenology, 10
Poland, 46, 252
Policies, 140
Policy gap/clash, 141
Policyscape, 137, 141, 155
Policyscaped environment, 139–140
Polish pedagogy, 61
Populism, 20, 45
Populist movements, 46
Positivist position, 69
Positivist scientism, 68
Possessive individualism, 47
Post-colonialism, 84
Postsecondary institutions, 176
Asian civic values, 180–181
civic and citizenship education in
universities, 182–184
civic roles, 180–191
conceptual framework, methods,
and data sources,
179–180

Confucianism on postsecondary/
 HE, 181–182
East Asia, 180–184
Europe, 184–191
North America, 187–188
serving society/state and
 strengthening democracy,
 188–191
social roles of postsecondary
 institutions, 177–179
Poverty, 206–208
Pre-formal education, 6–7
Primary school, 60
Primary Years Programme (PYP), 257
Principle of subsidiarity, 185
Private education, 205
Private schooling, 205
Problem-based method, 59
Programme for International Student
 Assessment (PISA), 158, 160
Property control, 87
Public education, 205
Public space, co-option of, 86–88
Public sphere, 86–87, 94
Punctuality scale, 162

Quagmire of advocating for
 supporting student mental
 health, 144–145
Qualitative Evidence Syntheses
 (QES), 75
Qualitative research, 69
 in comparative studies, 74–76
Quantitative analyses, 102
Quantitative Critical Race Theory
 (QuantCrit), 100–102
conscious approach, 112
data, 104–105
descriptive statistics, 113, 127–129
education outcomes, 109–113
educational attainment at age 20,
 111
empirical strategy, 105–108
explanatory variables, 111–113
handling missing data, 105
linear regression output, 130–131

mathematics score at age 12,
 109–111
methodology, 104–113
Oaxaca-blinder decomposition
 results, 113–121
Peruvian context and
 operationalizing
 indigeneity, 102–104
principles, 100
results, 113–121
variables, 108–109
Quantitative methods, 68–69, 101
Quantitative paradigm, 69

Race/ethnicity, 102
Racial capitalism, 238, 243
Racial/ethnic minorities, 47
Racism, 102
Rainbow Friday, 256
Rationalization of authority, 43
Reconstructionism, 63
Reconstructive approaches, 75
Reducibility, 63
Reflexivity, 102, 151
Region, 19–20, 29
Regional Comparative and
 Explanatory Study (ERCE),
 161
Regression models, 162–163
Rehabilitation, 242
Reliability, 70
Reparations, 238, 242–246
lens of, 238, 242
linking reparations in education as
 global project, 244–246
Reparative justice, 238
Representativeness heuristic, 66
Research, 75
Research methods employed by
 scholars, 8
 Comparative Education Review, 10
data collection methods, 8–9
data interpretation methods, 10–11
data processing methods, 10
narratives, 11–12
phases, 12–13

Reservation System, 92
Reverse causality, 202–203
Right to education, 51
Right to Education Act (RTE), 221
Right-ward shift of politics, 82
Right-wing populists, 46
Rule of domination, 59
Rural-urban migration, 211
Rurality, 208–211
Rural–urban divide, 210

Sarva Shiksha Abhiyan (SSA), 221
Scape, 139
School attainment, 204
School culture, 139
School curricula, 183
School Statutes, 259
Science, 62–63
Scientific expertise, 49
Score difference, 105–106
Score gaps, 105–106
Secondary school, 60
Self-identification, 104
Service learning, 183, 189–190
Serving society/state and
        strengthening democracy,
        188–191
Settler colonialism, 238
Sexual and gender diversity (SGD),
        255
Shadow education system, 13
Similarity, 64–65
Skype, 220
Small group instruction, 205
Social actions, 70
Social justice, 11, 183
Social psychology, 67
Social science research methods, 6
Societies, 49
Socioeconomic differences in learning
        outcomes, 158–159
Socioeconomic inequality
    database, 161
    descriptive analysis, 163–165
    limitations, 172
    lit review, 158–160

methods, 161–163
multilevel model results, 165–168
OB decomposition, 163
regression models, 162–163
research objectives, 160
results, 163–170
sample, 161
scales, 161–162
variance decomposition, 168–170
Socioeconomic scale, 161
Sociology, 70
Sojourner, 137, 155
South Asia, 200
    education's effect on gross domestic
        product, 201–202
    gender, rurality, and
        marginalization factors,
        208–211
    inputs and outputs, 204–206
    poverty, 206–208
    returns to education,
        203–204
    reverse causality, 202–203
Special education intersection,
        147–148
Special interests, 86
State-level initiatives, 227–228
Statistical/quantitative method, 71
Structural realism, 62
Student achievement, 158
Student mental health, 143
    before COVID-19 pandemic,
        143–144
    during COVID-19 pandemic,
        145–146
    Quagmire of advocating for
        supporting student mental
        health, 144–145
Student protection, 146
    and "duty to report", 148–149
    micro–meso-level and micro–meso-
        macro-level issues, 147
    and special education intersection,
        147–148
Support scale, 162
Suppression, 94

Index 281

Sustainable Development Goals (SDGs), 136, 158, 182, 222
Swayam Prabha TV Channels, 227
Switzerland, 71, 73, 184, 186
Symbolic interactionism, 10

Teacher belief for technology integration in classroom, 222–225
Teacher effect, 158
Teacher effectiveness, 159
Teacher quality, 158, 224
Teacher scales, 158
Teaching, 34
Technological Pedagogical Content Knowledge (TPACK), 223
Technological preparedness, 220, 226
Technology Enabler, 221
Technoscape, 139
Test scores, 205
Theoretical consensus, 61
Third Regional Comparative and Explanatory Study (TERCE), 161
Time-series analysis, 208
TIMSS, 160
Tradition, 176
Traditional societies, 22
Transformative power of education, 40
Transnational flows, 139–140
Tribal college movement, 191
True patriotism, 88
Tutoring, 205
Tversky model, 65

Understanding, 68
UNESCO, 45
Unexplained portion, 106–107, 115, 123
United Kingdom, 20–21, 49
United Nations Educational, Scientific, and Cultural Organisation (UNESCO), 12, 138, 226

United Nations International Children's Emergency Fund (UNICEF), 45, 226
United States (USA), 21, 23, 89–90, 242
Universalism, 22
Universities, 51, 184
Universities of Applied Sciences (UAS), 184
civic role of, 184–187
University of Chicago, 178
University Social Responsibility (USR), 182
Urban schools, 210
Urban slums, 211
Utopia of inclusion, 89

Variance decomposition methods, 163, 168–170
Verification, 63
Virtual learning models, 145
Vocabulary test, 110
Vulnerable students, 89

Weaponization of progressive educational practices, 88
Well-being, 137
Western rationality, 86
"Western" curriculum, challenge of, 92–93
Woke liberalism, 50
World Bank, 45
World Congress of Comparative Education Societies in 2004, 28
World Health Organization (WHO), 226
World Illiberalism Index, 47
World society, 41

Young Lives project, 104–105, 109, 112

Zhi-Xing concept, 181

www.ingramcontent.com/pod-product-compliance
Lightning Source LLC
Jackson TN
JSHW011916131224
75386JS00004B/219